This is the first book on the general history of US sociological research methods. It provides systematic archival, documentary and interview data which question many conventional views and it raises wider issues of method in the history of ideas. Special attention is paid to commonly neglected themes: foundations other than Rockefeller ones, 'case-study' method and the Lundberg circle.

Jennifer Platt discusses the production of methodological writing, showing that neither it nor theoretical work adequately describe research practice. She also investigates the dominance and meaning of scientism, and the impact of research funding. The book evaluates the significance of schools of thought and suggests that processes of social construction and memory lead to uneven emphases in the folk history of the discipline. This detailed study develops our understanding both of the history of social thought, and of the settings in which social research is produced.

IDEAS IN CONTEXT

A HISTORY OF SOCIOLOGICAL RESEARCH METHODS
IN AMERICA 1920–1960

IDEAS IN CONTEXT

Edited by QUENTIN SKINNER (*General Editor*)
LORRAINE DASTON, WOLF LEPENIES, RICHARD RORTY
and J. B. SCHNEEWIND

The books in this series will discuss the emergence of intellectual traditions and of related new disciplines. The procedures, aims and vocabularies that were generated will be set in the context of the alternatives available within the contemporary frameworks of ideas and institutions. Through detailed studies of the evolution of such traditions, and their modification by different audiences, it is hoped that a new picture will form of the development of ideas in their concrete contexts. By this means, artificial distinctions between the history of philosophy, of the various sciences, of society and politics, and of literature may be seen to dissolve.

The series is published with the support of the Exxon Foundation.

A list of books in the series will be found at the end of the volume.

A HISTORY OF
SOCIOLOGICAL RESEARCH
METHODS IN AMERICA
1920–1960

JENNIFER PLATT

University of Sussex

CAMBRIDGE
UNIVERSITY PRESS

Published by the Press Syndicate of the University of Cambridge
The Pitt Building, Trumpington Street, Cambridge CB2 1RP
30 West 20th Street, New York, NY 10011–4211, USA
10 Stamford Road, Oakleigh, Melbourne 3166, Australia

First published 1996

Printed in Great Britain at the University Press, Cambridge

A catalogue record for this book is available from the British Library

Library of Congress cataloguing in publication data
Platt, Jennifer.
A history of sociological research methods in America /
Jennifer Platt.
p.   cm. – (Ideas in context; 40)
Includes bibliographical references.
ISBN 0 521 44173 0
1. Sociology – Research – United States – History. 2. Sociology –
United States – Methodology – History. 1. Title. 11. Series.
HM48.P53 1996
301'.072073 – dc20   95–21429 CIP

ISBN 0 521 44173 0

Contents

List of tables	*page*	viii
Acknowledgments		ix
List of abbreviations		xi
1	Introduction	1
2	Writing on method	11
3	Scientism	67
4	Theory and practice	106
5	Funding and research methods	142
6	Social structures of academic life	200
7	Reputation, exemplars and origin myths	240
8	Conclusion	271
Appendix: Interviews		276
References		282
Index		316

Tables

1 Monographs and specialist texts on method   *page* 14–15
2 Methods textbooks   35
3 Trends shown in methods used in journal articles,
   various studies   124–5
4 Proportions of articles not externally funded   192
5 Proportions of funded and unfunded empirical
   articles whose data were quantitative   193

viii

Acknowledgments

The work on which this book is based has been in progress for a long time, and so has incurred many debts. Many colleagues have offered constructive and critical support. Particularly prominent among these have been Howard Becker, Martin Bulmer and Robert Merton, who have encouraged the enterprise as a whole and commented on drafts of earlier papers. Charles Crothers was especially helpful in providing swift feedback on drafts of book chapters. Help of other kinds, both intellectual and practical, has been provided by Robert Angell, James Beckford, Janet Billson, William R. Catton Jr., Jean-Michel Chapoulie, John Clausen, Jean Converse, James Davis, Jay Demerath, Otis Dudley Duncan, Gary Fine, Herbert Gans, Alice Goldie, Janet Griffith, Helen Haste, Roscoe Hinkle, Simon Hopper, Marie Jahoda, Barbara Laslett, Kate Neckermann, Charles Ragin, Lyle Shannon, David L. Sills, Stephen Turner, Norbert Wiley, Everett Wilson, Mary Yurko and many anonymous departmental secretaries. Special thanks are also given to the Archives I have used, and more particularly to individual archivists whose advice, assistance and expertise have been invaluable to me. These include Daniel L. Daily of Duke University Archives, Alan Divack of the Ford Foundation's archives, Gary Lundell of the University of Washington's Manuscripts and University Archives Division, Daniel Meyer of the University of Chicago Regenstein Library's Department of Special Collections, Earl Rogers of the University of Iowa's archives and Tom Rosenbaum of the Rockefeller Archive. My husband, Charles Goldie, made the ultimate sacrifice in support of the book: he gave me priority on our home computer every day for several months. I would repay this in kind, were it not that we now have two computers.

Several funding agencies have provided grants to support parts of the work: these include the American Philosophical Society, the British Academy, the Economic and Social Research Council (grants G00242008/1 and R 000 23 4322), the Leverhulme Foundation, the Nuffield Foundation, the Radcliffe Research Support Fund, the Rockefeller Archive Center and the Research Support Fund of the University of Sussex.

This book is dedicated, with gratitude and appreciation, to all my living respondents, and to the memory of those now dead.

Abbreviations

AAAS	American Association for the Advancement of Science
AAPOR	American Association for Public Opinion Research
ACSS	American Catholic Sociological Society
AES	Agricultural Experiment Station
AJC	American Jewish Committee
ASA	American Sociological Association
BAE	Bureau of Agricultural Economics
BASR	Bureau of Applied Social Research
CABS	Center for Advanced Studies in the Behavioral Sciences
DPS	Division of Program Surveys
ISR	Institute for Social Research, University of Michigan
JPA	Juvenile Protective Association
LSRM	Laura Spelman Rockefeller Memorial
NIMH	National Institute of Mental Health
NORC	National Opinion Research Center
NSF	National Science Foundation
ONR	Office of Naval Research
OPOR	Office of Public Opinion Research
SAA	Society for Applied Anthropology
SRA	Sociological Research Association
SSRC	Social Science Research Council
UCLA	University of California at Los Angeles
UNC	University of North Carolina
USAF	US Air Force
USDA	US Department of Agriculture
WPA	Work Projects Administration
WPOL	Washington Public Opinion Laboratory
YMCA	Young Men's Christian Association

CHAPTER I

Introduction

This is a book about the history of sociological research methods. As such, it approaches the history of sociology from an unusual angle; history of sociology has most commonly been written as the history of theoretical ideas. This has sometimes included methodological [1] ideas, treated at an abstract and philosophical level, but has seldom given attention to practical research methods or, indeed, to empirical research. The history of theoretical ideas is an interesting and important area, but there has been proportionately too much of it for justice to be done to sociology as a whole. This emphasis is understandable in relation to the early ancestors of present-day sociology, since in their time such empirical research as took place was normally located outside the academy, and might not go under the name of sociology; it makes little or no sense for more recent times. It is also puzzling given the extent to which methods have been discussed within sociology, which has had more explicit concern with method than have most other disciplines. The time has come to shift the balance of historical concern further in the direction of empirical research and ideas about its methods.

That shift is needed not only to complete the picture of what has happened, but to combat the naive assumption, often implicit in writing on the history of theories, that theoretical positions determine or summarise the whole of sociological practice. If this were so, that would make additional historical work almost redundant. I

---

[1] English creates a terminological problem here, and at many other places through the book. This book is primarily concerned with method, rather than with its analytical logic and justification, methodology. The adjective 'methodical', however, does not have the right meaning, so one is compelled to use 'methodological' to correspond to both nouns; this is likely to mislead, but cannot be avoided. The reader is requested to bear this problem in mind, and to interpret the adjective as referring to method unless there are specific contextual clues implying that the other meaning is intended.

hope to show that it is not redundant, and that there is ample scope to investigate and describe research methods in their own right, as both theory and practice. This area is particularly interesting in that it provides both the opportunity and the obligation, as purely theoretical enquiries do not, to ask questions about the relationship between theory and practice, including ones about why it should be that some areas of practice have been more heavily theorised than others. This book is, therefore, very much interested in method-ological thought, but does not take for granted that this either follows directly from general theory, or in its turn directly deter-mines methodological practice. It also tries, without venturing onto the territory of the classic sociology of knowledge in its concern with diffuse social influences, to take into account, at the level of proximate causes, the practical social constraints which affect empirical research in ways which are not relevant to purely theoretical activity.

The book takes as its remit the period in American sociology from around 1920, when university sociologists started to carry out empirical research and to write about research methods, until around 1960. This is at present an unfashionable period, but that does not make it historically unimportant and, as is shown later, such fashions change. It was a period during which American sociology became dominant quantitatively and qualitatively; since then other national sociologies have grown, but the directions in which they have moved cannot be understood without under-standing what happened in America, even if they have often reacted strongly against American influence in general, as well as particular American tendencies. Especially important in this has been the flow of migration created by Hitler and the Second World War, which led many European sociologists to the USA; there they made significant contributions drawing on their original intellec-tual backgrounds, but were also changed by the new experience. After the war, both the contacts which this established and the American political position in postwar Europe had considerable influence on European developments, particularly in diffusing survey method at the height of its novelty and vogue.[2] As European

---

[2] There have been a number of valuable studies of American influences and their reception in Europe. See, for instance, Chapoulie 1991, Mazon 1987, Münch 1991, Sulek 1994, van Elteren 1990. On the diffusion of the survey, see also Capecchi 1978, Pollak 1979.

sociology has expanded, American sociology has naturally become quantitatively less dominant. It has also, in what could be seen as part of the normal process of reaction against previous generations, been in some ways rejected by European sociologists – but even that rejection has often followed American oppositional models.[3] If we are concerned with influence and causes, the American empirical tradition cannot be ignored.

It is observable that much writing about the history of sociology (as no doubt also of other disciplines) starts from the moving frontier of the contemporary, and works forward to it from ancestors chosen for their perceived contemporary relevance. It is striking, thus, how the acknowledged theoretical ancestors of American sociology change from prewar accounts stressing early Americans such as Giddings, Ward, Ross and Sumner, to postwar accounts where suddenly the Europeans Marx, Weber and Durkheim figure (though Gumplowicz, Ratzenhofer and Tarde are now largely forgotten), and the only earlier American theorists mentioned prominently are Mead, Cooley and Thomas. (Of more recent figures, it has often been noted how Parsons moved from hero of the 1950s and 1960s to villain of the 1970s and 1980s, and is now being taken seriously as an ancestor again by at least some contemporary writers.) This sort of process also affects the treatment of whole national traditions, and of methodological strands within them. The shift, even within American sociology, away from interest in its own more direct ancestors, has led to a general downgrading of the historical significance of American sociology in relation to theory which is surely not justified. Least of all is it justified in relation to empirical research and its methods.

How have these figured in general histories? Far more has been written about theories, even when the title refers to 'thought'. Some standard works, chosen to exclude those with 'theory' in the title whose remit could make the question irrelevant, have been examined. Those of Beach (1939), H. E. Barnes (1948), Nisbet (1966), Coser (1971), Hawthorn (1976) and Szacki (1979) have no, or negligible, reference to any empirical matters. Works which do give

---

[3] One interesting example of this sort of process is the recent strong growth of interest among some European sociologists in the interwar Chicago school; this is associated with active support for qualitative methods of empirical research not previously well known in those countries.

some serious attention to empirical work have included those of House (1936), H. E. Barnes and H. P. Becker (1938), Bernard and Bernard (1943), Odum (1951), Hinkle and Hinkle (1954) and Mitchell (1968). These are almost all, however, in one way or another in the genre of the textbook, and so give little researched detail. There are also a number of books specifically about empirical sociology; these include Madge (1963), Oberschall (1972), Easthope (1974) and Ackroyd and J. A. Hughes (1981). Only Oberschall's rests on original research, and its period finishes in 1930. Other serious historical studies of broad scope, such as Furner (1975) and Dorothy Ross (1991), stop at the same period or earlier. The interwar period has in general been much neglected in recent writing, except in the large number of works on the Chicago department – Faris (1967), Bulmer (1984a), Kurtz (1984), Harvey (1987b), D. Smith (1988); Hinkle (1994), though focusing on theory, is a very welcome exception to this. Another shining exception is S. P. Turner and J. H. Turner (1990), which describes itself as 'an institutional analysis', and is centrally concerned with empirical work from before the First World War until the present day.[4] Another source of material is the 'sociology of sociology' literature, such as Friedrichs (1970) and Gouldner (1971), though this has often been at least as much concerned with drawing morals for the present as with understanding the past. There have, of course, been many relevant publications of narrower scope, often articles rather than books, but still with a marked shortage of serious historical work on the period since 1930 or on empirical research and its methods.

This book does not attempt to fill the gaps with a complete narrative history, but draws on narrative materials in relation to key thematic issues. (This means that some of the same material is referred to more than once, in different connections.) Many of the themes pursued are interpretations put forward by other authors, whether or not those were grounded in detailed research; this is part of a continuing discussion. The uneven spread over the field of work by others is taken into account. Jean Converse's really excellent history of the social survey (1987) makes much work unnecessary which would otherwise have been called for; that and other existing work are freely drawn on. To complement what has

---

[4] It is unfortunate, for historical purposes, that legal difficulties with the use of archival material (S. P. Turner 1994: 64) made it necessary for many of its sources not to be cited.

been done already, a special effort has been made to provide here more extended documentation on some groups and topics relatively neglected by other writers; these include the interwar 'case study method', the intellectual circle of George Lundberg, and foundations other than Rockefeller ones. This may have risked creating an impression skewed in an unconventional direction, but that seems a risk worth taking.

This risk has been taken not only to fill out the descriptive picture, but because the pattern of existing historical work – some done as a minor part of other enterprises – is itself part of the phenomena we are concerned to explain. Why, for instance, do the 'Chicago School', and Paul Lazarsfeld's version of the survey, loom quite so large in customary accounts? This and similar questions do not apply only to formally historical writing, but also to the amateur history of unresearched introductory comments, taken-for-granted textbook versions and orally transmitted understandings. There are things all sociologists know which are probably misleading, and there has been a shortage of systematic historical work to examine them.

One obvious possible answer to the question of why some parts of the history have received more study is that most attention has naturally been given to the best work. I certainly have my own evaluative judgments of methods and methodological writing, and have not always concealed them in this book. But, while I would not entirely subscribe to the 'strong programme' in the sociology of science,[5] I accept as a methodological imperative in writing on the history of knowledge its injunction to regard every outcome as requiring explanation, independently of its intellectual merit. The merit or demerit may constitute part of the explanation, but it cannot be the whole of it. It cannot be taken for granted that only the best has survived – and if it had, it would still be of interest to document how the best came about, and the processes by which that

---

[5] The 'strong programme' in the sociology of science, especially associated with the Edinburgh group of sociologists of natural science, is defined by Bloor as consisting of these tenets: it is causal, i.e. concerned with the conditions which bring about belief or knowledge; it is impartial with respect to truth or falsity, success or failure, rationality or irrationality, in that it sees both sides as requiring explanation; it is symmetrical, in that the same type of cause is assumed to explain both true and false beliefs etc; it is reflexive, in that its patterns of explanation are also seen as applicable to itself (Bloor 1976: 4–5).

outcome is ensured. It is evident that evaluative criteria have changed over time and differ between subgroups. Moreover, the ephemeral and second-rate is, by whatever evaluative criteria, a high proportion of the total work done; the historian, especially the sociological one, should be interested in this work too. To focus only on what is seen as important is more appropriate to the seeker for exemplary ancestors, or others with normative agendas. Normative agendas are rightly common in writing on research methods, but this book does not aim to meet the needs to which they respond.

The discussion starts with an overview of the types of method-ological writing done over the period, and the circumstances under which it was produced; it shows that the sets of concepts used have changed over time, so that what are in one sense the same practices can form part of different 'methods', the boundaries between which are drawn in shifting ways. Writing followed practice at least as much as it led it, but not every practice has figured equally in methodological writing; what gets written about has been to a surprising extent dependent on the enthusiasms of strategically placed individuals. The question of theory and practice is con-sidered further by an examination of the scientism often seen as dominant for much of this time. It is shown that even its keenest proponents in principle, George Lundberg and his circle, did not agree among themselves on what it consisted of, and did not necessarily exemplify what they preached in their practice; it was a slogan and a dream as much as a clear message. A more general discussion of theory and practice shows that some theoretical positions commonly seen as underlying particular methods cannot be causally responsible for them, and that the balance of quanti-tative and qualitative empirical work probably does not correspond to the balance in methodological writing. Methods in practice are caused by, and chosen for, a whole range of reasons, many of which have little to do with theory of any kind. One explanation offered for the overall trajectory of methodological change has been the pressure of funding bodies for quantification. The pattern of research funding is reviewed. The plausibility of accounts which rest on the interests of capitalists and the capitalist state is questioned, and it is argued that foundation behaviour can be better understood in terms of the immediate situation of foun-dation officers – who were not very clearly distinct from those they funded. It is possible to interpret the course of events as revealing manipulation of funders by social scientists as much as vice versa. It is shown that there is reason to believe that methods would have become more quantitative even without their funding, though not in quite the same way. Some other social structures relevant to academic life are sketched, suggesting that these form part of the relevant background; real social groupings are more consequential than the factitious 'schools' of thought sometimes proposed as the relevant units. Finally, it is argued that collective memories, reputations and the choice of exemplars are socially structured so that they are much more likely to preserve some parts of the whole past than others; our unresearched shared knowledge of the history of the discipline is the product of such processes, creating stories and stereotypes, and selecting ancestors suitable to provide the origin myths we need to legitimate current stances.

METHODS USED

The data in this book come from diverse sources. Published work has of course been examined. The study started, some years ago, as one of methods textbooks, and there are few enough of those for it to have been possible to examine all of them, as well as all the monographs on method. Empirical studies have also been examined and occasionally, when the topic and the practical possibilities justified it, aspects of their methods have been analysed quantitatively. Archival sources have been extensively drawn on and, for materials not often systematically archived – such as teaching documentation – the unofficial archives of departments have been used wherever possible, although what has been kept may be largely accidental. In addition, a considerable number of interviews have been conducted with sociologists (and occasionally also others involved in related activities) professionally active before 1960.

These interviews have been unstructured in form, though I have come to each with an agenda; inevitably, that agenda became more sophisticated as I learned more. In general, however, each respondent was asked to tell me the story of their life from a methodological point of view, and I would then pick up particular points for further enquiry or ask about matters not spontaneously mentioned. Topics normally covered included their initial methodological training and the publications emphasised in its setting, the methods used in their subsequent research and the reasons for that, their evaluations of well-known works and writers and their influence, and how it came about (where applicable) that they had written on methodological matters. I prepared for each interview by checking publicly available sources about that person's career, and asked in some detail about aspects of particular methodological relevance in it. I also made a special effort to elicit comments relevant to my emerging ideas on particular points. People were used as informants about the social settings they had experienced, as well as about their own careers. (Some colleagues, usually emeritus, occupy unofficial positions as custodians of departmental history, and they were particularly valued inform- ants.) In a few cases, as when the interview was an opportunistic one snatched at a conference, the focus was more narrowly on the special reasons why I had chosen that person to talk to; very brief or casual encounters are described in the bibliography (where only those directly cited in the text appear) as 'conversation' rather than 'interview'.

Some respondents spoke freely and at length, others were more restrained. The answers were recorded as near as possible to verbatim, by hand. Several testimonials to my ability to get the material down have been received, and one respondent's tape recorder confirmed my general accuracy. That was not usually the final version, though, as my normal practice was to send a transcript with a request for any necessary corrections, after- thoughts, or answers to questions which occurred to me after the event, so that the eventual version would be a full and agreed one. Many responded to this invitation, and in doing so some chose to 'improve' their oral English and to remove the original indis- cretions, with which I have parted with some regret.

How were respondents chosen? Several criteria intersected, and the eventual sample cannot be seen as a representative one from a defined population. (It has not been used in ways which make that assumption.) The first criterion was to include as many people as possible who were especially associated with research methods: writers of textbooks, articles or monographs on methodological topics, authors whose substantive work has been seen as method- ologically important, people who had worked in units or on projects significant in the history of methods. The second criterion was to represent graduate schools, or other groupings such as research units, firstly those seen as methodologically significant, and secondly others from the same period which might have been different. On the latter principle, some more 'ordinary' people were included to insure against the possible bias of picking only those well known for particular stances. The third and fourth criteria were practical ones, geographical and demographic. The USA is a large country, and my research funds were restricted; I therefore made a special effort to plan trips so that the maximum number of respondents could be found for one fare. Thus otherwise equally relevant respondents had a greater chance of inclusion if they were in the same area as an archive or someone else I wanted to see, though efforts were made to counterbalance the consequent skew to those located at the time of interviewing in large departments or major metropolitan areas; I visited Missoula, Montana, as well as Boston. Conferences were very helpful in this respect, since they gather people from all over the country in one place, and advantage was taken of this. I also developed a useful conference strategy of offering papers likely to interest different constituencies – participant observation one year, Stouffer and Lazarsfeld's contributions to the survey another – as a way of making contacts and establishing credentials, or eliciting corrective comments to tentative interpretations. My response rate was excellent, with few refusals, though in one or two cases a mutually convenient time could not be found or a home turned out to be too inaccessible. However, some people I would have liked as respondents were dead, or too old and ill. (At one stage I wondered if those left alive were not a skewed sample, biased against more quantitative styles. When I mentioned this to a respondent who had seen the anti-positivist light, his face lit up and he said yes, of course, qualitative methods are life-enhancing! I have not attempted a systematic check of this interesting hypothesis.) The names of all those interviewed are given in the appendix, with some basic background information about their affiliations. In the text, their names have generally been used, with their permission; who they are is often significant to the meaning of what they said, and it would do them little credit to treat them as interchangeable anonymous subjects.

This book strives to provide well-grounded descriptive material, and that has often implied sticking rather close to details, and exercising restraint in either supporting or rejecting large, macroscopic interpretations. I hope that, when a choice had to be made, restraint has been chosen, even if that may have been done at a cost. But that is not the book's only aim for its own method, and it is not unconcerned with larger theses. Historical work is seldom framed as testing hypotheses, and it is often not appropriate that it should be, but even for historical topics the kind of intellectual discipline which that strategy implies can be valuable. To make an interpretation convincing, or justify an explanation, it is not sufficient to show that it fits a reasonably large body of relevant data; other explanations might fit them as well or better, and further data might create a different impression. Too many of the 'explanations' in this field have started from a known outcome and worked backwards to earlier factors which can be connected with it, without considering whether other outcomes would have been more likely if the general interpretation implied were correct, or the same outcome equally predictable from another theory. Insufficient attention has been given to the counterfactual conditional – what would have happened if things had been otherwise. In some cases, too, the connection between cause and effect has been taken as almost self-evident, rather than requiring investigation. One version of this is where apparent similarity of ideas between two thinkers is assumed to show that the first influenced the second. Another version is that where normative links are made: theory must have led to method, because that is the way it should be; capitalism and quantification must go together, because they are both bad things. We attempt to identify and to avoid such questionable structures of argument, and to take seriously the search for negative cases and alternative possible explanations. If that sometimes leads to more negative arguments than positive ones, so be it. In writing a book, there is a strong temptation to make everything fit a neat template and lead inexorably to the foreseen, overdetermined conclusion. There is also a place for untidy antithesis to follow tidy thesis. The reader who reads on will see that this set of decisions fits into an established historical pattern.

CHAPTER 2

Writing on method

One kind of account of the history of research methods would look at the sequence of methods which have been invented, independently of the nature or prevalence of their uses. This is the kind which might be expected to follow from the study of methodological writing alone. Such an account would be of interest to the history of ideas, whatever the relation of the ideas to research practice. But it cannot be assumed that practice directly reflects precept, any more than it can be assumed that the pattern of methodological writing directly reflects research practice, although they are of course related. (For a general discussion of these relationships, including data on changing patterns of practice, see chapter 4.) S. P. Turner (1994: 48–51), indeed, suggests that there is a practically dominant methodological tradition, transmitted through apprenticeship relations, which has not been explicitly intellectualised and so does not appear in the methodological literature. This chapter, without making assumptions about the relation to practice, looks at methodological writing as an independently existing intellectual product, considering how it arises, what ideas are expressed in it, and how they can be accounted for. It is concerned both with 'inventions', the first introduction of novelties, and with the systematisation and routinisation of novelty. First, the patterns shown in the contents of the writing are reviewed; the emphasis is on the foci of interest shown and the stances taken, and the ways in which these have changed over time.

MONOGRAPHS ON METHOD: CONTENT

Our review starts with monographs; it is assumed that this approximates an overview of significant new written contributions.[1] A listing of every monograph published over our period has been attempted. The line between general textbooks and monographs or readers on method is not always clear; doubtful ones have been counted as monographs, since we wish to reserve for discussion as textbooks those which claim to cover the whole field; textbooks are treated later. Some of the 'monographs' are more like textbooks of limited scope, while others are advanced technical treatments close to the frontiers of knowledge. Omitted from the list are works exclusively on statistics, apart from Zeisel's unusual book, primarily because most are not specific to sociology; included are, nonetheless, a few others which are interdisciplinary in character, or might be regarded as belonging equally to another discipline such as psychology,[2] but which are known to have been treated as significant in sociology. Also included are a few books which are not wholly methodological, but have been important in methodological discussion. Merton and Lazarsfeld (1950), Christie and Jahoda (1954) and Himelhoch and Fava (1955) appear, despite the fact that they are critiques of published work by others and their contents are only in part methodological, because such important contributions to the methodological discussion of the time were made by those parts or, in the case of the last, by more widespread reaction to the work in question. The 'monographs' thus identified are listed in table 1, and are discussed in broadly chronological order.

The general trends shown in the monographs are in the direction of increasingly detailed, practical and analytical discussion of methodological issues; one might reasonably describe this as progress on the theoretical level, whether or not the later methods discussed are better than the earlier ones. Although such progress may not be inevitable, it is not surprising over a period when the numbers of sociologists, and the extent to which they took part in

[1] There have certainly been articles too which have made important contributions. The practical difficulty of listing from a so much larger category would be almost insuperable; fortunately it seems likely that most of the influential articles will have been incorporated into monographs, if with some time lag. This of course neglects articles which were not influential, equally part of the total range of methodological writing; I plead guilty, but in mitigation invoke again the magnitude of the task. Some articles are mentioned in the discussion.

[2] Others which might have been included here, but were excluded on disciplinary grounds, are Thurstone and Chave (1929) and Chapple and Arensberg (1940).

empirical research, increased dramatically, and the discipline became securely institutionalised.

Looking more closely at the content of the discussion, we can see shifts of other kinds. The period up to the early 1940s shows a marked quantitative/qualitative, humanistic/scientific controversy, with substantial technical work on both sides of the line. (See below for detailed discussion of this.) The most prominent topic is the uses of personal documents, though the importance of Social Science Research Council (SSRC) committees led by Ernest Burgess in initiating these publications (on which see below) is such that one hesitates to assume that this characterised the whole field, of interest or of practice. At the beginning of the period social-work interests are represented, while at the end their place has been taken by the concerns of the commercial research agencies. After the war, work on purely qualitative topics almost vanishes, though many issues relevant to qualitative work are still raised. The dominant themes are to do with survey research and with experimentation and measurement. To a significant extent this reflects the leadership of Lazarsfeld,[3] against the background of the spillover from the wartime research and the growing commercial interest in surveys. (However, our chronological dividing line has been drawn at what is here a misleading point; we have stopped just when a significant revival of methodological work on qualitative issues was starting, led by articles published in the 1950s, though now that was concerned with participant observation rather than with documentary sources.) Much empirical research on method is now being reported. Within the postwar work, there is much more than before on the highly quantitative themes of scaling and sampling, but also much more on the more philosophical aspects of the logic of design and analysis,[4] and on practicalities of interviewing technique. Below, this outline is filled in with details of the particular books.

Before 1940, the literature is thin, and there is little which was

---

[3] This is not meant to imply that Lazarsfeld himself was only interested in quantitative work, which is certainly not true. His qualitative interests are, for instance, reflected in his publications with Allen Barton (1951, 1955), and are symbolised in the decision by those closest to him to call his festschrift *Qualitative and Quantitative Social Research* (Merton, Coleman and Rossi 1979).

[4] Rossi (1959: 36) points out that survey method places a premium on *post hoc* interpretation, so that analysis is more salient than design in relation to surveys.

Table 1. *Monographs and specialist texts on method*

Date	Monograph author	Title	Field	Origin, stimulus[a]
1916	Aronovici	The Social Survey	Old survey	Not known
1917	Elmer	The Technique of Social Surveys	Old survey	Author
1929	D. S. Thomas and associates	Some New Techniques for Studying Social Behavior	Observation	Author
1931	Rice	Methods in Social Science	Various; critiques	SSRC
1933	Ellwood	Method in Sociology: A Critical Study	Metasociology	Author
1933	Hader and Lindeman	Dynamic Social Research	Various	Not known
1933	D. S. Thomas, Loomis and Arrington	Observational Studies of Social Behavior	Observation	Author
1934	Moreno	Who Shall Survive?	Sociometry	Author
1934	Znaniecki	The Method of Sociology	Metasociology	Author
1935	Dollard	Criteria for the Life History	Life history	SSRC/author
1939	Blumer	An Appraisal ... 'Polish Peasant'	Critique	SSRC
1939	Lundberg	Foundations of Sociology	Metasociology	Author
1941	Horst	The Prediction of Personal Adjustment	Various	SSRC
1942	Allport	The Use of Personal Documents	Documents	SSRC
1942	MacIver	Social Causation	Metasociology	Author
1945	Gottschalk, Kluckhohn and Angell	The Use of Personal Documents	Documents	SSRC
1945	Greenwood	Experimental Sociology	Experiment	Author
1947	Cantril	Gauging Public Opinion	Survey	Author

Table 1 (*cont.*)

Date	Monograph author	Title	Field	Origin, stimulus[a]
1947	Chapin	*Experimental Designs*	Experiment	Author
1947	Zeisel	*Say It With Figures*	Statistics	Lazarsfeld
1949	Hovland, Lumsdaine and Sheffield	*Experiments on Mass Communication*	Experiment	SSRC
1949	Mosteller, Hyman and McCarthy	*The Pre-Election Polls of 1948*	Survey	SSRC
1950	Bales	*Interaction Process Analysis*	IPA	Author
1950	Merton and Lazarsfeld	*Continuities in Social Research: Studies in the Scope and Method of 'The American Soldier'*	Various	SSRC
1950	Parten	*Surveys, Polls and Samples*	Survey	Author
1950	Stouffer, Guttman, Suchman et al.	*Measurement and Prediction*	Scaling, measurement, prediction	SSRC
1951	Payne	*The Art of Asking Questions*	Survey	Author
1952	Berelson	*Content Analysis*	Content analysis	(Lazarsfeld)[b]
1953	Hansen, Hurwitz and Madow	*Sample Survey Methods and Theory*	Survey	Authors (Census)
1953	Moreno	*Who Shall Survive?*, 2nd edn	Sociometry	Author
1954	Christie and Jahoda	*Continuities in Social Research: Studies in the Scope and Method of 'The Authoritarian Personality'*	(Sampling, scaling, coding, analysis)	Authors
1954	Hyman	*Interviewing in Social Research*	Survey	Lazarsfeld, SSRC

Table 1 (cont.)

Date	Monograph author	Title	Field	Origin, stimulus[a]
1954	Lazarsfeld	*Mathematical Thinking*	Models, scaling, measurement	Lazarsfeld
1954	Riley, Riley and Toby	*Sociological Studies in Scale Analysis*	Scaling	Not known
1954	Zetterberg	*On Theory and Verification*	Research design	Author
1955	Himelhoch and Fava	*Sexual Behavior in American Society*	(Interviewing, sampling)	Society for the Study of Social Problems
1955	Hyman	*Survey Design and Analysis*	Survey	Lazarsfeld
1955	Lazarsfeld and Rosenberg	*The Language of Social Research*	Various	Lazarsfeld
1956	Merton, Fiske and Kendall	*The Focussed Interview*	Interview	(Lazarsfeld)
1957	Kahn and Cannell	*The Dynamics of Interviewing*	Interview	Authors
1958	Stephan and McCarthy	*Sampling Opinions*	Survey	SSRC
1958	Torgerson	*Theory and Methods of Scaling*	Scaling	SSRC
1960	Adams and Preiss	*Human Organisation Research*	Fieldwork	SAA
1960	Junker	*Field Work*	Participant observation	Hughes

[a] This refers to the way in which the publication was initiated and/or sponsored; details are given in the text.
[b] Brackets indicate that the methodological categories deemed most relevant have been provided by Platt.

both practically oriented and specific to sociology. (Ellwood's, Znaniecki's and Lundberg's books are meta-sociological, while Aronovici and Elmer are writing for the pre-sociological survey of community reform (on which see below) and an audience of social workers,[5] while Hader and Lindeman, from a social-work background, focus, despite the general title, on modes of studying joint committees.) Ellwood attacked contemporary conceptions of the scientific approach as unsuitable to sociology, on the ground that 'the social sciences are much more sciences of culture than of nature' (Ellwood 1933: 64). He opposed behaviourism, empiricism, quantophrenia,[6] and the collecting of facts without synthesising them, and expressed disagreement with Ogburn, Rice and Lundberg. He was not at all hostile to scientific method in the sense of testing bold hypotheses; indeed, he counterposes this favourably to the perceived alternative, associated by him with his opponents, of collecting data without hypotheses. He advocates the relevance of imagination, history and psychology.[7] Lundberg's book, of opposite tendency to Ellwood's, was very influential in the sense that it was widely cited, though also highly controversial. It lent closely argued support and intellectual legitimation to the 'scientific' approaches which it advocated, and even if it did not go into their technical details it made critical comments on methods of data collection. It was strongly in favour of quantification, dismissing alternatives with adjectives such as 'mystical', and taking the extreme operationist position that the question of 'what' scales measured did not matter. Robert Lynd's *Knowledge For What?* (1939), though only in part metasociology rather than cultural critique, can be seen as part of the same discussion, in which he comes down on the humanistic side, but with a special emphasis on the use of social science for desirable social goals rather than the empiricist pursuit of pure science for its own sake.[8]

---

[5] 'Social work' at this period was taken to include kinds of community activism, as distinct from individual case work, no longer normally covered by the term or role.

[6] Sorokin's term (Sorokin 1958) for an excessive use of potentially meaningless quantification.

[7] S. P. Turner and J. H. Turner (1990: 65–6) see this as part of a controversy with the SSRC establishment, on the 'science' side, and specifically associated with funding politics. See their book, *passim*, for more about Ellwood.

[8] It might also be relevant to mention here Alihan's *Social Ecology* (1938). This is mainly theoretical in orientation, and has commonly been seen as Columbia attacking Chicago. It did attack an important Chicago tendency, the ecological approach, on the unusual

Znaniecki, like Ellwood, expressed disagreement with many tenets of contemporary scientism, emphasising the distinction between cultural and natural systems as leading to the need for sociology to be concerned with meanings. He put forward the innovatory idea of 'analytical induction' as a preferred alternative to statistical method, and his emphasis on the significance of personal experience led him to see 'personal documents' and participation in the life studied as preferred data sources. Analytical induction made a modest impact as an idea at the time. Angell (1936) used it in a prominent book, though he said that he had been working along those lines before he read Znaniecki's book and learned the name; Sutherland diffused the idea more widely by mentioning it in the latest edition of his well-established textbook *Principles of Criminology* (1939); Lindesmith used it for his Chicago doctoral thesis submitted in 1937, though the book version of this was not published until after the war (Lindesmith 1947); Cressey, a student of Sutherland's, used it for his doctoral thesis, published as *Other People's Money* in 1953. It was taken up as a topic for discussion, initiated by Robinson, in the early 1950s (see W. S. Robinson 1951, Lindesmith 1952, Weinberg 1952, Angell 1954, R. H. Turner 1954.) Some of this discussion is reproduced in a well-known reader on participant observation (McCall and Simmons 1969). Its requirement that every case be accounted for is a very strong one, which few researchers would find it easy to meet; Angell handled this problem by developing a typological strategy, so that different types could be dealt with in different ways. (When Glaser and Strauss put forward a similar strategy in their 1967 book, at a time when there was a clear dominant philosophy-of-science orthodoxy, they 'resolved' the problem by saying that they were concerned with the creation of theory rather than its testing.) The idea has never entered the mainstream as a normal topic or practice; it was overtaken by probabilistic approaches to sampling and analysis, which treated 'deviant' cases as normal rather than an intellectual problem.

Of the more technical work, Dorothy Thomas' came from an

---

ground that it was inappropriately 'scientific' in that it took over a biological and terri- torial model which did not fit social subject matter. Lynd and Znaniecki were both also at Columbia, though the Chicago/Columbia division has certainly not normally been seen as one where Chicago stands for science and Columbia for a humanistic approach – rather the reverse, though that refers more to the postwar period.

interdisciplinary research unit (Yale Institute of Human Relations) and was influenced by psychology. The two books both reported results, but are included here because they also had quite extensive discussion of method, especially the problem of observer reliability and how to deal with it, and were used by others as work on method. Thomas developed techniques for systematic observation of small units of behaviour which could be reliably classified into categories so that the results could be quantified; this was very much in a behaviouristic scientific spirit, omitting those aspects of behaviour which did not lend themselves to such treatment. She saw this as necessary to overcome the problems of existing descriptive accounts of behaviour, relying mainly on case histories and diaries, which were at best likely to be selective and inconsistent in what they observed and thus not give quantifiable data. She defined what she was doing as experimental, in the sense that it involved control of the observer rather than of the situations observed, which were naturally occurring ones. What she achieved was technically impressive, and treated as exemplifying scientific quantification, though it does not seem to have had much effect on general sociology. That is probably in part because such observation could only be done in special situations, of a kind which seldom occur or can be created outside the nursery school setting where the original work was done[9].

Moreno's *Who Shall Survive?* is a highly idiosyncratic work; insofar as he can be regarded as having a disciplinary affiliation, perhaps it was social psychiatry. (For more about him and his context, see chapter 6.) The book had many components, some of which, like his 'psychodrama', have much more to do with practical applications than with research. Indeed he was probably much more interested in social intervention, with other concerns a means to that end; it just happened that some of the techniques he developed lent them-

---

[9] Her work was treated as important enough at the time for a Symposium on the Observability of Social Phenomena with Respect to Statistical Analysis, at which the discussion was initiated by her, to have been organised in 1930 at a joint meeting of the American Sociological Society and the American Statistical Association; this is published in two issues of *Sociologus*, starting with Dorothy Thomas in 1931. Much of her other work was in demography, where it was also recognised as important. Although she was well established in her time, becoming President of the American Sociological Society in 1952, she seems to make very little appearance in historical accounts; this may have something to do with her marriage to W. I. Thomas, which has somehow subsumed her under his penumbra despite the very different style of her work.

selves to research uses. In particular, he employed the technique of collecting data on individual choices of, or links with, others to create graphic plots of group relations; such data can be manipulated in many creative and mathematically interesting ways. Perhaps the fact that he chose for this the name 'sociometry', which had previously meant social measurement in general, also did something to promote its perceived relevance to quantitative sociology. At any rate, for a time he had a great vogue, among several otherwise rather distinct constituencies, of which the committed quantifiers are methodologically the most relevant.

Dollard's *Criteria for the Life History* set out to systematise the requirements for an adequate life history, taking it for granted that life histories are a valued data form. The disciplinary orientation is psychiatric and anthropological as much as sociological, and the work was initiated by a group in which psychologists were prominent, so it is not surprising that it is not distinctively sociological in content, though it was much referred to by sociologists. One may suspect, however, that it has been referred to and taught more than used, since it appeared after the heyday of life-history data in sociological research.

Dollard's book consisted primarily of analysis of respected published work, as did the two critiques. The collection edited by Rice contains fifty-two chapters, each by a different author, analysing another author's well-known work; the examples chosen were across the whole range of the social sciences. This represented the failure of an attempt to reach a consensual synthesis on scientific method in social science; the chapters vary considerably in style and coverage, since there was not even agreement on what was meant by 'method'! Considerable use was, nonetheless, made of this as a source of teaching material. Blumer's contribution, in contrast, was a close analysis of one sociological work generally agreed to be of great importance and methodological interest – although that work was, by the time Blumer dealt with it, twenty years old and no longer in the forefront of methodological development. Blumer was known for his stand against scientism and his commitment to close qualitative data, though he had done little empirical work himself. *The Polish Peasant* (W. I. Thomas and Znaniecki 1918–19) was chosen as the subject of his critique because it was still regarded as an outstanding work, with methods of special interest; these methods rested on 'personal documents', letters and autobiographical material. One reason for its method-ological reputation is that it includes a long 'Methodological Note' which lays down general principles. This is somewhat ironic in that the Note was (as Thomas explained at the conference to discuss Blumer's critique, reported in the monograph) written after the work was essentially complete, and its standpoint is not system-atically followed in the substance of the book.

Blumer's discussion is both sympathetic and critical. Although he looks with favour on the use of personal documents, he concludes (and the authors accept this as fair comment) that the documents were not suitable to test the interpretations put forward, and that the conclusions could not have been derived from them, but were drawn by unsystematic methods from a much wider body of knowledge; moreover, the documents did not meet the scientific criteria of representativeness, reliability and adequacy. This critique too became regarded as an important contribution to methodological discussion; it is not clear what morals others drew from it, but it seems possible that these may have supported the kind of quantitative technique which Blumer himself did not favour. The critique could be used in that way, though it could also be used as an endorsement of the importance of Thomas and Znaniecki's methods, and as a source of guidelines on how they needed to be improved rather than abandoned. Nearly forty years later, Blumer wrote an introduction (Blumer 1979) to a reissue of the original critique in a series of 'social science classics'. In this he argues that human documents are valuable because they, unlike data sources now more fashionable, provide naturalistic data on subjective factors in human action. As he sees it, they – and hence *The Polish Peasant* – have lost interest for sociologists as the assump-tion that action depends on culture and structure has become predominant. However, the fact of the reissue suggests that there was still some market for discussion of such matters.

In the 1940s, there was a higher proportion of specialised and technical work. The only metasociological work is MacIver's, which argues against the behaviouristic, natural-science approach as represented by Lundberg and his sympathisers. Of the other work, some is following up prewar concerns while some introduces new themes. The two volumes on personal documents relate to themes raised by Blumer's cited work. The Horst volume is also marginally connected, in that it contains a substantial section on the prediction of individual behaviour from case studies, which might use personal documents; the whole volume is located within the framework of the controversy between case study and statistical method, on which see below. More of its contents are, however, oriented to statistical techniques and formal analysis of the prediction process, modes of scale construction and so on.

It is significant that there is a book from the emerging commercial survey industry: Cantril's unit, on the edge of academia.[10] The blurb on Cantril's dust jacket claims, justifiably as far as books are concerned, that it furnishes 'the first systematic examination of the highly important and widely misunderstood new methods of surveying public opinion'. The topics covered include question wording and the development of scales, interviewing technique and training, sampling and the use of 'breakdowns' of respondents in analysing the determinants of opinions; they are illustrated with copious examples, drawn from both the routine work of the Office of Public Opinion Research and other polling outfits and from its methodological research.

Zeisel's semi-statistical work, which went through many subsequent editions, is about the analysis and presentation of numerical data; it relates particularly to the needs of survey data. It is a thoroughly practical book, treating a topic not previously dealt with, whose enormous success shows that it met a felt need. Mosteller, Hyman and McCarthy is addressed to technical issues raised by surveys of the kind used in election polling, especially interviewing, question wording, sampling and the prediction of outcomes from responses; although it is a post mortem on a failure, the conclusions are relevant prospectively as well as retrospectively.

Finally, there are two books on experimentation from the 1940s. Chapin's is one of the first books to provide a rigorous and systematic analytical discussion which is closely related to research practice; it reports on a long-term programme of empirical work which he and his students had carried out, as well as analysing a few studies by others. It is particularly interesting that all the cases he deals with are of studies carried out in normal community

---

[10] Works such as those of Blankenship (1943, 1946), outside in market research, might also have been mentioned here. These are referred to in academic sources, and included several chapters contributed by Lazarsfeld as well as others then more securely in academic life; they are much more focused on survey methods than the titles might suggest.

situations, not in the laboratory or special settings such as class-rooms. Its main concern was the logic of design, but it also has material on measurement. He had introduced in an earlier work (Chapin and Queen 1937) the new analytical category of the *'ex post facto'* experimental design, in which it is attempted to trace an observed effect back to its causes, and in this book he fleshed that out with empirical examples of that and other types of design. Most of the studies reported on had already been published as articles, if not in quite the same form, so this is a book which systematises and illustrates rather than introducing innovations for the first time. For Chapin, the programme of work reported is an attempt to make 'an adaptation of the experimental method of physical science to the study of the problems of human relationship' (Chapin 1947: viii). Greenwood's book has more the form of a critical review of the literature (it was presumably his doctoral dissertation). It shows that 'experiment' has been defined in a variety of ways, and offers as his definition one which emphasises the testing of a hypothesis by the comparison of situations controlled on all factors except the hypothetical cause or effect. It provides a typology of experiments in terms of whether they start with cause or effect, and whether they commence before the effect has occurred, and goes on to discuss problems such as randomness and artificiality; it criticises the *ex post facto* design on practical grounds.

In the 1950s, there is a spate of publications. Two of them, Bales and Merton, Fiske and Kendall, present at least partly new tech-niques developed by the authors. Bales offers a system of categories for the classification of interpersonal behaviour in small groups, an enterprise somewhat analogous to Dorothy Thomas'; his aim was to find general categories applicable across a wide range of contexts, and these were used in such a way that the results could be quanti-fied to establish regularities and test hypotheses. His own data came entirely from small groups of Harvard students, whose inter-action while carrying out a discussion task was observed in a special room. This represents one manifestation of the strong interest at this period in small group behaviour,[11] which may in part account for the second edition of *Who Shall Survive?* Merton, Fiske and Kendall present techniques of relatively unstructured interviewing. These were originally devised to deal especially with the impact of

[11] For a general account of this, see Mullins 1973, chapter 5.

communications, but were seen as appropriate to any problem to do with subjects' experience of a particular situation on which the interviewer already has some hypotheses. (In practice, at least some aspects of what was proposed have almost certainly been used more widely than that would imply.) Kahn and Cannell write from a psychological perspective, aiming to create understanding of the dynamics of the interview process in order to improve technique. Though they wrote from the Michigan Survey Research Center they were not only oriented to the survey type of interview, but also discuss personnel, medical and social-work interviews. The considerable level of interest in interviewing at this time is also shown by Hyman's volume, which takes a much less psychodynamic approach; it reports a large number of planned empirical studies on sources of error in interviewing.[12]

A batch of publications arises from the 'American Soldier'[13] research: Hovland, Lumsdaine and Sheffield, Stouffer, Guttman, Suchman et al., and Merton and Lazarsfeld. (Another book which in a sense draws on wartime work is Berelson's, since content analysis techniques, though not without prewar roots, had been enormously refined and extended during the war as they rose to the challenge of reaching conclusions about the enemy from available written material. Merton, Fiske and Kendall (1956) too was first drafted for use by the Army research team.) Hovland, Lumsdaine and Sheffield was mainly concerned with the effects of communications on their audiences. In addition to the material exemplifying leading-edge methods – to do with such matters as the formulation of appropriate questions, the relevance of background variables, and the use of controlled variation to distinguish causes – there are substantial appendices on measurement problems which address

---

[12] There were some prewar books on interviewing – e.g. Bingham and Moore 1931, Young 1935 – which are referred to in the methodological literature of sociology before such works as these became available. They are not listed as sociological monographs because they were either explicitly concerned with social-work interviews, or treated research interviewing as just one kind along with interviewing of job applicants, journalistic informants, etc. The emergence of research interviewing as a special type is part of the story of the separation of social science from social work.

[13] This name is customarily used for the programme of social research done in the Army during the Second World War; it appears in the title of two of the books on it published after the war, but is commonly taken to refer both to all four of the books, which include Hovland, Lumsdaine and Sheffield and Stouffer, Guttman, Suchman et al., and to the whole undertaking. Stouffer is especially associated with it, because he directed the programme, but many others were involved.

general issues of experimental design and the measurement of change. Stouffer, Guttman, Suchman et al. is more intensively methodological in its content. The bulk of its material is about the theory and practice of attitude and opinion scaling, but there is also a substantial section on the prediction of future behaviour. Although several novelties are introduced, among which the Guttman scale (a technique for ranking qualitatively different attitudinal items so that underlying dimensions could be identified and the strength of individual attitudes measured) was probably the most consequential, these concerns are recognisably in the line of earlier traditions. From the point of view of development of methods, one of the most important features of the Army research was simply the opportunity it gave to carry out a very large number of empirical studies so that alternative strategies could be put to the test, although there was little time for methodological reflection or deliberate experimentation.[14] The enormous impact of the series was, one may safely presume, helped by the recent practical significance of the substantive subject matter as well as the striking nature of some of the findings.

The Merton and Lazarsfeld volume, whose authors had been very close to the *American Soldier* research team when not formally members of it, is in the tradition of critiques of published work, but not so much attacking it as drawing out its implications further. As Hyman (1991: 86) points out, it performed an important function in summarising the major findings in shorter and more accessible form and so assisting their diffusion; this was part of its declared object. It also helped to make its potential relevance to people not interested in the military evident by analysing the general theoretical ideas. Methodologically, it is significant that it presents *The American Soldier* as 'the first major work which enables the reader, not specialising in social-psychological research, to learn the details of the more advanced methods in the relatively new field of attitude sampling surveys . . . social scientists themselves . . . have

---

[14] As Converse (1987: 224) points out, there was no equivalent of the American Soldier volumes for the civilian research effort during the war, which is a major reason why its contribution is much less known and, presumably, its ideas might have spread less widely among those not directly involved. Important work was done there on the use of more qualitative styles of survey data and their coding and analysis. However, communication among survey researchers at this stage was good, so this may have made little real difference.

yet to work out the numerous relations of this newer kind of analysis to more traditional problems of research in the social sciences', and later it is pointed out that survey analysis has been little discussed so far because so few surveys have been published and are available for discussion (Merton and Lazarsfeld 1950: 12, 133). Only the chapter by Kendall and Lazarsfeld on 'Problems of survey analysis' is specifically on method as such, though Stouffer also comments on it in his 'afterthoughts'. Both hold out experiment as the ideal, and indeed Stouffer says that '*The American Soldier* will have a dangerous influence on future research if the survey methods on which it relies for so much of the data are regarded as the ideal' (1950: 210). Kendall and Lazarsfeld characterise the kind of analytic technique they offer as unnecessary when one is testing prior hypotheses, but valuable in extracting the maximum of theoretical generalisation from existing empirical data when enough is not yet known for the testing of hypotheses.

Following Merton and Lazarsfeld, two more volumes provide critical analysis of the methods and conclusions of major and controversial empirical works, *The Authoritarian Personality* (Adorno, Brunswik, Levinson and Sanford 1950) and the Kinsey Report (Kinsey, Pomeroy and Martin 1948). Neither of these is concerned only with method, but it is a significant component of both, and in each case some serious criticisms were made. Kinsey was particularly open to attack for his unsystematic 'sampling', though the chapter on his statistics in Himelhoch and Fava concludes that his methods were superior to much previous sex research, and for interviewing techniques which, although he had a rationale for them as facilitating the statement of sexual material which would otherwise be concealed, were plainly leading. *The Authoritarian Personality* was praised both for being a project which started from a well-developed theory, and for combining the previously separate approaches of statistical methods and intensive clinical case-study of psychodynamics. Adorno, Brunswik, Levinson and Sanford were, however, criticised for serious methodological weaknesses affecting the adequacy of the relations between data and conclusions. It is suggested that their sampling was biased, that the choice of scale items was sometimes unsuitable, that some of the procedures adopted in interviewing and coding were likely to skew material artifactually in the direction of supporting the hypotheses, that they fail to control for relevant variables such as education, and that qualitative data are over-interpreted to favour the thesis without scientific checks on the validity of the interpretations or attention to plausible alternatives. It is indeed a devastating critique, distinguished by its close attention to detail and its consistent focus on the relation between method and justification of conclusions; it shows a highly-developed methodological culture and sensibility (from authors, Hyman and Sheatsley, who were both closely associated with survey work). It is likely that such critiques, though mainly negative in character, did a lot to draw attention to the concrete detail implied by high methodological standards, and the strengths and weaknesses of new and fashionable techniques. The association of each with a specific substantive subject matter, and one of wide interest and of a sensational nature, must have helped to diffuse methodological self-consciousness, bringing its implications to the attention of non-specialists.

Several other books took up various aspects of the now established survey method. Parten's is a sophisticated specialist textbook, reflecting her background in drawing on both academic and commercial experience. Payne's is a witty and informal guide to the formulation of questions, how to do it and how not to do it, sufficiently user-friendly and wise to continue to be referred to even now. Hansen, Hurwitz and Madow and Stephan and McCarthy are two thorough advanced texts on survey sampling, both written by acknowledged experts in the field with much practical experience. The former deals more with the mathematics of sampling. Stephan and McCarthy emphasise the relation between sampling and other aspects of survey design. About half the book reports the results of empirical studies of the sampling process as it operates in practice; work of this kind had not been done on that scale before. The suggestions made for procedure draw on these findings, and so take many practical contingencies into account. Converse (1987: 371–2) sees this book as a compromise designed to resolve the controversy between the mathematically sound probability sample and the cheaper and easier quota sample favoured by the commercial outfits, bringing the academic and the commercial together. In that context, she sees the use made of empirical studies as a rhetorical strategy, since these would be more likely to be persuasive to people not at home with probability theory.

Scaling is not exclusively relevant to surveys, and indeed much of it has been developed by psychologists not involved with the survey, but at this time it was very much related to the elaboration of survey techniques; several of the leading survey figures were particularly interested in scaling and, as sociologists sometimes tend to forget, psychological social psychologists have been at least equally prominent in survey history. Scaling is connected with the theory of measurement, and provides a relatively firm foundation for quantification, by making it possible to claim accurate and meaningful measurement of degrees of intensity; this translates attributes into variables, and means that the data collected can be much more effectively manipulated mathematically. Its relevance is more than merely technical, since it necessarily raises the issue of whether items intended to measure the same thing, or varying levels of it, actually do so, and indeed of whether that thing actually exists as an empirically meaningful entity. Riley, Riley and Toby's book is both theoretical and technical, and reports methodological research. The issues raised include the description, empirical representation and measurement of single variables. It claims to represent the convergence of the methodological thought of Lazarsfeld, Stouffer and Guttman with the theoretical line of Parsons, Cottrell, Merton and Moreno; the Guttman scale is the general model used, and a new use of it is made to study group situations sociometrically. Torgerson's book is an advanced technical review of the work done to date, which was mainly in psychology but seen as also relevant to sociology and other disciplines. Lazarsfeld's collection deals with mathematical models for different types of behaviour, a rather new theme in the literature, largely treated here by getting experts from other disciplines to suggest applications in sociology; it also covers scaling and measurement issues, especially in relation to attitudes. In relation to sociology, this was work at the forefront.

Hyman's *Survey Design and Analysis* is the first monograph not about experiments to treat the logic of design and the imputation of causes. Some of its concerns are also reflected in a rather different way in Zetterberg's book, though his work is not confined to any one method of data collection. Zetterberg draws together and formalises in a masterly manner themes in philosophy of science and research design which were in the air, but had not previously been so fully developed. His emphasis is on the need for explicit theorising, and the structuring of research to test hypotheses, so that general conclusions can be logically justified.

The book which has been seen by some as epitomising the 1950s is Lazarsfeld and Rosenberg's *The Language of Social Research*. This had tremendous success, one reason for which was surely that it was the first substantial reader on methods, and could be used as a main or supplementary textbook in graduate teaching. But it was far from being merely a summary of what had been learned about how to do various research tasks, both because much of it consists of concrete examples of good procedure, and because it was not without reason that the authors contemplated presenting it as a contribution to philosophy of science. Whatever the degree of theorisation of the examples offered, the authors' own framework is a strongly analytical one which locates them in the logic of conceptualisation, classification and causal explanation. This is partly because topics where there was already a standardised literature – sampling, questionnaire construction and experimental technique – were omitted. Also omitted were topics where they judged that systematic analyses of the methodological problems had not been made, and these included studies of formal organisations, participant observation in community studies,[15] and anthropological fieldwork. Although what is included is certainly not confined to survey methods, and much of it could in principle be relevant to data collected in any way, the examples given tend to come from surveys and the effect is skewed in that direction. The introduction suggests that it could be seen as a programmatic statement of the team working on the Columbia Project for Advanced Training in Social Research, Lazarsfeld's long-term enterprise. The mark of Lazarsfeld is heavily on the book as a whole; half the papers are by him or his close associates, some especially commissioned to fill a gap. Indeed, it could more plausibly be described as epitomising his personal approach rather than the themes of the 1950s, though his prominence was such that it is sometimes hard to distinguish them – but that prominence is in part the product of the apparent dominance which this book gives to his work and influence.

Junker's *Field Work* and the Adams and Preiss volume stand out from the rest in that they are unequivocally about qualitative styles

---

[15] The now-classic sources on this (Whyte 1955, H. S. Becker and Geer 1957, H. S. Becker 1958) were all published too late. One might, however, question Lazarsfeld's judgment on this.

or aspects of research. *Field Work* can be seen as essentially the product of Everett Hughes' compulsory Chicago graduate course on fieldwork methods, on which it draws for much of the data presented. The project which provided the material was one in which fieldworkers, beginners or experienced researchers, were interviewed about what they did, and many reports of fieldwork experience were collected; in the spirit of Hughes' teaching as his students describe it (J. Platt 1995a), it is heavier on examples than on detailed analysis. Although for Hughes this book merely continued his long-term commitments, it can be seen as a fore-runner, if not a part, of the flurry of systematic work on participant observation and related qualitative research styles which developed in the 1960s; this included Cicourel (1964), Bruyn (1966), Webb, Campbell, Schwartz and Sechrest (1966), Glaser and Strauss (1967), McCall and Simmons (1969), Filstead (1970), Jacobs (1970) and Lofland (1971).

Human Organisation Research is equally a forerunner. Its contents emphasise the human relations of research, an issue hardly touched on in the survey literature except in discussions of interviewer rapport, and under that head include a number of chapters on relations with clients and within research teams which raise quite new themes. The second part of the book deals with field techniques, and it is interesting that the great majority of the contributions specially commissioned for the book appear here; this presumably implies that fieldworkers had written less about that area, but it also represents a decision by the editors to cover some techniques (such as Q technique, sociometry, mapping) not conventionally used in fieldwork to broaden the repertoire which could be drawn on. As a matter of principle as much as possible of the material is presented in the context of concrete field situations actually experienced. The availability of many such situations to write about indicates that, even if dominant tendencies lay elsewhere, qualitative fieldwork research had been taking place.

It is evident that fieldwork makes issues of social relations more salient. This is both because there is no formal instrument of data collection to conceal them, and because they are commonly conducted by the researcher in person, not a lower-status employee regarded as merely an instrument. A whole literature of auto-biographical accounts of research experience came into existence after our period, and it seems likely that the new fieldwork literature helped to stimulate this by drawing attention to such factors.

Over the period as a whole, it is striking how much of the monographic writing on method is reviewing empirical work already done by others; critical analysis, whether hostile or friendly, is clearly a key mode of methodological advance. Very little of the work introduces novelties which have not already been tried in practice; that which does is normally abstractly philosophical or mathematical in character. Little presents novelties for which the author was solely responsible either; there is a research community with some cumulative work, even if it has subdivisions. It is not easy to draw convincing boundaries between sociological and other work, and important contributions were made or taken from other disciplines, mathematics and psychology in particular. (Let us hope that sociologists also contributed to those fields in return.) There was quite a lot of cross-disciplinary cooperation, and importation, perhaps with modifications, was one source of ideas and writing.[16] Thus the pattern of development is one in which thinking advances by reflection on practice drawn from diverse sources. To that extent writing does reflect practice rather than self-generating theory, but it does not follow that it is representative of practice.

Following the sequence of developments recorded in writing on method as they change over time tells one something about the available repertoire, though new practices may be well established in their places of origin long before publication. It is sometimes a good question to ask why a certain sociologist did not use a method which already existed and seems to us obviously appropriate, as for instance Selvin (1976) does in his article on why the statistical ideas of Yule did not reach Booth or Durkheim, despite their relevance to the concerns of the other men. What makes it a good question is that there were sufficient factors predisposing towards it, or making a real opportunity for its use, for the omission to be initially surprising; such factors are often not present. Those with expertise in statistics have regularly pointed out that well-established

---

[16] Blalock (1989: 447–8) suggests that the increasing size of cohorts of methodologists was important in making it possible for the field to have the resources to learn about and borrow from work in other disciplines. It may be that the rate of borrowing has increased – there could be a dissertation topic there – but such borrowing was important even when there were very few sociological methods specialists.

statistical principles are not being followed by sociologists – see, for instance, Dewey 1915, Woofter 1933, Hagood 1947. Ignorance seems as likely a reason as any; the existence of a technique of unquestioned validity for those who are aware of it does not guarantee that it will be applied where relevant by others. But ignorance too invites explanation, which is likely to involve academic social structures and/or cohorts.

Thus not all methods known are practised; conversely, it need not be the case that all aspects of method actually practised are written about, or conceptualised as distinct. Hempel (1966: 3–8) has used Semmelweis' work in the 1840s on childbed fever to illustrate correct scientific procedure in the testing of hypotheses; there is no reason to believe that Semmelweis had any abstract knowledge of the principles which Hempel enunciates. Beatrice Webb used participant observation before 'participant observation' had been 'invented' as a recognised technique (J. Lewis 1991: 156). Selvin (1965) showed how Durkheim used analytic strategies which noone had formalised at the time. Lazarsfeld pointed out how Stouffer did novel things which he did not himself label as such, and for which Lazarsfeld received credit:

When you go through Stouffer's papers, you find at every point an interesting new contribution, but it is never tagged . . . While Sam and I worked on various similar matters, most of the time in complete agreement, he did it and I added a slogan to it . . . he didn't recognise, so to say, the important things he did, and therefore impeded in a way his role in the history of sociology. (Lazarsfeld 1961: 339).[17]

It became harder to commit the ecological fallacy (of assuming that group-level correlations convey information about correlations at the individual level) after W. S. Robinson (1950) had identified it and given it a name. These instances are easy to identify because they have now been written about; who knows how many others there are yet to be identified? The introduction to Lazarsfeld and Rosenberg (1955: 4) observes that in the search for suitable material to include they had found that 'the number of studies making use of sophisticated research practices is far greater than the number of papers which articulate or codify or discuss the procedures themselves'. Erving Goffman, asked about his own

---

[17] For further discussion of the relationship and contributions of the two, see J. Platt 1986c.

method, says that he can recognise instances of it done well, but cannot provide the rules for doing it well and does not trust anyone else's explication (Verhoeven 1993: 341). Hyman mentions in passing several cases where innovatory practices were not written up, referring to one survey unit's staff's 'persistent attention to methodological problems but their chronic failure to disseminate the scientific by-products through scholarly publications' (Hyman 1991: 38). These examples make clear that the identification, labelling, elaboration and formalisation of existing practices[18] is an important function of methodological writing, but not one which is automatically performed when an advance has been made.

TEXTBOOKS: CONTENT

When we turn to the textbooks, the picture is filled out. Textbooks are central to a discipline, if seldom at its cutting edge. Individually they may be idiosyncratic, but collectively they express some sort of consensus on the ordinary, shared positions which are taken for granted by most teachers and transmitted by them to their students; popular and successful textbooks must be taken to express this better. We may assume that researchers have read textbooks and are influenced by what they read, even if they no longer consciously remember it, so that this discussion is at least indirectly relevant to research practice. The history of textbooks throws light on the history of both mainstream methodological ideas and textbook writing as a genre, and is discussed below in relation to both themes. Textbooks are especially relevant for what they show about the sets of concepts used to describe and classify methods, since they, unlike monographs, aim to cover the field.

The large number of variants on a standard formula which exist among the textbooks suggests that significant originality is not a requirement of the textbook genre. Although it is not impossible that a textbook should be intellectually innovative, it is not to be expected; the prime scope for originality is in the arrangement and conceptualisation of the material, but too much originality might

---

[18] Sometimes the relevant practices come from another discipline, and what the writer does is to introduce them to sociology; this can be of the utmost importance, as when O. D. Duncan (1966) drew attention to the applicability of biologist Sewall Wright's path analysis to social data.

run the risk of not covering the conventional syllabus and so being rejected by teachers as unsuitable (Rothman 1971: 126–7).[19] Graduate textbooks are, however, more similar to monographs: closer to the newer and more esoteric knowledge of those at the cutting edge, and directed at students more likely to apply what they learn from them within the discipline, or at all.

Every sociological methods textbook published in the USA up to 1960 is listed in table 2. The first book which could be regarded as a methods text in anything like the modern sense is Bogardus (1918, 1925).[20] This, however, is very vague about practical details, presumably because, although some empirical research was by then being done, it was not yet sufficiently institutionalised in the universities to be within the sphere of a professor or to have standard models and terminologies to draw on. Anyone wishing to find out how to do research work would have needed a lot more guidance than such a book provided. Nonetheless, Bogardus may have been first because the orientation of his department was to practitioners rather than academics.

The sense that the weight of empirical conclusions rested on the merit of the methods by which they had been reached was not yet clearly established in the 1920s, and even at the University of Chicago, where much important research was done then, the publications based on it were often extremely vague about the status and origins of their data (J.Platt 1994a). However, the Chicago department produced an early textbook (Palmer 1928), which brought together a body of practical research experience; another early one is Odum and Jocher (1929), from the department at North Carolina which was another major contemporary centre of research and training, though its contents are much less practically helpful.[21] The next prominent text was Pauline V. Young's, which

---

[19] For the more recent period, McGee (1985) has described the process of putting together a text, and the commercial pressure on publishers to cover everything that any subgroup might want in order to maximise sales.

[20] The first edition was in 1918, but I have not traced a single surviving copy in the libraries visited – with the exception of one found in Columbia University Library, which turned out to have only its cover, with no contents remaining. Perforce, the discussion draws entirely on the second edition.

[21] Giddings' *The Scientific Study of Human Society* (1924), though hardly a practical textbook and hence not included in the listing, could be taken to represent the Columbia department, though Mayo-Smith's (1895) book on social statistics might be at least equally eligible for that title.

Table 2. *Methods textbooks*

Date	Author	Title	Target audience
1918	Bogardus	*Making Social Science Studies*	?(Not seen)
1920	Chapin	*Field Work and Social Research*	?
1925	Bogardus	*Making Social Science Studies*, 2nd edn	Students
1926	Bogardus	*The New Social Research*	?(New methods)
1928	Palmer	*Field Studies in Sociology*	Students
1929	Lundberg	*Social Research*	Students
1929	Odum and Jocher	*An Introduction to Social Research*	Students and specialists
1934	Fry	*The Technique of Social Investigation*	Graduates, executives
1936	Bogardus	*Introduction to Social Research*	Students, general reader
1939	Elmer	*Social Research*	?General sociologists
1939	Young	*Scientific Social Surveys and Research*	Students (intermediate)
1942	Lundberg	*Social Research*, 2nd edn	Students, teachers
1949	Young	*Scientific Social Surveys and Research*, 2nd edn	Students, teachers, social-work administrators, researchers
1950	Gee	*Social Science Research Methods*	Graduates, researchers
1951	Jahoda, Deutsch and Cook (2 vols.)	*Research Methods in Social Relations*	Graduates
1952	Goode and Hatt	*Methods in Social Research*	Students
1953	Ackoff	*The Design of Social Research*	Graduates
1953	Festinger and Katz	*Research Methods in the Behavioral Sciences*	Graduates
1953	Furfey	*The Scope and Method of Sociology*	(Not specified; ?graduates)
1954	Doby	*An Introduction to Social Research*	Students
1956	Young	*Scientific Social Surveys and Research*, 3rd edn	Students, teachers, social-work administrators, researchers
1958	McCormick and Francis	*Methods of Research in the Behavioral Sciences*	Graduates
1959	Selltiz, Jahoda, Deutsch and Cook	*Research Methods in Social Relations*, 2nd edn (revised edition of Jahoda, Deutsch and Cook)	Undergraduates

went through a series of revised editions; this came out of Bogardus' department, but also had strong Chicago connections. Lundberg's contribution did not represent any significant department – he was based at Pittsburgh at the time – but a younger man's enthusiasm; it showed familiarity with a wide range of work, related theoretical issues to empirical practices, addressed hot contemporary issues such as the case study versus statistics, and did give a fair amount of guidance on details. His scientistic approach was shown by the space devoted to scaling, measurement and operationalisation, treated for the first time in the textbook literature. It was perhaps the first really modern textbook, running ahead of the available monographic literature, and as such deserved its success.

It will be noted that for a decade there was an almost complete hiatus in the production of new textbooks, which helps to account for the marked change between prewar and postwar. The new post-war texts include three generally recognised as classics: Jahoda, Deutsch and Cook, Festinger and Katz and Goode and Hatt. The first two came out of milieux where the new survey was prominent, Columbia and Michigan, and give emphasis to survey issues; both are also strongly social-psychological in orientation. Goode and Hatt, with one author at the time of writing based at Columbia and the other with experience in the National Opinion Research Center, is also heavily skewed to survey issues. The presence of three postwar volumes (Jahoda, Deutsch and Cook vol II, Festinger and Katz, Doby) which collect chapters by different authors is suggestive of emerging specialisation and division of labour within the field of method.

'Science' is an important theme in the texts, and there are important changes over time in the conceptions of scientific method shown there (and in a range of other methodological writing touching on this theme which is taken into account here). Although even the early textbook writers generally recognise the desirability of testing hypotheses, induction to establish laws is heavily emphasised. 'Induction' was for that generation the virtuous alternative to 'deduction', the latter referring not to empirical work, but to system-building without benefit of system-atic data. When one considers what they were reacting against, one can understand why they took positions which to later generations merely look like mindless empiricism. (It was only later, when 'theory' had become something that produced propositions for empirical testing, that it was rehabilitated for people seriously committed to scientific empirical work.)[22] There was also considerable emphasis on having an objective attitude, without personal bias, as part of being scientific;[23] for later writers the emphasis shifted to suggested intellectual procedures.

All textbooks after Bogardus' first put a heavy emphasis in their chapter titles on modes of data collection, although the modes distinguished change over time. These chapters are conventionally preceded by general material on scientific approaches, and succeeded by something on analysis and presentation. Only in the postwar period is it taken for granted that students will learn statistics, and then some texts assume that another book will be used for that while others include chapters on it. (Changing standards of statistical sophistication are shown by the movement under that head from the use of official statistical sources, tabulation and graphs to modern mathematical techniques.) A distinguishing feature of the postwar generation of texts is their heavy emphasis on (modern) survey method, and a tendency for the whole structure and ordering of the book's material to follow the sequence of phases conventional in surveys.[24] There is also the appearance for the first time of research design as an important topic. Sampling, scaling and indexes, measurement and operationalisation are also given heavier weight than was usual earlier, and the terminology of 'variables' becomes normal. Another major transition is marked by the decline of serious treatment of 'case study', life histories and 'personal documents', and the correlative emergence of 'fieldwork' and participant observation as standard topics. (For more on this, see below.)

Sales figures for most texts have not been found, but the available course reading lists and the issuing of reprints or revised editions support the comments of my respondents on the textbooks to which they were exposed in indicating that Young and Jahoda et

---

[22] C. Wright Mills is perhaps reverting to an earlier tradition of counterposing systematic data and theory when he makes his very questionably well-founded attack on Lazarsfeld for 'abstracted empiricism' (Mills 1959).

[23] A number of my postwar-student respondents mentioned Weber's methodological essays on the role of values and politics (in Gerth and Mills 1946, Weber 1949) as having been important to them in connection with these issues; hence what might otherwise seem a rather puzzling association of Weber with positivism.

[24] Gee's book follows the earlier model, but it had been written earlier and its publication was postponed due to the war.

al. were especially prominent; these will, therefore, be examined more closely.

The character of Young's book, plus the timing of its revised editions, makes it a particularly useful source for plotting the course of change. It is in many ways a compilation work, though formally written by one author with a few additional chapters by others, in that it draws heavily on both printed sources and brief statements by leading figures especially written for it. Thus it has a strong tendency to reflect whatever were seen as the tendencies of the time, and may to that extent be taken as an index of the sociological community's perception of those. Pauline Vislick Young worked for many years at the University of Southern California, where she submitted her doctoral thesis,[25] which appeared as *The Pilgrims of Russian-Town* (1932). She is not generally known for any later empirical work, but made a career as an author of textbooks, most of them addressed to social workers. One may presume that much of her teaching was to social workers, and *Scientific Social Surveys and Research* shows signs of that orientation. The first sign is in the title of the book, where 'survey' refers, as the dedication to Beatrice Webb as well as the earlier chapters show, to the old, reformist model:

a study – generally a cooperative undertaking which has social implications and significance – of current foci of social infection, of pathological conditions, having definite geographical limits and bearings, for the purpose of presenting a constructive program for social advance arrived at by measuring social conditions and comparing standards with an existing unit which has been accepted as a model towards which to strive. (1939: 54–5)

The second part of the title is also historically significant, because it is distinguishing 'survey' from 'research', which she goes on to discuss and define as systematic study concerned to theorise, generalise and predict across the whole range of human behaviour

---

[25] Faris' book on the Chicago department refers to her as if she were one of Park's students (Faris 1967: 71), though she does not appear in his list of those who received degrees there; the influence is, at any rate, plain. Her thesis was published in the University of Chicago Press monograph series, the only work in it by someone not formally associated with the department. Her husband was Erle Fiske Young, who got a Chicago PhD in 1924 and then taught there for four years before moving to the University of Southern California (USC); perhaps she transferred her registration to follow him? Bogardus, the head of the USC department, had Park of Chicago as his mentor, and worked with him on the Pacific Coast Race Relations Survey.

without special reference to pathology or amelioration. The third edition of 1956 still starts with a chapter on the history of the survey movement, and 'survey' is still seen as oriented to social problems and practitioners, but the contrast, and the emphasis on the 'survey' part, is much less salient.[26] The same transition is indicated in the pictures provided of heroes of social research. In 1939, only John Howard (the prison reformer), Charles Booth, Beatrice Webb and W. I. Thomas appear; by 1949 Robert K. Merton, W. Lloyd Warner, Margaret Mead and Dorothy S. Thomas have been added, as well as several of the leading interwar sociologists.

Apart from the social-work orientation, we may note as features old-fashioned by the 1950s the emphasis in the chapter titles on data-collection at the expense of design and analysis, and the continuance of a chapter on 'case-study method'.[27] The original chapter on 'sociometric scales' did not refer to Moreno's sociometry, not generally known at the time; this appears in the revised edition under 'scaling techniques' which, while still a short chapter (now by Schmid), has been technically updated to take into account the work of Guttman. The chapters on ecological methods and on graphics are not ones which have typically appeared in texts of any period;[28] they may be taken to represent both a Chicago affiliation (for ecology and the mapping techniques which form part of the graphics shown) and the special interests and expertise of Schmid.[29] Looking more closely at the contents of the chapters, we can trace how Young has followed the emergence of fresh research. If the classic Chicago monographs figure largely in the first edition, that is because little other empirical work had been published in book form at the time of writing. It is not surprising that *Pilgrims of Russian-Town* bulks large as a source of examples and illustrations. The initial chapter on field observation draws almost entirely on Young's own fieldwork; the 1949 one has been extended to cover the more 'scientific' observational studies of Dorothy S. Thomas –

---

[26] For detailed material on the history of the early survey, see Bulmer, Bales and Sklar 1991.

[27] An amusing minor aspect of modernisation is the later addition in the title of the chapter on community study (in the part omitted for reason of space in the table) of 'rural' to the original 'urban'; this may be taken to signify recognition that Chicago is no longer the one university taken as model.

[28] The headings appear in several course lists – but they are ones which draw on Young's text.

[29] Schmid was a specialist in demography and ecology, whom (he told me in conversation) she recruited to contribute his chapters without being personally acquainted.

published in 1929, so not new, but perhaps more up to date in spirit. In each edition participant observation is mentioned, but briefly and without special meaning attached to it; *Street Corner Society* (Whyte 1943) is mentioned only in 1956, and given a few lines. The book as a whole could hardly be said to have an intellectual standpoint. It puts together carefully collected fragments and statements by other people, and conscientiously mentions the works it has become customary to mention even if they make little impress on the ideas stated. Despite these deficiencies, not present in Schmid's contributions, it does give quite a lot of detailed technical and practical advice on how to carry out research procedures; it was not without reason that it was well used.

Research Methods in Social Relations is a very different sort of book. Its authors were social psychologists. Marie Jahoda had been Paul Lazarsfeld's wife and collaborator in Vienna, and had stayed in touch with his intellectual milieu while also gaining other kinds of research experience in England before going to America and joining New York University, where her collaborators were located. The book was under the auspices of the Society for the Psychological Study of Social Issues, and had been initially planned as one on the measurement of prejudice; the original editorial committee had reflected this in its composition, including representatives of Jewish and Christian/Jewish bodies. It was, though, eventually decided to make it a general book on the research process, but with a special emphasis on prejudice and on the practical application of research; it was intended to be suitable for introductory graduate courses in research methods. It was in two volumes; the first dealt with the major steps in an inquiry in order, while the second dealt with some specific problems in more technical detail.[30] It conscientiously ensured that qualitative techniques were covered, but the basic structure as well as the overall content is one appropriate to the model of survey or experimental research, where one starts from a clear problem, forms hypotheses, collects all the data to test the hypotheses, then analyses the probably quantitative data.

[30] In 1965 a revised one-volume edition (Sellitz, Jahoda, Deutsch and Cook) was issued, somewhat modified to make it suitable for the by now commoner undergraduate courses in research methods. Most of the background information given here comes from the Prefaces to the two editions.

Jahoda, Deutsch and Cook are much more sophisticated philo-
sophically than Young, as well as aiming at a more sophisticated
audience, of graduate students in social science rather than under-
graduates and social workers. It is particularly notable that in the
first volume two full chapters, after the general introductory one,
are devoted to the formulation of problems and to research design,
with serious coverage of the logic of experimental design. (Young
treats the topic as too difficult to deal with in her book.) The final
chapter returns to the theoretical purposes of research by treating
the relation of research and theory. The theory of measurement
as well as practicalities of scaling is covered, and there is a whole
chapter on projective and other indirect methods. Sampling and
analysis are dealt with more extensively than in Young's second
edition, and there is a section on coding which does not appear at
all in Young. Rather than Young's whole chapter on 'case study
method', there are just five pages, and in a section on 'insight-
stimulating examples'.

The second volume is an intellectually substantial one, with each
chapter by people prominent in relation to its theme. Most of these
themes are, if not new, up-to-date, reflecting the latest developments; several chapters are thick with formulae. The topics are
questionnaires and interview schedules (Arthur Kornhauser),
interviewing and interviewer selection and training (Paul B.
Sheatsley), observational field-work (William F. Whyte), systematic
observation of small groups (Alvin Zander), content analysis of
mass media (Donald McGranahan), analysis of sociometric data
(Charles H. Procter and Charles P. Loomis), panel studies (Morris
Rosenberg, Wagner Thielens and Paul Lazarsfeld), community
self-surveys (Margot Haas Wormser and Claire Selltiz), sample
design (Philip J. McCarthy), scaling (Samuel Stouffer) and
assumptions underlying statistical techniques (Leon Festinger).
The chapter on 'community self-surveys' is significant; it sounds as
though it were a survival of the old type of 'survey', and indeed what
is described has considerable resemblances to it, but the text and
references show no awareness of the existence of that tradition.
From the point of view of method, the focus in that chapter is on
using the technique of the modern survey, but simplified for the use
of amateurs, and, unlike in the typical old survey, it is assumed that
the data collected will be on one particular theme rather than
giving a general picture of the community. That is new, but the aim

of community self-improvement, and the use of community participation to promote the aim as well as instrumentally to collect data to be used toward it, could have come from Elmer's 1917 book. One can only guess why there should have been this apparent ignorance of earlier work; perhaps it can be attributed to the different frames of social and intellectual reference of circles skewed towards psychologists, Jews, cities and recent immigrants rather than the older social worker/sociologists, social Christians, rural areas and pioneers.[31] Although not all the authors come from the same institution, this is a group largely drawn from those based in or near New York and connected with the Lazarsfeld/survey circle, while Young's book is, apart from its early Chicago connection, oriented to the West coast, which was relatively distant from the main centres of development at the time.

So far the differences between Young and Jahoda, Deutsch and Cook have been emphasised, but there are also similarities,[32] whose presence despite the important intellectual differences tells us something about the process of construction of textbooks. Each shows a range of material which in principle attempts comprehensive coverage, but in practice is weighted in the direction of areas and examples closest to the authors' personal concerns; the authors' own material is supplemented by only partially integrated contributions from others seen as expert on the topic in question. Each draws on as examples, and holds out as exemplars, empirical work some of which is the product of disciplinary consensus, but some of which is idiosyncratic or local in its use; the latter is drawn from the work most familiar to the authors, because done by themselves or their close colleagues.[33] Each carries traces of its time of origin in the conceptualisation and organisation of the material even when (in Young's case) a later edition has updated the

---

[31] Perhaps it might be regarded as an ignorance symbolic of another discontinuity with earlier work that Dorothy Thomas, Loomis and Arrington (1933) is mentioned – and the authors referred to as 'these men'! (Zander in Jahoda, Deutsch and Cook 1951: 531).

[32] One of these is coincidental; most textbooks are not, like these two, written so specifically with a social-problem orientation for research in mind.

[33] Seymour (1982) reports that in his time as a graduate student at Stanford – relatively close to USC – in the mid-1950s *Pilgrims of Russian-Town* was still treated as important; no other respondent ever mentioned it.

examples used.[34] There is nothing surprising in such features – indeed, it would be more surprising if they were absent – but they are inconsistent with the normal self-presentation of textbooks as comprehensive and non-partisan. In general, textbooks draw their material from work already done by those who write articles and monographs or who publish substantive work which is regarded as methodologically interesting. The characteristic textbook has strong elements of *bricolage* in its composition, piecing together standard examples and available fragments of systematic work already done by others to cover – and to define – the field. This is often done with a greater cultural lag behind the moving frontier of new thinking[35] than can be accounted for by the length of time needed to produce a new book; where editions are revised, there is an understandable tendency to insert minor revisions into the old framework rather than changing the basic structure.

In addition, Young's chapters (by Schmid) on quantitative methods articulate very poorly with the earlier ones on data collection; Jahoda, Deutsch and Cook's chapter on analysis and interpretation gives no clue how to analyse data not essentially of the type provided by surveys, despite their conscientious earlier references to qualitative modes of data collection. This is a common kind of discrepancy, which indicates not only which model of the research process is really dominant in the author's mind, but also in which areas techniques have already been explicitly theorised. It is commonplace in modern texts to discuss design in terms of experiments, and sampling and analysis in terms of surveys, while other modes of research appear only in the chapters on data-collection.

Obviously new features cannot appear until the practices they discuss have been invented; for textbook writers to have effective access to them, they typically also require to have been written about in ways which draw attention to them and systematise them.

---

[34] There have been several revised editions of Jahoda, Deutsch and Cook; postwar changes have been less marked than those between prewar and postwar, so within our period there is less scope for such features to reveal themselves. Comparison is also complicated by the fact that its second edition combined the two volumes into one, and adapted the material to be more suitable for an undergraduate audience.

[35] An example of this in recent texts is the use of Campbell's earlier work to criticise case-study designs, in apparent ignorance of the fact that his more recent work has argued along quite different lines. For more about this, see J. Platt 1992c: 42–3.

Where there is a neat schematic formulation, it is highly likely that texts will draw on it. Thus R. L. Gold's (1958) distinctions between types of role played by participant observers are now almost universally used. The rather more complex formulations by Lazarsfeld of distinctions among specification, interpretation and explanation in his elaboration model (Kendall and Lazarsfeld 1950), and by Campbell of threats to validity in experimental design (Campbell 1957), have had if anything even more success. This success must also, of course, owe much to the felt intellectual merit and timeliness of the content of these formulations, but I think that one can be reasonably confident that if anyone had produced an equally tight and comprehensive list of types on other topics it would also have been widely used, and in consequence its theme would have bulked larger in textbook contents.

CHANGING CONCEPTS

The concepts used to describe the methods current have changed historically, so that the same practice can not just have a different name but be part of a different set of ideas; this makes any consistent set of categories potentially misleading about methodological thought. The task of tracing change over time, especially if done quantitatively as in the studies cited in the next chapter, entails using the same categories at each period. This forces such studies to apply their own concepts – which normally implies those current at the time of writing – rather than those which would have been used by many of the researchers whose work they are classifying. In addition, even the same names for methods may change their meaning over time.

This can be documented with a few examples. In the 1920s, 'personal documents' regularly appears as a type of data. The term covers diaries, letters and autobiographical accounts, possibly commissioned by the researcher; such materials have seldom or never been used in more recent times, and the category postwar exists only with a selfconsciously historical reference. 'Participant observation' was done in the 1920s but, as is shown in more detail below, it was not then called that, or given the full significance it later acquired until the 1940s; nor was it seen as clearly distinct from modes of data collection now regarded as quite different. 'Survey' was used as a category from the earliest days, but not to refer, as it does now, to a particular mode of data collection. What it used to mean laid the emphasis on the purpose (which was social reform and local community self-improvement), and on the coverage of a limited geographical area; the typical early 'survey' collected facts about a town by whatever means came to hand. It had in common with the later 'survey' that it often employed a schedule, though usually one completed by an enumerator, and without questions with a fixed wording to be addressed to individual subjects. It had nothing to do with attitudes, and the jokingly pejorative reference to this sort of activity as 'outhouse-counting' was not without foundation. Holt, discussing the usefulness of 'case' records on religious experience, brings this out by remarking that:

if the commonly accepted survey which has been staged in America had been carried on in Jerusalem at the time of the early church, it would never have discovered any difference between the Scribes and the Pharisees and the goodly company of the Apostles. It would have catalogued them all as church members and let them go at that (Holt 1926: 228–9)

The meaning of a name, and the location of its conceptual boundaries, thus depend on the understood other members of the set of conventional alternatives to which it belongs.

We need, therefore, to look more closely at the conceptualisation of methods.[36] Over the whole period with which this book is concerned a distinction between quantitative and qualitative methods has been conventional, if sometimes disputed, and there has been a conflict between the supporters of the rival alternatives. This continuity, however, conceals significant changes. Before the Second World War the cleavage was understood to be between the case-study method and the statistical method. (This received a happy symbolic representation at the Chicago department's student–faculty picnic in the 1930s, where baseball sides were

---

[36] The reader will appreciate that there is no way in which to conduct this discussion without using concepts; the author has a problem here which is shared with those she appears to be criticising. It would be tiresome to place every methodological concept in quotation marks, or repeatedly insert phrases to indicate that one is aware that other terms could have been used and would give a different impression. The reader is invited, therefore, to credit the author with remembering the problem without such signals. The terms used are the conventional ones used in modern texts.

picked on the basis of case study versus statistics.)[37] After the Second World War, only the older generation remained aware of 'case study method'. It was no longer a subject of professional discussion, and was not taken seriously as a 'method' at all; if mentioned, it was only as an optional part of exploratory work in the early stages of a project. Now, however, the cleavage was understood to be one between the survey and participant observation. This shift was not just one of names. What had happened?[38]

The origin of the term 'case study' probably had a lot to do with the social worker's 'case history' or 'case work'. Sociology and social work took a long time to become disentangled; in the 1920s people called social workers were equally or even more likely to carry out empirical research, and university sociologists very frequently drew on their case data whether or not it had been collected for research purposes. But origins do not account for the way in which 'case study' was elaborated and theorised. The term may appear to refer to a design feature, the number of cases used and the intensiveness with which each is studied. This meaning was present, but it is certainly not the only one. Another key theme is the idea that it gives data of a special kind. This is indicated in the earlier literature by treatment of 'life history' and 'personal documents' as interchangeable with 'case study'. What these were seen as having in common was that they gave access to the subjects' personal meanings, while alternatives are seen as dry, narrow and giving access only to external data. When 'case-study' data were especially collected (rather than found) what was envisaged seems to have been a process of semi-structured interviewing, possibly leading to the production of a document written by the subject rather than recorded by the researcher. (Thus the classic exemplars of the method include the autobiography of Wladek presented in *The Polish Peasant in Europe and America* (W. I. Thomas and Znaniecki 1918–20), and *The Jack-Roller* (Shaw 1930). The letters also used in

---

[37] This story from his student days was told in one of Philip Hauser's classes which I attended. He did not say who usually won. He, as a demographer, was probably on the side of statistics, while Herbert Blumer, a serious sportsman (he supported himself as a professional football player for some of his time as a graduate student), must surely have appeared for the case study; my bet would be on the case study.

[38] Much of the discussion which follows summarises the more detailed and closely documented version given in J. Platt 1992c.

The Polish Peasant, however, as 'personal documents' contributed further to its exemplary status.)

To the modern reader, the virtues imputed to this sound very much like those now especially associated by its proponents with participant observation – but those ideas were not then attached to that practice.[39] Some observation was certainly done in the 1920s by people who took part in the life they studied – though less than is often imagined (J. Platt 1994a) – but this was not seen as especially associated with access to meanings and, indeed, it was hardly given attention as a distinct practice. (The name was not widely used until later and, when first introduced, referred to the use of existing participants who would report to the researcher rather than to participation by the researcher.) The focus, as with the early 'survey', was not on the manner in which the data were collected, but on what the data were about. Insofar as participant observation as such was commented on, it could be seen as providing accurate and systematic observational data, even analogous to those of the natural scientist, rather than access to meanings and understanding. The term 'participant observation' did not become current and institutionalised in its modern sense until the late 1940s and early 1950s.[40] It was then rationalised and advocated in terms of access to meanings. Meanwhile, in the 1930s the strong association of meanings with case study died away before the term went out of use. Why did this happen?

It can probably be understood by the antithesis which implies that quantitative methods could not deal adequately with meanings; this antithesis was eroded from two directions. There had always been criticisms of the case-study camp, eventually supported by empirical evidence of the limitations of some versions of case-study method,[41] and an effort was made to respond to them.

---

[39] For more detailed presentation of material in support of the argument here, see Platt 1983.

[40] The textbook by Fry (1934) shows a transitional usage, where the primary reference of the term is to participation by the researcher, but meanings are not salient and direct observation is seen as in vogue due to the influence of behaviourism. Fry came from a background in the Institute of Social and Religious Research and, although he shows knowledge of academic work, his approach is a rather practical and commonsensical one. He is not concerned with the nuances of the issues of method salient to Chicago people, and so 'case-study method' is not given serious attention.

[41] For example, Stouffer (1930) showed that a simple Thurstone scale could give essentially the same results as judgments based on case histories, and Sarbin (1943) showed that an actuarial method using a regression equation predicted an outcome better than case-study material.

On the one hand, it became clear to proponents of case studies that these raised two key problems of analysis: how to describe their contents sufficiently objectively, and how to justify generalising from them to a wider population. Work was done on these issues. The answers developed for the first problem led inexorably to a convergence with 'statistical method' as modes of classifying the content in replicable ways were attempted. On the second, there came to be some consensus that individuals should be seen as representative of larger classes, that typical cases should be distinguished from others, that cases should be classified into types and that the numerical prevalence of different types was relevant; once the consensus had got that far, it was evident that the distinction from statistical method was no longer clear.[42] Thus the boundary between the two categories was eroded from the case-study side.

Simultaneously, however, it was being eroded from the other side. Questionnaires became much more complex and capable of dealing with motives and feelings, and techniques of depth interviewing were developed using ideas from clinical psychology; at the same time techniques were being worked out for the precoding of attitude questions and the postcoding of open-ended questions in surveys. This meant that the old distinction between simple factual questionnaires and the intensive exploration of attitudes no longer held (cf. Homans 1951). At the same time great technical advances were made in statistical theory, especially in relation to representative sampling. One can, thus, tell a plausible story of case-study method fading away for internal reasons, even an old-fashioned story of progress in which crude early methods are replaced by better ones. But it is much less certain that all the practices

---

[42] Some of the most sophisticated proponents of the case study, such as Angell, saw accounting for every observed case as necessary for adequate theorising: Znaniecki's 'analytical induction' provided a strategy which fitted this need. But the gradual diffusion of probabilistic ideas (Stephan 1948) made the feeling that a generalisation was threatened if any exceptions to it were found out of date, at the same time as the theory of sampling just starting to be seriously applied in sociology provided a different basis for general conclusions. Moreover, the development of the analysis of deviant cases as a strategy within quantitative methods undermined this objection. The transition is nicely demonstrated in the section on deviant case analysis in *The Language of Social Research* (Lazarsfeld and Rosenberg 1955), where a piece by Horst (who had worked with Burgess, a key figure in the case-study discussion) appears along with items by colleagues of Lazarsfeld who see such analysis as merely a stage in the construction of modified general rules to include the deviant cases.

vanished from research than it is that the term vanished from methodological discussion, where the striking discontinuity invites explanation in terms of historical events; we can, indeed, also construct a quite plausible purely external explanation, as follows.

The Depression, and the governmental response to it, enormously increased the external demand for social research, as well as providing a labour force to collect data in relief projects; this gave more sociologists access to quantitative data sets and experience in dealing with them. At the same time, some sophisticated sociologists, like Philip Hauser at the Census, were recruited to answer the need for improved government statistics on such matters as true unemployment levels, and they did much to make those statistics more relevant to social science. These movements prepared the way for change. The case-study tradition had been especially associated with the Chicago department. In the postwar period, this became less dominant numerically (J. Platt 1995a), and most of the senior figures interested in case studies had died (W.I.Thomas), retired (Burgess) or left (Blumer) and had been replaced by younger people from other intellectual backgrounds. Angell at Michigan, another leading figure, spent several years abroad working for UNESCO, and was now working in quite different ways on topics related to tensions and international understanding. If they had been succeeded by those they had trained this coincidence would not have created such a break.

But here the war played a crucial role. It emptied the graduate schools of young men, and placed many of those who would return to the universities in the exciting and cohesive environment of the wartime research effort. There the main emphasis fell on public opinion research, because the felt need to mobilise the civilian public's cooperation and the practical constraints of work in the Army, combined with the importance of the ideological theme of democracy, meant that attitudes were to be studied and heads to be counted. The unprecedented research opportunities and resources led to many technical advances. A contribution to this was also made by the intellectual exiles fleeing Hitler; Lazarsfeld was the most prominent in this context, but Kurt Lewin and the Frankfurt School of Adorno and his colleagues were also relevant. The charisma and institution-building of Lewin and Lazarsfeld helped the impulse of the wartime groups to stay together when the war was over. All this combined to establish and give hegemony to the new model survey, and to the departments where its leaders were now located. It also, more particularly, helped to generate a large body of methodological writing by them to diffuse the innovations made and to train the enormous cohorts of new students filling the universities, writing which was naturally done within their terms of reference.[43]

Possibly either the internal or the external explanation would be sufficient alone to account for the course of events; together, they seem more than sufficient to explain the disappearance of 'case study' as a category, covering both the intellectual developments and their social bases. Its boundaries were eroded conceptually, and a new set of practices which straddled them became institution-alised. A new set of categories then emerged, shown in the modern textbooks, in which 'participant observation' has replaced 'case study' as the 'qualitative' alternative which offers access to meanings. The grounds on which this access is claimed are, however, different, in ways which redraw the boundaries and allow superiority to the new survey to be argued. The basis of the distinction between major categories has become the manner in which the data are collected, which previously had not been treated as important.[44] At the more specialised level, a new body of writing started to develop which on the one hand chose ground on which participant observation was plainly distinct from the survey (H. S. Becker and Geer 1957), while on the other it tried to demonstrate that its conclusions were well founded in ways which had something in common with the survey approach (H. S. Becker 1958). The issue of representativeness and generalisability ceased to be addressed, except by the other side in dismissing such methods as useful beyond an initial exploratory stage of work.

---

[43] The explanation offered here is paralleled by that offered by Hinkle (1994: 333–5) for the important shift to a more Europeanised social theory over roughly the same period.

[44] It is odd that this shift should occur when much of the prewar methodological writing had been about how to collect data, though research reports did not usually treat how the data had been collected, often not made clear, as important to the support of the conclusions reached. Postwar methodological writing shows much more concern with design and analysis issues, though the categories used do not reflect this. One may, however, detect some textbook writers struggling with the problem of finding consistent principles to rationalise the distinctions current among different types of work. 'Experiment', 'documentary' and non-participant observation are normally included among the types to be covered, and it is evident that no one *fundamentum divisionis* is adequate to deal with this set.

Abel's book on Nazi life histories (Abel 1938) offers an interesting example relevant to this discussion. Abel was of Polish origin, and before coming to America in 1922 had studied for a year with Znaniecki in Poland. Znaniecki had, of course, worked with W. I. Thomas on *The Polish Peasant*. This became the classic exemplar of life history and case study in the Chicago tradition. When Znaniecki returned to Poland in 1921 he instituted a programme of research which regularly involved the collection of solicited life-histories, and this was very successful and encouraged by the government. Abel and Znaniecki were good friends who spent much time together later when both were at Columbia after Hitler's invasion of Poland, as Abel's diaries show. This might be seen as a strong Chicago connection, and moreover Abel knew leading Chicago figures. However, when asked, he did not seem to connect what he had done at all with Chicago, except in the person of Thomas received via Znaniecki (Abel 1983). When, years later, he wrote an article about the method he had used he called the device of soliciting life histories, as he had done, by the new name of 'biogram', not 'life history', 'personal document' or 'case study' (Abel 1947). He indeed distinguished it from those, stressing as differentiating factors that the biogram is written at the request of the researcher in order to address a chosen problem, and is solicited in large quantity from members of a specific social group who are given directions on the desired content and form. He refers in the article to some of the Chicago and other earlier literature, but takes as his main model the work done in Poland. It is hard not to think that anyone from a Chicago background would have seen what he was writing about as essentially indistinguishable from the American tradition, despite some minor variations on its typical details. Chicago sociologists had, for instance, solicited life histories, had given some guidance on what they should cover, and had collected relatively large numbers of them (Bulmer 1984a: 106–8). What we are seeing is a choice to draw boundaries between categories to correspond to social boundaries. Whether the social boundary in question is Chicago/Columbia or USA/Poland is not clear; it could be either.

These conceptual changes do not directly tell us anything about what was happening in research, but they have implications for the manner in which researchers are likely to have conceived of what they were doing, and so for what the standard packages of practices were. One larger change has been in the extent to which method has been theorised and systematised. This has increased so hugely that it is only to be expected that methodological choices by non-methodologists should also have become more theorised and systematised; at earlier times the terminology with which to describe some choices hardly existed, or was not widely diffused. Occasionally some of my older respondents found themselves slightly embarrassed because my questions raised issues which had not been treated as such at the time we were talking about. Thus Leonard Cottrell, when pressed on the early significance of the idea of participant observation, said

Being around with a family, is that participant observation or isn't it? I never got awfully excited about it. I came along at a time when we never worried too much about what was a method or wasn't. Park was a newspaperman, you went out there and got the story (Cottrell 1982)

At no time have the standard sets of methodological categories covered the whole range of research that was actually being done, any more than standard textbook topics have dealt with all the phases of research required to complete studies using the methods they name.

CAUSES OF METHODOLOGICAL WRITING: TEXTBOOKS

Why was so much methodological writing done? One obvious reason is simply the growth and differentiation of the discipline, which made room for more specialists, in method as in other fields. Another is felt teaching needs, which are likely to be affected both by student numbers and by the expectations of what the students should learn. All college student numbers rose in the 1920s; the rising trend was set back by the Depression and the Second World War, to be followed by massive expansion in the 1940s as the soldiers returned and veterans were funded to go to college under the GI Bill. After that bulge had worked its way through the system there was a relative drop, but to a much higher level than before. In terms of sociology, this meant a number of doctorates per year which was in the tens and twenties until the 1930s, when it rose to *c.* 45; then in 1947 there were *c.* 135, dropping to 55 in 1948 and rising to 135–40 in the later 1950s (Turner and Turner 1990: 30, 63, 87). Membership of the American Sociological Association

(ASA)[45] was 1530 in 1930, then rose between 1949 and 1959 from 2,673 to 6,436 (Rhoades 1981: 11, 42). Odum (1951: 13–25) provides other data to show the increasing scale and range of sociological activity, including increasing numbers of different courses.

A review of the graduate course listings of a number of universities[46] reveals a pattern of development in the provision of courses on research method. In the 1920s, there are very few methods courses, and those there are sound extremely elementary. Over time the number increases, with the largest expansion in the 1940s. Thus, for instance, Chicago had 5–8[47] in 1929–30, and the impressive total of 18–20 by 1954–5; Harvard had 4–6 courses in 1935–6, and 11 in 1960–1; Iowa State had two in 1930–1 and seven in 1960; Washington had 2–3[48] in 1925–6 and 11 in 1950–1. This was in part because total numbers of courses of all kinds increased with student and faculty numbers and the increasing differentiation and professionalisation of sociology,[49] but it also reflected the increasing orientation to empirical research and the increasing

---

[45] At the beginning of our period, this was called the American Sociological Society; the name was changed to American Sociological Association in 1959. In the interests of simplicity, it is referred to throughout in this book under the latter name.

[46] Universities for which at least some material is available are Chicago, Columbia, Harvard, Iowa State, Kansas, Minnesota, New Hampshire, North Carolina, Washington and Wisconsin. This has little claim to be a representative sample, but it seems reasonable to regard trends found in it as likely to be more generally present. It would be desirable in principle to present some of the material in quantitative terms, but so many questionable decisions would be needed to do so that the meaning of the figures would be doubtful. The data were in some cases incomplete, and the time spans covered varied and were grouped differently. It is also not clear in a number of cases whether a course should be classified as a 'methods' one; this usually arises when it either takes the form of critical analysis of published work, or relates explicitly to a narrow substantive field. In addition, some courses listed are provided by staff in other departments, and there is reason to suspect that varying catalogue conventions may mean that such courses are not always mentioned under Sociology when they are available.

[47] This mode of describing the number of courses has been chosen to take account of the fact that there are some course titles which leave it ambiguous how specifically methodological their content is; the lower number refers to those where this is clear, the higher one adds others which might also be appropriately included.

[48] The third course is called 'Social Aspects of Publicity', but its content includes 'Technique of preparing and exhibiting social data pertaining to community problems. Publicity devices, exhibits and campaigns.' This clearly relates to the older survey tradition.

[49] A study by Kennedy and Kennedy (1942) of undergraduate sociology courses offered in 1939–41 showed that the courses on method made up the sixth commonest type, with 5.2% of all courses; the larger the college, the higher the frequency of methods courses. A study by Bernard of the courses offered in more than 200 colleges, comparing the pattern in 1909 with that in 1940–4, showed that the average number of courses approximately quintupled; among the most marked increases was that in methodology, which provided 7.66% of all courses after 1940 (Bernard 1945: 547).

elaboration and theorisation of method; courses of a type previously only offered to graduate students are now being provided for under-graduates, and can be treated as prerequisites for the graduates. Before the war, there were few general methods specialists nationally either, so the ability to offer advanced courses was unevenly spread; visiting professors in the summer quarter could help out, but not change the underlying situation.

One noticeable transition in the courses, paralleling that found in the textbooks, is from the assumption that quantitative method is a special method ('the quantitative method') to what looks more like the reverse, with courses such as those on field methods treated as being about specialist topics divergent from the mainstream. By the 1950s, all these places had specific instruction in the techniques of the modern survey, and the number and level of courses on statistical topics had increased dramatically, with sampling some-times figuring as a separate course; other modern topics included scaling, and machine processing of data. Despite these common-alities, departmental differences remain, some visibly due to the special interest of one member of the department: Bales at Harvard offers a course on Research Methods in the Study of Small Groups, while Calvin Schmid at Washington offers one on Graphic Techniques in Sociology. Those departments that had relatively sophisticated courses on statistics earlier were those with faculty with skills then not widely spread. (One can, thus, see a local tradition in the Wisconsin catalogue for 1947–8, which shows one–three courses in general research methods, but no less than six on topics classified as statistical.) In this context, some writing is generated by immediately practical motives: authors see a gap which they think it would be desirable to have filled, or are not satisfied with the material available for their own methods teaching. Thus Doby (1991) says he felt that none of the available books integrated the different aspects of methodology successfully, and James A. Davis (1984) thought that they rested on what now looked like amateurish work and needed to be brought up to current professional standards.

The distribution over time of texts and of monographs is some-what different: there is a spurt of textbook publication in the 1920s, before the monographs had started to appear, which implies that there was at least a student market at that period. This is confirmed by the statements made by some of the authors that their book was written to answer the needs of their own students. Odum's and Lundberg's correspondence with publishers (HWO and GAL, *passim*) makes clear that from a commercial point of view the prospect of a large demand from the author's own institution was a relevant consideration, so it is not surprising that the authors come from departments with more students.[50] One may suspect that empirical sociology was not yet widespread enough, or its practice among sociology professors rather than their students common enough, for there to be a significant market for more specialised work on method at that stage. There was some method-ologically quite sophisticated work being done in sociology (and discussed in journal articles), but the profession was not large and did not have many methods specialists. The archival corre-spondence between sociologists and their publishers suggests that it was expected interwar that any book which was not a textbook, and could expect reasonable sales on that ground, would only be accepted by publishers if they could anticipate sales to general educated readers; obviously work on method, except that on the non-professional community survey at the height of its vogue, was not likely to meet that criterion. However, it will be noted that earlier textbooks quite frequently mention people outside academia as part of their target audience, and one may infer that there was a market among the non-academic researchers,[51] as their numbers increased, since a number of books on such topics as market research were published. After the war, the huge expansion in student numbers made a serious market where there had hardly been one before. The role of the Free Press, founded in 1947, which specialised in publishing academic sociology and was not wholly profit-driven, was also important; 7 of the 23 monographs on our list were published by them.[52] (A further 6 came from university

---

[50] Among the interesting books which might have been is *Methodology in Sociology* by Robert Park and Floyd House, offered for the series Odum edited for Henry Holt. There is no indication why it never appeared; Odum thought the Chicago following alone would justify its publication (Odum 1928).
[51] Paul Horst, trained as a quantitatively oriented psychologist, was seconded from his job with Procter and Gamble to work on the SSRC monograph on prediction; he worked in personnel at Procter and Gamble, devising tests for selecting and evaluating employees, and reported that since they were leaders in that field people from other companies often came round to ask about their methods (Horst 1982).
[52] For a brief outline of the history of the Free Press, see Lipset 1993. Its special initial relationship with sociologists at Chicago probably helped to diffuse its books; not only were the first produced in direct response to their teaching needs, but as a graduate

presses, and Moreno's appeared under the auspices of his own enterprise, so all other commercial publishers together barely outnumbered their contribution.)

These considerations explain demand, but do little to explain why particular people come to write. A range of motives has been reported by authors of various types of methodological work. Of course some authors write on methodological topics because they have a strong personal interest in them, and see that as a significant part of their intellectual work, but that is not at all the only reason. Some did so to meet a need they themselves felt in their teaching. Odum wrote that his planned text 'grew out of a sort of desperate need which we had here in getting our research assistants and our graduate students in shape as quickly as possible to do first-class work. We have given the course for two years, and we have been very much handicapped by having no guide' (Odum 1926). Palmer's book (1928) arose from the felt teaching needs of Park and Burgess' programme of research on the city. Some of the practical proximate causes were, however, simply a request by someone else: people may start to write on method because a publisher offers them a commission to do so, as for example Bernard Phillips did (Phillips 1984). Anyone whose initial effort is successful, especially in the textbook market, is likely to be asked to revise and update or to write on related topics. Alternatively, a colleague may suggest it or invite a contribution to some planned enterprise; Lazarsfeld was the cause of much methodological writing by others, and some texts are edited collections of contributions by different authors. These people would probably not have done such writing if they had not come within the orbit of those issuing the invitations, even though their acceptance of the invitations implies motives which would appear under one of our other heads. Obviously more than one of these motives may well apply.

Different genres of methodological writing are typically produced by writers who play different roles in the academic division of labour; the nature of these varying career roles is relevant to the intellectual content of the writing and how its representative status

---

student there I experienced the system by which we all got their list and submitted a block order at a discount price. I do not know if other graduate departments had the same system.

should be interpreted. Broadly, non-innovative methods specialists write textbooks, innovative specialists write monographs, and non-specialists write only autobiographical reflections or methods sections in substantive works. In practice, of course, some individuals play multiple roles or cut across conventional boundaries and transcend these stereotypes, but the stereotypes still correspond usefully to large parts of the social reality. (The only authors who appear on our lists as authors of both a textbook and a monograph are Chapin, Elmer and Lundberg.) We can be fairly certain that the highest direct financial return comes from writing a widely adopted textbook, so that the author aiming for maximum royalty income would write a textbook. However, writing a textbook can be looked down on as a low-level academic contribution in settings where original research is important and other forms of writing are dominant and can in more recent times, as Blalock (1988: 113) found, actually impede career advancement. This probably contributes to the predominance among textbook authors of those not widely known for their other work, or located at departments in the first rank for research.[53]

CAUSES OF METHODOLOGICAL WRITING: MONOGRAPHS

We turn now to consider how it came about that the various monographs were produced, and to locate them socially. Information about the personal motives of the authors, beyond that provided in the books themselves, is seldom available,[54] but a considerable amount can be said about the institutional context. The SSRC (on which see chapter 5) figures very prominently in this. Before 1940, much of the more practical and social-scientific work was elicited, in whole (Rice, Blumer) or in part (Dollard),[55] by the SSRC in response to what its activists saw as needed for the advancement of research; the favourable reception and widespread use in teaching

---

[53] Not all textbooks are just another textbook, and particularly unlikely to be such are those written from evangelistic motives, to draw attention to and advocate (as well as perhaps serve the market for) a preferred standpoint. Lundberg's *Social Research* and, more recently, Denzin's *The Research Act* (1970) provide us with examples of this genre.

[54] In some cases my interviews provide data, but many authors were dead by the time my work started.

[55] Dollard's work was initially commissioned for internal use by an SSRC subcommittee working on a substantive topic; he then decided to work it up further for publication.

of what was thus produced suggests that others welcomed their initiatives. It continued to be important later, though more others then entered the field. In the 1940s there were another four books generated by SSRC committees,[56] though not all in the same way. Allport and Gottschalk represent the sequence of SSRC-initiated work on documentary and life-history methods which followed up the issues raised by Blumer. This in part reflected the personal interests of Ernest Burgess, who led the relevant committees. Burgess was a colleague of Blumer, and personal documents have been especially associated with Chicago, but it would be misleading to see this as simply showing Chicago influence; Burgess was equally responsible for the quite differently oriented volume edited by Horst (1941), which expressed his concurrent deep involvement in work on quantitative methods of prediction.

For the remaining SSRC-sponsored work, its Committee on Measurement of Opinion, Attitudes and Consumer Wants was important. Even before the 1948 poll fiasco (on which see below) there had been criticism of surveys and reservations about their adequacy,[57] and it was in all parties' interest, reputational and commercial as well as purely academic, to try to explain and justify the new methods to those not involved with surveys and to find ways to improve methods. Moreover, the records of the SSRC show that in the 1940s the commercial survey researchers were making representations about their need for guides to the new developments. The Committee on the Measurement of Opinion, Attitudes and Consumer Wants started in 1945, and brought together leading survey workers from academia and the commercial sector. It commissioned Hyman's work on interviewing and Stephan and McCarthy's on sampling as well as Lazarsfeld (1948) on panel study methods. The rivalry between different survey outfits and their associated departments may have been one element in producing the large total of postwar writing, creating a motive for diffusing and justifying the practices which distinguished each (cf. Converse 1987: 385–7). But there were high levels of cooperation among the

---

[56] It is appropriate also to mention here the important SSRC monograph, exploring the possibilities of case-study method, which was never published and may never have reached a final written version. This was the product of an elaborate re-study of Angell's cases from *The Family Encounters the Depression* (1936). For details of this episode, see J. Platt 1992b.

[57] Some of these are reviewed in McNemar (1946), which criticised much current practice; this had been commissioned by the Committee on Social Adjustment.

leading survey workers in the postwar period, following on from the spirit of the war work, and a sense of shared interests reflected not only in these activities but also in the foundation of the American Association for Public Opinion Research (AAPOR), to which they all belonged, and the *Public Opinion Quarterly* in which they all published. Torgerson's monograph arose separately; it was commissioned by SSRC's Committee on Scaling Theory and Methods, to make the advances in that field available to students. Mosteller, Hyman and McCarthy's monograph, unlike other SSRC-promoted work, was a response to a crisis. The failure of the 1948 pre-election polls to predict Truman's victory had led to so much criticism of polling and survey methods that it was felt to be urgent that the errors should be identified and corrected; a strong working party was set up, with active cooperation from all the key polling agencies, and this report was produced with great speed.

In the 1950s the SSRC again figures prominently in the production of methodological work, though largely in relation to the drawing out and publication of what had been learned or become defined as interesting during the wartime research in the Army. It was generally known that much important work had been done there, and that there had been significant methodological advances, so the desirability of recording and systematising this for the wider social-scientific community was obvious and funding was found to support the enterprise; this accounts for Hovland, Lumsdaine and Sheffield, Stouffer, Guttman, Suchman et al. and Merton and Lazarsfeld. In some cases this systematisation had already started during the war, in response to the urgent need for training of new research workers. Obviously the topics covered by the work for the Army depended on its perceived needs, and the methods used were constrained by the practicalities of studying an army in the field. To that extent the methodological developments possible were determined by the setting. However, there is no reason to believe that, for instance, conventional Army top brass contributed new ideas which were taken up, and the continuities with earlier academic work are evident, so not much can be accounted for in that way. It might be interesting to speculate how different the research could have been if the social scientists had approached it with different backgrounds. Would there, for instance, have been so much on the impact of communications if Lazarsfeld had not done so much earlier work in this area, or on scaling if little had been done on it previously? Might there have been more, and more systematic, participant observation if the later analysis and elaboration of its techniques had already taken place? If one inclines (as I do) to answer these semi-rhetorical questions no, no and yes, then one will conclude that the Army experience led to change primarily by the distribution of the research opportunities it provided.

But that answer deals only with what was done, not how it was used by the sociological community. Merton and Lazarsfeld's volume includes a very interesting analysis by Lerner of the reception of *The American Soldier*. He argues, plausibly, that this was moulded by the nature of the extensive advance publicity for the book, whose leading themes were its uniqueness, magnitude, and, most importantly, its scientific status and use of new methods. Thus reviewers responded to it as 'the new social science', whose modern method is: 'the rigorous testing of explicit hypotheses on largely quantified data accumulated by structured observation in empirical situations approximating (with specified deviations) the model of controlled experiments' (1950: 220). In responding to this image, reviewers drew on their stock of existing attitudes. From within sociology, there were prominent and favourable reviews in the journals. There were also criticisms, both from those such as Blumer who preferred a more humanistic and qualitative approach, and from those such as Robert Lynd and Alfred McClung Lee whose critique, an essentially political one, was of its technical efficiency as having the potential for manipulative social engineering. This was the traditional quantitative/qualitative divide. It is probably fair to say, as Lerner did not, that the meaning of *The American Soldier* within sociology became the basis for treating the survey as the leading method of data collection. This was despite the contents of Hovland, Lumsdaine and Sheffield, and the repeated comments of Stouffer about the superiority of experimental method. The Merton and Lazarsfeld volume must surely have contributed significantly to this by its survey orientation and its accessibility.

The survey field also produced books independently of SSRC. Some came from polling and market research. Cantril's draws on the experience of his Princeton-based Office of Public Opinion Research (OPOR), and Payne's, though not evidently initiated by anyone else, has a foreword by Cantril and is published by Princeton University Press, so may be regarded as also associated with OPOR. Others came from the more academically oriented units based at universities after the war; Kahn and Cannell's book came from the Institute for Social Research at Michigan. There are also several associated with Lazarsfeld's Bureau of Applied Social Research (BASR) at Columbia, though these should probably be treated as due to Lazarsfeld's personal role rather than the organisation. Great man theories of history may be unfashionable, but they are hard to avoid here; the whole pattern of publication after the war is marked by Lazarsfeld's influence. As several of his colleagues have described, he had not only an extremely strong interest in method, but a style of operation which recruited many others to work on problems and develop ideas in which he was interested. (See chapter 7 for more on this.) He also had a commitment to the analysis, systematisation and documentation of procedures, and managed to raise funding to support this enterprise. The result was that, of the 29 monographs listed for 1947–60, he was the joint author and/or editor of 4, was directly responsible for the production by other men of 2 more, was important in initiating and/or involved with the enterprise of 3 others,[58] and was a member of the SSRC committees which commissioned a further 2. Zeisel's book, which went through many reprints and revised editions, was to a considerable extent Lazarsfeld's; as the preface to the fifth edition of 1968 explains, it expounded practices which Lazarsfeld had started to develop when still in Vienna (where Zeisel was a colleague), and which had become the house rules of BASR. This is an astonishing record, reflecting not only Lazarsfeld's personal interests and charisma but also the institutional setting which he created. In the Bureau of Applied Social Research there was a continual flow of projects which provided research experience and challenges, as well as a large and changing research staff, many of them graduate students, who needed training; these provided much of the material drawn on in the methodological work, as well as the demand for training materials. But BASR and its training needs cannot explain the outcome; the

[58] Greenwood acknowledges a primary debt to him for his whole enterprise, and he provided a foreword to the book. Berelson's book states in its preface that Lazarsfeld 'was instrumental in its inception and invaluable as adviser throughout its development' (1952: 10). This was based on work which was part of the wartime effort in the analysis of propaganda, etc., and was a revision of a mimeoed document produced in 1948. In addition, Zetterberg acknowledges the influence of Lazarsfeld, and of his close colleague Merton.

other comparable survey units did not have a comparable scale of production of methodological writing.[59]

Field Work, or at least the project on which it rested, was funded by a Ford Foundation grant to Everett Hughes of Chicago, who employed Junker as his research officer (and Ray Gold in a more junior capacity). Hughes was a key figure in encouraging and inspiring participant observation among students at Chicago, and then at Brandeis (Reinharz 1995). Several of those active in fieldwork-based studies at the Chicago department were also members of the Society for Applied Anthropology, which held many sociologists. William F. Whyte, then at Chicago, had the idea of producing the *Human Organisation Research* volume (Adams and Preiss 1960), which drew on articles from their journal (initially called *Applied Anthropology*, then *Human Organisation*). Thus both these qualitatively oriented books were connected with the group within Chicago (at the faculty level, Hughes, Whyte and Lloyd Warner, under the umbrella of the Committee on Human Relations in Industry) which combined a commitment to occupational and industrial sociology with a preference for participant observation methods.

One may speculate that such books would have been less likely to be produced if there had not been so much other methodological work of a very different tendency going on; Howard Becker and Ray Gold, who worked closely with Hughes and have made leading contributions to the literature of participant observation, say that those working in this style at that time were under attack from those who saw only other approaches as legitimate, and so felt they had to justify what they were doing (H. S. Becker 1982, R. Gold 1984). There is no specific evidence that either of the two books was trying to rise to the challenge of Lazarsfeld by starting to systematise fieldwork methods – but they could well have been.[60] The paper by Becker and Geer in Adams and Preiss refers

---

[59] Since the period we are are concerned with, BASR has ceased to exist, and the Survey Research Center at Michigan has produced a considerable number of methodological publications.

[60] Whyte (1981: 359) says that the appendix to *Street Corner Society* was written to respond to the need for teaching material for his seminar on field methods; this is very close to Lazarsfeld's declared motive for much of what he did, and shows a convergence stemming from a shared situation even if the content of what was written was very different in style. He has also said that he felt a need to explicate the logic and procedures of participant

to Lazarsfeld and points out (1960: 272) that the issues they raise parallel those in his discussion. Patterns of departmental rivalry certainly continued, but the explanation of the writing in terms of these would not fit the data well, even if the period in question was extended to cover the renewed flowering in the 1960s of writing on qualitative methods, because no department was predominantly qualitative in character. The Chicago-based writers were defending themselves against Chicago-based critics too – though some of those (e.g. Ogburn, Rossi) had been trained at Columbia – and between the wars there were qualitatively or anti-scientistically inclined writers at Columbia (Lynd, MacIver, Znaniecki) whose disagreements were as much or more with Lundberg, who at that stage had strong Columbia connections.

CONCLUSION

It is evident that, whatever the patterns of individual interests and motives, social factors such as the size and structure of the student market have had an important influence on the writing published. Less obviously, it seems likely that teaching needs may have contributed to the prevalence of conceptualisations of the range of methods which are simplistic and stereotype practice; such material is easier to teach. As research and research jobs expanded more, and more sophisticated, methods became established, and at the same time there were more people who needed to know about them. More diversity (combined with improved communications) creates scope for more controversy, greater sophistication leads to the availability of more complex criteria of criticism, disciplinary growth provides a basis for departmental market rivalry.[61] It is not surprising that the amount of methodological publication should have increased. However, the pattern of development cannnot be explained only in those terms, and internal factors in the intellectual life of the field were also relevant.

Before the war, Burgess felt that case-study method needed not

observation and fieldwork, seen as new. (Chicago graduates might have been less likely to see this as new.) One should also, however, mention the practical stimulus to write an appendix at all: his publisher asked for additional material to justify a new edition.

[61] Mulkay and Turner (1971) provide some ideas suggestive in this context, arguing, on the basis of three examples, that competition among those with expertise leads to intellectual innovation in pursuit of new audiences and new sources of support.

just to defend itself but also (since he was by no means hostile to other styles) to improve itself to rise to the challenge of its critics. Lazarsfeld and others in the postwar period had what they felt, with good reason, was an important innovation; they also felt that it was not yet widely understood, and that developments which had started outside academia or on its fringes required justification of their appropriateness and relevance to academic theory-driven work. Obviously neither could have had a significant impact if there had not also been contextual factors such as their institutional locations, and funding opportunities, which enabled them to operate as they did. It does, however, appear that Burgess and Lazarsfeld did, by their personal interest in eliciting research and writing on methodological problems by others as well as by their own writing, make a real difference to the pattern of development. It does not follow that they and that work had a correlative influence on research practice, or directly reflected it. Indeed it seems likely that Lazarsfeld's inspirational dominance of postwar methodological writing has led to a disproportionate picture of methodological practice. The existence of a large body of work on related themes suggests that they are dominant; the examples it uses are likely to become seen as the important and typical ones; practices not recorded and analysed in this way sink from view as distinct practices, even if they continue to be created and are known as concrete cases. What started as a marginal practice becomes in its turn one which others see as the dominant orthodoxy to be attacked.

Lazarsfeld himself was not as singlemindedly committed to the survey as his diffuse public image in the discipline implies. That suggests that the reception of his influence has been somewhat selective. There could be a number of reasons for that, but one of them would be the skew of the writing for which he was responsible. That surely did influence practice to some extent, despite what is argued above. In addition, survey method is intrinsically easier to systematise, and so to learn from reading as well as to write about, than some 'qualitative' methods, which respond more to the situation studied rather than being superimposed upon it. It is not by chance that fieldwork has generated both less writing, and a literature of more anecdotal character which often deals with personal experience. This is more fun to read, but gives less :tion on how to deal with a fresh research situation.

Chapter 4 discusses some aspects of the relation between practical method and methodological theorising. Here we note only that, while when an innovation is made it may well get written up, this is by no means an automatic process.[62] Writing is more likely to be produced when the innovation is one in which there is much external interest, or when its proponents feel that it is unappreciated or under attack. There is a related tendency for writing in one area to generate further writing by those working in other areas, to defend their stance against attack or to demonstrate that alternative claims can be justified. These processes too tend to encourage the creation of polarities. This may be connected with the ambitious general argument of Collins (1989) that intellectual creativity requires rival positions, which grow along the lines of greatest organisational rivalry and define themselves by their opposition to each other.[63]

But there seems to be a more general intellectual need for simple modes of organising thought by polarities. Quantitative/ qualitative is one of these; similar polarities are good/bad, Columbia/Chicago, or Blumer/Lundberg. Part of Lundberg's fame or notoriety must surely be due not just to his inherent distinction as a thinker, or the extent to which other people agreed with him, but to the relatively extreme and very clear position he took, which meant that he was eminently available as a symbolic marker. (His inclination towards controversy was such, indeed, that he could serve this purpose in more than one area: Lundberg vs. MacIver is also useful in more metasociological discussion.) Gehlke (1935) referred to the early use of Durkheim's *Rules* as 'one of the punching bags of the graduate seminar', and the role of punchbag is, indeed, a highly institutionalised one. Extreme cases serve this function well and, like very clear instances of types, are liable for that reason to be referred to disproportionately often, and so to give

---

[62] Conversely, what is written up may not correspond closely to practice. For some minor topics, one may observe the process by which, once something has been published on a particular theme, whose author *ipso facto* becomes the expert on it, that becomes seen as suitable for further treatment. Thus work by Schmid on graphics appears in several places, including an item in the *International Encyclopaedia of the Social Sciences*, which one can be fairly sure would not otherwise have had such an entry; similarly McKinney's (1954) work on typology generated other versions of it by him.

[63] However, Collins also says that there are normally from three to six concurrently active schools of thought in creative periods; either our period was not a creative one, or his model does not clearly fit it as it has often been described.

a misleading impression of the true range of activity. This point has a bearing on writing, but also on our historical accounts. There are recurring themata (Holton 1988, Nisbet 1976)[64] and stories which are culturally embedded in our imaginations, and become super-imposed on a wide variety of subject matter, including disciplinary history.

---

[64] Nisbet suggests (1976: 39) that the distinctive themes of substantive sociology have been community, authority, status, the sacred and alienation. Any comparable list for method would surely include science, quantitative/qualitative, representativeness, meaning, probability.

CHAPTER 3

Scientism

It is commonly assumed, and not without some reason, that American sociology of the 1950s and 1960s was dominated by scientism, and interpretations of the period tend to associate theoretical writings about the idea of scientific method with leading empirical work of the period, especially the survey of Lazarsfeld and Stouffer. There have been different versions of the story. In particular, there is on the one hand the triumphant story of the successful development of a truly scientific sociology (e.g. Madge 1963), and on the other hand the unhappy stories of the emergence of a sociology which had abandoned a humanistic concern with qualitative meanings, and/or had succumbed to a political agenda masquerading as scientific neutrality but actually supporting the capitalistic interests of the status quo (e.g. Fisher 1993). Each of these versions, however, as well as less value-laden ones, typically makes similar assumptions about the connections between theory and practice – and between theorists and practitioners; these assumptions can be questioned. Surprisingly little attention has been given to the detail of what happened – and, until the recent work of Bannister (1987), Hinkle (1994) and S. P. Turner and J. H. Turner (1990), the interwar period has been largely neglected, which reflects the extent to which much 'historical' discussion has been motivated by the concerns of the late sixties and early seventies with their proximate past.

In this chapter we consider the specific topic of scientism, especially in the postwar period, before going on to discuss the relation between theory and practice more generally in the next chapter. 'Scientism' is usually a term with pejorative overtones, so it was not used by those to whose ideas it is used to refer; they talked of 'science'. Its meaning overlaps with that now attached to 'positivism'. It is associated with a commitment to making social science like natural science, and thus with themes such as empiricism, objectivity, observability, operationalism, behaviourism, value neutrality, measurement and quantification. Bannister's *Sociology and Scientism* (1987) is a valuable study of major 'objectivists' in American sociology from *c.* 1880 to 1930, presented mainly in biographical terms; he sees the main impulse of the movement as having become less important by the later 1940s, though it was kept alive by Lundberg. This is much the most substantial work done on the topic, though there are many other writers who touch on it in the course of discussions centred elsewhere; prominent among these are those, such as Fisher and Silva and Slaughter (1984), who associate it with 'technocracy' and hence with modes of political domination to which they are unsympathetic. (Dorothy Ross (1991) treats it in her chapter on the 1920s, in a book also covering a longer period and other social sciences, but this draws so heavily on Bannister and Bryant for its interpretations of sociology that it cannot really be treated as a separate case.)

Even some of the most detailed and sophisticated accounts of particular periods, such as those of Bryant (1985) and Hinkle (1994), give them general characterisations, under labels such as 'instrumental positivism', which imply essential unity among groups and individuals whom we shall treat as divergent. This picture of unity is in effect achieved by starting from the implicit presupposition that an era can be characterised as a whole, so that, for instance, one group's metatheory can be treated as characterising another group of contemporaries who did empirical research without stating a metatheoretical position. Here this assumption is taken as problematic. A detailed case study of the group most securely to be described as scientistic questions whether even they meant the same thing by 'science', and consistently expressed their theoretical positions in their empirical work. If they did not, it seems *a fortiori* less probable still that their positions informed the work of others. Were their ideas really dominant? Their social location in the discipline makes this seem unlikely. There were also a multiplicity of other scientistic ideas in circulation, associated with diverse empirical interests and theoretical stances and, indeed, diverse natural sciences. The implications for our account of the period are considered; we are led to question the assumption that scientistic theorising can do much to explain methodological developments.

POTENTIAL INFLUENCES: DURKHEIM

Explanations of scientism in terms of the history of ideas have attributed important influence to Durkheim's *The Rules of Sociological Method* (1938), to the Vienna Circle of philosophers of science and to Lundberg, the well-known sociological evangelist for science. Each of these possibilities is reviewed below; none looks very convincing when studied more closely.

Durkheim's influence can be dealt with fairly briefly.[1] For most of the interwar period Durkheim was not regarded as a pre-eminent classic, and his methodological ideas, when mentioned, were usually heavily criticised; the 'group mind' was salient in interpretations of his thought. It may be assumed that relatively few read the *Rules* for themselves, since it was only in 1938 that the first English translation appeared. In the late 1930s the substantial works of Parsons (1937) and Alpert (1939) came out, and reinterpretation commenced; the *conscience collective* is no longer seen as a group mind, and 'treating social facts as things' is now understood as having weak meanings such as an emphasis on observability or a forswearing of *a priori* analysis. By the 1950s, he had become a figure normally treated as important and in the 1960s, helped along by the marking of his centennial in 1958–9, he became, with Weber and Marx, a member of the 'Holy Trinity' (Bierstedt 1981: 91). It is evident that this was not simply because more specialist work had been done, but because what he had to say spoke to concerns which were now current in ways they had not been previously: Merton's (1949) development of anomie theory in relation to deviance, a growing area of empirical research, was important here, and the ascendance of functionalist theory directed much more attention to a writer who now became generally seen as an ancestor of functionalism. Durkheim's *Suicide* was translated only in 1951, and from then on the *Rules* was usually understood in conjunction with it. *Suicide* was well adapted to use in relation to the current interests in comparative method and in techniques of multivariate analysis, and the brilliant article by Lazarsfeld's associate Selvin (1958) making this connection helped to seal it. From then on the *Rules* makes a regular appearance in methods texts, though it could not be said to be really used in them, except to provide diffuse

---

[1] For an extended and documented account of the argument here, see J. Platt 1995b.

legitimation; given the emphasis there on data collection, rather than meta-sociological issues, that is not very surprising. Thus the pattern is one in which, rather than Durkheim's ideas influencing methods, changing current methods and theories determined not just the level of interest in Durkheim but the understanding of what those ideas were.

POTENTIAL INFLUENCES: THE VIENNA CIRCLE

The Vienna Circle looks like a more plausible candidate. Among those who suggest that developments in sociology were caused or influenced by the Vienna Circle are, for example, Bryant (1985), Friedrichs (1970), Halfpenny (1982) and Sjoberg, Williams, Vaughan and Sjoberg (1991). The connection is normally made through the idea of positivism: the Vienna Circle were (logical) positivists, who in their well-known philosophical writings developed the idea of scientific method, and aspects of sociological practice are defined as positivistic. (This conception of 'positivism' is itself a product of the period after the one with whose history we are concerned, and has commonly been used as a term for positions from which the writer wishes to be dissociated (J. Platt 1981); different authors have, thus, given it different contents. Insofar as it has implied treating as part of the same syndrome – whatever the specific content of that – the ideas between which a causal connection is suggested, the conception is inappropriate for our purposes here since it begs the historical question.) The imputation of connection has not, however, been grounded in systematic research on methodological writing or empirical research in sociology.

It is a precondition of Vienna Circle influence that sociologists must have come across their ideas, directly or indirectly, and had the opportunity to become familiar with them. Most of the members of the Circle migrated to the USA in the 1930s and 1940s, and many of them became prominent there.[2] But before the migration their work was little known to sociologists, not least because it was published in German, and in natural-scientific and

---

[2] These include Gustav Bergmann, Rudolf Carnap, Herbert Feigl, Carl Hempel and Hans Reichenbach. Ernest Nagel, an earlier migrant, became closely associated with them.

philosophical contexts; by the time they were publishing original work in English, and giving more attention to the social sciences, they had spent some years in the USA and their ideas had been modified and responded to the context they found there.

Given familiarity with the ideas, influence requires that they made a difference to the thought or practice of those familiar with them, which implies that they were novel – but they were not totally novel. A number of social scientists actively welcomed the Circle's ideas because of their compatibility with those they had already been developing themselves. J. B. Watson, the originator of behaviorism, was no longer in academic life, but behaviorism was still a significant movement in psychology with its admirers in sociology, and operationism (originating with the physicist Percy W. Bridgman)[3] was also widely influential: these tendencies combined with a more generalised support for the idea of being 'scientific' to make the welcoming context in the social sciences. Feigl (1969: 643) remarked that 'The closest allies our movement acquired in the US were undoubtedly the operationalists, the pragmatists and the behaviorists.' The Vienna Circle and these US movements appear to have originated entirely independently of each other, although the Mach and Russell/Whitehead connection made some contribution to the origins of each. Watson's *Psychology from the Standpoint of a Behaviorist* was published in 1919, Bridgman's *The Logic of Modern Physics* in 1927 and Lundberg's *Social Research* in 1929. The Circle's manifesto appeared only in 1929, and when Feigl visited the USA in 1930–1 he met Watson and Bridgman and discovered sympathetic thinkers whose work was not familiar to most members of the Circle and who did not know of the Circle's work. L. D. Smith's important book (1987) on the relation between behaviourism and logical positivism shows convincingly that the leading US psychologists Tolman, Hull and Skinner, who have been assumed to have been strongly influenced by the Circle, had all developed the ideas which most resembled theirs independently. That is, there were home-grown American movements already under way, specifically in the social sciences as well as in philosophy, which both sides saw as in some sense related or

---

[3] As Walter points out, however, its meaning to Bridgman was very different from the meaning it had for his supposed disciples in sociology and psychology, and he was not happy with what others made of his original ideas (Walter 1990: 164–89).

sympathetic. In addition, less theorised tendencies to quantification and the idea of science were already current and affecting practice. In these circumstances only direct evidence that those potentially influenced drew on the work in question, and that this in particular made a difference to what they did, can show that it had independent influence.

A review of all the textbooks on research methods published between 1930 and 1960 shows minimal reference to works by the Circle – or to any other works of technical philosophy; more elementary and popularising works are used, and technical issues are seldom referred to. Where textbooks have general discussions of scientific method, it is rare for them to treat its definition as controversial or to outline the positions of rival schools of thought. Zetterberg said in the introduction to his well-known book (1965: ix):

I am well aware that this text does not take into account all, or even most, of the niceties elaborated by various philosophies of science . . . However, in a text for sociology students, the details of philosophy of science are out of place, and many of the points made in works on the logic and philosophy of science have little or no relevance or consequence for sociology as it is currently practiced.

Other authors could well have said the same. This means that, if they are taking a stand in relation to these, it may need to be inferred. Sometimes, however, the ideas used and the authors cited are drawn quite eclectically from different schools, or the issues are discussed in such a broad and superficial way that no position in relation to the questions disputed is implied (see e.g. Young 1949). Broadly speaking, in the earlier period 'science' was seen as 'inductive' – by which opposition not to the hypothetico-deductive approach, but to non-empirical work, was intended, and the importance of an objective attitude – i.e. one not directly reflecting religious or political concerns – was stressed. After the war, the hypothetico-deductive approach comes into view and the general discussion is somewhat more sophisticated. However, the main focus of most textbooks is on methods of data-collection and statistics, and there is not necessarily a close correspondence between the general principles declared and the concrete methods recommended. Even, for instance, the well-respected textbook by Goode and Hatt (1952), which starts with several chapters on issues of scientific method, rapidly moves on to concentrate on survey-related techniques, with little attention to their relation to the experimentation advocated earlier or to the validity of their operational definitions. Of the few more monographic treatments of relevant issues, those not by Lundberg (e.g. Ellwood 1933, MacIver 1942, Znaniecki 1934) are often actively hostile to scientism.

It is not practicable to provide systematic data on research practice specifically related to the Vienna Circle's focuses, so this must be dealt with more impressionistically. The major changes over the relevant period are the emergence of the modern survey and the replacement of the 'case study' by 'participant observation'. The survey has often been described as positivistic; the validity of that description can be questioned, but even if it is accepted Converse (1987) makes it clear that it emerged as the product of a wide range of influences, most of them non-academic. Participant observation is a more plausible candidate, in that it entails direct observation which could be (and sometimes was)[4] thought of in behaviouristic terms, but it has normally been theorised as strongly anti-positivist. More relevant to the Circle's concerns than modes of data collection are theory construction, research design and operationalisation. It is not so easy to make plausible generalisations about these. There has certainly, however, been the growth of a greater self-consciousness about method, manifested in the increasingly felt obligation to describe it in research reports, and an increasing tendency to associate the idea of being scientific with testing hypotheses rather than just being 'objective'; the latter is associated with recognition of the weakness of induction as a programme, and preference for a hypothetico-deductive strategy. It is, though, unfortunately notorious that the hypotheses reported as tested have often been derived from inspection of the data rather than formulated in advance to guide the work, so it cannot be assumed that references to such themes show much about research practice, as distinct from presentation. They do, however, show a shift in the grounds of legitimation felt to be appropriate.

My interview respondents, like the textbooks, showed far more interest in specifically sociological sources. The only interviewees

---

[4] See chapter 2. Argyris (1952) wrote of Whyte's *Street Corner Society* as based on a position following that of 'Bridgman and other positivists'. See also J. Platt 1983.

who spontaneously stressed anything to do with the Vienna Circle as an influence were Bernard Phillips (1984) and John Doby (1991), the authors of two leading methods textbooks (Phillips 1966, Doby 1954), Lyle Shannon (1993) and Robert Ellis (1991). As a graduate student at Washington State in 1952–3 Phillips was taught philosophy of science by Wesley Salmon, one of Reichenbach's students. This, however, was for him only one contributory strand in a general pattern of 'positivistic' influence in which the American Soldier research, Parsons, social psychology and statistics courses were also important. Doby did his graduate work at Wisconsin, chosen because he liked what he saw as its rigorous and empirical – rather than philosophical – style, and the method-ologist/statistician T. C. McCormick was his mentor. He described the Vienna Circle as favourites of his, and said: 'I think their way of putting the emphasis on hypothesis construction and theory construction interested me more, because for the most part the emphasis had been on testing without regard to the origin of the idea.' Shannon was a graduate student under Lundberg and Dodd at the University of Washington, and described Lundberg as setting people onto 'the logical positivism approach'. Elaborating what logical positivism meant to him, he said 'you create definitions of the variables to be used in hypothesis testing based on what you can observe, not saying this is the ultimate reality, just that this is what you can observe'. Clearly this, though in a broad sense compatible with the Vienna Circle's ideas, is hardly a position distinctively associated with them, and owes at least as much to operationism as understood among sociologists. Ellis came into sociology from psychology, and had a course in 1952 at Yale from Hempel, whose ideas he associated with the tradition of experimental psychology rather than with sociology as he found it in his early years in the discipline.

   The reading lists for graduate courses that I have been able to obtain show that, although some works from Circle members are cited, they are normally those written at a time when they had adapted to the American setting and social-scientific interests; the overwhelming weight is on more practical and specifically socio-logical sources. This suggests that the message received was heavily mediated in form, as well as sufficiently modified by interaction for a description in terms of one-way influence to be misleading.

Lundberg was one of the mediators, but Lazarsfeld might seem a more likely source for direct mediation of the authentic message. Lazarsfeld was, of course, himself also an émigré from Vienna and had moved to some extent in the same environment as members of the Circle, although he said that some writers about the Viennese milieu had exaggerated the extent to which different intellectual groups overlapped, and described his own circle as 'socialist empiricists' (1961: 52). However, Bergmann was a good friend of his, and he was even involved in a discussion group there in the 1920s with some Circle members. Zeisel (1990) reports that the Circle's new ideas were there 'fairly generally accepted as gospel'. Lazarsfeld in the USA kept in touch with Hempel and Nagel, especially the latter, with whom for many years he taught a joint seminar at Columbia which examined social-scientific work in the light of philosophical ideas, and he acknowledged a vital influence on work at the centre of his interests from Hempel and Oppenheim's (1936) monograph on typology. Thus he had the intellectual skills and interests, the background and the contacts to expose him to Circle influence. However, it would be highly misleading to describe him as a logical positivist, and he criticised Hempel and other philosophers of science for not paying sufficient attention to what actually happens in the social sciences: 'Philosophers of science are not interested in and do not know what the work-a-day empirical research man does' (Lazarsfeld 1962: 470). He appears to have influenced the philosophers as much as they influenced him,[5] and he focused selectively on those of their ideas which related to his own concerns and showed little interest in others more central to their distinctive position.

Thus the case for any simple causal relationship between the Vienna Circle's migration and the prevalence of scientistic ideas cannot be sustained, even though their work was referred to by sociologists.[6] This does not mean that they had no influence, but that their work was mediated to the point where a purist might regard it as no longer recognisable, its reception was selective, and

[5] The analysis by Nagel of the logic of functionalism was part of Lazarsfeld's Ford-funded Documentation programme; there is a section on social-scientific explanation in Nagel's *The Structure of Science* (1961) which acknowledges discussions with Lazarsfeld. Hempel (1959) too wrote on functional explanation, in a symposium on sociological theory.

[6] For a more detailed discussion of the Circle's influence, see J. Platt and Hoch 1995.

its reception and use depended on the presence of other tendencies which might alone have produced very similar outcomes. We have shown that one reason for the implausibility of that causal relationship was the importance of already existing intellectual movements, originating outside sociology but significant within it. The movements mentioned so far are those which they recognised as akin, and are ones which were relatively metatheoretical in their interests. But, as Bannister (1987) has shown, there were before the Second World War not just such movements from outside, but prominent sociologists with more home-grown scientistic positions. Those who were most relevant to the development of research methods are Giddings, Chapin and Ogburn.

Giddings was hardly an empirical researcher himself, and wrote about method only in a broad programmatic way, but he led the important Columbia department from 1896 to 1928 and there played a key role in inspiring others (including Chapin and Ogburn) to undertake empirical statistical work. He identified himself as a behaviourist, and was influenced by Karl Pearson's work to adopt an approach which advocated correlational statistics as the basis for theory-free measurement and description (Bannister 1987: 70–86). Chapin headed the important department at Minnesota from 1922 to 1953, and held a series of leading positions in the discipline nationally over his years there. He was strongly influenced by evolutionary theory, and again by Pearson, and in the later 1920s became committed to a severe scientism. He was particularly known for his 'living-room scale', which gave numerical scores to items of furnishing in order to arrive at an index of socio-economic status, and also for his efforts to develop ways of applying controls in sociological research so that it could approximate the logic of the laboratory experiment (Bannister 1987: 151–60). Ogburn too was prominent in the discipline, especially in roles connected with the governmental statistical data on which he normally drew for his own work; after a few years in minor institutions, his appointments were at Columbia from 1919, and then Chicago from 1927 until his retirement in 1952. He was Research Director for Hoover's President's Research Committee on Social Trends (Bulmer 1983a), reporting in 1929, which collected massive bodies of statistical data, and edited the *Journal of the American Statistical Association*. As Bannister (1987: 161–87, 222–7) documents, he took the statistical approach even into his personal life. He consistently advocated quantitative methods, although he did not publish significant methodological work. However, in his 1929 presidential address to the American Sociological Association he took an extreme scientistic position, emphasising the need for the accumulation of objective facts. In a properly scientistic sociology, articles would be 'wholly colorless', with more tables and less text, and the emphasis would be on demonstration and verification. 'There will inevitably be a great many unimportant and uninteresting things verified', often by dull or stupid people, and 'everyone will be a statistician'; this will give a high scientific return (Ogburn 1929). The deliberately controversial tone of this makes it clear that Ogburn did not expect universal agreement from his audience.

Bannister (1987: 231–8) concludes by arguing that the interwar 'objectivism' that he describes arose from the response to a variety of factors characterising the American social situation which converged to shape academic culture at the time; these included, in particular, the sense of a growing lack of shared social values. I would be inclined to stress, in a way that he does not, the significance in those circumstances of the many attacks on social scientists made in the name of religion or vested interests in lending attraction to an appeal to objective truths independent of values. Whatever the specific causes or reasons, it will be noted that the content of the work of these writers owes little to philosophers.

LUNDBERG, DODD AND THEIR CIRCLE

A yet more promising candidate than Durkheim or the Vienna Circle for the role of key intellectual influence is George A. Lundberg. He emerged against the background described above, and in his own right is widely recognised as the leading spokesman of his period for 'science' within sociology.[7] We start by considering his position and that of his immediate associates, and their relationship to the wider discipline; no previous close work has been done on them, so this is dealt with in some detail.

Lundberg was born in 1895 and, in a pattern typical of the period, worked his way up from a humble background of immigrant

[7] See, for example, Simpson 1949: 303, Timasheff 1950: 26, Westie 1993: 262–3.

farmers to win himself an education and an academic job. He became a well-known figure in the discipline, and in 1943 he was elected (in the first such election conducted by secret ballot) as President of the ASA. From 1940 to 1945 he edited the journal *Sociometry*. After jobs at various other universities, he was called in 1945 to the headship of the department at Washington, where he spent the rest of his career, retiring in 1961 and dying in 1966. As a doctoral student at Minnesota he had been converted to the cause of science, and was convinced that the future of sociology was scientific (Larsen 1968); he became a tireless lecturer and polemicist in the cause. His main relevant publications include: *Social Research* (1929), a methods text which appeared in a revised edition in 1942; *Foundations of Sociology* (1939a), a metasociological manifesto; *Can Science Save Us?* (1947), a relatively popular polemic whose rhetorical question was, inevitably, answered with a yes; there were also articles such as 'The growth of scientific method' (1945) and 'The natural science trend in sociology' (1955). The account which follows starts by describing his work from my point of view, and goes on to consider what he meant to his contemporaries.

Lundberg's detailed statements of his views developed over time, largely in response to his reading of changing (he would have said improving) contemporary metatheory and empirical research; for our purposes here the general statements made in the 1942 edition of his *Social Research* are the most useful. There he describes the most advanced level of scientific research as one with 'experiments or other crucial compilations of data . . . directed by systematic and integrated theory'. The steps which make up scientific method are: the working hypothesis; the observation and recording of data; the classification and organisation of the data collected; generalisation to a scientific law, applicable to all similar phenomena in the universe studied under given conditions (1942: 7–11). This he sees as applicable to social just as much as natural science. He frequently criticised those who argued that social and natural science differed, responding that they failed to appreciate that the points they made were either erroneous or applied to natural as much as to social science (see e.g. Lundberg 1945).

From the 1930s onwards he showed an enthusiastic interest in the Vienna Circle's work, and drew on it much more than most other sociological writers (J. Platt and Hoch 1995); in the 1950s he regularly referred to their *International Encyclopedia of Unified Science* as an authoritative source for currently accepted theory of natural science (1955:196).[8] Lundberg's general statements about scientific method somehow always have a hint of greater emphasis on the inductive phase than is compatible with the strict hypothetico-deductive approach of the Vienna Circle tradition; he seems more at home with the accumulation of empirical data than with the testing of general theories, even when he is formally advocating that. (More on this below.) He saw the use of explicit operational definitions as an important part of scientific procedure, and quantification as highly desirable. He dismissed the objection that a 'scientific' approach cannot deal with language and meanings by saying that 'the symbols and the symbolic behavior by and through which man anticipates future occurrences or "ends" can be as objective and tangible "empirical facts" as any other phenomena whatsoever' (Lundberg 1955: 194), since speech is behaviour which can be observed and so does not cause a problem for a behaviourist stance. He regularly praised the general work of Lazarsfeld and Stouffer, and in several places cited Stouffer's 'Intervening opportunities: a theory relating mobility and distance' (Stouffer 1940) as exemplary;[9] other work that he praised was in demography/ecology or sociometry, took a deliberately exper-imental form, used scaling techniques, or provided instruments of prediction (e.g. Burgess and Cottrell 1939). In sum, he declared in favour of every tendency seen as particularly scientific. It may be questioned how far, in doing so, he was always consistent. Russett (1966: 128) argues that he showed a theoretical confusion in

---

[8] The Vienna Circle members were keen proponents of the unity of science in all fields, including the social, though most of them were trained in physics or mathematics and they typically drew on physics for examples and exemplars. They were committed to physicalism, as part of the perceived need for an intersubjective observation language, and sympathetic to operationalism and behaviourism. The appropriate model of theorising and explanation for them was a deductive one. They saw only synthetic-empirical propositions as adding to knowledge of reality, although their own work emphasised formal logical analysis. For a detailed discussion of their views, see Achinstein and Barker 1969.

[9] This was a paper which set out to test the proposition (presented in the form of an equation) that 'the number of persons going a given distance is directly proportional to the number of opportunities at that distance and inversely proportionate to the number of intervening opportunities'; this was seen as a basic theory open to verification, and a candidate new sociological law. Data about migration patterns within the Cleveland area, dealt with in careful detail, showed an 'encouraging' fit between expectation and observation.

supporting both the biological and the physical model of equilibrium although they are incompatible. It is also hard to reconcile the curve-fitting of the associates whose work he supported (see below, pp. 85–8) with the hypothetico-deductive approach, or the survey or sociometric work he approved with an experimental model.

Given the relationship between Lundberg and Dodd (on which see chapter 6), to understand his position it is also appropriate to look at Dodd's work. The obvious starting point for this is Dodd's *magnum opus*, *Dimensions of Society*. (The 'dimensions' of the title are any measurable societal phenomena (1942: 16); the fact that the term was salient in contemporary physics – cf. Bridgman 1931 – is not coincidental.) The book aims 'to begin constructing a *quantitative systematic science* of *sociology*' (1942: 3); to that end, he presents his 'S-theory'. This is a theory in a somewhat unusual sense:

> The theory tells little of what relationships to expect between phenomena. One cannot solve for unknowns from it without further data . . . It takes whatever data the observer records, good, bad, or indifferent, and describes in definite symbols the operational degree of precision of those data, tells how they may be classified, and prepares them in standardized and parsimonious form ready for further manipulation to discover deeper relationships in those data. The function of the theory is thus, largely, to improve methodology systematically, more than to immediately state a system of generalisations about the behavior of social phenomena.

The system developed is one in which symbols are provided for twelve basic concepts, whose permutations ' . . . will be shown to define by formulae more than four hundred derived concepts which summarize and comprehensively classify quantitative societal phenomena'(1942: 18). The symbols used are T for time, I for indicators of the societal residue of characteristics of people and their environments, L for length, P for population, plus those for the operators adding, subtracting, multiplying, dividing, aggre-gating, cross-classifying, correlating and identifying, and various exponents and scripts specifying the kind and number of classes, class-intervals and cases of what the index denotes. This leads to formulae such as this, which is one of those Dodd offers as examples (1942: 76):

$$S_3 = {}^{a:z}_{t}T^{-1}:(\underline{P}, \underline{P}_{n}^{-1}T^{-1})$$

(That summarises a table showing the changes over time in the ratio of marriages to divorces.) The 'quantic formula', derived from the T I L P description, gives the 'quantic number' which:

serves to classify every S that can exist into a single, definite, unambiguous category according to its combination of indices and exponents. *The quantic number thus provides a thoroughgoing basis of classification for all quantifiable societal phenomena.* (1942: 41)

It is not hard to find apparently inconsistent statements in Dodd's work, which imply something nearer to novel substantive claims for this system, and he sometimes implies that the manipulation of such formulae could lead to new findings.[10] His habit of referring to it as 'a system of hypotheses' is confusing, though the sentence continues 'which assert that combinations of these basic concepts ... will describe and classify every ... set of quantitative data in any of the social sciences' (Dodd 1942: i). (In presenting his material, he also used many verbal neologisms such as 'plurel', 'interactance', 'addend'; these would presumably be justified as new concepts needed to express his ideas at the required level of generality, though I have not found a passage where he says so, but one may question whether they always add useful meaning to the words already available.) When pressed by critics, he and his supporters regularly defended the system by saying that it aimed only to provide the prolegomena to substantive work, and that it was concerned to establish a language which would unify disparate conceptual schemes and make it possible to express findings unambiguously; it was about the analysis of data already collected, not about the facts themselves to which the data referred.

This system in itself of course does not constitute a version of scientific method, though it is certainly the kind of thing which he thought was appropriate as part of that. In the first chapter of *Dimensions of Society* he proclaims his general allegiance to Lundberg's position as stated in *Foundations of Sociology*. He goes on (1942: 5–12) to specify that the scientific method consists of problem, observation, systematisation and verification. The problem could be a hypothesis to test or could be a field to explore or a

---

[10] He maintains in an article about 'the interactance hypothesis' (which predicts the number of interactions between groups) that it can be deduced from the definitions of his dimensions independently of empirical observations (Dodd 1950: 255).

technique to be developed. Observation collects the facts on all the relevant phenomena. The facts are then summarised; generalisations are made and principles are induced. Verification determines the truth of a generalisation or theory by checking its capacity to predict and control in particular situations to which deductive applications of the generalisation are made; crucial experiments or, when the conditions cannot be deliberately varied, statistical manipulation to isolate the required characteristics are used. Most importantly for his distinctive style, he adds that a mature science does not, as sociologists tend to do, move too fast to immediate application of theory to concrete situations, but builds up operationally defined principles 'general [in the case of sociology] to any societal content' (1942: 11).

DODD AND LUNDBERG'S EMPIRICAL WORK

We turn to consider the empirical work of Dodd and Lundberg, and relate it to their methodological manifestos; we might expect that this would throw more light on what they meant by their general statements. We shall concentrate on the work which appeared after 1940, which is the most relevant to the period with which we are concerned here. However, the first work to be considered is Lundberg and Steele's 'Social attraction-patterns in a village' (1938), since it was Lundberg's most cited and reprinted paper (de Grazia, Handy, Harwood et al. 1968: 15). This presents the data from a sociometric study of friendship patterns in a Vermont village. Friendship was measured by responses to a question asking for friends to be named; the results were analysed to show membership of networks defined by mutual choices, and the groupings established were correlated with other data such as socio-economic status, church membership and the cultural content of periodicals taken. Detailed diagrams are presented which show the positions of individuals and the structure of groupings. The declared purpose of the study was methodological experimentation as much as substantive interest. (This probably reflects his stated interest in sociometry as a technique which 'helped open up and objectify a large area of important phenomena which had hitherto been largely subject only to imaginative and subjective approaches.' (de Grazia, Handy, Harwood et al. 1968: 14).) In the conclusion it is stated that

When fundamental groupings have been located, their classification and the objective analysis of the nature and laws of their interaction is in order . . . It must be the aim of sociology to formulate increasingly broad generalization comprehending common sequences...That aim can be furthered by first formulating generalizations that are demonstrably sound for the smaller and simpler types of grouping. (Lundberg and Steele 1938: 418)

Thus this study is presumably to be seen as one which provides data for later theorisation. However, it is related to theory in another way. The introduction sets the scene thus :

Underlying the more obvious social events there are undoubtedly processes that correspond to the atomic structure and behavior of the so-called material world. Our understanding and control of the latter are recognized to be dependent upon our understanding of the former. Likewise there are in all communities subtle patterns of social attraction and repulsion, friendships, groups, cliques, etc., the existence of which may not be discernible to the casual observer. These groupings nevertheless explain to a great degree the more overt and obvious organization and functioning of the community . . . If we choose to regard any social group as a system of energy flowing through a more or less intricate pattern of intersecting channels, then the charting of these channels becomes a primary problem in the explanation of the behavior of the group . . . In general, science has found that the distribution and flow of energy is most conveniently studied under the categories of attraction and repulsion and these terms also describe a basic social phenomenon . . . The behavior most directly available and interpretable in this respect in the case of human beings is their verbally expressed attractions and repulsions. (Lundberg and Steele 1938: 375–6)

This shows that the study was defined by Lundberg as one with an agenda which made his social data reveal processes directly analogous to those of physical science, conceivably even to be subsumed under the same general laws. From our point of view, the problem is that there is nothing about the main body of the study which distinguishes it from many others which collected similar data without seeing it in that light. If he had not made the comments quoted above, we could have said with some confidence that this was simply a descriptive empirical study.

Lundberg had few later empirical publications, and these too are concerned with patterns of attraction and repulsion. (They probably arose in part from his political interests (Catton 1968: 31–2), which are discussed below.) Two related publications (Lundberg and Beazley 1948, Lundberg, Hertzler and Dickson 1949) look at this in a small college and a large university. Each collected data on the preferred social contacts of students, and analysed them in terms of characteristics such as year and subject of study and place of college residence. It is concluded that propinquity was a particularly important determinant because of its effect on opportunity, though it would be desirable to hold that constant so that other factors could be isolated. What types of membership are associated with strong in- and out-group feelings, and how these arise, is seen as an important scientific issue, potentially open to reliable prediction; the methods used are seen as also applicable to religious, racial, ethnic, political, etc. cleavages. Another study was of patterns of association among ethnic groups in a high school, and this led to two articles (Lundberg and Dickson 1952a, b). The data were sociometric, collected by questionnaire, and assessed the degrees of ethnocentricity shown by different groups and related ethnocentrism to other characteristics. The bulk of the material presented gives details of the specific data, and frequently also offers speculative interpretations (e.g. about possible reactions to minority or majority status) which might explain the observed patterns. No pronouncements are made about scientific method; instead, issues of policy and its consistency on matters to do with discrimination are raised. No hypotheses are tested, and each article remarks that the generalisability of the findings to other contexts depends on further study. Once again, therefore, there is nothing to distinguish this from any routine descriptive study.

Thus Lundberg's later empirical work does not, as far as its logical structure and its methods are concerned, show the features one might expect from his programmatic statements about scientific method, except insofar as he quantifies his data and provides summary indices, although it does itself include some programmatic statements and some comments suggesting ways of theorising the data which, while they have made no detectable difference to the content of the studies, hint at convergences with abstract theories of a nature sufficiently general to cover natural-science topics too. That is, the 'scientific' parts seem like *post hoc* comments and future aspirations rather than visibly informing the research practice. Perhaps more striking still is that the work shows no trace of Dodd's distinctive contribution; Lundberg does not use his S-theory notation, or offer mathematical models or even formulae to summarise his findings.

Dodd's empirical work was of a very different character. Most of what was published in the journals revolves around 'Project Revere', which studied the diffusion of messages, usually delivered by leaflets dropped from the air, and was funded by the US Air Force. An enormously painstaking series of experiments attempted to isolate different variables in the process, defined in terms of the S-theory, and fitted the outcomes to curves. One is struck by the discrepancy between the weight of the theoretical apparatus and the banality of the substantive data, on topics such as the proportion of housewives who, with the incentive of the reward of a free pound of coffee, by a specified date knew a slogan advertising the coffee. It is reported that various aspects of the results showed an extraordinarily high fit to harmonic or logistic curves,[11] and such findings are related to much more general modes of diffusion such as those applicable to fruit flies or gas molecules (see e.g. Dodd 1955); Dodd sees such applicability of theory across social and non-social science as an ideal.[12] What he actually does empirically seems to vary. In one paper (Dodd 1951) he starts by giving a hypothesis to be tested: 'that human interacting tends to decrease as the first power of the distance it travels'. He goes on to treat the testing of hypotheses using statistical data as starting with finding the best curve to take as the candidate law to describe some regularity in the data already collected, then testing its goodness of fit. No fewer than 12 types of curve were tried on the data in question, and it was found that 11 of them fitted about equally well! One was chosen 'on grounds of parsimony and of consistency with previous studies and theory in physics, geometry, and social physics' (1951: 282, 287). This seems a curious mixture of genuine hypothesis-testing and

---

[11] Dodd was not the only writer who took an interest in logistic curves and their fit to the pattern of various kinds of data; Hart (1946) reviews 12 series of statistical data to show the effect of war and depression on the logistic trend, and Pearl (1924), a population biologist referred to by some of the later social scientists, shows that the same curve fits the growth of a range of populations – both human ones and fruit flies. He enters various methodological caveats about the lack of light thrown on causes by such demonstrations, pointing out (p. 558) that the same curve can fit phenomena with quite different causes, but nonetheless suggests that it may be 'a descriptive law of population growth' (p. 637) and that 'the search must be thrown back to more fundamental natural causes, biological, physical or chemical' (p. 585).

[12] This tends to lead to propositions which would commonly be regarded as of rather little sociological interest, such as the 'hypothesis of interactance', which 'states the factors determining the *quantity* of group interaction regardless of its quality or form, i.e., regardless of whether it is cooperating, competing, conflicting' (Dodd 1950: 245).

inductive empiricism. He was certainly strongly interested in finding general formulae which would fit empirical data – so interested that it is not always easy at first, or even second, glance to tell whether particular papers should be regarded as presenting empirical work or as elaborating his theoretical scheme. This is especially so given that some of his propositions come near to being true by definition, so that he is spelling out the implications of the initial assumptions.

Dodd's commitment to the accumulation of large quantities of data, normally assumed without discussion to come from surveys, is theorised in his accounts of the 'pan-sample' to which he aspired:

a study of a sample of persons each of whom is observed in hundreds or even thousands of ways . . . a representative panel of persons must be recruited to be interviewed and tested, each for several hundred hours . . . towards cumulating eventually every measurable index known to any social science on one and the same set of persons . . . pan-sampling would make exactly known all *the conditions under which any generalization held good* . . . The conditions for each variable are simply all the other variables that show correlation indices with it. (Dodd 1948: 310, 311)

(As that quotation implies, he rejected the concept of cause, and preferred that of correlation as permitting more rigorous reasoning and prediction via regression equations (1948: 318).)[13] This proposal must surely be the ultimate in inductive social science – although, once again, one's perception of that as its character could be shifted by a statement of how such data would be used. It is not very surprising that he was never able to raise the enormous sums of money needed to put the pan-sample into practice.

In the light of this material, it does not seem appropriate to characterise Dodd's position or style by any one project report or statement that he makes; there are conflicting themes. His empirical practice is subservient to his theoretical interests, but those often lead him to what might be regarded as atheoretical accumulation of data. Should we take what he says at face value, or should we observe his practice? In my judgment the weight of the distribution of his effort, as distinct from his declarations

---

[13] His conception of causation is elaborated in more detail in *Dimensions of Society* (1942: 313–14). Although he refers to this in the article cited, the two discussions do not seem altogether consistent, since in the book he proposes experimental or statistical techniques for isolating 'true causes out of all the frequently concurrent conditions'.

of principle, comes down on the side of inductivism rather than theory testing, and the creation of (dubious) theoretical propositions rather than merely the elaboration of a system of symbols to integrate available data. Thus neither Dodd's nor Lundberg's work appears altogether consistent with their declared principles – or, alternatively, if we take their practice to define what they meant by their more general statements, those mean something rather different from what one might have assumed. This may seem a harsh judgment; it is made by what is perhaps an unreasonable standard, ignoring the difficulty for pioneers of living up to goals which have as much of aspiration as they do of the immediately attainable.

Lundberg and Dodd belonged to an intellectual grouping, described in chapter 6, which was vital to their conceptions of science and striving towards what they saw as its goals. It makes sense, therefore, to look at what the group shared. Zipf and Stewart were other central members. What did these men have in common in their intellectual practice? It is striking that Zipf and Stewart, despite their very different academic backgrounds, worked in highly similar styles. Each acquired huge amounts of data, often already available from such sources as the records of banks or telephone companies, and looked for empirical regularities in them for which simple abstract summarising formulae were then sought.

Zipf in his last book (1949) enunciated the 'principle of least effort', seen as governing all individual and collective behaviour. Data are presented on an extremely large number of phenomena shown to fit a straight-line rank-size distribution quite well. On the one hand he says that all his own data in the book show tests of hypotheses first worked out theoretically, then tested on data compiled by students who did not know the hypotheses; on the other hand, he asserts that 'we may claim in all modesty to have increased the number of our observations to such a point that they may be viewed as empiric natural laws, regardless of the correctness of any of our theoretical interpretations. In other words, by means of the accepted methods of the exact sciences, we have established an orderliness, or natural law, that governs human behavior' (Zipf 1949: 543, ix).

Stewart did not invent his own new natural laws; he, rather, as a physicist by training, applied those of physics in novel social contexts. His method emphasised the search for quantitative regularities independent of theoretical rationale.[14] He saw the history of physics as proceeding from such observations to 'their condensation into empirical mathematical regularities' and the 'theoretical interpretation of the latter', and concludes that 'if there is to be a social physics, its beginnings must follow the same standard pattern' (Stewart 1947: 179). Fortunately, however, for the unification of science, he found the existing laws of physics in the data he studied! He became particularly attached to the concept of 'demographic gravitation'[15] and its consequent 'population potential' (Stewart 1948a), relating population distribution to spatial distance. Number of people substitutes for mass in physics, and the density of population in an area is its potential, or influence at a distance on other points; the interesting concept of the 'human gas' is introduced to account for the apparent resistance to social gravitation. ('Were it not for the expansive force of the human gas, representing the need for elbow-room, the center-seeking force of gravitation would eventually pile everyone up at one place' (Stewart 1948b:23).)

The empirical work of Zipf and Stewart has little or nothing in common with that of Lundberg, though much with that of Dodd, whose research reports predictably make many references to theirs and who also regularly uses physical terminology and ideas. Perhaps for Lundberg it is more relevant to compare his scientific method than his empirical work. At the level of practice, he collects data but goes only a short way in the direction of proposing general theories of them, though he indicates that as the long-term goal; his statements of principle are more consistent on minor points such as the desirability of quantification than on major ones of intellectual strategy. This indicates a more general issue about the group: how far did they really share a conception of 'science'?

[14] He defined his own position as Leibnizian rather than Newtonian, which was of course idiosyncratic – as well as showing that he had probably thought about these matters more than most of his colleagues. Cartwright (1987), in a paper on the response of American physicists to quantum theory, suggests that there was widely diffused in the American physics community at the time when Stewart was trained a version of operationalism which saw the task of physics as description rather than explanation, and was hostile to the postulation of hypotheses; against that background, Stewart's approach sounds relatively conventional.

[15] He was, as he acknowledged in the paper cited, far from the first to use this idea – though the record shows that he several times started lines of thought without realising that social scientists had already done related work, so his ideas were not altogether novel. Moreno (1953: 447–51) is one of those who offered a version of 'social gravitation'.

The extent to which they did so is open to question, despite their very active cooperation and solidarity, as a sampling of quotations from the archives will reveal. First, some which express reservations about each other's work:[16]

Lundberg, replying to Chapin (1938) who criticised Dodd for converting qualitative terms into quantitative ones by arbitrary assignment of weights on an uncalibrated scale, agrees that 'unless measuring scales are developed to a very much higher degree than at present most of his formulations cannot be practically applied' (Lundberg 1938).

Theodore Abel reports in his diary on a 1941 meeting with Dodd: 'I was surprised to find that Dodd has not read Lundberg's book, and disapproves of his identification of the social with the physical, and of George's conception of definitions . . . Dodd's system does not presuppose Lundberg's metaphysics. In fact, Dodd is opposed to its assumptions and he accepted my suggestion of separating his book from Lundberg's'[17] (Abel 1941: 8, 127–8).

Lundberg writes to Robert Bierstedt: 'Zipf's contribution is important for its empirical contribution rather than for his theorising, although as a speculative thing, the latter is not to be sneered at' (Lundberg 1951).

Stewart writes to Dodd: 'Doggone, Stu, wish you'd learn "the calculus and the physics"! They are easier than symbolic logic. The latter tempts one to over-generalisation, and to mistaking the symbol for the thing, seems to me.' (Stewart 1957); Warren Weaver reports in his work diary that Stewart 'thinks that Dodd is too verbose and too much enamored of fancy symbols, etc.' (Weaver 1949).

---

[16] Similar comments can also be found about Moreno: Lundberg, writing to Zipf about his tactical reasons for allying himself with Moreno's sociometric group, describes some of them as 'outright mystics' (Lundberg 1941). Dodd, writing to Lundberg, says of Moreno's *Who Shall Survive?* that: 'the sweepingness of his concluding chapter is not justified from the simple tests of psychological distances with which the book deals . . . [though] I have the greatest admiration for its having manipulated into objective and quantifiable form interperson choices from life situations' (Dodd 1936).

[17] Dodd in a public presentation gave a different account of the reasons for the separation of the two books, attributing it to problems of distance and mailing – and then the further delay of his volume by wartime hazards (Dodd 1967: 5). However, by 1941 Lundberg's book had already been published, so perhaps the separation referred to by Abel is not the physical one. When Dodd's book did appear it described Lundberg's book as a 'companion volume'.

We can also find passages which suggest that members were not competent in fields which they purported to practise, or advocated as a basis for practice by others:

Stewart writes to Bridgman: 'Dodd has not made a correct transfer of physical thinking about dimensions . . . He has used the term dimension very loosely, and often as a mere synonym for variable' (Stewart 1951).

Stewart also corrected Lundberg on his use of some definitions in physics – but nonetheless closed this letter by saying that 'I cannot overstate my admiration of your point of view, because it is unbounded' (Stewart 1949).

Lundberg writes to Bentley re various authors in the philosophy of science, some from the Vienna Circle: 'when it comes to the rarified atmosphere in which you and Dewey move, I am not even sure I follow the fine points. Carnapp [sic]and Kaufman [sic] likewise leave me a good deal in doubt as to what they are doing part of the time though I must admit, I have not made any thorough study of either' (Lundberg 1944b).

Bergmann writes to Lundberg about his Foundations of Sociology: 'you would not expect me to say that you do full justice to all the possible epistemological niceties, sophistications, and precautions. But . . . such criticism . . . usually comes either from philosophical busiebodies [sic] or from ideological saboteurs. So I shall not split the epistemological hairs with you' (Bergmann 1944).

Lundberg writes to the mathematical biologist Rashevsky: 'Since I consider myself entirely incompetent to judge the mathematical part of [Dodd's] manuscript, I am very glad to get your reaction to it . . . I am entirely in agreement with you as to the difficulty of reading the symbolic part of his manuscript, although I was inclined to attribute this in part to my own unfamiliarity with that type of expression' (Lundberg 1939b).

Thus it seems that the natural scientists and philosophers had doubts about the adequacy of the sociologists' grasp of the material from their fields which they drew on, while the propagandists did not necessarily wholly approve, or even fully understand, the detail of what they advocated. None of this, though, shows in the published material; they kept their doubts and reservations among themselves. Moreover, although some of the critical points they made look severe indeed, this was for them quite compatible – as some of the quotations above also show – with fullhearted support for their colleagues' general enterprises.

THE SOCIOLOGICAL RECEPTION OF THE LUNDBERG CIRCLE

How were the ideas of this group received in sociology generally? For Lundberg, we can say with confidence that he was very prominent and taken seriously, with his textbooks widely used,[18] even if he was a controversial figure. The main attention was given to his theoretical/methodological rather than his empirical work; indeed, in my interviews respondents repeatedly referred to him as not doing research, only writing about it. (For some this was enough to discredit his views.) As Rossi (1984) said, 'There are persons who are ideologically important, and Lundberg was ideologically important, but mainly in putting across an epistemological point of view...'. The fact that he wrote on general topics meant that he provided a convenient reference point in discussion for both supporters and opponents, and was commonly regarded as among the symbolic leaders of a tendency. Although he was quite frequently attacked – see, for instance, Simpson 1949, Timasheff 1950 – the attacks treated him as important and not isolated. A summary of the citations of his work in the main journals from 1936 to 1964 shows that he was mentioned by 178 authors in 186 articles; in their 334 references to his work, 159 agreed with him, 78 disagreed and 97 were neutral. The ratio of disagreement to agreement was highest for metasociological topics; the book most frequently referred to was *Foundations* with 71 citations (Lundberg, no date).

The reviews of *Foundations* were mixed in character. Donald W. Calhoun (1942) reviewed *Foundations* and *Dimensions* together for *Social Forces*. He saw Lundberg's view as basically fairly acceptable, useful in its general scientific framework if going rather far in its relativistic stance; Kirkpatrick (1940), similarly, saw the book as

---

[18] Correspondence with his publishers shows that the second edition of *Social Research* sold 12,541 copies from 1942 to 1952 (GAL 8). A report of research on the circulation of introductory texts shows Lundberg, Schrag and Larsen (1954, 1958) as the fourth most popular, with 8.2 per cent of the total reported circulation (Hart 1960a: 1). Odum's (1951: 253) listing of the most widely used texts includes Lundberg's *Foundations*, and also shows Lundberg as one of the writers cited often enough by other text authors to be mentioned in that connection.

vigorous and stimulating despite having some strong criticisms of it. Sorokin (1940), in a way typical of his idiosyncratic style, attacked it violently for its distorting imitation of natural science, but declared his respect for its enterprise at the same time as he judged the implementation a failure. *Can Science Save Us?*, also reviewed in the major journals despite its popularising character, also had mixed reviews. H. P. Becker (1948), a theorist, saw it as a profession of religious faith; Freedman (1948), a demographer, saw its methodological position as one widely shared, though the statement of that was mingled with controversial material about foreign policy and the social role of the sociologist; Hertzler (1947) – perhaps the husband of Lundberg's collaborator Virginia Beazley Hertzler? – gave the book his full support as 'a brilliant, earnest, concise exposition and summary of the status of social science', and asserted that most sociologists would be in entire agreement with its tenets. The revised edition of *Social Research* is favourably reviewed as a very competent textbook (Provus 1942, Davis 1943). There are recurring references in the reviews to his evangelistic tone,[19] and also to the more or less explicit political positions which could be inferred from both his general statements on the desirability of a technical, instrumental role for the social scientist and his choice of examples; we return below to the implications of these.

Shannon, a Lundberg student, describes his message as 'operationally defining the crucial importance of variables, extending theory on the basis of research etc., basing research on testable theories' (Shannon 1993). Larsen, another Lundberg student, described his message as more diffuse:

the inspiration of making sociology a science, a new religion and he was the Messiah . . . Lundberg was an advocate, not a practitioner of those things [experiments, statistics, etc.]; he understood some of them, and did some interesting practical work, but that wasn't really his expertise – he knew that scientific methods were the right medicine. (Larsen 1984)

William H. Sewell, a leading figure in the practical application of quantitative methods from the 1940s on, speaks approvingly of Lundberg, but as 'philosopher':

[19] E.g. 'Lundberg might be regarded as the John the Baptist of sociological positivism who cries the gospel of quantification, baptizes with operational definitions, and heralds the coming of S. C. Dodd as a methodological Messiah bearing the perfected doctrine' (Kirkpatrick 1940: 438).

I don't know what influence George Lundberg had on me, except in his explication of the philosophical background of sociological science . . . He had a big impact throughout sociology at a time when everybody was ready to have a philosophical basis for sociological pragmatism and empiricism. (Sewell 1983)

Hubert Blalock, another leader in quantitative methods, saw Lundberg as an extreme operationalist, supporting *ad hoc* procedures and measurement by fiat; he disliked what he saw as an atheoretical approach (Blalock 1984). This shows the unfavourable reaction to what others, especially from the Washington department, experienced as attractive encouragement to get out there and collect data without being delayed by pointless theoretical discussions of what were essentially empirical questions.[20] James Davis, a graduate student at Wisconsin and Harvard in the 1950s who then went to Chicago, and yet another leading quantitative figure, says that work in distant Seattle 'hardly swam into our ken' (J. A. Davis 1984); those of my respondents most prominent in statistical techniques, Otis Dudley Duncan and Leo Goodman, did not mention him. A theme stressed by those close to Lundberg as a key part of his message (Alpert 1968: 56–7, Catton 1968: 33, L. Shannon 1993) is the irrelevance of ethical and moral concerns to scientific work; this had greater significance at a time when religious motives for interest in sociology were still common among students, and should not be seen through the spectacles of the extensive discussions sparked off in the 1960s. However, some of the same issues are raised by this stance in connection with his political views (on which see chapter 6), and again there is a division between those who read it in favourable (scientific) and unfavourable (political) ways.

Dodd published large numbers of articles in the most respected sociological journals, so his work was certainly taken seriously in that sense, though Lazarsfeld's reported difficulty in deciding whether he was a genius or a madman (Glock 1984) seems to represent a common position – indeed, one shared even by Lundberg (Larsen 1984). Many reviews of *Dimensions* contain the

---

[20] 'Instead of getting all involved in what the real world is and so on you create definitions of variables based on what you can observe . . . If somebody didn't like your operational definition, George always said let them produce another definition and conduct research and see what they come up with' (Shannon 1993).

most biting criticisms, some from natural scientists as well as sociologists. In the *American Sociological Review* his *Dimensions* was reviewed both by Talcott Parsons and by mathematician E. T. Bell (Bell 1942, Parsons 1942). Parsons says that what Dodd has developed is not a theoretical system but a language; it is too general to describe a determinate class of empirical systems, and selects phenomena to describe simply because they can be stated in his notation, ignoring significant sociological problems and existing work in systematic social theory. Bell concentrates on the 'mathematical' aspects – but concludes that there is no real mathematics in the book, only 'a feeble mathematical pun'; the symbols are not useful because there are no processes for combining them which give rise to new and interpretable combinations. In the *American Journal of Sociology* Ethel Shanas wrote an extended critique (Shanas 1942). She sees the symbols and definitions as arbitrary and sterile, adding nothing to our understanding; she also points out that the residual 'everything else' covered by Dodd's 'I' includes most of the characteristics of people in which sociologists are normally interested.[21] Calhoun (1942) again saw Dodd as providing a language which added nothing and as having too much in his residual 'I', as well as using old-fashioned physics and drawing inappropriate analogies from it; despite failing in its central aim, though, the book makes some useful incidental contributions. Woolston (1942) lists assumptions made in Dodd's book which many will not share, though he also suggests that the enterprise is potentially a helpful one.

For more recent times, a search of the *Social Science Citation Index* for 1980–93 shows 39 references to Dodd's postwar work, only 7 of them in mainstream sociological journals. (Most of the others are in papers which appear to be about diffusion of practices or innovations.) This suggests rather small lasting impact in sociology. His S-symbolism has probably not received any significant public use since his death. It may also be noted that, while Lundberg did not himself aspire to the kind of research which needed external funding, Dodd did, but after the initial postwar flush of money from sources associated with the military Lundberg did not succeed in

---

[21] Henry Ozanne, then working with Dodd, replied to this review, arguing that Shanas had seriously misunderstood the nature of his enterprise, and Shanas made a rejoinder (Ozanne 1943, Shanas 1943).

raising it for him from the more conventional academic sources.[22] This cannot obviously be accounted for by the nature of foundation agendas, since at that period they were extremely interested in improving research methods, in 'scientific' work and the application of mathematics to social science, and in interdisciplinary work. Given that at the relevant period foundations were funding most of the prominent sociologists respected within the discipline, often with money which they could use for purposes of their own choice, and making much use of advice from the discipline in deciding whom to support, it is suggestive of attitudes towards Dodd that he did not do well. The somewhat grandiose eccentricity of his pet projects towards the end of his career – he was developing a theory ('Epicosm') to encompass the whole cosmos[23] – may have had something to do with it, as may, more mundanely, the East Coast location of the major foundations, and the relative geographical isolation of Seattle before the age of easy air travel.

Stewart published articles in respected social-science journals, though not in sociological ones apart from *Sociometry* (initially when under Lundberg's editorship), and attention was given to his work by some sociologists outside the Dodd/Lundberg circle. However, that attention did not take the form one might have expected if there was a keen commitment to natural-science models and theories. The writers who drew on his work are all ones in fields such as demography and ecology (in the USA closely linked with sociology) where data similar to his were routinely used, and on the whole it was his data rather than his theories which were used in sociology.[24] The distinguished demographer/ecologist and

---

[22] Later projects were funded by the American Council for Judaism (an anti-Zionist group which approved Lundberg's political stance on issues where other Jewish groups perceived him as anti-Semitic), and the Behavioral Research Council.

[23] 'this deals with a mathematical model for the organizing of activity at all levels in the cosmos from protons through electrons and atoms, molecules, cells, brains, societies and scientific systems. With the aid of the newly developing dimension of *complexity*, measured in bits or logarithms to the base 2, it is proving possible to unify the sciences thus. This develops an isosceles triangular distribution of everything nameable in the cosmos' (GAL 10).

[24] 'In sociology', because the *Social Science Citation Index* reveals that his work has been drawn on quite heavily in more recent years, but this has been almost entirely in geography and related fields such as urban planning. Further investigation shows that he played a significant role in the quantitative and 'behavioural' revolution in geography which started in the late 1950s. Although his theories were used there, the link through his use of spatial data is obvious.

methodologist Otis Dudley Duncan, then at the beginning of his career, was one of those who took a more active interest; he had personal contact with Stewart, reprinted an article by him in a reader which he co-edited (Spengler and Duncan 1956), and used his work and referred to it as potentially valuable in his own writing (Duncan 1959: 688, 692; Duncan, Scott, Lieberson, Duncan et al. 1960: 139, 257, 553). The last reference cited, however, implies that Stewart's work was not altogether being used as he would have hoped: 'we have not emphasized the physical science analogues of population potential to which the inventor of the concept refers. Instead, we have . . . simply thought of population potential as a convenient indicator of generalised accessibility.'[25] Donald J. Bogue, a distinguished demographer, says that Stewart's work was taken very seriously in social ecology, and appealed to those who aspired to rigorous quantification and/or the unity of social and natural science, but even by these it was treated as naive in relation to the subject matter and requiring translation into sociologically relevant theoretical terms (Bogue 1992). But it could also be rejected for reasons specifically to do with alternative conceptions of scientific method or approach. A leading social ecologist, Amos Hawley, who might well have been one of those interested in Stewart's work, felt that concern with spatial distribution was a theoretical cul-de-sac, and that a bio-ecological model which laid more stress on social organisation was more appropriate (Hawley 1992: 3). Fred Strodtbeck, whose later work is in other fields, started his academic career with an MA thesis which drew on Stewart's work and led to publications; however, these addressed the issue of migration and preferred Stouffer's (1940) approach. In an auto-biographical account he explains how he came to this under the influence of his teacher Bain, and later at Harvard with Stouffer was converted to experimental work, which he saw as of a different style (Strodtbeck 1980: Introduction). More systematically, a search of likely articles[26] in the main sociology journals up to 1970 shows that although there were a number of references to Stewart few of

---

[25] In a recent letter responding to an enquiry by me (Duncan 1992), Duncan remarks that Stewart 'had good ideas and a sense for pattern in data as well as a sense of the limitations of data', though he went too far in his enthusiasm for Zipf who was 'all but a charlatan', as was Dodd.

[26] 'Likely' represents my judgment, and other judges might differ; for that reason no figures are offered, in order to avoid a misleading level of precision.

those were made by people other than our heroes or their students, and a fair number of opportunities to cite him in reasonably appropriate contexts were missed.

Zipf's work too was regularly reviewed in the sociological journals, and he also published in them. The only favourable review found, however, came from a member of the Lundberg circle. Bain (1950) saw his *Human Behavior and the Principle of Least Effort* as 'an impressive contribution to the rapidly growing literature of the unity of science', and finishes by saying:

His PLE may or may not attain a place in the history of science comparable to that of gravitation, atomic theory, or relativity, but it does seem to be a conclusive answer to those who contend that there are no constant universal relationships between social phenomena capable of being expressed in rigorous logico-mathematical terms.

A rather different impression is given in the review by Rashevsky (1951), a distinguished mathematical biologist who had himself applied his natural-scientific approach to social topics. He sees the book's aim as desirable, but as merely stated rather than achieved; there are a number of interesting conclusions, but they do not clearly follow from the assumptions and there are no mathematical derivations; no clear-cut propositions have been proved. The latter part of his review shows a tone, characteristic from some of those who wished to be generally sympathetic to parts of this enterprise but had doubts about the outcome, of polite uncertainty whether the fault may not lie in his understanding.[27] Later, in an encyclopaedia entry, Rashevsky's close colleague Rapoport (1979) gives a sterner verdict, condemning Zipf's work on rank-size relations of inadequate understanding of statistical processes and failure to recognise that there could be many other rank-size laws, while theoretical conclusions could only be justified if some reason was offered why the curves must belong to a certain class. Hollingshead (1949), an empirical sociologist, finds that Zipf ignores the relevant work of sociologists in his field and, more seriously, that in most cases the empirical data he presents do not

---

[27] Cf. a letter from Henry Margenau, a physicist, to Dodd: 'your model . . . surely deserves much more study than I have been able to give it. But it is also true that every beginning effort I have made to understand it has bogged down in my failure to comprehend your language. I try to grasp a mathematical formula and the significance eludes me. Your math is either too profound or too trivial to arouse my enthusiasm' (Margenau 1969).

support his argument. A similar judgment is made by McCormick (1941b), a methodologist, in his review of *National Unity and Disunity*. He also points out that no reason is offered why the size of cities or incomes should follow a law of harmonic relationship, and that the implied superiority of a balanced harmonic series has no justification. The problem is not adequately approached by 'the spectacular manipulation of an unresisting mathematical formula'. Riemer (1942), in his review of the same book, not only argues that the data do not support the claim to have observed an empirical regularity, but strongly asserts that a political agenda appears to have influenced the interpretation: 'Under the cover of a scientific attitude that stresses unbiased empirical observation, the author proposes a system of social and political propaganda which coincides closely with Axis publicity'. (In support of this, he reports Zipf as arguing that the Treaty of Versailles should be blamed for breaking the sequence of community size in Germany, and that Hitler may be restoring a natural balance in Europe.) The *Social Science Citation Index* shows 274 references since 1980 to Zipf's work, but of these only 11 are from sociological sources. Apart from those which come from linguistics, and may well draw on aspects of his work other than those of concern to us, the main interest appears to be from areas related to geography and information science.

The general sociological reception of the group's ideas was, thus, at least mixed, even if the political reactions are ignored. It can be summarised as showing that there was a nucleus of strong supporters, an outer circle of people who either diffusely favoured their enterprise without necessarily sharing their more distinctive positions or were interested in their data rather than their theoretical and/or methodological ideas, and a number of strong critics and opponents; some seem to have been uncertain whether parts of their enterprise should be regarded as brilliant or as fundamentally misconceived. The picture is surely not one of consensus around an emergent orthodoxy, even if only the sociologists are considered.

OTHER STRANDS OF SCIENTISM

There were many other strands within sociology, in addition to those mentioned above, of what could be seen as scientism, so to see our group as distinct is not to deny the broader significance of scientism. Some of these others, such as the movement to small-group research in laboratories, were already established at an earlier stage or originated quite independently. The modern survey had quite other origins (Converse 1987), in no way especially associated with 'science', although it came to be associated with scientism by many among both its friends and its foes; however, Bain (1928) and Sorokin (1956: 407) from their very different stances can represent those who argued that to collect data in that way was particularly unscientific. It is puzzling that Lundberg and Dodd came to draw so heavily and uncritically on survey data; in this they seem simply to have followed the times, happy with the quantification and explicit operational definitions and not making any novel contributions; they were on good collegial terms with the leading survey figures, but not members of their intellectual circle[28] – and not really sharing their intellectual preoccupations.

To what extent were the circle we have focused on influential in the mainstream of postwar American sociology? It is clear that Lundberg was in many ways close to the centre, though he regarded himself as having a mission to convert it to the true gospel. He was personally popular, and much admired by his students, many of whom remained in touch and continue still to associate themselves with him.[29] His published work was widely mentioned, and admired by many. It does not follow, however, that the distinctive aspects of

---

[28] It is potentially relevant that Lundberg's friendship with Lazarsfeld dated from the period early in Lazarsfeld's career when he had not yet become fully established in US sociology, when Lundberg was personally involved in a project employing large-scale data collection, and when both of them were based in the New York area and took part in some of the same activities there. My interviews show that the Washington Public Opinion Laboratory (set up by Lundberg and Dodd) was not taken seriously as an intellectual contributor by other survey units, and indeed some of those active in survey work denied having had knowledge of its existence.

[29] It is instructive to look, when considering influence and the forms it takes, at the careers of some of those who were students of Dodd and Lundberg and associated themselves with their ideas. W. R. Catton was a graduate student and then for some years a faculty member in their department, and accepts identification as a member of their group; he worked on Project Revere and his thesis topic arose from it. Like every good student, however, he did not follow his mentors blindly, despite accepting the shared goal of building a scientific sociology. His very interesting book *From Animistic to Naturalistic Sociology* (Catton 1966) starts from a problem (substantively, about the explanation of visits to national parks) with which Dodd's theory could not deal, and criticises his version of social physics; he does so, however, only to suggest an improved set of axioms for a 'naturalistic' sociology. In his later career, the interest in issues connected with national parks led him to a concern with ecology and to involvement with biologists' ecology and 'environmental sociology'.

his views were dominant, or that agreement with them in principle led to concordant practice. His well-known support for Dodd, whose work was much more controversial – though its hermetic incomprehensibility both exposed it to and protected it from criticism – may not have advantaged his standing. Zipf and Stewart were connected with the centre mainly through the Lundberg science circle; although they had a vogue in limited sociological circles, they often ignored earlier sociologists who had done related work, and did not make connections which sociologists felt appropriate.

Why, despite a collective atmosphere of support for scientism, were the Lundberg group and its more idiosyncratic ideas not more widely influential within sociology? Some intellectual reasons and some social ones may be suggested. The concrete work of the group tended to link data on topics which many would regard as either trivial or uninteresting with theories of such high levels of abstraction that it was not easy to see what other topics they had implications for.[30] This provided few opportunities for those starting with other interests to link them with those of the group, as well as suggesting grounds on which their work could reasonably be criticised. Dodd's personal symbolism was of extreme complexity (and, presumably, expense in typesetting) and also used many verbal neologisms. These were hard to understand, and required training and practice – which might not seem worth the investment – if they were to be grasped. Insofar as they drew on theories and equations from natural science, many sociologists probably felt incompetent to understand or imitate their work; they also, naturally, tended to see its claims as inappropriate or threatening from a disciplinary point of view. Those who did understand their work and feel competent often saw reason to reject it. Moreover, when all due allowances have been made, it must be admitted that some features of their work had elements of numerological fantasy, and other features which even at the time most sociologists would have regarded as eccentricities; there was also a cultish and evangelical style, with hints of the inappropriately religious, which must surely have deterred those who were not actively attracted by that or other features. Finally, the University of Washington was, in

---

[30] This does not, however, in itself seem to have impeded the acceptance of the general systems theorists as important.

Seattle, distant from the East Coast and even the Midwestern centres of disciplinary and funding power, and the group's political stance also set it apart from the leading figures in ways described in chapter 6.

There were also other lines of natural-scientific interest in the social and vice versa. Prominent among these was the 'general systems' movement. The Society for General Systems Research started as a group within the American Association for the Advancement of Science (AAAS), initiated by the biologist and polymath von Bertalanffy,[31] Rashevsky and another colleague who met each other at the Centre for Advanced Study in the Behavioral Sciences. Rapoport was a leading figure in it, and the society included a number of social scientists (among them Dodd and Lundberg). This was part of the same impulse which led to the development of cybernetics, also involving a different set of social scientists (Heims 1991). (The descendants of both these movements seem to be in information theory and artificial intelligence.) A statement in the first (1956) volume of its yearbook says that mathematicised social science occupies a pivotal position in its approach, because this puts to a severe test the conviction that mathematical methods are universally useful. An editorial in a later volume suggests that 'Perhaps the strongest theme running through past volumes . . . is the organismic viewpoint' (Meier 1961: iii). This draws attention to the idea of system as it has been used in sociology more generally, especially in Parsonian functionalism. (Parsons' pupil Marion Levy was a member of the society, though Parsons was not.)

It is well known that Parsons was much influenced by the thinking of the physiologist L. J. Henderson, as well as by his own early studies in biology.[32] Less attention has been drawn to his other scientific interests. (Though Russett (1966) analyses the use he, as well as other writers, have made of the concept of equilibrium.) His collaborator Pitts tells how his political championing of Robert Oppenheimer led him, during the writing of *Family, Socialization and Interaction Process* (Parsons and Bales 1955) to go on such an 'atomic

---

[31] Von Bertalanffy's version of the unity of science is described (Laszlo 1979) as not reductionist to physics, but searching for isomorphism of laws in different fields.

[32] Robert Park of Chicago, not commonly associated with scientism by those with methodological interests, was also strongly influenced in his theoretical ideas by biological ecologists; he attended an ecological discussion group at Chicago.

kick' that he had to be discouraged from excessive use of the word 'fission' (Hallen no date: 445). Lundberg (1956) argued that there had been a marked convergence in the theory of Parsons and Dodd, shown in particular in the *Working Papers in the Theory of Action* (Parsons, Bales and Shils 1953). His detailed argument can be questioned, but he is certainly right that there Parsons presents an extremely 'scientific' programme, with obvious analogies to physics shown in its terminology of dimensions, coordinates, forces, energy, etc..[33] This is, thus, another line of 'scientific' thought.

Bales, Parsons' collaborator, is famous for his collection of systematic data on small group interaction, which represents a further scientistic theme. His work was not strictly experimental, but links with the small group laboratory work very fashionable at the time in sociology as well as psychology (on which see Mullins 1973, chapter 5). Another figure prominent in the study of small groups was Kurt Lewin, whose 'field theory' and use of topological modes of presentation (Lewin 1951) show yet another mode of appropriating aspects of natural science. From a quite different direction and research tradition comes the 'scientific' work of the Yankee City project led by Harvard anthropologist W. Lloyd Warner. Its conception of science is explained in an introductory statement in the first volume (Warner and Lunt 1941: 8–14). Durkheim is invoked,[34] and Radcliffe-Brown is an immediate ancestor. It is an intensive community study, with much relatively traditional anthropological data, but a lot of the analysis is quantitative and diagrammatic and it uses a conception of social structure which is expressed in matrices. It was not without reason that early reviewers (Opler 1942, Mills 1942) criticised its mindless accumulation of data, though eventual theorisation is the declared goal. It is clear, from this incomplete list of examples, that the Lundberg group by no means subsumed the whole of the tendencies to scientism, some of which were carried by people working in quite different styles and moving in quite different socio-intellectual

---

[33] In my judgment there is not so much a convergence in the sets of categories used, as Lundberg argued, as a longer-term similarity in the basic enterprise: each was, in his very different way, constructing a set of high-level abstract categories designed to cover everything – and suffering from severe difficulties in establishing clear relations between those empty general boxes and specific empirical contents.

[34] As he also was by Bales (1984) in relation to his totally different work; the connection for Bales was an interest in *rates* of behaviour.

groups. It is argued, therefore, that, despite Lundberg's prominence, he was in an important sense only a member of one small and idiosyncratic circle among others also in different ways committed to scientism: all shared a beautiful dream, but that did not mean that it had a clear consensual content – indeed, we have seen differences even among the members of the inner Lundberg circle.

A shared dream of unity with natural science need not imply truly shared conceptions of what that would entail. A key interpretive issue, arising in relation to much of the material of both Lundberg's and other circles, is how far terms such as 'force' were meant literally, and how far they were purely metaphorical; if they were meant literally, the next question is what they literally (operationally?) meant in a social-science context. The answer is frequently not obvious, and it seems probable that the authors who used them might not have been able to answer it themselves. Only if they were meant literally, at whatever level of theoretical abstraction, could there have been a justified claim to substantive unification with the natural sciences, in the sense that the same laws and propositions applied to both. Dodd and Stewart plainly did mean them literally in this sense, though most others probably did not, and this could help to account for the extent to which their work was not incorporated into the mainstream except in incidental ways.[35] (It should be noted that their programme was not a reductionist one: it did not treat social events as directly determined by events at the atomic level. When that is done, the element of metaphor does not arise.)

The claim to *methodological* unification with the natural sciences, the centre of Lundberg's contribution, is less problematic and so he was easier to take on board. But in what capacity was he taken on board? Perhaps the thoughts on metaphor above may be allowed to suggest that it was as a figurehead, rather than as the pilot or the captain, that he joined the ship. That is, it is suggested that his role should be regarded as legitimatory rather than fundamentally causal of research practices. Relatively few sociologists shared his metasociological interests, and he wrote with clarity and

---

[35] Physical theory seems especially likely to raise problems. Some aspects of biology, however, especially evolutionary theory, deal with units which do not require to be treated metaphorically to be applied to sociological topics, and so cause much less difficulty.

enthusiasm, so a division of labour in which he wrote persuasively to show that science was a good thing and their practices were scientific, while they got on with doing them, was an attractive one. As his own empirical work shows, studies can be interpreted in one methodological framework which could equally have been done in another or in none.

In addition, we should not forget that Lundberg's prominence was as a controversialist, and the other sides in the controversies were not powerless or insignificant, even if his side seemed to be winning on 'science' after the war.[36] The classic debate was between him and Herbert Blumer of Chicago, who had his ardent followers while at Chicago and then left in 1951 for Berkeley to found what became probably the leading department at a slightly later period. Interwar, there were significant figures who objected to the new emphasis on 'research', and did not define empirical work as an important part of university sociology's mission. (Some of the pressure for 'science' should be seen, against that background, as simply proposing that general statements should be supported with data.) Some of my postwar respondents, perhaps especially those who were graduate students at Chicago, speak very dismissively of Lundberg and all his works and say that in their experience such ideas were not taken seriously. Although the uniformity and qualitative commitments of the postwar Chicago department have been exaggerated, it was the training ground for important sociologists, among whom Howard S. Becker and Erving Goffman are especially prominent, who researched and wrote in styles which, while rigorous in their own way, have nothing to do with scientism. Those present in the department at the time describe its ethos as one where there was enthusiasm for being scientific about society. However, the conception of science was not one which rested on any philosophical prescription, but emphasised the value of staying

---

[36] Gouldner and Sprehe's 1965 study falls after our period, but is close enough to it to be worth mentioning here. This used a postal questionnaire, sent to ASA members in 1964; about half responded. Some questions were about 'scientific method'. The responses show that 80 per cent or more thought that the coming generation of sociologists would need much more mathematical training – and that inventiveness was at least as important as rigour in the design of research. Something over a third agreed, and disagreed, with statements about the importance of precise measurement and the relative fruitfulness of field and laboratory work. These are not data of a quality that can be taken very seriously, but for what they are worth they suggest a divided or ambivalent profession rather than one with a dominant research style.

close to the data and only making grounded assertions; this ethos was held as much by the demographers and other quantitative workers. At the level of practice, too, any view of the discipline as a whole needs to take into account what Feagin, Orum and Sjoberg (1991: 270) call 'book sociology' (as distinct from 'article sociology'), which they see as less quantitative and hypothetico-deductive, more diverse and qualitative in style.

Thus scientism of whatever hue was not quite so overwhelmingly dominant as has sometimes been suggested; indeed, our perception that it was so comes in part from the protests of contemporaries who objected to it, and were thus themselves part of other tendencies. Similarity and difference are matters of perspective, and there could be senses in which the differences emphasised are less important than similarities which distinguish all those focused on from others; here and now, however, it is the differences which need emphasis. It is misleading to imply that, for example, Dodd's approach was the same as that of Lazarsfeld, that sociologists who claimed to be following natural science were necessarily really doing so, that all those who invoke 'science' actually meant the same thing by it, or that the styles of practical researchers – even when they invoke 'science' – can be accounted for by metatheoretical ideas. The link between theory and practice is, as we argue in the next chapter, weaker than ideologists, of whatever persuasion, like to suggest. Insofar as there was consensus in sociology on the desirability of 'science', it was not a consensus with an agreed content.

CHAPTER 4

Theory and practice

Theories take positions with potential implications for method. Metatheoretical and methodological works take positions with implications for research methods, and introduce new methods. But what is the relation between such general statements and research practice? It cannot be taken for granted that theory guides practice normatively, or leads it causally. Our concern here is with the determinants of practical methodological outcomes. We start with general theory, and then go on to consider the role of methodological theorising in the determination of method. There is a common implicit assumption that theory can be inferred from practice, or vice versa, so that only one needs to be studied to consider their relationship. Since this approach is so common, the general arguments it involves are discussed first. The assumption could only be shown to be justified by not initially acting on it, but studying both to investigate their relation, and this will be our main strategy.

MUST METHOD IMPLY THEORY?

It is often asserted in the more recent literature that every research method implies a theoretical position, whether or not that is stated by the user. The normal assumption is that the relationship between method and theory is one of elective affinity, but not symmetrical: theory is more fundamental, and leads to the corresponding method or, to put it as Bryman (1988: 123–6) does, the epistemological leads to the technical. Among those who spell out their stance on this orthodoxy, it takes a range of more specific forms. At one extreme, the link is seen as involving the most fundamental aspects of world-view and epistemological assumptions (e.g. Gouldner 1971, Phillips 1976: 21, Ritzer 1975), while at the other it is seen as involving only 'theories of instrumentation' (J. A. Hughes 1976: 273), although these may imply theories of a broader kind. Different writers define the relevant theories, or types of theory, differently. Phillips and Ritzer, for example, while they agree that basic paradigms are involved, each offers his own typology of what those paradigms are. There are also many writers with more philosophical concerns who see logical connections between broad (meta)theoretical and methodological positions, with 'positivism' usually seen as one of the key alternatives (see Fay 1975, Filmer, Phillipson, Silverman and Walsh 1972, Hindess 1973, Keat and Urry 1975). The picture is one where particular methods follow from the general methodological positions, which themselves follow from or are part of the (meta)theoretical positions. Alexander (1982) and Alexander and Colomy (1992) have spelled out their version in unusually explicit and helpful detail. They use a diagram of a continuum from abstract, general and metaphysical elements at one end to observational statements and other concrete and factual matters at the other end. They assert that 'every social scientific statement contains implicit or explicit commitments about the nature of every other element on the scientific continuum'[1] (Alexander and Colomy 1992: 34). For our purposes here, the issue can be taken at a sufficiently general level for all these distinctions not to make a difference to the argument. It should be noted that the argument is one of principle, not of history, though historical data bear on the points about what has happened in practice. The positions sketched above are distinctively postwar positions, and their emergence from some of the changes in methodological thinking which we have sketched elsewhere could be traced.[2]

The general assertion that the choice of method implies a theoretical position depends on a number of (usually implicit) assumptions. The first of these is one about the intrinsic nature of methods and theories: any one implies only one member of the other class, or at least is only compatible with a limited range of its

[1] Elsewhere, they add detail to their picture which is not altogether consistent with what this suggests; this is discussed in chapter 6.
[2] Hinkle (1994: 9–11) provides a useful outline of changing meanings of 'theory' in the interwar period, showing a gradual shift away from an association with 'general sociology' in the direction of an emerging association with the idea of theories to be scientifically tested.

members. The second is that fundamental theoretical commitments necessarily determine particular sociological practices, and that particular sociological practices are determined by theoretical commitments. The third is that everyone has fundamental theoretical commitments, preferably but not necessarily conscious ones, with which to determine their practices. Let us examine these assumptions in turn, in reverse order.

Does everyone have fundamental theoretical commitments? To the extent that any practice whatever logically implies some theoretical position, or at least is inconsistent with one or more other theoretical positions, every researcher has at least one theoretical position. But it does not follow that practitioners exemplify the same position on different occasions of practice, or that they consciously hold that position, or would endorse it if it were put to them in the abstract (or that the abstract position already exists as a recognised body of thought with a name).[3] One cannot, therefore, be justified in imputing a general set of theoretical beliefs to a practitioner without evidence independent of their research that she or he holds those beliefs. At this point one runs into a practical difficulty in treating the issue as an empirical one, since most researchers do not provide general statements of their philosophies; it is not the convention that this is required in empirical articles or books, so few provide it, and the division of labour within the discipline means that few of those who carry out research also write general works. When they do, their practice may not be consistent with their precepts, as in the previous chapter I suggested happened in the case of Lundberg. Danziger (1990: 13–14) has suggested, moreover, that practice involves taken-for-granted tacit knowledge, so that investigators may be poor sources of information on their own practice; discourse about practice needs to be distinguished from practice. In the absence of appropriate evidence, imputations of theoretical commitments come from the observer rather than the actor, and so are normative rather than empirical.

The next question is whether fundamental theoretical commitments necessarily determine particular sociological practices, or particular sociological practices are determined by theoretical

---

[3] Would those who impute implicit theoretical positions to practitioners accept the corollary that nothing can be described as 'atheoretical'?

commitments. In the abstract the answer is self-evident: of course the fundamental theoretical commitments held must determine practice. Sociologically, however, this has several implications which do not necessarily hold. It implies not only that everyone has fundamental commitments, but that they are conscious of them,[4] make correct derivations from them, always act with complete consistency, choose methods on theoretical grounds unconstrained by any practical considerations, and use methods only in contexts to which they are appropriate. I may be excessively cynical, but I find these further conditions implausible as universal empirical generalisations.

Does each method or theory imply only one member of the other class, or a limited range of corresponding ones? 'Theory' in this context has been used to mean anything from a fundamental philosophical stance to specific middle-range propositions about, for example, the extent to which language can be taken as an indicator of thought (J. A. Hughes 1976: 148). The latter type of proposition is self-evidently relevant, in that to say that it is implied amounts to saying that the method used is believed by the user to be valid, but for just that reason it is of little interest – and its relation to more fundamental positions is likely to be unclear.

Fundamental philosophical stances may not have precise implications at the level of practical method or, if they do, these may not distinguish between what sociologists conventionally treat as distinct methods in empirical work. As an example of this point we may take 'positivism', probably the general position most often mentioned in recent discussion. This is used in different senses by different writers; when the definitions given of it by a number of authors were analysed, it was found that they were not sufficiently

---

[4] There may be some meaningful sense in which unconscious commitments can influence practice, but it would be extraordinarily hard to *show* that they did so (Rhoads 1972: 153). It is, of course, not acceptable in this context to infer commitments from observation of practices; because that would take as given what requires to be demonstrated. Unless the commitments exist independently of the practices, they cannot *determine* them.

Verhoeven (1995: 13–16) provides some amusing examples of his difficulty in trying to get leading symbolic interactionists to declare their basic presuppositions, while they deny any interest in the question, or sufficient knowledge of the philosophical literature to confirm or deny his uses of it in relation to their work. The collective stance is indicated when Gregory Stone agrees with Verhoeven's summary of his views as being 'we don't agree with assumptions, we just want to be empirical', and Eliot Freidson says 'I resent the necessity of choosing [between philosophical positions] . . . I think the necessity of choice is created by people who are occupied with words, not with action.'

precise to be usable to distinguish between positivistic and non-positivistic *practices*, as distinct from declarations of principle (J. Platt 1981: 74–5). However, these authors probably all have in common the idea that positivism dictates that the method of natural science should be followed in social science. But this idea is vacuous, since there is no such thing as *the* method of natural science; work in sociology of science (e.g. Latour and Woolgar 1979, Gilbert and Mulkay 1984) has amply demonstrated that what natural scientists do may have little correspondence to the 'scientific method' described in textbooks – and there are differences of opinion even in them. If one wants to do what natural scientists really do, should it be what is done by theoretical physicists, astronomers, field biologists . . . ? Whichever one chooses, it is probable that the divergence of subject matter will mean that detailed methods cannot be the same; some other technique or device will be substituted for the astronomer's telescope. Within sociology, the attempt to be scientific has been associated with each of laboratory experimentation, the survey and direct naturalistic observation, which are radically different methods. Declarations of positivistic principle, then, might mean that their authors intended to be 'scientific', but give little clue what that would be taken to imply.[5]

Several writers have argued, sometimes drawing on systematic data, that there is not in practice a perfect match between theory and method, whatever logic might suggest. Mann (1981: 548–9) argues that different epistemologies do not lead to different research practices because epistemologies of objective knowledge are no longer regarded as tenable but relativism does not provide a basis for research, so all actual research now rests on 'as if positivism', whatever the formal position of the researcher. Bryman (1984) shows that discussion in the quantitative/qualitative debate has regularly confused epistemological and technical issues, and argues that in research practice there is not a neat correspondence, of the kind posited in the debate, between epistemological position and technique. Alexander (1979) maintains that it is normal for

[5] Imputations of positivism to others, much commoner in recent times than declarations of affiliation made on one's own behalf, are normally meant as abuse. The others grouped together under this heading, from whom the writers are dissociating themselves, often have little in common with each other.

theories to have a number of different components – one of them methodological assumptions – each concerned with distinctive problems, and hence each with relative autonomy[6] in relation to the other components. In his more recent formulation, he maintains that the basic elements cannot be combined in an infinite variety of ways, but that 'although in principle there is no intrinsic relationship between the different elements arrayed across the scientific continuum, there is a clear tendency for certain kinds of commitments to hang together' (Alexander and Colomy 1992: 34–5), linked by the beliefs within intellectual traditions about elective affinities between different components of their positions. This is an argument for matching in the eyes of participants, but not of the observer. J. Berger, Wagner and Zelditch (1989: 20) argue, drawing on the example of one particular theory, that it is normal for metatheoretical positions to guide theoretical and empirical work – but that these then lead to revisions at the metatheoretical level, so that it is not a matter of one-way determination. Phillips (1976) and Ritzer (1975), while both maintaining that theoretical paradigms logically imply methodological choices, recognise that in practice they do not predict them perfectly; indeed, Ritzer says (1975: 68) that those he classifies as following the 'social factist' paradigm typically prefer methods not appropriate to their theoretical commitments. (Oddly, he does this in the context of a book organised in terms of paradigms which are defined as including methods.) Snizek (1976) and Freidheim (1979) show empirically that there is even less association between Ritzer's theoretical paradigms and the methods employed than he maintains. Menzies (1982), studying a sample of articles and books, showed that there was a significant gap between theoreticians' theory and researchers' theory; cross-references between theoretical and research articles were few, and the distribution of intellectual positions held or used differed between the two fields. These writers are not all addressing exactly the same issue, but each seems persuasive in relation to his or her particular concerns. To their arguments we may add some further ones about the nature of actual methods and theories.

It can be questioned whether every set of ideas commonly referred to among sociologists as a theory actually has a stance on all the issues relevant to choice of method, and it can be argued that

---

6 But how much autonomy is relative autonomy?

one of the differences in practice among theoretical schools is the level of attention they give to different aspects of the grounds that a 'theory' can in principle cover.[7] It can also be questioned on other grounds whether every actual theory implies a method. It has, for instance, been argued by some critics (Mills 1959, Black 1961) that Parsons' theory was formulated in such vague and abstract terms that it was not clear what its implications were. Other theoretical positions, such as postmodernism or Althusserian Marxism, have denied the possibility of empirical knowledge of the world, and so are incompatible with any method.

Analogous questions may be raised about the nature of methods in principle; one may also query whether the current methods generally recognised at any one time are invariably differentiated with respect to the relevant factors – and especially whether they are differentiated in such a way as to give a tidy one-to-one correspondence with the current generally recognised theories.[8] (Is there, for instance, a clear distinction between Marxism and functionalism in their relation to content analysis?) If every theory automatically generated an appropriate method it would indeed be so – and how convenient that would be for those of us who give lectures and write textbooks – but that cannot be taken for granted. To take it for granted is to imply that no additional creativity is required to develop a method, and that methods have no social base or process of development independent of that for theories. This would mean that, even if they were intrinsically connected with theories, they could never lag far behind or anticipate theoretical movements. It is also assumed that the same methods, taking 'method' in the sense of practical technique, lend themselves to only one interpretation. But perhaps the same technique does not always constitute the same 'method'? One could, for instance, very

---

[7] The point here is closely analogous to that made by Skinner (1969) about the danger of assuming that each classic writer on political theory must have had something to say on each of what are now seen as the standard topics of that field and, if appropriate statements cannot be found, supplying the appropriate features perceived as consistent with what was stated.

[8] There are obvious points to be made here about what counts as 'method' or 'theory'. It would be very reasonable to argue that the distinctions among modes of data-collection are far from the most significant ones, and I would agree; it is, however, in relation to those, or to the quantitative/qualitative distinction, that the matter has most commonly been discussed. Another reason for maintaining the discussion at that level is, however, that, unlike some more sophisticated focuses, it does clearly discriminate between *explanans* and *explanandum*.

plausibly hold that a survey questionnaire with simple yes/no questions on factual matters is quite different from a well-piloted one with open-ended questions on subjective experience where the answers will be classified into categories derived from the data. The case of participant observation demonstrates how the same technique may, over time, change meaning for its users in terms of theoretical categories from behaviouristic to phenomenological. The assumption is implausible.

Once these assumptions have been exposed to view, it is apparent that much of the force behind the commonplace that method depends on theory is normative, not empirical. Method ought to depend on a conscious and coherent theoretical position; what is logically prior should also be causally so. One does not need to dispute the desirability of such a relationship[9] to doubt its automatic occurrence in practice. For historical purposes, is must be distinguished from ought.

Against the background of these general points, let us turn to consider particular methods and their relation to theories. The most commonly argued connections are between functional theory and survey method, and between symbolic interactionism and participant observation; each is explored below.

FUNCTIONALISM AND THE SURVEY

There are several versions of the assertion that functionalism and the survey are connected. One is the 'radical' version, which sees both as serving the needs of corporate capitalism (e.g. Szymanski 1971) or some related conservative purpose; this need not imply that they have shared intellectual characteristics. A second version is one which sees them as linked by their 'positivism' (e.g. Eisenstadt and Curelaru 1976); this view has been shared by writers, such as Keat and Urry (1975) on the one hand and Filmer, Phillipson, Silverman and Walsh (1972) on the other, who differ considerably in what they count as 'positivist'. In the same general category are views such as those of Ritzer (1975) or Phillips (1976), who see them as sharing a paradigmatic position defined in some

[9] One may, however, dispute it. It does not seem realistic to think that theoreticians will be better at devising creative methods than practical research people whose interest is focused in that area.

other way. A third view, exemplified by Baldamus (1976) or Schatzman and Strauss (1973), sees a detailed intellectual compatibility resting on their internal structures. Finally, there is a now very dated version (e.g. Lipset and Smelser 1961: 4, Ben David 1973: 470–1) which sees the two together as simply constituting modern sociology, without spelling out a rationale. The first two versions have in common an explanatory shortcoming as accounts of a specific connection between functionalism and survey, in that they treat them as members of broader categories also containing other theories and methods; this means that something further would be needed to account for a specific conjunction, and at that point it seems likely that the argument would need to invoke socio-historical circumstances and so would become sociological rather than philosophical.

There are good grounds for questioning the special compatibility-in-principle of survey and functionalism. Functionalism explains particular social patterns by the functions they perform for larger social units, and in that sense is intrinsically macroscopic; the typical unit of the survey is the individual, giving a microscopic and non-social focus. Functionalism attaches importance to latent functions, not dependent on the consciousness of societal members; surveys are commonly concerned with the overt attitudes and intentions of those studied. Functionalism attaches special importance to 'key' roles and institutions, which define the central character of the social system; surveys commonly aim for representative samples in which every individual is treated as equal.

But whether or not there is compatibility-in-principle, the views of actors are more important than those of outside commentators in the determination of practice. My interviews show that at least some key actors were far from seeing a connection; none of those who have played a leading role in surveys saw one. Peter Rossi, who got his doctorate at Columbia in 1951 and then went to Harvard, said that:

one of the tensions that existed both at Harvard and Columbia was exhibited in students as they would go from Stouffer's [survey methodologist] classes to Parsons [functionalist theorist] and backwards and have to live with those methods that did not connect, and also Merton's [functionalist theorist] mind and Lazarsfeld's [survey methodologist] except to the extent that Merton became a Lazarsfeldian. (Rossi 1984)

James Davis, talking of his time in graduate school at Harvard in the 1950s, said that the official ideology of the department was that:

the good sociology of the future would take Parsons' wonderful theoretical ideas and Stouffer's research methods, but there was no very concrete idea how to do it . . . it was like saying that it would be nice to combine survey research and the Bible: sure it would be nice, but how would you do it? (J. A. Davis 1984)

Haller, who got his doctorate in the same period in the Wisconsin department, which had a strong survey tradition and no recognised functionalists on the staff, said 'We read Parsons very seriously, and then didn't use him for anything' (Haller 1984). Robert Merton, perhaps the strongest candidate for the combination of the tendencies, says of his work with Lazarsfeld that:

At no point did we ever conclude that the multivariate analysis of sample survey data was specifically or uniquely appropriate for the kind of functional and structural theoretical orientation that I was trying to develop. Nor have I ever had occasion since for adopting such an opinion. (Merton 1984)

To the extent that such views were held, those who adopted theory or method will have done so for independent reasons.

But actors' views are not everything, and the individual level is not the only relevant one. It is certainly true that there was a period, roughly 1950–65, when functionalism and survey were leading tendencies in the discipline. For functionalism to have led to the emergence of the survey, as the theory-led model implies it should have done, it must have existed first in at least a rudimentary form, and here there are serious problems with dates. If 'functionalism' is defined to include the anthropological version, that was highly developed in the interwar period – but closely associated with participant observation, not surveys. But what is usually intended in this context is the Parsons version. This only started to be published at the very end of the 1930s, and it was first systematically expounded in print in 1949 (*Essays in Sociological Theory*) and 1951 (*The Social System*); he was not widely known until after the war, and it was only then that Stouffer, who had not previously figured in his personal network, moved to join his department at Harvard. (Once there, they had sufficient difficulty understanding each other for Merton to be invited back to Harvard for sessions in which he would translate one to the other in the hope that they would see how to collaborate productively, but even this did not achieve the desired effect (Merton 1984).) The Merton/Lazarsfeld partnership started when Lazarsfeld drew Merton into some work of his which was already under way (Hunt 1961: 60). The components of what became the modern survey were already present in the 1930s, and were consolidated in wartime research; most of its early development was entirely outside academic sociology, and early leading figures in it came from psychology, statistics or market research. Thus the chronology and the networks involved make a causal sequence highly implausible.

If a strict causal process is rejected, it could still be that functionalism was responsible for the *prominence* of the survey rather than its origin. That would surely require that functionalists preferred surveys. We cannot provide complete evidence on this, but a brief overview of the work of some leading functionalists is sufficient to suggest otherwise. Parsons had little personal involvement with empirical work, but when he draws on data in his publications it comes from a whole variety of sources: historical, anthropological, psychoanalytic, laboratory studies of small groups. Two of his former students say that:

He had no objections to any of the established methods of research ... so long as it was rigorously applied. Indeed, he supervised dissertations that were based upon a wide range of different methodologies without showing any generalised preference for a particular approach, qualitative or quantitative. (B. Johnson and M. M. Johnson 1986)

Merton has had, in addition to his survey work, a sustained interest in historical topics, and much involvement, in his leading role in the sociology of science, with the documentary technique of citation analysis. (For detail of more cases, see J. Platt 1986b.) Wells and Picou's data on articles in the American Sociological Review (1981: 141–3) show the survey as the dominant method from 1936–64 among those adopting 'standard American sociology', in which functionalism is the leading tendency – which would support the connection, were it not that it is also the dominant method in each of their other theoretical groups.

That suggests the conclusion that, while functionalism and survey were both very important at the same time, the relationship between them is more like a merely ecological correlation than a causal or logical connection; where the two coincided, at the level of individuals or departments, it was to an extent no greater than would be expected to follow from a random distribution of two important tendencies; to understand the growth and diffusion of survey method we need to look elsewhere. The role of the argument for their connection in the literature might be taken to provide an *a fortiori* basis, given this conclusion, for rejecting the whole idea of connection between theory and method; we shall, however, look more briefly at other pairings.

WEBER AND PARTICIPANT OBSERVATION

Not all such pairings have been suggested on the basis of an intellectual relationship between general theory and practical method. In the case of both Durkheim and Weber, it has been suggested that their broad methodological (rather than 'theoretical') stances inspired recent American work: Durkheim, generalised scientism, and Weber, qualitative methods generally but especially participant observation. The evidence about Durkheim was reviewed in the previous chapter. For Weber, the case rests on the perceived affinity of his idea of *verstehen* and the rationale of participant observation. Once again, though, there are grounds for scepticism.[10]

First, for Weber to have been influential he must have been known; however, few US sociologists of the cohort in question read German well enough, and his major relevant works were only translated into English after the Second World War. Those who were actively interested in his work usually had German connections and a special interest in German sociology, and were interested in theory or economic history rather than empirical work in sociology; they were located at institutions where the dominant style was quantitative or theoretical, not qualitative. It is agreed that key works in the history of participant observation came from the University of Chicago, with prominent monographs before the Second World War and both monographs and methodological works after. Those among my respondents who were doing

---

[10] The discussion which follows summarises a detailed paper, J. Platt 1985, which presents the data in full.

qualitative work disclaimed influence from him, or perception of his *verstehen* as especially significant.[11] This is perhaps not very surprising when one recalls that Weber's own *verstehende* work was historical, while the US researchers in question were collecting their own data on the contemporary situation on the streets of Chicago. (The extent to which Weber was being used for independently developed purposes, when he started to be referred to, is indicated by the curious failure to invoke his name as a rationale for emphasising historical and documentary work.) It is also unsurprising, in relation to the earlier empirical work, for a quite different reason: not only was participant observation not then theorised as a distinct method, but participation was not seen as the strategy giving access to meanings and understanding (see chapter 2). It was only when Weber became better known, and the modern conception of participant observation was independently developed at postwar Chicago, that the two became associated.

Also important to the lack of interest in Weber was that, to the extent that theoretical inspiration or rationale was required, there was at least one appropriate theorist much nearer to home whose work *was* well known and taken seriously: Charles Horton Cooley. Several respondents mentioned that to them Weber's message was seen as nothing special, simply because it did not seem novel when they were already familiar with Cooley. This could be taken to show that theory *was* relevant – you just need to pick the right one. But the error in relation to Weber should make us cautious. If Cooley was the man before the war and Weber was the man after, maybe neither was crucial? The work of either Weber or Cooley is capable of inspiring or legitimating methodological approaches which emphasise the understanding of motives and meanings; it does not follow that they were causally responsible for them. The case against the relevance of Weber has been adequately documented above, but what about Cooley?

Some of those interviewed did feel that Cooley had been a real

---

[11] It is interesting that two historical works both make the same factual error, which leads to the impression that Weber was used to a much greater extent than he really was: both Easthope (1974) and Ackroyd and Hughes (1981) correctly cite a 1945 chapter by the German-oriented theorist Howard P. Becker as strongly emphasising the importance of Weberian method – but both assume, wrongly, that he is the same person as the (unconnected) advocate and theorist of participant observation Howard S. Becker.

influence. The nature of his ideas was such that they lent themselves well to relatively direct translation into empirical work and, indeed, the relevant ones might scarcely be regarded as 'theoretical' in the high philosophical sense: he introduced the concept of the 'primary group', and recommended the use of a holistic and qualitative case-study approach involving close observation and the use of life histories. His relevant work was published and known soon enough. But it is not clear that it was really of practical importance. To the rather limited extent to which anthropological practice affected the emergence of sociological participant observation, Cooley must obviously defer to Malinowski as a serious influence. Interestingly, one of the few discussions from the early period which relates to participant observation (Cressey, only published in Bulmer 1983b) mentioned Cooley briefly, as gaining insights from intimate association, but pointed out that most research will not be on intimates. For his own work, Cressey instead invoked Simmel on the stranger as helpful.

However, no theoretical background seems adequate to account for the emergence of the practice. Much of the participant observation of the classic Chicago monographs, such as *The Hobo* (N. Anderson 1923), was based on the recording of normally-lived personal experience rather than on the deliberate acquisition of experience for research purposes. It was only in the 1940s that the modern conception of participant observation began to emerge; the term had been current earlier, but its apparent inventor, Lindeman (1924), was not associated with Chicago and anyway employed it to mean the use of actors as informants rather than the use of sociologists as quasi-actors. The relevant methodological categories which were stressed and theorised at interwar Chicago were 'case study' and 'life history' (J. Platt 1983). Many other data sources were used by the Chicago authors, and experience was not specially privileged in presentation – or even always acknowledged as such. One highly important practical influence on them was the availability of data already gathered by social workers, which was heavily used by the sociologists (J. Platt 1992c, 1994a); the form this took was consistent with Cooley's advocacy of the life history, but one may doubt if so much of that type of material would have been used, given the novelty of the idea of university sociologists collecting their own data, if it had not been ready to hand.

SYMBOLIC INTERACTIONISM AND PARTICIPANT OBSERVATION

Another line of argument is the one which sees participant observation as arising from symbolic interactionist theory. It is amusing to note that for symbolic interactionism, where it is arguable that a particularly strong case can be made for a close association between theory and practice, the argument has largely been developed by people (e.g. Blumer 1969, Rock 1979) who had to derive its supposed foundations from analysis of the practice of others, not their general statements. Rock at least is, then, not immune from the temptation of creating a kind of back-formation, in which an automatic correlation of theory and method follows when the theory seen as appropriate is imputed to anyone using the method. It is well known that Blumer invented the term 'symbolic interactionism' as a retrospective description of the work of colleagues at Chicago who did not apply it to themselves.[12] It is less well known that some of them, including some of those most strongly associated with participant observation, actually reject it or are unhappy with the implications of it as a description of what they have done.[13] Erving Goffman, interviewed by Winkin, said that there is no 'symbolic interactionism', and that the postwar students taught by

[12] Blumer 1937. Ironically in this context, Blumer, who was undoubtedly committed to symbolic interactionism as he defined it, did not see it as especially connected with participant observation. In my interview with him he said that 'Participant observation can be very dangerous to scholarship, in the sense that an individual who thinks he's really participating can be only doing so on the surface and misperceiving what's really taking place. In short, one has to be very careful to check up on participant observation and make sure it's not distortive' (Blumer 1982). Even those who admired Blumer and found inspiration in his ideas may say, as David Wellman and Howard Becker both did at the session in his honour at the American Sociological Association meetings of 1984, that he did not provide what are conventionally regarded as methods and that it was not clear how to translate his system into data; he published very little empirical research himself, and so did not provide exemplars.

[13] Ruth Shonle Cavan, a prewar Chicago PhD who was involved with much qualitative research, when I asked her if she saw herself as a symbolic interactionist, replied 'I don't think I qualify really as a symbolic interactionist. I asked Fred Seymour, who knows my stuff, whether I was' (Cavan 1982). Irwin Deutscher (1984: 71), a postwar Chicago PhD, describes being asked by Arnold Rose to contribute to his reader on symbolic interactionism. He asked what that was, and reports that Rose's 'face flushed as he angrily shouted "it is what they do at Chicago!"'. Rose himself, as Mullins (1973: 95) points out, became quite heavily involved in survey work.) These two vignettes sufficiently illustrate the point that, while some accepted the description for themselves, others from the same environment did not spontaneously do so. Whatever else these two were doing, it cannot have been deliberately steered by the imputed theoretical commitment. Cf. Verhoeven (1995), cited in note 4 on the attitude to philosophical stances of some seen as symbolic interactionists.

Hughes, Warner and Blumer, whom some have seen as part of such a movement, thought of themselves as occupational or industrial sociologists (Winkin 1988: 235). Eliot Freidson (1984) says he did not classify himself as one, though sometimes called such. Howard S. Becker (1990) says none of them used that term for a school of thought – it was just one of several key ideas in Blumer's theory – and he remembers being quite surprised at having it applied to him. Moreover, some of the leading figures in the formative practice of modern participant observation, even within the Chicago department, have never been regarded by anyone as symbolic interactionists. For example, Whyte was not an interactionist, and his participant observation came from other sources. Noone regards W. Lloyd Warner, who supervised many of the relevant Chicago students (including Goffman) as an interactionist, and it was clear that his participant observation came out of the anthropological tradition. Everett Hughes was very important in encouraging participant observation, but his style of teaching method was famously untheorised, resting on experience rather than precept; those closest to him have emphasised that he was not dogmatic about methodology, used demographic data, and expected students to be literate in statistics (H. S. Becker, Geer, Riesman and Weiss 1968: vii). Among the students in the postwar department, only 5 of the 21 generally known as interactionists used participant observation as the main source of data for their theses. (For a more detailed discussion of this cohort, see J. Platt 1995a.) Those who have shown a longer-term commitment to participant observation, whether or not it was used in their theses, were more often the students and co-workers of Hughes and Warner, who were actively involved themselves in projects based on fieldwork. Thus the supposed theory and the method were not closely associated in what has been presented as their key site. It is also well known that there was an Iowa school of symbolic interactionists, led by Manford Kuhn, whose main method was the 'Twenty Statements Test' on the model of a standard psychological test (Meltzer, Petras and Reynolds 1975: 55–67). Kohout (1993), of Iowa, describes his own work as using films of behaviour which would then be coded and analysed quantitatively. Meltzer, Petras and Reynolds suggest that methodology is a fundamental point of divergence between the Chicago and Iowa groups; they also identify as another group within symbolic interactionism ethnomethodology, and much if not most ethnomethodological work has used conversation analysis (with little concern over how the conversational data were collected) rather than participant observation. Symbolic interactionism is, thus, also an implausible candidate for a theoretical origin. Lofland (1970) has, indeed, suggested that symbolic interactionists (with whom he associates himself) have particular difficulties in carrying their work through to a successful conclusion because the detailed, codified accounts of method which are needed have not been produced; the perspective has remained too abstract to give guidance.

MARXISM AND FEMINISM

Turning to some more politicised versions of basic theoretical commitments, we may note that Erik Olin Wright both exemplifies the use by a Marxist of quantitative survey research methods, and addresses the question of whether, as some have suggested, they can be regarded as inconsistent with his theoretical stance. He concludes that there is nothing about them at odds with Marxist social theory or revolutionary praxis, and that the data used to address empirical problems should be determined by the questions being asked and the evidence required to discriminate between alternative answers to them (Wright 1989: 56–7, 68–73). Shulamit Reinharz treats the relation between feminism and method as an empirical one, and demonstrates in a comprehensive review that writers claiming commitment to feminist theory have not, as many have argued that they should, confined themselves to 'qualitative' approaches (Reinharz 1992); we may take it that it is no coincidence that her work is based on accepting the authors' definitions of what they have done as 'feminist', rather than applying her own prior criteria of orthodoxy. Hammersley (1992 – see also the critical discussion his article elicited) provides an example of the arguments for rejecting a more normative version of the claim that there is a distinctive feminist method, and suggests that the methodological ideas put forward by feminists are by no means exclusive to them. He also sees the feminist argument he rejects as just one instance of

an attempt to set up a separate methodological paradigm based on distinctive political and philosophical assumptions ... [which] suggests a stronger inferential link between political and philosophical assumptions, on the one hand, and research decisions, on the other, than is to be found in reality and than can be justified. (Hammersley 1992: 202–3)

Our conclusion here on the wider issue concurs with Hammersley's. Sufficient examples have been provided to demonstrate that the link between theory and method has been a loose one. It does not follow that it is insignificant, or equally loose in all cases, but it is clear that we need to look elsewhere to explain both the origins of particular methods and the choice of method made in individual projects. But what about methodological theorising? This is prima facie much closer to practice. We have reviewed the development of methodological writing, and turn now to consider its bearing on practice.

METHODS IN USE

It may be taken as evident that the broad pattern of change in *practice* over our period has been towards increasing quantification in an increasing body of systematic empirical research in which sociologists have created their own data. This is documented in a number of studies of aspects of research method used in practice, normally those shown in papers in the major journals. A summary is presented in table 3. Journal articles are an important part, though not the whole, of sociological research; 'major' journals are an important part of journal work, though it would be rash to assume that they contain a representative cross-section of it. The studies use different categories and periods, and each has its limitations, but in combination they give a reasonably convincing general picture of the work they cover. The precise figures should not be taken too seriously, given the unavoidable problems of categorisation in compiling them, though the overall pattern conveys some information, especially about the direction of change.[14] To the extent that they overlap, the broad results are in agreement. It is no surprise to see that surveys have become

[14] Any reader with a specialist interest in method who is familiar with the period discussed will note that this chapter does not deal with many of the more refined distinctions between methodological positions which are of interest to her. Among the topics not discussed at all, or barely mentioned, are the significance test controversy, analytical induction, survey versus experiment, ecology and the ecological fallacy, open versus closed questions and so on. It would indeed be desirable to look at such issues in historical detail; that is an area for further research.

Table 3. *Trends shown in methods used in journal articles, various studies*

Author	Sources used	Findings					
McCartney[b]	AJS[a], ASR, SP	Empirical articles reporting:					
			1915–24 %	1925–34 %	1935–44 %	1945–54 %	1955–64 %
		Case study	35	31	27	24	18
		Statistics	53	65	66	66	76
		Both	12	5	8	10	6
Brown and Gilmartin	AJS, ASR					1940–1 %	1965–6 %
		Substantive and research articles:					
		Quantitative				53	85
		Hypothesis-testing				46	68
		Data sources:					
		Observation (mainly participant)				13	4
		Questionnaire or interview				26	49
		Census				18	12
		Other documentary				38	15
		Other investigators' data				6	20
Snizek	AJS, ASR, SF, SP, Rural Sociology, Sociological Inquiry, Social Research, American Sociologist, Sociometry			1950–5 %	1956–60 %	1961–5 %	
		Method of data collection:					
		Historical		46	31	34	
		Informants, observation, interview		25	34	29	
		Questionnaire, experimental, census		29	36	38	
		Statistical procedure:					
		None		69	48	51	
		Chi squared, etc.		14	31	34	
		Analysis of variance		8	12	9	
		Correlation, regression		9	10	6	
Wilner	ASR	Methods used in empirical articles:					
			1936–41 %	1942–6 %	1947–56 %	1957–75 %	
		Survey	23	28	38	53	
		Other quantitative	55	52	43	33	
		Qualitative	21	19	19	13	

Table 3 *(cont.)*

Author	Sources used	Findings				
Wells and Picou	*ASR*			1936–49 %	1950–64 %	
		Method: 'Interpretive'		50	27	
		'Survey'		48	71	
		'Experimental'		1	3	
		Empirical tests of theory:		16	36	
		Data analysis:				
		Multivariate		0	8	
		Distributional and bivariate		58	71	
		Sample quotes and typical statements		42	21	
Platt	*ASR, AJS, SF*	Empirical articles:	1920s %	1930s %	1940s %	1950s %
		Quantitative:	40	51	40	63

[a] *AJS – American Journal of Sociology, ASR – American Sociological Review, SF – Social Forces, SP – Social Problems.*
[b] McCartney (1970) used a random sample of one-third of all articles and research reports in *AJS, ASR* and *SP* from when they started. J. S. Brown and Gilmartin (1969) took all the articles in *ASR* and *AJS* in 1940–1, and in 1965–6. Snizek (1975) took all the articles in the fields of stratification and mobility, deviance, industrial and organisational sociology, religion and the family. Wilner (1985) used all the articles in *ASR* over the period she covered. Wells and Picou (1981) used a random sample of *ASR* articles over their period. Details of Platt's sample are given in chapter 5. Another article, which would have been included if it had given trend data, is David Gold (1957). He looked at *ASR* articles from 1944 to 1953 to see what kinds of statistical analysis were used. He found that *c.* 52% used material which could not be subjected to any statistical analysis. For the remainder, he found that when the 11% which were demographic were omitted 55% of the rest had nothing but qualitative data, and these were seldom analysed in statistically appropriate ways. (By 'qualitative' data, he means that the variables were operationally treated only in terms of nominal classification or ordinal levels of measurement.)

increasingly prominent. More informative are the more detailed findings showing the employment of more sophisticated statistical methods in the quantitative work, and the increase in work which gives empirical tests of theory. It should be noted, however, that Wilner (1985: 15–18) also presents data about books, which give a somewhat different impression. The books she looked at were only the ones which had won American Sociological Association prizes from 1956 to 1979; these can most certainly not be taken as representative of all books, but, like articles in leading journals, tell something about disciplinary standards and ideals. Among these books, only 7 per cent were based on survey research, and qualitative macro approaches were the commonest; all quantitative methods were rare. This provides a caveat for any hasty assumption that articles alone are a good basis for generalisation about the methods in use and respected.

The distinctions made in the quantitative data are inevitably crude, even though in some cases more detailed than is common. Their utility in making sense of what was done in the publications analysed depends on whether those particular distinctions are the relevant ones for the purpose in hand. Some of them, like quantitative/qualitative, are hackneyed, and others are idiosyncratic, but different ones could always have been made. McCartney is addressing the question of a putative trend towards 'science', towards which he is not sympathetic, in part at least because he associates it with external pressures on sociology. Brown and Gilmartin are criticising the range and balance of contemporary sociology, seeing in it a neglect of historical and macroscopic problems, of other countries, and of topics other than those conveniently investigated by interview. Both are critical of the shortfall in qualitative work – and clearly classified the articles as quantitative/qualitative because they were interested in making that point – but only the latter raise the issue of coverage of other countries, and so only they have data on it. Wilner is also critical, but she is the only one who (fifteen years later, with the women's movement established) raises the issue of gender, giving figures on women authors. Wells and Picou, and Snizek, are particularly interested in the ways in which methods are related to theoretical positions, and so choose their categories accordingly. In each case there is obviously some sort of compromise between the focus of interest and what it is easy to classify and count, but different focuses lead to different selections of categories.

If we wished to divide research into that using analytical induction versus probabilistic sampling and analysis, or that which did or did not use factor analysis when it could have been applied, or snapshots versus historical designs, we would have to undertake our own studies; if we wished to divide it into what did and did not use machine methods of processing the data, or employ a commercial agency to collect them, or where the author did or did not personally take part in the fieldwork, we would probably not be able to rely on published sources, since these are not conventionally automatically reported. It cannot, therefore, be assumed that even the most detailed of the breakdowns quoted 'really' summarises the total pattern of what was done. They do provide information on certain conventional and widely recognised distinctions, and we shall have to settle for that, even at the price of being less relativistic in practice than we are in principle. Fortunately our main focus is on the adequacy of accounts given in terms of the conventional distinctions, so this does not create excessive problems for the argument.

RELATION BETWEEN WRITING AND PRACTICE

How far can methodological theorising explain how the patterns of methods in use, however these are categorised, have come about? The potential role of research funding is discussed in chapter 5; here we are concerned with other factors. It would, of course, be possible for such changes to take place without any intellectual novelties having been introduced; all the methods employed could have been available from the beginning of the period, and any changes in those used could reflect only changes in taste (of researchers, or of those they write for). We know that some novelties were in fact introduced, but need to bear in mind that this may not be the only relevant factor. Can the pattern be described as one showing the gradual growth of knowledge and improvement of technique?

The approach via theory blurs the distinction between origin and use, since it implicitly assumes that the same model is appropriate in both cases, and does not treat as problematic the existence of methods to match theories. Life is not so simple; wishes are not horses, and the methods actually available may all have evident theoretical defects, if not ones so severe that they prevent those who want to do empirical work from undertaking it.[15] The methods

---

[15] It is not uncommon for writers to report results with considerable expressed reservations on the methods which have generated them, which they may try to take into account in evaluating the data to reach conclusions; under those circumstances preferred methods were not available, and it is not the method used from which any inferences to the writer's underlying position should made.

defined by and treated in writings on method necessarily exist, though how prevalent they are in research practice is another question. However, explaining the origins of methods is not the same as explaining their subsequent use by others. That is the key reason why the kind of history which chronicles inventions or steps forward (e.g. Madge 1963),[16] and then treats that as the history of the matter, is little help here.

If theoretical work on method led directly to practice, one would expect that patterns of practice would correspond to patterns of writing, though with a slight lag to allow for diffusion. Temporarily suspending disbelief in the meaning of the figures in table 3, and allowing them to be supplemented a little by general knowledge, we can compare this record of practice with the trajectory of methodological writing. We do not observe a fresh flush of life-history studies after Dollard's book appeared in 1935, or of work with personal documents from the mid-1940s, or of focused interviewing after 1956.[17] Those movements in the publications seem to reflect what has already happened rather than to predict it. We find that over the time span when 'case study' was theorised as a serious rival to statistics, and meta-sociological work evenly divided, statistical work was always commoner, with no change in its proportions over the period of crucial conceptual shift away from the idea of the case study. We also find a decline, not an increase, in the amount of participant observation between the time when it was just starting to be theorised as a distinct practice and when the key articles favouring and analysing it had been written. Experiments have always been more favoured in principle than they appear to be in practice. There is a time in the 1950s when both writing and practice are heavily skewed to the survey, but this correspondence is the exception. The data are crude, and the inclusion of books and/or other journals would surely change the picture, but at this level it seems that theory is led by practice rather than vice versa. This is less surprising than it might seem when we recall how much of the methodological writing was shown to analyse practice rather than to introduce new inventions.

[16] The text accepts Madge's self-characterisation on this point, but that is questionable. What he actually does is to examine a series of well-known exemplars, without raising the question of invention. This is probably a sociologically more realistic strategy than the one he claims.

[17] Except in market research, as described by Merton (1990) in his foreword to the second edition.

METHODS IN PRACTICE: SUB-PARADIGMS

Much of this chapter, and of this book as a whole, treats 'method' as a distinct and unified category with its own history. That is the natural perspective for an author setting out to write a book on this topic. It is, however, the perspective of the methods specialist rather than of the ordinary user of methods. Several of my respondents expressed mild disapproval of the idea that one method could be intrinsically preferred to another, seeing it as obvious that the method one would choose would be the one appropriate to the problem so that, for instance, if your problem was to do with public opinion you would do a survey. This is surely sound in principle, though it leaves unanswered questions about how one decides which method is appropriate, or whether the known repertoire of methods may not do something to determine what one sees as a researchable problem. But sociologically it does indeed indicate an important practical ground for the choice of method: whether or not a method is inherently appropriate, substantive specialisms or narrower topics develop their own mini-traditions of how things are done. One might not dignify these with the name of 'paradigm', but there is in effect a package which most specialists buy. Such packages change from time to time, as for instance when demographers started using surveys rather than available Census data, introducing what was a novelty in that subfield even if it was not so in sociology generally.

For the ordinary user, methods are instrumental, not of interest in their own right, and it is normal for them to come as part of a package where there are also substantive and theoretical elements of equal or greater interest. After the stage when they take compulsory courses in method, many of these people will do little reading of purely methodological writing. Instead, they will receive methodological messages from what they do read, which will mostly be substantive and theoretical work in the fields of interest to them. Hence community exemplars are important in the formation of the methodological ideas and practices of ordinary sociologists, whether or not they are referred to in methodological writing.[18] It

---

[18] By 'community exemplars' is meant those substantive works which become treated as exemplary or classic for their methods, and are regularly used by others as sources of

seems likely that those who – like Howard S. Becker, Ernest Burgess, Otis Dudley Duncan, Paul Lazarsfeld and William H. Sewell in their very different ways – have been both active empirical researchers and active in methodological work are most likely to influence practice among non-specialist researchers, since they provide their own worked examples as well as abstract principles.[19]

This mode of transmission is a basis for methodological differentiation between sociological communities, which may relate to the problems with which different subfields deal, or whose origins may be intellectually accidental. Thus the existence of a parole system for prisoners provides criminologists with an incentive for concern with prediction problems; the commitment of Agricultural Experiment Stations (for more on which see chapter 5) to the improvement of agricultural practice has meant that rural sociologists are likely to take a special interest in the diffusion of innovations and methods of studying them; the existence of democratic elections, where individuals vote separately and privately and the majority wins, creates a natural affinity between political sociology and a survey method which samples individuals, explores their opinions and motives and quantifies them. Arguably more accidental, though detailed study might show good reasons, are the ways in which industrial sociology for a while developed a tradition of participant observation of work-groups, analytical induction became mainly associated with work in criminology, or stratification became heavily quantitative. However such packages arise, once they have been created most people will work within them. Blalock (1989: 454) has pointed out that methodological discussion of closely related or identical general issues may be taking place in different substantive specialties – for instance, demography and sociology of education – without participants

---

methodological recommendations. These do not constitute methodological writing for their authors, but they become used as a functional equivalent of it by others.

[19] These generalisations should, perhaps, be modified by adding that abstract methodological considerations are much more salient and interesting to some people than to others. In my sample of interviews Robert Ellis, for instance, made it clear that they had been important to him in guiding his research practice and defining his intellectual identity, while others politely responded to my questions but made it clear that for them method had been very much secondary. Impressionistically, it seems likely that method as such has been more salient for those active in heavily quantitative fields. If so, that would correspond to the degrees of formal elaboration of the literature on different topics, though it would not indicate which was cause and which effect.

being aware of the literature of the other field. Recent data on the patterning of expressed interests within the American Sociological Association (Ennis 1992: 261) show that specialties can be grouped to bring out affinities, and that 'methodology: qualitative' appears in a cluster with a quite different group of substantive fields from that of 'methodology: quantitative'.[20] Thus at any one period different specialisms are likely to have somewhat different patterns of method in use.

The same data draw attention to the fact, bearing on our discussion earlier in this chapter, that 'theory' is also treated as a specialism. Although in principle it may be equally relevant to all substantive topics, the structuring of sociologists' expressed interests does not define it as such. Ennis' data show 'theory' as belonging to a cluster consisting mainly of areas in the sociology of knowledge and culture – plus qualitative methods; it does not occupy a hierarchically central position, and multidimensional scaling shows it as having low proximity to quantitative methods and the majority of substantive specialisms. Cappell and Guterbock's data (1992: 269–70) show theoretical sociology as belonging to a critical/political/macro subgrouping quite separate from applied, funded research areas, with neither it nor methodology central to the structure of the discipline. Perhaps not all 'theory' relevant to our purposes here is covered by the theoretical commitments operationalised in these studies, but it is hard to reconcile such findings with a model in which theory leads practice.

PRACTICAL INFLUENCES ON CHOICE OF METHOD

When respondents described their methodological careers and choices, a range of factors quite separate from theory was mentioned. Influences from other disciplines play a prominent role; the contact could come from undergraduate work, from a graduate optional course or required minor, from a job setting which created

[20] Another article in the same issue (Cappell and Guterbock 1992) concluded that the quantitative/qualitative distinction was not important in structuring the discipline; this conclusion was, however, reached on the basis of fitting a statistical model to the distribution of co-memberships in ASA sections and inferring the underlying dimensions. Since there is only one 'methodology' section, while Ennis' data were self-identifications, the latter are more relevant and convincing for our purposes.

new contacts, or from a more accidental or personal contact. Thus
James Coleman had undergraduate work in chemical engineering,
which gave him experience in using graphs which he naturally
applied when he became involved in the analysis of the data
for *Union Democracy* (Lipset, Trow and Coleman 1956); his mathematical skills were picked up by Lazarsfeld, who gave him
problems to work on which led to further contributions (Coleman
1984). Hubert Blalock came into sociology from a mathematical
background, was required to take a minor for which he chose
statistics, and was subsequently influenced by work outside
sociology like that of Herbert Simon (Blalock 1984). Robert Ellis
came into sociology, initially rather accidentally, from a strong
background in experimental psychology, and remained influenced
by the conception of experimental design which that gave despite
also being exposed to quite different methodological influences
(Ellis 1991). Eliot Freidson took the not especially congenial jobs
he could get, and found himself learning from linguists and rat-
running psychologists (Freidson 1984). Samuel Stouffer, who had
strong statistical and measurement interests, used the psychologist
Thurstone as his mentor, since no member of the Chicago sociology
department when he was a student had the level of skill required.
Such factors can be relevant well past the student stage. As Bernert
(1983: 240–3) shows, in the area of quantitative techniques path
analysis, factor analysis and causal modelling theory were each
imported into sociology from another discipline. Those who
imported them made a valuable contribution to sociology, but it was
not an invention; what requires explanation in sociology is, thus,
how the importers became aware of the technique and how they
came to see it as applicable to sociological problems.

Methods were not always consciously chosen, especially when the
people concerned, or their mentors, had little interest in method as
such. This could mean that the contemporarily obvious method was
chosen without reflection, or it could mean multiple methods even
if theorists might regard them as inconsistent. For instance, the
Chicago department is repeatedly described by people who were
there as encouraging going out and getting the data, in a way which
was scarcely theorised. Eliot Freidson, a postwar Chicago student,
describes quite a lot of methodological themes in teaching, but did
not see them as taken seriously in relation to practice, seeing
choices made unselfconsciously 'in a pragmatic and unreasoned

kind of way' without explicit rationale, especially among those doing less quantitative work (Freidson 1984). Gans (Becker, Geer, Riesman and Weiss 1968: 301) remarked that 'When I was a graduate student at the University of Chicago just after World War II, no-one talked much about participant observation; we just did it'. Edward Gross (1984) paints a similar picture, emphasising how undue concern with method as such would have been seen as letting the tail wag the dog. Interestingly, Kent Geiger picked up a similar message as a student at Harvard around the same time, though there Chicago empiricism was despised:

If there was any doctrine or theme, it was that research methods are always there, you can go and pick them up when you need them, but it's much more important to get a good theory and then think about methods . . . like statistics, it was not a proper thing, unless you were some sort of genius, to make a career out of. (Geiger 1984)

That stance could be seen as a necessary one in a multidisciplinary department where students were exposed to a range of different disciplinary styles, as well as one which went with the emphasis on theory as the unifying theme.

Where there were strong departmental traditions, graduate students could simply be unaware of other styles, or those other styles could be very little salient for them while locally favoured ones were actively cultivated. Thus, in quantitative work, at Columbia in the 1950s significance tests were not used, and analysis was based on percentage differences with clearly distinguished independent and dependent variables, while elsewhere the emphasis was on measures which expressed only degree of association; at North Carolina, the demographic orientation to the study of regions meant that a multiple regression approach was dominant, which to Coleman (whose background was at Columbia) seemed like a novelty in sociology in the mid-sixties (Blalock 1984, Coleman 1984). The Michigan style of survey research, meanwhile, stressed area probability sampling and open-ended questions, which distinguished it from Columbia's BASR (Rossi 1984).

Whatever the personal position taken, the method chosen in a particular project could reflect not that but the perceived audience for the results and its likely reception of material gathered and presented in one way rather than another. James Bennett (1981) has shown, in a detailed historical study of the use of oral histories of delinquents, how these have been produced under circumstances where there are increasing rates of juvenile delinquency, a cleavage between a powerful middle class and the lower-class delinquent which makes him invisible to them, and reformers who wish to promote social change by showing the factors affecting individual offenders and so altering the middle-class public's perception of crime. In my sample, Lee Rainwater (1984) explained how the Planned Parenthood organisation pressed him to quantify the data in the work which became *Family Design* (Rainwater 1965) because they knew that some people in the audiences relevant to them would not otherwise be persuaded of the findings; similarly with other studies done for Social Research Inc., Burleigh Gardner's commercial qualitative research outfit, where from the point of view of the researchers the quantification was unnecessary. Such decisions may not always be made so consciously, and for more exclusively academic work orientations to an audience shade over into perceptions of what is customary or prestigious among colleagues, but they surely have some significance.

A yet more practical ground for the 'choice' of method is that one has no choice; a few respondents described this situation when they perforce took research jobs where the method was already set, whether or not they liked it, and this is also common with commissioned research. The extent to which it is likely to happen depends on the job situation. Similar but less severe constraints, positive or negative, can be set in other ways. A 'positive' constraint to adopt one particular method exists if, for instance, one has a survey unit with a complex division of labour and a body of specialist permanent employees to support. Under those circumstances one looks for surveys to do, not for interesting problems where the method remains to be decided. A large-scale bureaucratised research organisation has considerable advantages, in that its specialisation produces high levels of technical skill and experience. Less obviously, its social needs can have intellectual consequences. It was found in the wartime Division of Program Surveys (DPS) that a continuing commitment in principle to intensive interviewing with open-ended questions had to be increasingly diluted or abandoned, in face of the difficulties in training and supervising an interviewing force spread across the country to administer such questions satisfactorily (J. Platt 1986a: 99). A milder form of the positive constraint occurs when there is the opportunity to get access to better-quality or larger-scale data than one would otherwise have if one joins an ongoing project or, as has been done with increasing frequency, makes secondary use of available data. (The latter has, of course, been very much encouraged by the emergence of the institution of the data bank, linked to the computer technology which provides access to it from a distance, but this did not exist in our period.) Larger departments may institutionalise such arrangements for their students, using them as part of the labour force and in return giving them access to material they could not have gathered themselves; one model for this was the Local Community Research Committee at Chicago (Bulmer 1980), while a later one has been the programme in the Institute for Social Research at Michigan (ISR) (Converse 1987: 346). Less elaborate versions of this have also of course been widespread, and where they exist students who do not work on faculty projects may lose a major source of funds with which to support their continuing study. Such structures may constrain not only the students, but also faculty, who need to maintain a flow of suitable projects.

There is a negative constraint if one does not have access to the resources needed to employ a method one might otherwise have preferred, or if those resources do not actually exist. Goffman suggested that the methods of his first articles were determined by his lack of funding.[21] Rossi (1959: 14, 21), writing on the history of voting research, draws attention to the way it was transformed by the introduction of survey method, which made it possible for the first time to have attitude data on non-captive populations and to compare the characteristics of individual voters. Numbers of respondents referred to the almost impossible task of using statistical methods such as multiple regression, which were well known in principle, before the computers (or more modest earlier machines) had been invented which reduced the enormous task of doing the calculations required to manageable proportions. (One reason why statistical work was developed much earlier in government settings was simply that there they sometimes had the resources, maybe in size of clerical staff before the machines could

---

[21] 'At the time I began my career professors got big grants, and students worked for them. And I tried to do it without grants, so my first couple of papers were just sort of papers I wrote off the top of my head' (Verhoeven 1993: 321).

be substituted.)[22] Haller (1984) described how, in his time as a graduate student at Wisconsin, they were able to use statistics which were very advanced for the 1950s, because there was a numerical analysis laboratory run by the mathematics department as a service to the university community generally; they could go directly to multiple correlation and regression, while Stouffer and Lazarsfeld were still devising techniques to deal with two-way tabulations of categorical data which became irrelevant with the emergence of computers. Those who had not had such advantages in some cases continued to use the older techniques, which those at the forefront regarded as outdated. Similarly, Merton (1990) describes how what eventually became *The Focused Interview* (Merton, Fiske and Kendall 1956) emerged gradually in the circle of enterprises with which he and Lazarsfeld were connected, starting in prewar days and going through two xeroxed editions internal to the BASR before it was formally published and entered the public domain, and Hyman (1991: 212) mentions several other such examples. Several respondents report being familiar with materials known in their departments well before they were published, or which sometimes were never published.[23] Thus publication may confirm for some what it introduces to others; people in locations with distinctive resources, personal or mechanical, have the opportunity to learn and apply methods which those elsewhere may not be aware of. This creates a time-lapse between possible uses of the method by insiders and outsiders, so that when significant innovations are developed practice is uneven, at least in the short term.

Several respondents mentioned such accidental factors of

---

[22] The Census, in particular, also had the evident need for mass data processing which led to the encouragement of the development of computing machinery suitable to deal with it. Truesdell (1965) documents the gradual process, starting with the punched-card machine devised by Hollerith, to meet their needs. Once it had been invented, others could make use of the technical advance if they could get access to the machinery. However, like other machines developed for particular types of user, they were not necessarily optimal for academic research purposes, and so could constrain in that sense. Similarly, statistical techniques developed in the context of certain problems and concerns will set limits, of kinds of which their later users may not be conscious, to what can be done with them (Mackenzie 1981).

[23] Thus Reiss (1984) mentioned that the re-study of Angell's cases from *The Family Encounters the Depression* (on whose history see J. Platt 1992b), which was never published, was available as a mimeographed copy in the library at Chicago, and was seen as important and morals drawn from it among his cohort of graduate students.

location as relevant in their own methodological careers. But they were not always accidental, since at least a few people were sufficiently interested and well-informed on methodological issues to choose where to do their graduate work on such grounds. This could be the basis for one of those recognised successions of discipleship which are important in the formation and diffusion of traditions.[24] On that basis or not, such personal transmission of ideas and practices has taken place in the field of method as in other fields, and sometimes quite non-academic aspects of relations play a part. Thus, for instance, Giddings can be seen as the origin of one set of relationships. (S. P. Turner 1994: 49–51 traces part of this network with reference to the intellectual detail of what was being transmitted.) Giddings' graduate students at Columbia included F. Stuart Chapin and William F. Ogburn. Lundberg, Sewell and Guttman were all students of Chapin's at Minnesota; Sewell says he went there to work with him. Sewell did not himself make methodological breakthroughs, but kept up with the latest developments in other fields as well as sociology, applied sophisticated thinking in novel ways to interesting problems, and so inspired others to imitation, and taught many students techniques and standards of rigour which they went on to apply and develop. One of his fellow graduate students was Otis Durant Duncan (father of Otis Dudley Duncan) who invited him to his first job in Oklahoma. There Sewell met O.D.D. junior, who used to babysit for him – and reports first encountering a key book at his house while doing so! – as well as taking some of his undergraduate courses. He also taught Guttman, then in psychology, and helped to recruit him to sociology, in which he went on to take his doctorate at Minnesota. (He had a subsequent career as a methodologist of great distinction, in the Army wartime research and at Cornell before moving to Israel; he appears to have been recruited to this via Chicago-centred networks.) It was largely on Sewell's recommendation that

[24] However, in several cases where a choice had been made because the student wanted to develop quantitative skills they report that they found that the great man whose reputation they had followed did not himself have sufficiently advanced knowledge to be really useful; for that they had to go elsewhere, maybe to another department. Another unexpected outcome is mentioned by Heaven (1975: 183). Many bright prewar graduate students went to Harvard from large state universities because it appeared strong in *rural* sociology, with Sorokin and Zimmermann there, but many of these were then converted to other interests.

Duncan then went to Minnesota for his MA, and he continued to regard Sewell as a mentor, though he also was much influenced by Ogburn during his doctorate at Chicago. Thomas C. McCormick, who had studied at Chicago with Ogburn, was at Wisconsin. McCormick wrote an early book on statistics (McCormick 1941a), and was primarily a methodologist; Roy Francis, one of his graduate students, married his daughter, and when he died before completing his methods textbook took it to publication (McCormick and Francis 1958) and continued his own career as a methods specialist. Haller was taught by Chapin, and then chose, informed by contact with two previously made friends now there, to move to Wisconsin, in part because Sewell was there, as well as McCormick; his and Sewell's shared interests in quantitative methods, and in topics in stratification to which they could be applied, led to many years of joint work of a pathbreaking kind on 'status attainment'. Who babysat for whom is intrinsically trivial, but such trivia of networks add up to a real component of the hidden side of the social structure of academic life.[25] Moreover, when the normal mode of recruitment to jobs was – as at least in the interwar period it was – to write between senior acquaintances about likely candidates, and it was treated as perfectly acceptable to mention men's [sic] religion, ethnicity, appearance and private morality, particularistic criteria could make a considerable difference to career paths.

CONCLUSION

Thus we see that a whole range of non-theoretical factors can be relevant to the choice of methods in practice. No sociologist who reflects on her or his own lived experience will be surprised by this, though it has been common for such factors not to be taken into account, or to be mentioned only in the self-critical autobiographical literature. Theorists – a category which tends to encompass

---

[25] Vaughan and Reynolds (1968) show (though on the basis of data only on institutional locations) that there have been multiple bonds among those symbolic interactionists who believe that symbolic interaction is a general theory capable of dealing with social change. They suggest that the strong social support provided by such bonds may be a necessary condition for the development and maintenance of an unconventional intellectual stance. Burt (1982) has documented the network of elite methodologists in 1975 and shows, using sociometric data on personal communication and the soliciting of comments on work in progress, that the network has many connections, and that teacher–student relations are one basis of its formation.

those who write on the history of sociology – are not character-
istically interested in method as such, so they treat it as though
other people worked on the same level as they do. But many
practical researchers and methods specialists make methodological
decisions in untheorised ways, and /or draw on the methodological
work of others. In drawing on it, they may engage in *bricolage* to put
together fragments of ideas which serve to justify what they were
doing anyway. Theories currently 'in the air' are particularly likely
to be plundered for fragments (like my use of *'bricolage'* above?)
which imply no commitment to it as a general theory from the user;
it would be naive to assume that every passing reference should be
taken seriously as an influence.[26] Techniques may be treated in
analogous ways, sometimes being applied to unsuitable topics or
used without full understanding of what they can and cannot do.
It is notorious, too, that methodological claims such as that
hypotheses have been tested may be added after the event rather
than having guided practice.[27] Rationales used in publications
cannot be taken as a sure guide to the processes by which original
research decisions were made.

Blalock (1989: 450) suggested that 'methodological ideas are
adopted when it is relatively easy and costless to do so, but . . .
resisted or totally ignored when it is to the investigator's vested
interest to do so'. He says this in the context of pointing out that
fairly sophisticated statistical techniques which do not need hard
calculations have been widely adopted, but that measurement
errors which vitiate their application have been effectively given no
attention because they are difficult to deal with. The availability of
computers for high-speed and elaborate calculation, with programs
that can be used as cookbooks, plus easy access to large quantitities
of data already collected by others, make quite different styles of
work easy now from those that were in the past. (Perhaps in that
sense the old style of using data provided by social workers is a

---

[26] For the theorist, the writing is the work; for the empirical researcher, what has been done
to collect the data has an existence independent of the writing and so, despite the
familiar more sophisticated points to be made about the decisions and meanings
involved, a real sense remains in which any particular written version can be seen as
epiphenomenal.

[27] For a striking and closely documented case where it is shown how the written version of a
research project had a highly creative and tendentious relation to the literal findings, see
Gillespie 1991.

direct functional equivalent of superficially very different work.) It would be too cynical, as well as very weakly explanatory of what has actually happened, to take ease of adoption as the prime factor. Blalock's statement does, however, usefully emphasise the importance of practical considerations, including technological ones. Over our period, it did become much easier to apply some methods which had been invented earlier. These were quantitative, and that surely goes some way to explain the trend to more quantification; it has not become any easier, or less labour-intensive, to carry out qualitative work.

The scepticism expressed about the significance of written methodological theorising as an independent cause of developments is not intended to imply that it has been merely epiphenomenal, but that it has been closely linked in a dialogue with practice in which the practice has commonly come first. This suggests that for those who have been recognised as important innovators – a recognition which to a large extent depends on their methodological writings – practice leads, while rank-and-file researchers are more likely to be influenced by their prestigious writings, even if the limited resources at their disposal sometimes make it hard to follow the standards set in principle.

At the level of the disciplinary community, theoretical changes have at best only a rough fit to changes (of the kind discriminated) in the methods in use. This indicates the limited utility of the normative/Whig style of history, primarily employed for professional socialisation, which traces technical advances made by important people and treats each contribution as embodying logically appropriate commitments. To understand how things happen we need to look below the level of the whole disciplinary community. There we see how the division of labour between theorists and methodologists, or methodologists and researchers, means that it is commonly different people who theorise explicitly and who engage in research practice.[28] We see, too, how the discipline is divided among specialisms, cohorts and institutions in ways which promote differentiation. (For more discussion of this,

---

[28] Collins (1977: 150) suggests, very plausibly, that Merton's professional eminence is largely due to his unusual role in consistently linking theory and research: 'Merton situated himself at the crossroads of a discipline of almost mutually oblivious approaches, and thereby managed to come as near as anyone to directing the traffic.'

see chapter 6.) The total picture is made up of the sum of these groupings, but it is a classic methodological error to assume that the group-level correlations can be imputed to the individual or subgroup. The historian is tempted to assume disciplinary unity because that allows data deficient in one place to be supplemented by what is available elsewhere, to make the picture complete, but to succumb to this temptation is to risk missing the expediency of many alliances and the untidiness of life, even intellectual life, in progress.

CHAPTER 5

Funding and research methods

The institutions which fund research are an important part of its social context. Much empirical work can only be carried out if funding is available to cover its expenses, and for work on any scale few sociologists are able to provide such funding themselves. The question of how research is affected by the patterns of available funding is, thus, a significant one. The major external sources of research funds have been foundations and government. There has been considerable discussion about the role of foundation funding in the development of sociology (e.g. Alchon 1985, Arnove 1982, E. R.Brown 1979, Bulmer 1984b, Fisher 1980, 1983, 1984, 1993), much of it critical in tone. It has been argued that the course of empirical work in sociology has been influenced by patterns of foundation and governmental funding, often in ways which the writers see as undesirable. Research methods have not been central to this discussion but, insofar as the argument relates to them, such funding is seen as having played an important role in promoting quantification and other 'scientific' aspects of method[1] – which the writers commonly characterise as a distortion. (The idea of distortion obviously implies a judgment, and the role of such judgments will be discussed below.) First, a brief and roughly chronological outline of the funding situation will be given, with

---

[1] This has sometimes been associated with the puzzling idea that quantification is inherently especially associated with the interests of the state – see, for instance, Irvine, Miles and Evans 1979. Similarly D. Ross (1991: 429), to pick another instance, associates 'behavioristic premises and replicable, exact methods' with the desire for control. The association is puzzling because it is presumably in the interests of any person or institution to have valid data of good quality which cover the points of concern to them; where quantitative data are appropriate, as where qualitative data are, it is not evident why the interests of the state should differ from those of any other user. (For further discussion of the general issue and some cases, see J. Platt 1986a). If those studied made the association, this requires explanation rather than just acceptance.

special reference to its bearing on the development of research methods; against that background, the theoretical and empirical plausibility of the arguments about funding will be evaluated.

PRIVATE FUNDING

The occasional individual benefactor funded a project; notable cases are Helen Culver's support of W. I. Thomas' (and F. Znaniecki's) work on *The Polish Peasant in Europe and America* (1918–20), and Ethel Sturges Dummer's funding of W. I. Thomas' *The Unadjusted Girl* (1923).[2] More significant in scale than such individual arrangements were the relationships between local notables, involved in clubs and committees concerned with social problems, and social scientists. In the Progressive era there were innumerable such groupings, often focusing on 'vice' or delinquency, and not always clearly distinct from the organs of the local state which they lobbied and by which their initiatives might be taken over. These groups sometimes undertook research in pursuit of their concerns, and the people who did the research for them could well be, or become, graduate students who might also use the work for more academic ends; it was not always clear where the boundary lay between university and community either, especially since professors might be social activists in their private lives.[3] This was most marked among those who taught social work, which at that time was socially rather than individually oriented and in that sense less distinct from sociology; the settlement houses with which they were closely associated also sometimes undertook research on their areas and clients. Thus social research was quite often supported by funds committed to local social problems. Such money did not normally support professors, which may help to explain why so much of the officially sociological work of the time draws heavily on data originally collected by social workers for their own purposes (J. Platt 1994a).

The leading foundations have had enormous sums of money at their disposal, rather small proportions of which have been devoted to social science; the amounts involved have, however, been enough to make a significant difference to the research opportunities of

---

2 For details on these cases, see Haerle 1991, J. Platt 1992a.
3 For the case of the community in Chicago, see J. Platt 1994a.

those who could get access to them. Sociologists may obtain money under the heads of programmes not primarily intended for social science, or even for research, but we are concerned here with the major amounts intended specifically for social research. (No such programme has been confined to sociology.) Initially, the Laura Spelman Rockefeller Memorial fund (LSRM) was of overwhelming importance;[4] later, others came on the scene.

The LSRM's history has been documented in great detail by Bulmer and Bulmer (1981), and their basic facts are not disputed, though Fisher (1983, 1984, 1993) argues strongly against their interpretations; that account is drawn on here. LSRM was founded in 1918, and in 1929 was consolidated with the Rockefeller Foundation and ended its separate existence. Only in 1922, following the appointment of Beardsley Ruml to head it, did it start to fund social-science research. It was run relatively informally, and Ruml had more or less a free hand. At that period university sociology was little developed as an empirical subject, and most universities had not themselves developed mechanisms for funding faculty research, so those who undertook it had to do all the work – often much more laborious than later, when efficient machinery for processing data existed – without assistance. LSRM made available very large sums of money to support empirical research in social science: $112 million over six years. This was widely distributed, but the main recipients relevant to US sociology were the University of Chicago, Columbia University, Harvard University, the University of North Carolina (UNC), and the Social Science Research Council (SSRC). There was a general policy of strengthening or helping to establish great national centres (also shown in the provision of large funding to the London School of Economics); UNC was chosen because of the felt need to build a regional centre in the South, while the other three universities produced the largest numbers of doctoral candidates in the social sciences at the time. The University of Chicago was particularly well treated, and this was vital to its role

---

[4] This perhaps does insufficient justice to the Russell Sage Foundation and its programme of community 'surveys' (not using survey method in the modern sense of the word); for details of this, see Harrison (1931) and Glenn, Brandt and Andrews (1946). These were undoubtedly of some importance, though largely run by amateurs. Some leading sociologists, such as Ernest Burgess and Manuel C. Elmer (author of Elmer 1917) were involved in such 'surveys' at early stages of their careers, but these were more associated with social work than with sociology.

in building empirical social research. (On this, see also Bulmer 1980, 1984a.) A key feature of LSRM policy was that it gave block grants to institutions, which they could spend as they chose; this meant that specific project proposals did not have to be submitted for evaluation before a grant would be given. A separate major enterprise was the Research Committee on Social Trends, initiated by President Hoover as a background to his plans for social reform, which was funded by Rockefeller; this reported in 1933, and led to a number of publications.[5] When LSRM ceased to exist the main Rockefeller Foundation took over social science funding. It moved in the 1930s to programme and then project funding, as well as showing more interest in initiating work on its own choice of fields and problems.

The SSRC was (and is) a federation of learned societies, in whose foundation and early funding Rockefeller foundations were prominent, which funded research in social science by providing both project grants and individual fellowships for young researchers. (At later periods its funding base was broader, and it funded a changing and wider range of activities, including some to provide training in research methods.) It was run by representatives of the learned societies, with a small office staff. Most of its work has been done through committees, manned by academics and serviced administratively by members of the office staff. Each committee is responsible for a particular programme, which could be a general one like 'Grants in aid' or a very specific one like 'Pressure groups and propaganda'. The latter type have usually existed only for a few years, and then been discharged when their remit has been fulfilled. Some have dealt with current social problems, while others have had more inward-looking remits such as the ones concerned to improve social-science data sources or to raise standards of training in social science. The great majority, however, has been on substantive research topics, and as such has not had any methodological definition.

But research method has been an area of continuing interest. One of the first committees was on 'scientific method'; it did not reach any agreement, but commissioned a remarkably eclectic collection of examples of method (Rice 1931). More consequential for sociology was the promotion of a series of appraisals of what

---

[5] For details on this, see Karl 1969, Bulmer 1983a.

were recognised as key works; the work chosen for sociology was Thomas and Znaniecki's *The Polish Peasant in Europe and America*, and Blumer's influential critique (Blumer 1939) was the result. This led to the commissioning of major publications on 'personal documents' (Allport 1942, Gottschalk, Kluckhohn and Angell 1945) which became the standard references in their field. A related project restudying Angell's cases from *The Family Encounters the Depression* (Angell 1936) was also funded, but never reached publication, though it appears nonetheless to have had some influence. There can be little doubt that this programme of work was generated internally to the SSRC, and responded to the personal interests of Chicago sociologist Ernest Burgess, who chaired the Committee on the Appraisal of Research and its successors (J. Platt 1992b). There have been several efforts to improve mathematical standards in social science. Two important postwar committees, addressing issues arising from the ideas developed during the wartime research experience and reflecting the concerns of what had by now become survey professionals, were those on Measurement of Opinion, Attitude and Consumer Wants and on Scaling Theory and Methods. Of great importance postwar was the field of foreign-area studies, which came to dominate the Council's activities (Sibley 1974: 89–106). This was not in itself in any way methodological, but it has had the consequence of encouraging more interdisciplinary work in the 'area studies' tradition, and more comparative designs.

Fisher (1993), in his general account of the SSRC in the 1920s and 1930s, sees it as playing, under Rockefeller hegemony, a key role in forming the development of US social science, although he also, somewhat contradictorily, says in his conclusion that it did not succeed in making much difference. Unsurprisingly, the official history (Sibley 1974) paints a rather different picture, in which the issue of support is not mentioned; SSRC appears as autonomous. There is room for disagreement over the extent to which it was subject to control by its funders, and this has probably varied over time, but they were certainly not involved in the detailed decisions on which projects and candidates for fellowships to support. Sibley reports (1974: 6–7) that, if a distinction is made between areas where aid was given to individuals to pursue their own interests and those where the SSRC organised work on problems it had identified, the former took about 30 per cent of expenditure until the mid-1940s, rose to a maximum of 67 per cent in 1961, and then declined again. This gives a minimum baseline of social-science work supported but not controlled; the other category includes areas where the initiative was taken by the social scientists of SSRC rather than by its funders. Louis Wirth of Chicago, who was no establishment timeserver despite his long-term involvement with SSRC and related bodies, concluded in his report on its history that if the SSRC had been completely independent of foundations:

the Council's program would probably not be very much different from what it is, or at least what it has recently come to be, with the possible exception that this program would have a more continuous and long-range character and would be relatively free from some of the uncertainty that has marked it during certain periods. (Wirth 1937: 125)

In many ways the Council and the foundations have had shared objectives.

The range of work funded between the wars by Rockefeller sources was so wide that there is some excuse for the tendency in the literature to make generalisations based only on its role then – and for sociology this matches well with the tendency in historical work to treat the University of Chicago as though it were the only university. Both tendencies fit the interwar period much better than they do later, though even for that period they are of course quite misleading. Governmental funding at the time is dealt with below; considered here are other major private sources.

The Carnegie Corporation initially funded social science more spasmodically than Rockefeller, though it was an early contributor to the SSRC; its most dramatic role was in the commissioning and support of the large-scale project which produced *An American Dilemma* (Myrdal 1944). After the Second World War it became more consistently prominent in funding social science, but its single major contribution was to fund, via SSRC, the enormously influential *American Soldier* volumes (Stouffer, Guttman, Suchman et al. 1949–50), which drew out for publication the findings and implications of the wartime research done for the US Army and reported on the methodological advances made. Connected with this was Carnegie's funding for the Laboratory of Social Relations at Harvard, headed by Stouffer.

The really big new postwar player was, however, the Ford Foundation, whose Program for the Behavioral Sciences was especially important and relevant to our concerns here. This ran from 1951 to 1957, spending nearly $40 million, and when it closed there was a five-year programme of 'terminal grants' so that those who had come to rely on it were phased out gradually. Although its remit was not at all confined to methods, there was a strong interest in methodological advance, as well as some fairly marked preferences for quantitative and 'scientific' methods among key staff.[6] It supported many important research centres, contributed to SSRC programmes which included some summer workshops on mathematical methods, and founded the Center for Advanced Studies in the Behavioral Sciences (CABS) where chosen groups of scholars could spend a year together working on their own concerns. In relation to research methods, its most important contribution was to fund much of Paul F. Lazarsfeld's 'Documentation in Social Research' programme (to which Rockefeller also made a large initial grant). This ran for the whole of the 1950s, and served his agenda for methodological work, creating training materials in research method which took the form both of analysis of cases drawn from published work and of the systematisation and exposition of the state of knowledge in various areas of method. From this programme came many of the well-known methodological monographs and advanced textbooks of the period (on which see chapter 2). Foundations at this time were actively concerned with the USA's lack of background for its new world role, and so initiated some programmes for developing area-studies knowledge; the politics of this (on which see Seybold 1987) are of much interest, but attention is drawn to it here simply because it probably did something to encourage and facilitate internationally comparative methods. It should be noted, however, that Ford grants were normally for programmes, or for the chosen individuals to use at their discretion, rather than for projects, in that respect resembling earlier Rockefeller ones.

Finally, a funding body which was not a foundation but for a time

---

[6] The term 'behavioral science', put in circulation by this programme, has contested implications and has often been seen as tendentious in academic politics. One of those most closely involved in the programme described it as including psychology, anthropology, sociology and closely related areas in such fields as biology and psychiatry, and distinguished from social sciences such as history, economics and political science by collecting original data to establish scientific generalisations about how people behave and why (Berelson 1968).

played a comparable role should be mentioned: the American Jewish Committee (AJC).[7] This was a voluntary organisation for the defence of Jewish interests[8] which in 1944, following a conference on social research in relation to anti-Semitism, set up a Department of Scientific Research and Program Evaluation, initially directed by Max Horkheimer. For a number of years this defined its remit quite broadly, since the issues were theorised as relating to minority groups generally. Its overall goal was seen as 'to establish on a firmer foundation principles of action leading to the reduction, elimination and neutralization of intergroup hostility, with special (although not exclusive) emphasis on anti-Semitism'. From this followed the more specific objectives of understanding the personality and group dynamics of anti-Semitism and the social structure within which it is located, of studying propaganda and action techniques for combating anti-Semitism, and of understanding Jewish family life to facilitate positive commitments to Jewish identity among American Jews (American Jewish Committee 1950:1–2). A research staff was employed, which included Marie Jahoda, and there was also active cooperation with university researchers. Paul Lazarsfeld was among the distinguished social scientists who acted as consultants, and his Bureau of Applied Social Research had a continuing relationship and interchange of staff with it; other well-known sociologists associated with it were Alvin Gouldner, Edward Shils, Morris Janowitz and Arnold Rose. The research funded ranged from psychological experiments to polls and community studies. *The Authoritarian Personality* (Adorno, Brunswik, Levinson and Sanford 1950) is probably the best-known single book to arise from this programme, but there were many other publications; the distinguished 1951 textbook by Jahoda, Deutsch and Cook, *Research Methods in Social Relations* (subtitled 'with especial reference to prejudice'), although not formally funded by AJC, was closely related to its programme. (The rather broad definition of AJC's remit is also shown, for instance, in the fact mentioned by Rainwater (1984) that he was employed on a small study they funded of employers' attitudes to Japanese

---

[7] Other large charities and professional bodies also funded research from time to time, but most of this stayed closer to the obvious spheres of the bodies in question.

[8] Other Jewish organisations had different political agendas; Lundberg and Dodd at Washington University received a large research grant from the American Council for Judaism, which supported their strong anti-Zionism and was hostile to the AJC.

Americans.) In the 1960s social research became less important to AJC, and there had also been internal political problems about some of the findings on contemporary Jewish life, so its funding role became less prominent.

GOVERNMENT FUNDING

Governmental funding has also played a significant and increasing role for sociology, its specific forms and sources changing over time. As with the foundations, it has seldom been provided with the simple remit of supporting sociology or social research for its own sake; more commonly it has been a by-product of policy concerns. Some has been for work done within government, though the sociologists involved may have moved between government and academia; some has taken the form of direct funding outside government; some has been commissioned from academia, and some has been made available for academic application.

Among the earliest government-supported work was that in rural sociology, often forgotten in general accounts of the history of sociology. Within government, there was what Larson and Moe (1990: 1) claim to have been the first, and initially only, unit in the federal government specifically for sociological research: the Division of Farm Population and Rural Life of the US Department of Agriculture (USDA). This was a division within its Bureau of Agricultural Economics (BAE), and it existed from 1919 until 1953. Well-known sociologists such as Charles J. Galpin, Carl C. Taylor, Kimball Young, Charles P. Loomis and Margaret J. Hagood[9] worked there, and staff members had often held university positions before joining it. In its early years funds were very modest, so studies were limited, but it played a useful role, by its policy of cooperative projects, in getting research under way in land-grant and other universities. It also contributed to methodological improvement by such activities as a methods training institute, with distinguished visiting academic instructors, in 1930. In the New Deal period from 1935 resources and activity increased significantly, as data were required for relief purposes; BAE became the staff agency to guide the planning and research of the

---

[9] Hagood was the author of *Statistics For Sociologists* (1941), the first such textbook specifically for sociologists.

entire USDA. (An important role was played in this by the
Secretary of Agriculture, Henry Wallace, who had strong Iowa
university connections and was an expert on statistical correlation
at a time when this was not a common skill (J. Platt 1986a: 102).)
Much of their work was of a routine practical nature, but there was
a continuing tradition of important qualitative and quantitative
studies of rural communities often drawn on by general sociologists;
in addition, there was pioneering work in the use of stratified
sampling techniques.[10] In the late 1930s what was initially a very
small unit, the Division of Program Surveys, was set up to collect
informal interview data on the opinions of farmers; Wallace felt
that detailed qualitative data on reactions to the many new
programmes were needed. It was gradually recognised that more
systematic sampling and data-collection would be desirable, and
Rensis Likert was employed to put it on a more 'scientific' basis.
With the US entry into the war DPS became responsible for much
of the official research on the civilian population; its methods
became recognisably those of the modern survey, but with a strong
commitment to open-ended questions and a more qualitative
approach. This unit, like the other wartime research groups,
recruited many bright young people from academia and took part
in lively methodological discussions which had long-term consequences; after the war was over, it metamorphosed into the Survey
Research Center at the University of Michigan (J. Platt 1986a:
96–9). This sketch should sufficiently suggest the extent to which
what was formally a policy unit of one branch of government
nonetheless took a meaningful part in the intellectual life of
academic sociology, and so can justifiably be mentioned in this
context.

Another aspect of government support for rural sociology is the
place of social science in the Agricultural Experiment Stations

[10] It is not coincidental that so much important work in statistics should have entered
sociology via routes associated with agriculture, given the salience in the history of
statistics of work on crops, such as that of R. A. Fisher.
   There was within USDA a Graduate School, sometimes offering courses to students of
local universities (Hansen 1987: 162), and a Department of Mathematics and Statistics,
under the direction of the distinguished statistician W. S. Deming, where R. A. Fisher had
given visiting lectures; Philip Hauser's papers show that in 1941 he himself gave a course
there on 'The planning and processing of statistical enquiries', while one on 'Theory of
sample surveys' was given by Madow and Hurwitz (PMH); BAE sponsored a conference on
sampling at the Statistical Laboratory at Iowa State in 1936 (Converse 1987: 46).

(AES) located at the state land-grant universities. Under the Purnell Act of 1924 there was a place there for sociologists, along with the other disciplines associated with agriculture. Although the AES were under considerable pressure to respond to local demands, they provided one of the few settings in universities at the time where there was time for research (Rosenberg 1976: chapter 2). As importantly, the dominance there of natural scientists also made them one of the few places where research funding and support facilities were automatically available, which made jobs there valued by those interested in research (C. A. Anderson 1984, Sanders 1984).[11] For the same reason there was a relatively strong and sophisticated quantitative tradition in rural sociology. William H. Sewell's important work on measurement and scaling started while he was employed at the AES at Oklahoma State. Archibald Haller, who has spent much of his career since 1951 based in an AES, said that his experience has been that he has been able to work directly on theoretical issues of interest in status attainment in both the USA and Brazil without having to associate it with solving other people's practical problems, indeed with enthusiastic institutional support (Haller 1984). Robin Williams describes rural sociology as having had the stereotype of dustbowl empiricism (Williams 1984) – and the stereotype was not wholly unfounded – but at least it had extensive empirical experience. Williams is among those distinguished people who started in the rural field and eventually moved over, partly on the basis of the participation in the *American Soldier* wartime research for which his background of rural work had made him well equipped.

All this meant that there was a more elaborated and cumulative early empirical research tradition in rural sociology than in most other fields and, although ecology and subject matter made this somewhat segregated from the sociological mainstream, and its importance declined with that of agriculture, enough people crossed the barriers for it to play its part in the general development of methods as well as in substantive fields such as stratification and community study. Government funding, stemming from the political importance of agricultural interests, was vital to this.

---

[11] There were also good and accessible publication opportunities in the AES Bulletins (Nelson 1969: 102).

Another major source of governmental funding for social research was the New Deal; it both led to studies planned to inform relief policy and, at least as important for sociology, also supported research under the Work Projects Administration (WPA), which ran from 1935 to 1943. The prime object of the WPA was to create useful employment for needy unemployed people; sociological research was just one of the forms which such employment took. Many university sociologists became involved in such research in one way or another, and there were unprecedented opportunities for those interested in empirical work related to social problems. This not only meant that much more of it was done, but also affected the character of the work done. For instance, Philip Hauser describes how on his doctoral dissertation he requested two assistants for a study of differential fertility and mortality in Chicago, and was asked if he could use more people; he ended up with 150 clerks, and so could use data on all births and deaths for 5 years instead of a sample (Hauser 1982). It became possible for the first time for sociologists outside government to collect data on a large scale, and to learn from experience about the practical as well as the intellectual problems of undertaking such work; significant advances were made in sampling and statistical methods, and in diffusion of understanding of them. Within the WPA there was also its own Division of Social Research, which undertook some large surveys, and was staffed by statistically trained sociologists (including the methodologist T. C. McCormick) many of whom came from an AES background (Converse 1987: 39).

This pattern of movement and collaboration between academia and government was also shown in the Bureau of the Census. Philip Hauser, a leading sociological demographer, between two periods at the University of Chicago spent 1937–47 associated with the Census in various capacities, and was Acting Director of the Census in 1949–50. There he put into practice what his colleagues William F. Ogburn (Chairman of the Census Advisory Committee) and Samuel Stouffer (a Census consultant, along with Frederick F. Stephan) had promoted, and introduced more sociological styles of work; over his time there the number of professional employees increased enormously. (Leslie Kish, who has played an important role in sampling for sociological surveys, was just one of those trained in this setting (Kish 1983).) The first serious use of large-scale probability sampling was within the Census Bureau in

1937–40, and this led to key technical developments as well as the diffusion of knowledge and the increased availability of high-quality data for secondary analysis by sociologists. Part of that initiative arose from the political need at the time for improved figures on unemployment; existing data were inadequate and disputed (Hansen 1987: 163–5, Kahn 1983). The monthly Current Population Survey, started in 1941, was the best sample survey at the time, and could cover many issues; it helped to open up jobs for sociologists in quantitative methods, and provided data which could be used in their own research (Hauser 1982). The considerable influence exercised by sociologists on Census concepts and categories made its data more useful to them for sociological purposes, and the Census monographs which a number of sociologists were commissioned to write were also contributions to sociology (Hauser 1968). Thus although the Census did not directly fund research by independent sociologists it did contribute significant resources which were available for sociological work.

The wartime sociological research effort has been so well documented that little time needs to be spent on it here – see, for instance, Converse 1987, Clausen 1984. However, it is sometimes forgotten that it did not consist only of the Army work using survey methods; the Army work did not use only survey methods, and there was important work outside the Army, especially that on civilian issues mentioned above. This research was, obviously, planned to serve immediate policy purposes, but methodologically it provided unprecedented resources and opportunities for experimentation with new techniques, and brought together in intensive cooperation all the leading figures in the field and some of the brightest young people who would otherwise have been their graduate students; those involved also, naturally, used the theoretical ideas they had in their work, and developed new ones to meet the circumstances. It had, thus, some of the same consequences as direct funding would have done, even if these gains could not be applied until the war was over. (We may also note that numbers of those not working in research branches drew on their experiences for sociological data – see, for example, Homans 1947, Turner 1947.) After the war, much of this new knowledge was put to work in sociology, and both the prestige of the successful application of sociology and science more generally, and the personal relationships established, had longer-term effects.

At the end of the war, military issues remained salient – encouraged by Cold War and Korean War – and some of the professional military had learned to value social research; there was, thus, a time in which military sources of funding were significant for academics. Most striking here is the Office of Naval Research (ONR).[12] Darley, in the introduction to a book which reports a conference on five years of ONR-funded research, tellingly remarks that:

For an indefinite moment, psychologists, anthropologists, and sociologists are enjoying a *succès d'estime* that is heady and gratifying ... We have been given the chance to produce our equivalent of the atom bomb. (1963: 10–11)

The recent role of physics in war technology had indeed given a new prestige and perceived practical relevance to science (or 'science') of all kinds; basic science was now seen as potentially useful (Converse 1987: 242). ONR supported much basic social-scientific work having no self-evident relation to naval needs, including some of Leo Goodman's statistical work. Darley (1963: 5–7) describes how the civilian advisory panel was set up which listed topics for appropriate research under these headings: comparative study of different cultures, structure and function of groups, problems of communication of ideas, policies and values, leadership, growth and development of the individual. ONR staff were so committed to research for its own sake that, when the Korean War made military relevance more salient, ONR

developed rationales ... that would link basic research directly to current and projected naval warfare needs . . . two titles and descriptions were prepared; one by the scientist directing the project, and the other, much more graphically military, prepared by the ONR staff . . . exploration of Pacific Island cultures became the study of favorable amphibious assault sites. (Sapolsky 1990: 63).

Darley (1957: 305) reports the Certificate of Appreciation given to ONR by the American Psychological Association, and as a

---

[12] Some of those involved argue that this happened because farsighted Navy men saw the need for a national body to encourage and coordinate scientific research, and set in motion the necessary plans while Congress and other powers closed existing wartime bodies and discussed what to do next: 'The world leadership of the US in basic research in the decade following World War II has been largely credited by many experts to the timely and effective work of the Office of Naval Research' (The Bird Dogs, 1961: 35). ONR has been widely seen as a forerunner of the National Science Foundation.

participant concludes that 'ONR's program *emerged from* the research interests of civilian scientists and was not *planned for* the institutions to which the contracts were given' (1957: 319; Darley's italics).[13]

The US Air Force (USAF), too, supported social-science research; Lyons (1969: 142–6) describes the complex and changing institutions, including the RAND Corporation, through which this was organised. One prominent example of its sociological work was Stuart C. Dodd's 'Project Revere', which studied the diffusion of messages from leaflets dropped by air; many journal articles arose from this, few of them showing any interest in the substantive topic in its own right; Dodd's intellectual programme (on which see chapter 3) was quite different.[14] The research on which Riley, Riley and Toby's book (1954) was based was largely funded by the Human Resources Research Institute of USAF. The Bureau of Applied Social Research held important USAF grants from 1950 (Converse 1987: 491). Delbert Miller held a grant to study the effects of isolation on men in the Air Force in isolated places from which Edward Gross got several articles on small groups including, for example, one on 'Symbiosis and consensus as integrative factors in small groups' (E. Gross 1956) which related data on Air Force personnel to the literature on the cohesiveness of small groups. It is of some relevance to the politics of such funding that he and his colleagues were shaken at the time when an Air Force Colonel visited them and said that, for the Air Force, the area they were working in was just interesting, not things that they must know or were even important. Gross naively asked why, then, it was subsidised. Over drinks later, the answer emerged:

he said suppose there's a war, and we lose the war, and after the war there's an investigation of why we lost the war – well, we think it essential for us to be able to show that we consulted with all the available experts, even sociologists! (E. Gross 1984)

---

[13] The State University of Iowa held a contract to furnish the advisory panel for Personnel and Training Research which evaluated grant applications under that head (Iowa 1), and presumably similar contracts were held at other universities.

[14] In fairness to both parties it should, however, be pointed out that if his abstract general theory were well founded it would indeed predict outcomes which would have included the specific ones presumably of interest to the Air Force.

Government funding expanded dramatically over time (Crawford and Biderman 1970: 62–4, Hall 1972: 195, S. P. Turner and J. H. Turner 1990: 134), and the military component became of decreasing importance as other agencies developed although, as Brooks (1983: 43) points out, the science support system that developed was largely a by-product of the Cold War. The National Science Foundation (NSF) was set up in 1950; this reflected an important change from the prewar period, in that federal research funds were now allocated to outside agencies such as universities, not just the government's own agencies (Converse 1987: 242).[15] Initially NSF had a remit which left little room for sociology or other social science, but by the mid-1950s it was starting to fund social research, at first in very restricted areas but gradually expanding (England 1982, Larsen 1992). This was confined, for political reasons, to work in a 'scientific' style, though that constraint has become weaker with time. Cautious moves were made in the direction of introducing elements of social science (Alpert 1954, 1955), but the external political climate continued to encourage caution, and the internal climate was dominated by the natural sciences. The net result was that social science there adopted what Riecken describes as 'a strategy of protective coloration, of allying one's cause with stronger others'; this, together with the felt need to differentiate social science from socialism or social reform (with which it was often confused), led to choice of the solution 'to emphasize the similarities between social and 'natural' science by focusing on methods of inquiry' (Riecken 1983: 40, 41). As an agency policy this did not so much express a taste as constitute a perceived condition of survival; the alternative was seen as no NSF money for social science. The consequence was, however, undoubtedly discriminatory by method. Interestingly, this was in the context of *basic* research, which was NSF's distinctive mission, not the policy-oriented work with which leftish commentators have traditionally associated quantitative methods, which Riecken points out are the domain of other government agencies.

Probably the single most important other federal sources were

---

[15] For a set of useful accounts of the social-scientific and governmental politics of NSF's emergence, see Klausner and Lidz 1986; for an insider's account of the progress of social science within it, see Larsen 1992.

the National Institutes of Health, whose Division of Research Grants was established in 1947, and in particular the National Institute of Mental Health (NIMH), whose budget rose sharply in the later 1950s (Greenberg 1969: 172). In a sample of sociological journal articles federal health agencies, among which NIMH contributed most, supported about 7 per cent of all articles in 1959–60, and in the following eight years this rose to 15–16 per cent. (Crawford and Biderman 1970: 62). As Lyons (1969: 235) indicates, NIMH had become not just a major funding source, but one which supported fundamental work not immediately related to its parent department's programme needs. Among the sociological work funded by it not of obvious direct relevance to mental health which was reported by my respondents are Mirra Komarovsky's *Blue-Collar Marriage* (1964), James Short's work on street gangs (Short and Strodtbeck 1963), and a community study by Irwin Sanders financed by a grant to train applied community sociologists.

COMMERCIAL FUNDING

Finally, the possibility of funding from directly commercial interests should be mentioned. This was not advertised as sums available for application, as with foundations, but nonetheless it was there, and some sociologists used it. Of course this was not always for strictly sociological purposes; it is well known, for instance, that Lazarsfeld at the Bureau for Applied Social Research frequently took on commercial projects simply to maintain the organisation when other sources were not to hand. He also, though, more importantly, found ways of using commercial projects to fund work he was interested in for his own ends; for instance, the data for *Personal Influence* (Katz and Lazarsfeld 1955) came from a study funded by *True Story* magazine, which he had persuaded that it needed to know whether their readers were opinion leaders (Glock 1984). Much less well known is the case of Social Research Inc., an agency set up by Burleigh Gardner, Lloyd Warner and clinical psychologist W. Henry to do qualitative research. Although this was a commercial agency undertaking market and similar research, numbers of well-known sociologists around Chicago, including Erving Goffman and Anselm Strauss, worked for it at one time or another. Much of the work done was, of course, not published, but some was and more is likely to have fed into participants' thinking.

Lee Rainwater was employed by them for 13 years, and in that time produced several sociological books, such as *Workingman's Wife* (work funded – again! – by *True Story*) drawing on their data. (Gardner 1982, Rainwater 1984).

FUNDING AND CAPITALISM

Against this background, we consider the significance of funding for research methods. There are two linked relevant lines of argument in the literature, the first a general one about the operation of foundations and/or the capitalist state, and the second specifically about the impact of funding on sociological methods; each is dealt with in turn. Both see foundations and/or the state as representing the interests of capitalism, as exercising control over social science through the distribution of funds, and as thereby distorting the pattern of sociological work in the direction of capitalist interests – which produces, among other outcomes, an emphasis on 'scientific' styles of work and on quantitative methods. One of the earlier writers to argue in this way was Gouldner (1971: 444–5). He sees a:

growing instrumentalism . . . [which] finds its expression in 'theoryless' theories . . . and a corresponding emphasis upon seemingly neutral methods, mathematical models, investigational techniques and research technologies of all kinds . . . their 'hard' methodologies function as a rhetoric of persuasion. They communicate an image of a 'scientific' neutrality . . . their conceptual emptiness allows their researches to be formulated in terms that focus directly on those problems and variables of administrative interest to government sponsors. They thus avoid any conflict between the applied interests of their government sponsors and the technical interests of a theoretically guided tradition.

Donald Fisher has been particularly prominent recently, and he argues similarly:

The commitment to 'academic science' and the strengthening of the professionalization process placed the social sciences above reproach. These 'new intellectuals' could then become the technical experts who would provide unbiased, objective solutions to social problems . . . Rockefeller philanthropy was actively involved in confirming through reproduction those parts of the dominant ideology that placed faith in objectivity, professionalism, science and the academy. (Fisher 1983: 224)

Fisher has since been involved in controversy with Martin Bulmer who, on the basis of his own research into the workings of the Rockefeller foundations, argues that they were in practice disinterested and that their very considerable financial support for sociology left sociologists able to pursue their own intellectual priorities. However, this led to more quantitative work because without such external support academic sociologists had simply not got the resources to collect large-scale data and compile figures from it (Bulmer and Bulmer 1981: 402–3; see also Bulmer 1984a, Fisher 1984). Bulmer has elsewhere (1984b) made an intensive study of one key department and its use of such funds. Michael Useem (1976), in a study of several social sciences, finds that the receipt of federal funds is strongly associated with conducting quantitative research, and concludes that federal research money does make a difference. Below, we assess the state of the argument and relate it to some systematic data on sociology. The emphasis of the discussion in sociology has been on the foundations, so that is where the emphasis here is placed.

A starting point in this argument is that the activities of foundations set up by capitalists are determined by the interests of their founders, and should therefore be accounted for in terms of the material interests which follow from their social location. (It is seen as following that the political tendencies of foundations are right-wing, so it is natural that this should lead to distribution of foundation funding in an elitist way which reveals anti-democratic bias.) It is also assumed that the availability and provision of foundation funding gives control over the pattern of research carried out and that, where foundation staff and social scientists interact, the former are inevitably dominant. Here we raise queries about the adequacy of every component of this argument.

First, a theoretical or methodological point. If we are interested in assessing the explanatory merit of the idea of capitalist interests as a way of accounting for social-scientific developments, it is necessary also to consider whether the same outcomes might not have resulted from other mechanisms. The development of US sociology certainly took place in a capitalist society with a capitalist state, but capitalist in practice does not necessarily mean exclusively capitalist in principle. Socialism or communism in power might have generated many of the same general interests, especially in methodological areas, if not substantive topics formulated in the same way: after all, socialism too is concerned with rational planning, and would benefit from efficient and accurate techniques of data collection as well as from well-grounded and practically relevant theories.[16] The socialist not in power might also be thought at least equally likely to show concern with solving current social problems; few actual socialists, especially in America, have taken the strong line that short-term problems are desirable for the long-term revolutionary unrest which they promote (Hyfler 1984), nor does objective interest clearly indicate a non-reformist strategy. If it can be argued with some plausibility that the outcome would also be consistent with non-capitalist interests, then the mere fact that it can be argued with some plausibility for capitalist interests cannot be a sufficient basis for imputing causation.

The critical work in question has commonly started from a general standpoint which sees class analysis in terms of material interests as fundamental to understanding social processes, and has observed what foundations actually did and interpreted it in the light of that standpoint. There is, however, a problem about this, which would be equally applicable to analyses starting from quite different standpoints: to look backwards from outcomes, with a predisposition in favour of particular interpretations, makes it too easy to find ways of interpreting almost any actual outcome as consistent with them – especially if the processes suggested do not have to be conscious or overt. (Apparently inconsistent facts can be interpreted as showing deliberate camouflage, or subtle legitimation strategies.) To say this is not only to make the case for giving more serious attention to actors' viewpoints, without abandoning a sensitivity to the possibility that there are important underlying causes, but also to point out that other structural interpretations might be equally or more consistent with the same data. Outcomes which fit are a necessary condition for satisfactory

16 The association of quantitative methods with an oppressive capitalist state bureaucracy, customary among those who emphasise capitalist interests as explanation and oppose quantification on that ground, is particularly odd. Unless the capitalist state is technically incompetent, in which case we can all relax anyway, it would be expected to utilise qualitative data for its oppressive purposes if they were technically superior to that end. If certain methods are more effective, they will be more effective for whoever uses them. (For discussion of two cases where states did use qualitative methods, see J. Platt 1986a).

explanation by the interests, though not a sufficient one to demonstrate that it is the correct explanation. If one is concerned to *investigate* whether the outcomes can be adequately explained by certain material interests, it seems logically more appropriate to specify what those interests would dictate first, and then to study the outcomes to see how far they fit the prediction.

What would a pure capitalist, motivated solely by material interest, have done in relation to sociology? A robber-baron capitalist (of the kind relevant when some major foundations were set up) who wanted to put his money to good use in furthering robbery would surely not have put any of it into sociological research. He would have used it (and did) for practical things, like bribing judges and politicians, hiring thugs to shoot union leaders, buying newspapers to put a favourable gloss on his dubious activities, advertising to create an attractive image for his adulterated goods. If he still had so much left over that a little social research might as well be done with it, one may safely presume that it would be results of business relevance that he would be interested in, though he would of course want to know that the conclusions were well grounded, and that shooting union leaders would indeed keep down the costs of labour. He would not, however, want to disseminate these results where they might benefit his competitors, so they would not be put in the public domain.

A rather more sophisticated and modern rational capitalist might take a less crudely direct approach, and so might put social research higher up his shopping list. He, too, would be primarily interested in results: immediately, for the recruitment and management of an effective and profitable workforce and for the marketing of his product, and less immediately for such matters as standards of training in the labour markets he draws on, political attitudes affecting taxation policy for business, and so on. He, too, would not want to put his results in the public domain, unless this was instrumental in putting together industrial or political coalitions on matters of shared interest. We might still think that he could spend his money in considerably more effective ways than on social research by academics. His social research would probably come mainly from market research agencies when it was not done in-house; his concerns for legitimacy and a favourable image would surely be catered for by spending money on donations to appropriate political parties and industrial interest groups, on public relations and personnel management functions, rather than through social science.

If this account of interests is accepted, it is clear that on their own they give little help in understanding why it was that foundations set up by capitalists funded enormous amounts of social research by academics, most of it not on topics of immediate business relevance and almost all of it published. Indeed, they give little help in understanding why any attention at all should have been given to social research and its methods rather than to more pressing concerns.[17] (They also give little help in understanding why foundations should have spent much larger amounts of money on support for the worldwide eradication of hookworm (Rockefeller), creating public libraries (Carnegie), the YMCA (Rockefeller), the civil rights movement (Ford), and so on – but that is not the subject of this chapter.) One might feel that a Veblenian account in terms of conspicuous consumption (Veblen 1931) was at least as relevant as a Marxian one. These considerations suggest that, though capitalist interests may have some relevance, they cannot provide a sufficient explanation of the actual outcomes in question; other factors are also logically required. One possibility that should be taken more seriously than it often has been is simply that, while those who set up foundations were undoubtedly themselves capitalists, it does not inevitably follow that that is all they were, so that this must explain their every action. I see no reason, for instance, not to believe that John D. Rockefeller was also a sincere Baptist, even if as such he showed ordinary levels of hypocrisy and inconsistency in his behaviour, and that his Baptism sometimes determined his choices. There is no reason why two motives or causes should not be present simultaneously. Real capitalists are not rational ideal types.

I conclude, thus, that the account in terms of objective capitalist interests is not logically convincing as an explanation, even though capitalist interests were present, and we may presume that such men would not have acted in a way directly counter to capitalist interest. One needs to look, without that preconception, at the

---

[17] No major foundation in fact defined social research as part of its basic remit; for them it was, at the highest levels of policy, instrumental to other ends, usually ones connected with social problems, and they typically devoted small parts of their total resources to it and moved in and out of programmes involving it over relatively short periods.

detailed mechanisms by which the outcomes were generated in order fully to understand what happened. It may be noted that, although the theorisation referred to above is commonly in terms of foundations generally, the data used come overwhelmingly from the Rockefeller foundations,[18] and the period focused on is very often the interwar one; empirical generalisations would be more convincing if given a broader base, and this chapter draws on material from other foundations heavily involved in funding social-science research, and from the postwar period. Heavy use is made below of archival sources about foundation policies and decision-making, especially the archives of the Ford Foundation, and the invaluable Oral History Archive of Columbia University, which contains extensive interviews with many leading postwar foundation insiders.

FOUNDATION OPERATING PRACTICES

We turn, then, to consider more detailed aspects of foundations' operation. We need, to understand their decision-making, to look at their internal power structures. In some foundations set up during his lifetime the founder played an active and dominant role; once he was dead, however, it was very much more likely that, even if family members were still involved, *de facto* control would rest in the hands of others. The others in whose hands formal control lies are the trustees, commonly drawn from businessmen (to whom an analysis in terms of diffuse capitalist interests would be as appropriate as to the founders). It would be unwise to assume, however, that the formal control exercised by the trustees means that what is done reflects nothing but their own priorities, especially given that they usually have many other commitments, meet infrequently and make decisions in the light of the materials presented to them. In these circumstances even an analysis purely in terms of interests cannot sensibly focus only on the trustees, let alone the founders.

It is the professional foundation officers (cf. Karl and Katz 1981:

---

[18] One reason for the focus on Rockefeller is probably the availability of their really excellent Archive Center, which gives free access to an enormous range of materials, and also has a scheme which provides grants to researchers to visit it. (Would a really single-minded capitalist provide such a facility?) If grants buy researchers to give conclusions favourable to the funder, I have been bought – but so has Donald Fisher! and that instance surely weakens the general argument.

263–6) who present issues to the trustees and implement policies, and they may have their own agendas; indeed, they can sometimes manipulate and mislead their trustees. This is exemplified in oral-history accounts by foundation insiders:

> In good season and bad we fought our trustees, who didn't understand what the social sciences were about, and got money for the Social Science Research Council. (CCOH 1:10)

> within the very strict limits of what they could do with their boards of trustees they employed the social sciences . . . , developed various aspects of social science. But always without mentioning its name, which was pretty much anathema to most members of the board. (CCOH 2: 90)

These quotations summarise the general impression gained from reading the whole set of oral histories, which is that interest in social science generally came from officers rather than trustees, and that they could and did use their positions to promote it, though within constraints set by the trustees, who did not always accept their recommendations. It is interesting, in the light of the assumption often made that the Behavioral Science programme of the Ford Foundation was the epitome of support for quantitative method in the interests of capitalism, that it was ended by the businessman trustees, who had difficulty understanding what it was meant to be for, over the resistance of the social-scientifically qualified officers of the Foundation.

Post-1968 comment among sociologists has tended to assume that foundations are obviously associated with capitalism, and so are prima facie right-wing in tendency if they are anything; it has also assumed that support for 'science' and quantification fit in with that.[19] It does not seem to be realised how curious this is, given that only a little while earlier, in the McCarthyite period, opposite assumptions were being made in powerful places. René Wormser, who acted as General Counsel to the Reece Congressional Special Committee to Investigate Tax-Exempt Foundations of 1954,

---

[19] Alchon saw a 'technocratic bargain' (1985: 52) between capitalist philanthropy and social science, in which political processes were replaced by capitalist planning to achieve depoliticisation. It is, of course, not only capitalists who traditionally plan, and replace politics. We may note, too, that the understood counter-factual is not just politics as it might otherwise have developed, but the victory of the politics the author prefers; whether that is an empirically plausible alternative may be questioned. 'Depoliticisation' is a word normally used to refer, not to change from a more politicised earlier situation, but a failure to be politicised as the user thinks appropriate.

published a book in 1958 which provides a convenient summary of this approach. Foundations are seen in it as potentially subversive bodies, promoting un-American values such as internationalism and collectivism, sometimes even supporting work by communists. They funded work by sinister men like Stouffer, who undermined US defence by providing data used to demobilise the army after the Second World War in ways which weakened it militarily; moreover, their dangerous commitment to 'scientific' method is not only elitist but, more seriously, un-American in that it implies a lack of prior commitment to American values, holding instead that:

there are no absolutes, that everything is indeterminate, that no standards of conduct, morals, ethics and government are to be deemed inviolate, that everything, including basic moral law, is subject to change, and that it is the part of the social scientists to take no principle for granted as a premise in social or juridical reasoning, however fundamental it may heretofore have been deemed to be under our Judeo-Christian moral system. (Wormser 1958: 105, quoting from the Reece Committee report)

That might almost be enough to make some critical commentators see previously unsuspected virtues in foundations! The then head of the SSRC found it necessary to defend it against the Reece Committee attack by producing figures to demonstrate that a majority of the projects it had funded recently had been non-quantitative (J. Platt 1986a: 104). The attack on foundations was part of a traditional populist hostility to big business, and there were of course also quite different strands of right-wing thought. The point of drawing attention to this version is not to assert that it is the correct one, but to demonstrate that different stories can be told about the same practices. If they can, something more than an adequate fit between one story and the facts is needed to show that the story is the right one. I suggest that each of the stories in question is plausible in its own terms, but wrong. Each moral is drawn by comparison with the author's preferred alternative, rather than reflecting a real historical concern.

Whether or not they were right-wing, foundations were often accused of elitism and prejudices in the allocation of grants, which certainly did tend to go disproportionately to a small group of elite research institutions. But this was an area where there were deliberate policies, resting on knowledge of the structure of the academic system. Carnegie had a strategy of placing grants in places which set trends or were at the centre of networks of scholars (Lagemann 1989: 154, 178–9); this to get the maximum return on their investment. Rockefeller in the 1920s had the strategy of 'making the peaks higher' because this was expected to raise standards generally. Berelson pointed out that

if you want to turn the system around, then you better try to turn it around at the top. And the top there covers a very large proportion of the field. The next ten wouldn't have covered nearly as many graduate students. (CCOH 3: 108)

Morrissett, of Spencer, makes a practical rationale explicit:

if a foundation decides that it wants to develop basic research outside the normal major research institutions, it's a very hard task . . . one way would be a sort of talent search . . . [which] would be time consuming . . . need staff and be difficult . . . Another . . . would be to say that in particular places you would promote special areas of basic research in order to build up facilities and people; that would take a great deal of perseverance . . . long-term support and careful nurturing . . . again, that's a high expenditure of staff time and effort to do that, with uncertain payoff because the social system that you're operating in means that for a whole variety of reasons, salaries, living conditions, colleagues, reputation, facilities, graduate students, you name it, people migrate towards the other kinds of institutions so if you want somehow to reverse that flow, it's a tough and long-term job. (SFOH 1: 32)

His junior colleague Carlson adds that fine scholars at what are basically teaching institutions often lack essential support mechanisms like reduced teaching loads, and are not on good dissemination networks (SFOH 2).

If these broad factors were not so important, how were foundation decisions made and whose ideas did they represent? We have shown the importance of the professional foundation officers as distinct from the trustees, but there are also innumerable examples in the archives which show academics being consulted about how money should be used, and their views being taken seriously. A sharp distinction between foundation officers and social scientists could be misleading. Some key ones were themselves social scientists by training, and some moved back and forth between the foundation world and academia. For instance, Bernard Berelson started as an academic, then was recruited to the Ford Foundation; Donald Young went to SSRC from the University of

Pennsylvania and stayed for 1932–48, still nominally on leave from the university, and then went to head the Russell Sage Foundation. Wormser (1958: 57–69) provides useful data on other such moves, as well as on links within the foundation community.

Sometimes the academics initiated an idea which a foundation took up; for instance, the Center for Advanced Studies in the Behavioral Sciences, funded by the Ford Foundation, was the eventual result of a proposal by Lazarsfeld and Merton for a professional school. Lazarsfeld and Merton also had an enterprise for advanced training in empirical social research which was undoubtedly their own idea, though funded by Ford and Rockefeller, and which led to many of the best-known methodological publications of the 1950s (Lazarsfeld and Rosenberg 1955, Hyman 1955, Komarovsky 1957, as well as a number of papers).[20] Ford's decision to enter the field of research training:

started from Mr Sibley's evidence of the lack of trained people, and was supported by further evidence from Messrs Parsons, Riley et al. of the critical lack of resources for the development of social science. At the conference sponsored by the Council to discuss these reports there was particular emphasis on the need of people equipped to do empirical research. All these influences led to the grants. (LW 3)[21]

Academic involvement could take the form of peer review procedures, or sometimes was addressed to more general policy issues and took the form of anything from private consultation to a specially arranged conference with papers on the state of work in various fields and its needs. A cynic could say 'which academics?' and, to the answer that it is the most distinguished ones, reply 'how did they become so distinguished?', or 'who says so?' On that there is a suggestive report (Berelson 1956) on a small empirical study of 'leading contributions' to social science over the period 1930–56 as evaluated by academic social scientists, which shows that a high

[20] It may be noted that this could not be regarded as showing simple personal favouritism. There is more than one reference in the files to reservations about Lazarsfeld's personal style, his possible charlatanism and excessive salesmanship – but these are overcome because he is also seen, surely rightly, as outstandingly dynamic and entrepreneurial as well as intellectually stimulating.

[21] A striking footnote to history is provided by evidence that W. I. Thomas was used by LSRM as a sort of academic spy, with a secret retainer to act on their behalf: 'Dr Thomas has been able to approach persons and representatives of institutions in the role of a private investigator known to be interested in the general field, thereby obtaining an insight into the situation that it would in some instances at least be difficult for a recognised staff member of the Memorial to acquire' (RAC 7).

proportion had received foundation funding, and it was higher among those more highly rated. (He was aware of the obvious problem of knowing whether the funding had actually played a causal role in producing better work.) Whether or not these findings are seen as convincing, such cynicism is not addressed to the immediate issue, which is simply that these were undoubtedly academics, not foundation officials.[22] Some critics might reply that the academics in question were elite members of the foundation-related establishment. That is simply a redescription (with critical overtones) of what they did; if 'establishment' is a reasonable description, some academics belonged to the funding establishment, and such an account is not compatible with one in which academia is simply the object of manipulation.

FOUNDATION CONTROL OF RESEARCH

Next we consider whether the availability and provision of foundation funding gives control over the pattern of research carried out. Obviously it does to the extent that work needing funding cannot be done without it (J. Platt 1994b), but it cannot be taken for granted that even the acceptance of a grant automatically determines what is done. In the simplest case, as Bulmer and Bulmer (1981: 381) have pointed out, this is because the grant was an open one given to be used as the recipient chose. It was the general practice of the Laura Spelman Rockefeller Memorial in the 1920s to give such block grants to institutions, and in the 1950s Ford gave such grants both to institutions and to individuals. Rockefeller and other foundations also made large donations to the SSRC, which took responsibility for deciding how to distribute them.[23]

---

[22] S. P. Turner and J. H. Turner (1990: 90–7) give a picture of the community of foundation officers and academics as involving considerable elements of patronage, and selection of which academics to consult, which could lead to long-term symbiotic relations. Although this is a critical account, it still supports the basic point that academics played a significant role in foundation decision-making.

[23] Some of these donations left more discretion than others to the SSRC. Fisher (1993) depicts it as a subservient body anxious to please its funders, with the apparent freedom a misleading façade; no doubt there are elements of truth in this, but as a total picture it seems overdrawn. Rockefeller appeared anxious to avoid direction of its activities. A paper for an internal LSRM meeting says, for instance, re funding for the SSRC: 'The objection to frequent returns is that they convey the impression of a desire on the part of the Memorial for review and appraisal in connection with applications for continued financial support. Any action which fairly conveys such an impression is to be avoided' (RAC 8).

There is also evidence that foundations deliberately refrained from even the appearance of intervention:

Our present highly concentrated program involves us in the danger of being interpreted as wishing to direct research into certain channels. The more information we give out needlessly, the more research is shaped to come within our favor . . . When in doubt what to say to questions, say nothing courteously. (RAC 3)

some of us asked him [Dollard] once why he didn't get over to see us [working on what became Myrdal 1944], and well, he thought it was better not to appear to be sticking his nose into the business over there; that Carnegie was financing it, but, after all, that was it. They were not trying to dictate what was done. (CCOH 5: 54)

At a later period, a senior officer enunciates the principles that:

When once we have made an appropriation . . . we should not attempt to manage or direct the work . . . nor should we make appropriations that leave in our hands a lot of managerial strings . . . when the appropriation is made it is for better or worse, and we must remain in the state of mind of accepting whatever favorable or unfavorable, satisfactory or unsatisfactory, pleasing or embarrassing results ensue. (RAC 4) (This related to the strong technical criticisms made of statistical aspects of Kinsey's work, which they had funded.)

Fisher interprets such statements by foundation officials as hypocritical or misleading. I do not see adequate grounds for rejecting the less cynical reading of them as accurately representing their conscious attitudes and policies, more especially when they were not made in public but appear in private internal papers.

Whether or not the officers wished to maintain tight control, some academics affected the practical outcomes, rather than the policies, of foundations, by taking the money and then not doing what the foundation had intended, whether deliberately or by accident. Even grants given for fixed purposes were not always used as the funding body had hoped.[24] Some examples of reported foundation disappointments from oral histories:

[24] Nor are block grants. Report on block grant to Harvard: 'It is difficult to explain the generous support of the work of Prof. Sorokin . . . except in terms of departmental considerations. Much of his work seems very remote from contemporary problems, and the statistical underpinning is regarded with considerable suspicion by competent statisticians' (RAC 9).

Clarence Faust at Ford 'had some very distinct, settled views on what higher education in the US should be. And he, in effect, was trying to buy that into existence with Ford funds, and in my view he failed . . . John [Gardner] was much better at sensing what people themselves wanted to do and giving them the funds to do it if it coincided with Carnegie's view of what was desirable' (CCOH 3: 100).

Berelson concluded that: 'the effort to get inventories of knowledge in particular fields failed. People didn't do it, or did what was not really intended, or even spent the money on something else' (FFOH 47–8), and 'Ford, of course, was so big that it was something of a threat in academia, and a lot of people didn't like things Ford was doing, felt . . . [it] was going to try to use Ford's millions to push them around . . . They weren't going to have it, and they didn't in the end. They got the money without being pushed, in effect.' (CCOH 3: 92).

Daniel Griffiths remarked of the Spencer Foundation that 'What they did was really to give the academics carte blanche', and some abused it (SFOH 3: 12).

A bit subtler than just plain not doing what the funding body intended – which may sometimes have happened by accident – is to find ways in which, when they have policies not exactly consistent with what you would like, what you want to do can be passed off as or combined with what they are interested in; surely most readers will regard this as a normal aspiration and common practice, and US sociologists generally have not been less alert to such opportunities. Peter Rossi, a man of much experience in the field, describes how it is done:

The game is 'Robin Hooding', taking from rich foundations and government support for non-financeable ideas. It's a trade-off: if the Ford Foundation is interested in X and you are interested in Y and you can see a way of coupling the two, you go to the Ford Foundation and ask for support for X and Y. (Rossi 1984)

He says he learned from Paul Lazarsfeld how to do this. Turner and Turner (1990: 101) describe how at Lazarsfeld's Bureau of Applied Social Research:

The paradigmatic kind of project was a survey with a highly practical purpose tailored to the specific concerns of some business, which was funded at a sufficiently high level to enable Lazarsfeld to add material and talented helpers so as to conduct an academic research project at the same time.

The journals provide many examples of purely academic socio-logical reports of work funded by bodies which were surely not primarily interested in that version of the results. For instance, the first issue in my office of the *American Sociological Review* provides an article (Form and D'Antonio 1959) presenting data in relation to the then important disciplinary debate on community power structure; the data-collection was funded by grants from Carnegie and the US Public Health Service to a third person for work on 'Anglo-Latino relations'. Raymond L. Gold (1984) describes how, after earlier lack of success in getting funding to do the kind of community study he wanted, the passage of the National Environ-mental Policy Act meant that he could 'bootleg good sociological research in' while conducting environmental impact studies.

On the second issue raised above, that of funding distorting the pattern of disciplinary interests, there are numbers of cases where it might seem as plausible to suggest that disciplinary interests are distorting the work done away from the funders' concerns. For instance, another issue of the *American Sociological Review* to come to hand provides us with these two cases:

Herman Turk, with funding from the US Public Health Service, does a study of doctor/nurse teams, and concludes that the results 'provide a case for the extension of current sociological theory into the following general proposition: *The cohesion of a structurally differentiated system rests on some tolerated variability in the values to which its various parts are oriented.*' [his italics] (Turk 1963: 37).

Jack Ladinsky, working under a grant to Harold Wilensky for a project on 'Labor and Leisure', funded mainly by NIMH, carries out a study of lawyers in which he shows the practices of recruitment and self-selection which lead some into solo practice and others into large firms; he relates this to general ideas about occupational recruitment, and also draws some implications for the way law is practised (Ladinsky 1963). It is not easy to see why NIMH should have funded such a study; the only themes which it raised that might connect with mental health are some minor references to the job satisfaction of lawyers.

It is, of course, possible, and indeed likely, that other reports made on the same data – in particular, those made direct to the funding agencies – will have emphasised other aspects and drawn out more practical themes. To the extent that both styles of reporting can be done satisfactorily, the interests of the funders and of the disciplines are compatible. If disciplinary interests are seen as lying in general theory, it is arguable that the specific substantive content of the data used is unimportant. But it would be a happy coincidence if the data which funding bodies were interested in were optimal for the advancement of general theory, so this kind of symbiosis is likely to be one which skews the development of theory and/or does not permit a true hypothetico-deductive approach to testing it.

However, we must once again draw attention to the fact that the absence of such funding would not necessarily improve the situation. A further point which needs to be made is that it is unrealistic to assume that no sociologists would have shown a practical orientation to social problems and social betterment in the absence of funding encouraging them to research such issues. An interest in such issues has probably always played some role in recruitment to the discipline, though no doubt a more important one earlier in its development as a distinct academic field, and many sociologists have not drawn a clear line between their interests as citizens and as researchers. (As Galliher and McCartney (1973: 78) point out, specialities whose boundaries coincide with those of the missions of existing agencies, e.g. sociology of medicine, are more likely to receive funding than those which have no corresponding agencies. It certainly does not follow that it is the funding which has created the specialities.) Roger Geiger (1988) however concluded, after a review of the relation between foundations and social science from 1945 to 1960, that the academics' preference to continue working within disciplinary traditions had prevailed over the foundations' efforts to increase knowledge for direct application to practical problems.

Foundation policies met university policies, and one could sometimes question who was manipulating whom at the institutional level. If a university did the research a foundation wanted because it wanted the money, clearly the foundation is setting the agenda – but universities did not only do the research the foundations wanted, when they did have clear wants, because of the money. The

174 SOCIOLOGICAL RESEARCH METHODS IN AMERICA

University of Chicago is an interesting case because it has been accused of being unduly dependent on Rockefeller money. The President's papers, and those of Wirth, show a less intellectually dependent relationship than this might suggest. There was, for instance, a meeting where it was reported that Rockefeller and Carnegie were seriously interested in their research plans:

Mr Wirth . . . warned that we should not . . . forget that the Division still has friends other than the Ford Foundation . . . proposed that we should regard the Ford money as presenting us with the rare opportunity to do what we really want to do in our fields, but have been prevented from doing by lack of resources. (LW 4)

Many projects considered for Ford funds were under way anyway – and those rejected often were referred to 'free funds'. It is suggested that they should 'have on hand definite projects in keeping with the University's policy of basic research ready for presentation at the right time to the right Foundations' (HHS 1). A letter reports apropos of another case that 'The President was much interested in this point of view and said he thought it would be a masterful stroke if you could put it in such light to Mr Ruml [of LSRM] that the suggestion might come from him rather than from us' (HHS 2).

The Chicago papers also show a striking cynicism in the instrumental pursuit of the university's own ends: there are regular reports of the discovery of hitherto unsuspected rich old people who should be cultivated, and whose tastes should be explored with a view to pairing them with some activity that the university wanted to develop. The whole spirit of these very private discussions is one of attempting to manipulate the various sources of funding, among which foundations are far from the only ones, in order to follow a pre-established university agenda. Funding bodies are not shown as powerless – but nor are universities.

The critical literature has tended to assume that it was self-evidently the funding bodies who were in control. A somewhat different perspective is given by looking at the matter from the point of view of a university. This might suggest that the archives of foundations, which not merely give details only on what they have funded, but are also records largely created by officials with a stake in demonstrating effectiveness to their trustees, cannot provide the whole story. The chance of foundations having a generalised influence on intellectual choices depends on the extent to which researchers depend on them and have no alternative sources of support. Our review above of the range of major sources implies that there will often have been some potential choice, though how much will have varied with the subject of research. A case study of a major researcher like Lazarsfeld shows that, even when funding was a continual problem and quest, there was a range of opportunities. For instance, the acknowledgments for *Voting* (Berelson, Lazarsfeld and McPhee 1954) include among others the Anti-Defamation League, the Carnegie Corporation, Columbia Broadcasting System, *Elmira Star-Gazette*, the Ford Foundation, the Readers' Digest Association, the Rockefeller Foundation and Time Inc. His colleagues have repeatedly told stories of his legendary ability to exploit other people's interests to enable him to continue the pursuit of his own agenda (e.g. Glock 1979), and this list surely shows a skilled operator at work rather than a pawn in the hands of the funders.[25]

It has been argued that control of research by funding bodies was not the whole truth, but let us now take a bolder step. There is a macroscopic structural conspiracy-theory story to be told which is consistent with the data, but which as far as I am aware has not previously been noted. It is this. There is a sinister hidden coalition, whose members share interests different from those of the general public; its ideological hegemony is shown by its success in convincing others, counter to their own interests, that its priorities are objectively correct. It has infiltrated the funding agencies, patiently using a variety of front organisations and its networks behind the scenes, to persuade public and altruistic private bodies to waste their money on often frivolously 'basic' research, sometimes even justifying subversive activities under a façade of support for capitalist democracy. Who are the members of this sinister coalition? They are academic social scientists.

What data support this interpretation? The key observation is that, since the 1920s, various agencies have funded social research; each of the private ones in turn has dropped out, only to be replaced by another (sometimes publicly funded) often using many of the

---

[25] Geiger (1988: 339) remarks, apropos of BASR and similar institutes, that 'the initiative for grants from foundations came largely from them, rather than from the foundations following their own independently conceived policies'.

same advisors. Thus early Rockefeller funding is succeeded by federal sources; the war effort is next exploited to the full, and then wartime prestige and Cold War politics are turned to advantage; as these recede or become problematic the Ford Foundation emerges as the vehicle of choice, and by the time it loses patience careful political work has ensured that the National Institutes of Health are supporting social science and the National Science Foundation is in place. The sociologist interested in the underlying social realities must surely regard such continuities as more than coincidental? Well, maybe. Joking apart, these facts do really suggest that social science is not such a powerless object of manipulation by funders as has been implied, even if its power rests on less tangible resources than money.

DETERMINANTS OF FOUNDATION BEHAVIOUR

The time has come to offer an alternative account of the reasons for foundation behaviour in relation to the social sciences.

Officers of the foundations we are concerned with constituted, at least by the 1950s, a professional community with its own occupational networks and standards; it was common for people to move from one foundation to another, and foundation representatives had meetings at which they compared notes on matters of shared concern and sometimes made deals about the division of labour between their organisations. They had the personal interests which followed from their own structural location, as well as the practical concerns of their organisations. These included an interest in developing a discrete area in which their achievement would be recognised, inside or outside the foundation. Those involved with funding the social sciences were often themselves social scientists by training, and some moved back and forth between the foundation and university worlds. Thus academic and funding networks intersected, and academic concerns had high salience for foundation officials, who surely identified more with them than with the interests of their founders. The picture is not one where officials foisted alien topics on reluctant professors, but where there was a high level of consensus. Insofar as it was an establishment, it was one not simply dominated by the foundation representatives.

Trustees were commonly business people, though some (like the remarkable Frederick Osborn or Chester Barnard)[26] took a strong personal interest in social science. Where no trustee took such an interest, their role in relation to social science was likely to be limited to approving or rejecting the officers' proposals; the somewhat spasmodic record of individual foundations shows how spasmodic their concern was, and how marginal social science was for them most of the time. The policy of foundations could depend heavily on the idiosyncracy of particular individuals, and so change if they moved or changed their minds (Lagemann 1989). But, given that many foundations had very broad remits, they could decide to support social science for other reasons. It appears to have been common for foundations to look for a gap to fill; this both justified the role of the foundation from the point of view of the founder and/or trustees, and catered for the officers' professional goal of being seen as responsible for distinctive achievements. Osborn

felt that there was no need for the Carnegie Corporation to involve itself with the physical sciences, because they were receiving such enormous sums through the government . . . the function of a foundation, even as large a one as the Carnegie Corporation, was to start new things and to develop new fields at a time when they weren't popular and weren't receiving government and other large backing. (CCOH 2: 31)

– so they went into social science. Sutton (1993) of Ford mentions that several times it chose a deliberate strategy of complementarity. Specialisation is, moreover, efficient from the foundation's point of view because it narrows the range of applications needing to be processed, as well as allowing the development of staff expertise.

Rather than showing ambitions to continuing control of university research, it is a recurring foundation theme that the institutions should do more for faculty research from their own funds rather than always coming to them for support; for instance, an internal report of the Rockefeller Foundation on a visit to Chicago ends by stating as the first of two objectives: 'Get

---

[26] Osborn was a wealthy man who left business in the 1920s for other interests; he became a Carnegie trustee, and in the war was the general in charge of the section carrying out the Army research (Lagemann 1989: 161–3). Barnard was president of a telephone company, but also the author of *Functions of the Executive* (1938) which made valued contributions to organisation theory, and had many connections with Harvard (Dubin 1961); he eventually became President of the Rockefeller Foundation (1948–52), and then Chairman of the NSF (1952–4).

universities to increase their support of SS research and, in particular, to provide funds for widely spread support among the faculty' (RAC 5). Admittedly this is favoured partly as a way of lightening Rockefeller's administrative load by making less sifting of relatively unpromising claims necessary, and it probably also reflects the desire for the prestige of being seen to be associated with the best and most successful work – but that once again demonstrates the relevance of internal organisational consider- ations, rather than a will to control. An additional such consideration is that foundations have often wished to maximise their effective- ness by flexibility in the disposition of their funds, shown in the conception of seed money or risk capital (Colvard 1976), and so not to have long-term commitment to any one object such as faculty research.

Geiger (1986: 145–6) argues that when in the 1920s the major foundations turned to funding research in the universities they had good political reasons not to attempt to influence its content, and this meant that those carrying it out had substantial power to decide what should be done and how. These good political reasons *were* ones associated with a felt need for legitimation of activity by capitalists, though it was not so much traditional capitalist activity as the activity of foundations which were, understandably, seen as alarmingly powerful in their wealth. In this context, with foun- dations under populist attack, legitimation needs were best met by non-interference – which also meant that they could not be held responsible for controversial outcomes, though part of the McCarthyite attack shows that this could sometimes backfire:

The headquarters of the Ford Foundation in New York said tonight that it had made the grant to the University of Chicago but that it has no control over the project. Which is all very fine, but don't forget that the Ford Foundation gave $15,000,000 to the Fund for the Republic . . . and it has no control over that 15,000,000 either. This is getting to be something of a habit on the part of the Ford Foundation. (Ford 2)

However, the archives show that open grants were also given for a simple practical reason: this entailed less administrative work by the foundation, which handed over responsibility for the detailed decision-making to the recipient. The use of intermediaries such as SSRC served the same purpose, making large amounts of free expert advice available.

The obverse of the concern to keep costs down is a desire to distribute funds so that the foundation would get the maximum bang for its bucks, and the evidence cited above shows that much 'elitism' can be accounted for by rational calculation of the way to achieve that. (Even in enormously rich foundations this is an index of professional competence for officers.) Some of it can also probably be accounted for in another way. Several writers have pointed out that there was a foundation/social-science establishment based in the East, with sociologists drawn from restricted circles used as advisors.[27] In the postwar period this, like other aspects of US sociology, had one striking feature: the prominence of those who had been involved in the wartime research effort. Clausen (1984) points out that close professional ties had been established among those working in the Army's Research Branch which influenced whole careers, and no fewer than seven of those there later occupied key positions in major foundations, while many others attained posts in leading research universities. Others who later became prominent in foundations (e.g. Bernard Berelson, who became director of Ford's Program for the Behavioral Sciences) or as advisors to them (e.g. Edward Shils) worked in other parts of the wartime research effort and, as Converse (1987) shows, were often involved in professional interchange with those in the Army. It seems probable that some of the 'elitism' was, therefore, causally more like the operation of the old boy network. This takes us back again to the social/intellectual networks in which foundation officers moved for explanation of the observed patterns.

It is concluded, therefore, that the practical activities of foundations in relation to social science can more convincingly be explained by looking at the patterns of social relations and incentives immediately relevant to the responsible actors than by invoking capitalist class interests. This fits the way actors saw it themselves, and is more consistent with the outcomes. It does not require ad hoc adjustments like the idea of contradictory class locations, as invoked by Fisher (1993: 240), to account for the behaviour by foundation officers which is otherwise inexplicable in terms of his class model. It does not entail abandoning the concept of interest, but invokes occupational and organisational rather than class interests.

[27] For material on some relevant networks, see Lagemann 1989, chapter 7.

OPERATION OF GOVERNMENT FUNDING

Data to give an equally detailed account of the administration of governmental funding cannot be offered; the archival resources are not available, or much harder to get access to. Hall (1972: 205) has argued persuasively that there is a typical pattern of 'institutional symbiosis', in which mutual dependence and influence develop between government agencies which need knowledge for their goals and universities which need money for their research. The result is that values come to converge, and 'Academic values, such as the development of knowledge for its own sake, are easily adopted as at least secondary goals in mission-oriented agencies which provide extra-mural research support' (Hall 1972: 207). Fisher (1993: 246–7) also sees a bargain as having been struck, though he assumes that it was one which subordinated social science to the state; this perception depends on regarding any research of practical use for current problems as serving the social control interests of capitalism.

It is hard, however, to reconcile his picture of social science as turned, by the postwar period, to practical applied work for the state with the observed patterns of government funding and their use. Crawford and Biderman, reviewing data on published articles, reach the conclusion that at least in terms of 'scientific' criteria 'Federal sponsorship seemingly has been accommodated more to academic sociology than academic sociology has accommodated to its federal sponsors' (1970: 76). Ploch (1978: 59) made a study of sociology proposals submitted to NSF in 1974–5 and concluded that 'award decisions were made in favour of those proposers . . . who directed their remarks to the central core of sociology as defined by major [sociological] journals', and that the power of the programme director was generally exercised only with the backing of peer reviewers. It is interesting to note the private view of a very experienced research unit director, in 1951, that federal contracts are to be preferred to foundation grants because they:

offer an opportunity for important research in which a staff member wishes to engage and which otherwise he could not undertake. It is not entirely a matter of pure service to a federal agency. On the whole, there need be little difference between federal contract projects and research financed by foundation grants, except possibly in the matter of amount of available funds and securing entrée for certain studies, contract research often excelling on both these counts. There is generally freedom of publication and no contract need be entered into with an agency which does not have sound policies in dealing with universities. (UNC 1: 3)

As Kohler (1991: 404) points out, government funding – and that of NSF in particular – relies heavily on peer review, and so the decisions made are less likely to be idiosyncratic than those of foundations, and reflect the views of the academic community to a greater extent. The material presented above is consistent with this interpretation. Once again, therefore, it looks as though sociologists have been users as well as used.

Government funding has become increasingly important, both absolutely and relatively,[28] and is provided by an increasing range of bodies. This institutionalisation and diversity may give some protection against sudden changes of policy, though it does not meet all felt social-science needs equally; Hall (1972: 194) describes it as a 'chaotic and pluralistic' situation, where accident has played a sufficient role for the term 'system' to be questionably appropriate. Historically, political caprice and extra-scientific considerations have often affected what has been on offer. Congress has been suspicious of rival claims to know what its constituents think or need, and has suppressed whole programmes if they gave results which were unwelcome. The 'Iowa Margarine Incident' (Kirkendall 1966: 327) is a well-known case in which local farm politics led to an attack on an AES (located in a dairy state) some of whose research had shown that margarine was nutritionally equivalent to butter, and therefore recommended that in wartime some taxes and legal restrictions on it should be removed. As a consequence of this a distinguished social-science research team dispersed (D. G. Johnson 1979,[29] C. A. Anderson 1984). R. B. Miller (1982: 208) points out that the enormous success of *An American Dilemma* (Myrdal 1944) had for many Americans created 'an association between social science research and attempts to improve the status of blacks in America' which made Southern

---

[28] Robinson's (1983: 36) figures show that estimated government funding for social science research rose from 31% of the total in 1956 to 44% in 1964 and 60% in 1972; the corresponding proportions for foundation funding were 22%, 16% and 8%, so that at each time government sources were more important. (The remaining proportions were made up by the colleges and universities themselves.)

[29] It is interesting to note that this led to the move of the economist Theodore W. Schultz to Chicago; one might speculate on the long-term intellectual consequences of that move.

Congressmen hostile to social research. Such hostility was also fuelled by some of the research carried out in the Department of Agriculture and the Division of Program Surveys, which drew attention to poor conditions in the black community. The dangerous word 'social' has, moreover, suggested 'socialism' or related themes.[30] In addition, tales circulate about, for example, the political necessity to draw samples which include the right districts even if sampling theory would make that quite superfluous (Lundberg 1956). These things do not happen, though, because politicians take a close interest in social science, let alone being concerned with its technicalities; in general, they have taken no interest in it, and their interventions reflect that. More consistent interest would have meant less caprice. Congress' concerns have been political, sometimes very locally so and sometimes more globally and ideologically, though normally having much more to do with specific constituency interests such as farming or race relations than with anything recognisable as generalised class interests. As Chubin and McCartney (1982: 234) pointed out, what had become the conventional wisdom about modern government's need for state production of social knowledge to support policy was sharply disrupted by the Reagan administration's hostility to social research and (not altogether successful) attempt to withdraw from funding it; this too was surely 'political', if more ideologically so. There is much more which could be said about the recent period, but that is outside our remit.

FUNDING AND RESEARCH METHODS

We turn now to review the evidence for the argument that funding agencies have been responsible for creating a distortive emphasis on quantitative and scientistic methods in sociological research. The idea of 'distortion' of course carries strong evaluative overtones, which will be discussed later. Initially, we deal with the empirical issue: have funding patterns brought about a situation where there are more of such methods than the spontaneous growth of sociology would otherwise have generated? Different

[30] Thus Robert Merton found it necessary to add a lengthy Appendix on 'Socialization' to *The Student Physician* (ed. Merton, Reader and Kendall, 1957) in order to make it absolutely clear that the sociologists' sense of the word had nothing to do with 'socialized medicine'.

authors have approached the issues in different ways, and have not always deployed the full range of material which their conclusions seem to require. We review the main works which have provided data potentially relevant to these questions, and consider how adequate they are.

McCartney concludes that major funding agencies have a preference for statistical and 'scientific' work which is skewing the methodological style of sociology. His evidence for the agencies' preferences is thin; the criteria for evaluating proposals which he quotes as an example (1970: 34) are quite ambiguous. The main weight of his data, however, comes from journals. He shows that an increasing proportion of articles used statistics, and that the statistics became more sophisticated. Over the same period, more articles come to acknowledge financial support, and the supported articles more often use statistics than the unsupported ones; moreover, the specialties with the higher proportions of support were more likely to be expanding. He concludes that the use of statistics is more attractive to sponsors, and that financial support is affecting the growth and decline of specialty fields. Unfortunately, however, although his data are consistent with these conclusions they are equally consistent with other conclusions; the causal connections are not proven. We do not know that funders rejected more non-statistical applications, or that financial support was not led by growth of interest rather than vice versa.

Fisher's work is on Rockefeller foundations between the wars. His 1980 paper shows that their policy for social science in Britain favoured the empirical, 'scientific' and 'realistic', although much money was given to institutions rather than specific projects. His analysis is at the institutional level, and does not look at specific works or systematically compare the funded and the unfunded. His assertion that there was control over methodology rests mainly on the foundations' stated preference for the empirical over the theoretical. He recognises that there was a general trend in that direction anyway (1980: 299). However, he does not provide any evidence of discrimination between projects on methodological grounds. His 1983 paper is explicitly concerned with the policy-making process rather than its impact, but sees Rockefeller as supporting a dominant ideology of science and objectivity which maintains the existing social order. He recognises that the policies and outcomes did to some extent serve the interests of the social-science community (1983: 222). His book (1993) focuses on the (US) SSRC and its relation to Rockefeller, arguing – though again there is little on outcomes at the level of method – that it moulded the social sciences to take an objective, scientific approach to suit an applied technical role rather than one which was critical or fundamental. Fisher recognises that some social scientists played an active part in this process.

Bulmer and Bulmer (1981) agree with Fisher that in the 1920s the Rockefeller foundations' funding had the effect of encouraging more systematic empirical research and, in particular, quantitative work, without giving detailed documentation. On research methods, however, they see the crucial difference made being 'to enable university teachers to do this kind of research within their own institutions' (1981: 403), rather than for it to be conducted elsewhere. Bulmer (1984a) has also made a detailed study of sociology at the University of Chicago, and shows how Rockefeller money was used there. It made possible relatively large-scale quantitative research, but was also used to fund a range of qualitative work which has become famous as characterising the 'Chicago School'. It was not methodologically discriminatory funding because, in line with general Rockefeller practice of the time, it was given as block grants to the institution. Bulmer (1984b) argues that Fisher's 1983 interpretation puts too much stress on the initiating role of the foundations, since social scientists influenced them as well as vice versa. Ahmad's review suggests that the truth lies somewhere between them, and rightly adds that they tend (1991: 516) to assume that foundation policies were necessarily successful. All these authors, although they suggest general conclusions, are writing only about the Rockefeller foundations and the interwar period; it would be unwise to assume without further evidence that even totally convincing data on that also cover later times and other funding agencies.

Michael Useem (1976) has questionnaire data on federal government funding in anthropology, economics, political science and psychology. He shows that for his subjects using quantitative data over the past five years was correlated with having received federal research money over the same period; he concludes that it is clear from this – which it is not! – that 'government money is preferentially allocated to social scientists involved in quantitative . . . research' (1976: 152). He shows that the correlation between receipt of funds and use of quantitative data is almost unaffected when recent citations in social-science journals – taken as a measure of recognised contribution to the discipline – are controlled, and concludes that the federal government's priorities in allocating its money are different from those of the discipline. However, the period over which funding was asked about is 1968–73, and the citations counted are from 1973; it would have been more appropriate to have a recognition measure which preceded the funding. (Lipset and Ladd's data (1972: 82–4) show that in sociology high achievers in the discipline more often received federal money.) Michael Useem's data on the effects of federal funding on research plans are more convincing. He asked whether recent reductions in levels of federal funding had affected research plans, and found that they quite often had, more often for those whose research expenses were high and for those who in the past had applied for federal funds and only sometimes been successful. He concludes that the situation is one where both substantive and methodological aspects of research are 'subject to government influence' (1976: 158). This is plainly true, although to summarize the findings in that way is rather misleading. The types of methodological effect which respondents had anticipated included 'reduction in research scale' and looking for 'new sources of funding' (1976: 154), both of which are obvious direct responses to financial cutbacks but need not imply any change in the basic character of the research; this is a very different picture from one where government actively intervenes to affect methods. From 11 per cent (Economics) to 26 per cent (Psychology) anticipated use of 'less costly research methods', but there is no indication whether these would be less quantitative.

It is noticeable that the writings divide into two camps: those which have detailed material about foundation dynamics but only broad generalities about the social sciences, and those which have detailed material about social scientists or their publications but little about the role played by funding in producing them. There are practical reasons why this should be so; different data sources need to be combined to give the full picture, and it is scarcely practicable to put together quantitative data on the processes by which specific publications were generated. Nonetheless this unfortunately means that no writer, except perhaps Bulmer in relation to Chicago, has built a fully convincing case connecting the two. An obvious limitation of agency-based research is that it naturally focuses on what the agency did fund, and does not show what was done without needing funding; this limitation is intensified when the agency files are mainly on proposals accepted, not those rejected. This makes the comparisons which are crucial to demonstrating a causal difference hard.

What would need to be shown in order to demonstrate that funding had made the imputed difference to research methods?

1 Funding activity had been present in the relevant field.
2 Funding agencies had followed policies which, whatever their controllers' conscious intentions, in practice discriminated between some methods and others, favouring the 'scientific' in what they chose to fund.
3 The research actually funded was consistent with those policies.
4 The funding was sufficiently influential to produce an outcome different from what it would otherwise have been.

For such a difference to have been made *intentionally*, we would need to add to that list:

5 Agency policies deliberately favoured some research methods over others.

Item 4 on this list is the one which raises the crucial difficulty, because it requires a counterfactual conditional: what would have happened if the agency funding had not been present? The other items listed are necessary conditions for the effect of funding, but without this one the set does not provide sufficient conditions for the proposition to hold. However prominent the funding, however discriminatory the funders' policies, however well the work funded fitted their priorities, whatever their intentions, if the net outcome was not different from what it would have been in the absence of that funding it cannot be explained by the funding's presence. Summarising the data presented by other authors on our questions, we find clear evidence that quantitative work has increased and is more often funded, little material on detailed methodological discrimination by foundations, and nothing systematic on ways in which the outcome differs from what might otherwise have occurred. We attempt below to take the issue a little further forward, but first some methodological problems in interpreting the data need to be considered.

A first problem in treating the issue empirically is that some kinds of research cannot be carried out at all without funding from somewhere, and others may be much facilitated by funding. If such research is done, it is highly likely that it will have been externally funded. It does not follow that the researcher would not have chosen to do such research anyway if she or he had been able to. Under those circumstances, the increased availability of funding will increase the amount of such research done, but will not have changed the underlying methodological preferences. This suggests that it is desirable to distinguish, in discussing the question, between research which did not require funding, or could have been carried out tolerably without it, and that which did require it. (Such a distinction would be relatively easy in extreme cases – say, an international survey versus participant observation in the researcher's normal environment – but many intermediate cases might make it unclear.) To the extent that such a distinction can be made, one could then draw a line between funding which merely made a practical difference and that which changed intellectual directions. A practical difference is still a difference, but maybe not a 'distortion'.

To decide where to look for the impact of funding, we need to think about how and why funding agencies might affect matters.[31] If agencies simply provide more money, impartially distributed, what would that buy? It could merely pay for a larger total number of separate projects, in which case there would be no direct influence on methods. Indirectly, however, there could be consequences. If the larger number of projects involved a larger number of individual researchers, there could be greater diversity of character than before. If the larger number of projects was achieved by the same researchers as before doing more each, each would gain more experience and technical skill faster; this might just mean efficient assembly-line production, but it seems likely that it would also lead to at least minor innovations producing technical improvements. (These two are, in fact, potentially connected, in that a continuing flow of research justifies establishing a relatively permanent

---

[31] Another issue is whether sociologists determined agency policy, rather than vice versa. Such an account would not make funding agencies causally irrelevant, but it would imply that their role was that of an intervening rather than an independent variable. The sense in which funding can be seen as making a difference, beyond simply facilitating work of kinds sociologists wanted to do anyway (Bulmer and Bulmer 1981: 402), would then depend on whether agencies showed differential receptivity to the ideas of some sociologists rather than others. This has been discussed above.

research capability with advanced capital equipment and specialists in a division of labour – but once such a capability is set up it
needs to be kept in use to justify its existence, and that may imply
continuing to do more of the same kind of research.)

If the money did not simply buy more projects, it could buy more
expensive projects: larger numbers of cases and more representative samples, more time in the field, more longitudinal studies,
more and more highly qualified hired hands, more complex data
processing, more cross-national research . . . and so on. Impartially
distributed money would buy more of whatever has fundable costs.
If, on the other hand, agency largesse was guided by specific
methodological tastes, it would produce more of whatever those
tastes favoured – but that might be the same things. Only when the
guiding tastes were not for the things which are more expensive
could one observe the difference between partiality and impar-
tiality. But the really inexpensive does not need external funding,
so it may not appear as funded research even if agencies are
thoroughly in favour of it. (If it is funded at all, the funding is likely
to take the form of fellowships rather than project grants.) These
considerations point to serious practical difficulties in using
outcomes systematically to evaluate the methodological tastes of
the funders.

What, then, is it practically feasible to look at in order to explore
further the questions raised? The first point on our initial list is
not problematic; it can be taken as given. The second has become
more complicated, because it has become evident that we need to
distinguish between discrimination between research which does
and does not need funding, and discrimination between fundable
projects using different methods. The fourth point has become both
simpler and more complicated. It is simpler because for research to
be funded whose methods could not be used without funding self-
evidently leads to a different outcome. It is more complicated
because funding may not change the intellectual choices of the
people doing the research, and so could be seen as irrelevant to
the character of the discipline. The gaps in the evidence already
available relate to discrimination in foundation policy, the
character of unfunded research and the counterfactual of what
would have happened in the absence of funding. Below some data
are deployed which bear on these issues.

Did foundations discriminate methodologically? It has been

pointed out above that no major foundation had the remit of supporting social-scientific research as an end in itself, and that for them other ends, most often related to social policy, were formally the salient ones. When they did support social science, that was often a minor part of their total portfolio, and they moved in and out of social science over relatively short periods; the decision to do so was likely to be the effect of the idiosyncratic interest of particular officers. This general background is not one which supports a picture of long-term trustee policy to develop a social science useful for their purposes, let alone to fund some types of social-scientific work rather than others. It is thus not surprising that no foundation had a general aim which related to research methods; any top-level policies they had which affected methods must have arisen for other reasons, or had the effect as an accidental by-product of other concerns. Moreover, officers often stated privately that methods as such were not of interest. Some quotations from records exemplify these points:

Principles governing the Memorial's [LSRM] programme in the social sciences: It is inadvisable to attempt to influence the findings or conclusions of research and investigations through the designation of either personnel, specific problems to be attacked, or methods of inquiry to be adopted (RAC 6)

the only way to judge a proposal is by virtue of the intellectual capacity, the record of imagination, of dedication, and of interest of *the man who proposes to do this work*. The specification of the problem is almost always unimportant. (RFOH 1: 430)

A propos of the famous methodological work of the *American Soldier* (Stouffer, Guttman, Suchman et al.1949–1950):

remember that the Carnegie interest in Stouffer started with the applied problem of morale ... The methodology was Stouffer's interest ... appropriations from the Carnegie Corporation ... were rarely ... for straight methodological development, they were always focused on an important social question. (CCOH 4: 77)

The foundations did play a significant role in the funding of quantitative work, and of the development and diffusion of quantitative methods, but it does not follow that they were thereby showing a bias in that direction. Two points demonstrate that they were not. The first is that they quite often gave grants in such a form that they had no control over what they were used for; the second is that they also funded much qualitative, and indeed non-empirical, work. The second point may be supported by a simple listing of some of the work that was funded, chosen from that not covered by block grants so that it is clear the foundation knew what it was funding:

> Ford, Behavioral Sciences, 1955: 'Support for work in social theory under the direction of Talcott Parsons.' In addition, Carnegie funded the production of *Toward A General Theory of Action* (Parsons and Shils 1951).

> Ford, Behavioral Sciences, 1952, inaugurated a programme part of which was to improve the ability of 'behavioral scientists' to share the contributions of disciplines such as history, philosophy and the humanities; under this there was a grant to the University of Chicago for a programme coordinating the humanities and social sciences.

> Howard S. Becker received several grants for his early work in association with Everett Hughes: a Ford-funded postdoctoral fellowship covered his work on choice of profession, and Carnegie money supported his and Geer's study of Kansas undergraduates (Becker, Geer and Hughes 1968).

> Ford, grant to support production of a volume on cases in field work (which became Junker 1960) to be used for training in methods of field observation.

We do not have numerical data on the proportions of work of different kinds funded, but such qualitative material is sufficient to show that, if they wanted to discriminate in favour of quantitative research, they were strikingly inefficient in implementing this policy.

We turn next to consider the character of unfunded research, and what happened in the absence of funding. These are addressed by analysis of a sample of articles for the period 1923–88, drawn from the generally recognised 'major' journals. This is not, and does not claim to be, a representative sample of research in American sociology. For the argument, however, it does not need to be, since it is generally agreed that the tendencies imputed to funding are most salient in hegemonic mainstream work, and in articles rather than books. This sample should, therefore, make the strongest case for the impact of funding. Each article has been coded as funded or not[32] and, where funded, the source has been categorised as foundation, governmental or other. Second, the content of each article has been categorised as empirical or non-empirical. For the empirical, the methods used have been divided into quantitative, qualitative and mixed. (Since most writers in this area have talked simply of quantitative versus qualitative work rather than making more sophisticated distinctions, we follow them in that.) It has also been noted whether the data used were the author's own, and whether they were collected on the author's own college. The non-empirical have been divided into those which favoured quantification and 'science', those which did not and those which were neutral. What do the results show?

First, the proportion of empirical articles has risen steadily; the largest jump is from the 38% of the 1920s to the 64% of the 1930s, and thereafter it increases by about 5% per decade until the 89% of the 1980s. In the earlier years, a negligible proportion of even the empirical articles appear to arise from funded work; in the 1930s and 1940s it was about 20% of the empirical, and almost none of the non-empirical. Thereafter it rose for the empirical to 40% in the 1950s, nearly 60% in the 1970s and nearly 70% in the 1980s, while for the non-empirical it reached around 20% in the 1960s and 1970s before leaping to over 60% (of a very small total) in the 1980s. Over the same time-span, the proportion of articles which are quantitative or favour quantification has risen strikingly, to include a substantial majority of the total by the 1960s. The rise has not, however, been even, with relatively large changes between the 1940s and the 1950s, and the 1950s and 1960s (see table 4).

How well does this pattern fit an explanation in terms of funding? We look first at data internal to the sample of articles. A higher proportion of the empirical articles was funded. In no year did more than 10 per cent of them have foundation funding; the main source of variation is in the proportion with government funding, which

---

[32] A problem for the adequacy of the data is caused here by the LSRM policy that their support should not be publicly mentioned (Bulmer and Bulmer 1981: 382); this, however, only affects the 1920s. As Crawford and Biderman point out (1970: 54–5), not all support is acknowledged, though the tendency has been for this to be regarded as increasingly an obligation – but it is not usual to acknowledge that from one's primary employer, so to that extent a count of acknowledgments gives only a partial picture. Another problem is that one can frequently not tell whether the funding acknowledged was for a specific project or given under some more general head; if the latter, the fact of funding of course implies less about the control exercised by the policies of the funding agency.

Table 4. *Proportions of articles^a not externally funded*

Date	Empirical articles		Non-empirical articles	
	%	N	%	N
1920s	94	50	100	81
1930s	81	102	98	57
1940s	83	121	98	54
1950s	60	116	100	41
1960s	41	108	84	25
1970s	41	134	77	26
1980s	31	126	38	16

^{a} The articles counted were all those appearing in alternate issues in years ending with 3 or 8 in the *American Journal of Sociology, American Sociological Review* and *Social Forces*.

rose markedly in the later 1960s when government became the largest funding source, a position which it has maintained. A very high proportion of the funded articles uses quantitative methods; it has been 90 per cent or more since the 1960s. However, as table 5 shows, this does not distinguish funded articles sharply from unfunded ones, since these too have been predominantly quantitative since the 1950s, although the proportion has been lower. Looking at the same data the other way round, we see that a higher proportion of quantitative than non-quantitative articles has received funding. It might be suspected that those without funding would be less likely to have been able to collect their own data, and a comparison between the funded and unfunded research very broadly supports that interpretation. However, there is a marked tendency from the later 1960s for the proportion of funded researchers using their own data to decline, until in 1988 it was only 44 per cent, the same figure as that for the unfunded. That clearly requires some explanation other than the mere presence of funding.

No account which stresses foundations as a funding source can do much to explain the overall pattern, since foundations have simply not funded enough of the articles;[33] it would need to be discussed in

[33] This picture is supported by the estimates of M. Robinson (1983: 36), which show the proportion of funding provided for social-science research by foundations declining

Table 5. *Proportions of funded and unfunded empirical articles whose data were quantitative*[a]

	Funded articles		Unfunded articles	
	%	N	%	N
1920s	(50)	2	41	41
1930s	(89)	9	47	73
1940s	60	20	35	88
1950s	74	43	55	65
1960s	92	68	67	42
1970s	96	75	78	50
1980s	92	85	74	35

[a] Articles with data of mixed character are omitted here.

terms either of government funding or of all sources combined. The proportion of empirical articles has increased rather smoothly over time, in a way which does not correspond to the more abrupt discontinuities in proportions funded. Even if the two had moved together, however, it would have been as compatible with an account which saw sociologists raising the money to do what they wanted as with one which saw funding as the motor of change – and even in 1988 a quarter of the empirical articles reported no funding, so it was possible to do publishable studies with limited resources. The increasing proportion of quantitative work among both funded and unfunded articles makes funding a poor explanation of quantification; the higher level of quantification among funded work could easily be accounted for by the greater costs of collecting quantifiable data – or of high-technology processing of available data.

One reason why numbers of highly quantitative empirical articles have not required funding is that their authors have not been using data which they collected themselves. In some cases this is demographic work using Census and related data. More recently, however, secondary analysis of large-scale data sets has become extremely common. This reflects the growth of computer technology, which makes access to existing data-sets easy. It also

from 22% in 1956 to 5% in 1980, while government funding rose from 31% to 61%. (The remainder is accounted for by university funding.)

reflects the emergence of social-research institutions: the data bank, and the public-use data set such as the General Social Survey. In combination, these open up a wide range of possibilities to researchers who could not themselves have collected such data. It is clear that, for instance, it is almost inconceivable that a graduate student could set up a study using a national representative sample for her dissertation. (My tables overestimate the number of projects receiving funding, because for some articles the funding recorded was a student stipend rather than financing the data.)

A qualitative scan of the journal articles over the period rapidly shows that a picture of the impact of funding which sees no alternative to accepting funding if one wants to undertake quantitative work, and sees that funding as automatically leading research in directions inconsistent with disciplinary interests, is misleading. First, there are, especially in the middle part of our period, ways in which sociologists managed to carry out quantitative empirical work without any significant external funding. On the one hand, they did relatively small, local studies, often using their students as either the subject or the research staff. It is not without reason that the sociology of sophomores has been mocked, but it certainly took place, and sometimes student subjects were used even when there was external funding. This did not necessarily lead to trivial work; for instance, R. F. Bales reports (1984) that the availability of a special laboratory at Harvard, and the use of students as subjects, enabled him to continue his well-respected work on small groups over many years without external funding. Russell Middleton (1984) can describe a sequence of imaginative small-scale projects, leading to publications in major journals, carried out with students as subjects and/or research staff while he was at Florida State with little access to external funds. On the other hand, many sociologists also made secondary use of data already collected by others. This has, of course, always been normal practice among demographers, who have applied increasingly sophisticated quantitative techniques to Census and other official data. It may reasonably be presumed that, in the absence of external funding, these would have been among the typical modes of empirical research; other patterns would be the one-person project drawing heavily on personal experience, and work using historical and other documentary sources. Work of a more parochial character would be likely to mean that researchers were compelled to rely more on the cooperation of officials who control access to situations and records, which would have had its own – undesirable – effects on what was done.

The careers of a number of the leading quantitative sociologists confirm that it was not necessary to have funding to pursue that line, and that their interest arose quite independently of any funding agency's attempt to stimulate it. In the older generation, Ogburn was a member of a cohort of Columbia students who were inspired by Giddings (and trained by econometrician H. L. Moore) to take up statistical methods, and who dispersed to train their students along the same lines; Chapin was another particularly important member of this cohort (S. P. Turner 1994: 42–6). They held to these commitments at a period when specific funding for such work did not exist, and it did not offer an obvious career strategy. Stouffer trained as a sociologist but, inspired by Ogburn (Hauser 1961: 364), became interested in quantitative methods at a very early career stage; a year's fellowship in London to study with British statisticians was significant in his development, but that was from a general programme many of whose other fellowships were used for quite different purposes, so the interest was strictly his own. Lazarsfeld was a forerunner of several who came to sociology from backgrounds in mathematics or natural science. Blalock, Coleman and Sewell followed the same pattern,[34] and either spontaneously carried on using the skills they had acquired or were recruited by colleagues to work on problems for which they were unusually well equipped. Leo Goodman started as a sociology major, but was encouraged to learn more mathematics to understand statistics; he ended with a joint major, and then did graduate work in mathematics but with a view to sociology. At that stage he held an SSRC fellowship, but again a general-purpose one.

SSRC ran summer workshops on mathematics in the 1950s funded by the Ford Behavioral Sciences programme, but initiated entirely from within the academic community. The initiative started with a symposium of the American Mathematical Society, the Econometric Society and the Institute of Mathematical

---

[34] Blalock's undergraduate degree was in mathematics with a physics minor (Blalock 1988: 108); Coleman came from a background in chemical engineering (Coleman 1984); Sewell had an undergraduate major in sociology but also had met the prerequisites for medical school with the intention of becoming a physician (Sewell 1983).

Statistics; this led to an approach to other learned societies, including the ASA. It was agreed that materials to raise standards should be developed, and the SSRC was approached. The numbers actually involved in foundation-supported mathematical pro-grammes were not large, though of course they probably had multiplier effects through their example and teaching. The 1953 summer workshop had only five sociologists among those admitted and awarded study grants, though one of these was Otis Dudley Duncan, who went on to play a very important role in quantitative sociology. However, he reports that he was attracted to this because he had always been oriented to quantitative training, starting an undergraduate minor in maths, but without finding very good teaching before: 'for me it just sort of solidified my grasp of what I could do already' (Duncan 1984).

It is not the fact of foundation funding which can account for the large number of applications from junior people for these work-shops, or the interest shown by the more senior fellows at the (Ford-funded) Center for Advanced Studies in the Behavioral Sciences in optional mathematical courses quite distinct from the activities for which they were selected for fellowships. There was by the 1950s a common, if not universal, feeling among sociologists themselves that it was important to acquire improved technical equipment for quantitative research. In funding much quantitative work, foundations were not so much pursuing their own agendas as taking the advice of leading academics who identified this as an unmet need. Lazarsfeld's programme of methodological codifi-cation and production of advanced training materials must have helped to make method more salient for sociologists generally. It could not have been carried out without significant funding, but it was very much his baby.

What, then, are the general conclusions to be reached about the relation between funding and methods? It has been repeatedly shown that US journal sociology has become increasingly empirical and quantitative in character. That may be taken as given. There can be no doubt that the total, and proportionate, amounts of external funding for sociological research have also increased over time, although its sources have fluctuated markedly, moving from Rockefeller to governmental dominance and with spasmodic but important interventions by other major foundations. The minimal condition for a causal relationship between the two is, thus, met, and we cannot doubt that the availability of funding made possible some research which could not otherwise have been done, and so shifted the balance of the whole. It is nonetheless argued here that the strong version of the causal proposition linking them cannot be supported, because the counterfactual conditional required will not stand up. Our theses are these:

It was not only quantitative work that received funding, and foundations did not in general have either a formal or a *de facto* methodological policy which discriminated at that level (though particular officers may sometimes have exercised their own intellectual tastes).

There were strong tendencies towards increasingly empirical and quantitative work in the discipline anyway, as is shown by the fact that unfunded work also moved in these directions.

Consequently, if external funding had not been provided research would probably still have been increasingly empirical and quantitative, though much of it would have had a different character: fewer national samples, less internationally comparative work, heavier secondary use of data originally collected for non-sociological purposes, more work done by and on students and college communities. (There would also have been less research carried out, of whatever kind.)[35]

However, such conclusions on the empirical questions do not dispose of all the issues raised by the literature. As Hawthorn (1991: 158) has pointed out, discussion of alternative possibilities 'should not require us to unwind the past. And the consequences we draw from these alternatives should initially fit with the other undisturbed runnings-on in that world'. Even sociology in the USA has a long enough history, sufficiently closely entangled with other academic and worldly developments, for it to be scarcely possible to construct a plausible alternative world where only the funding factor is missing. This difficulty is one that this chapter shares with those that it criticises, and we have tried to take it seriously by specifying a convincing alternative world.

Other writers have often had implicit alternative worlds whose

---

[35] It tends to be forgotten what a short while it is since research by faculty members was not taken for granted, and support of it not seen as the normal responsibility of a respectable university; Sibley (1974: 84) describes SSRC programmes as late as the 1950s designed to deal with this problem.

implications they have not seriously attempted to spell out, because the alternative is not really an empirical one. There is an ideological agenda which is as important to the overall interpretation as is the data, even if not all writers are as frank about this as Fisher (1993) in his Introduction, where he declares his commitment to a 'critical' approach and a Poulantzian-Marxist theory of the state. The idea of 'distortion' (applicable whether or not that word is used) implies more than just difference from what might otherwise have happened. The counterfactual state of affairs envisaged is the one which would be preferred, rather than the one most likely actually to have happened. One may infer that it has typically been one which would have had more theoretical work (of the right kind!), more qualitative research styles, more macroscopic and historical work, more work which is critical in its assumptions and more which is not directly useful to any part of the current power structure (but is useful to its opponents?). The intellectual evaluations made are not ones which every sociologist need share. (Is it necessarily so bad, for instance, to be a competent technician, even a 'mere' one?) But many of these changes might seem desirable from a purely disciplinary perspective, and to that extent this is invoked by these writers to support the claim that external funding has introduced distortions. This is hardly consistent, since they are themselves in favour of development in directions which favour their political agenda rather than a purely disciplinary one. This shows up in a particularly odd form when, like Galliher and McCartney (1973: 78), they appear implicitly to criticise more 'scientific' work on the ground that it is more accurate and predicts better. (This is criticism better addressed to the society which uses the sociology, since it is really about ends, not means. In this context political as well as historical counterfactuals become relevant, and one might wonder whether their preferred types of society might not also want or need research as effective as that provided by US capitalism.) Left and right have sometimes shared an objection to styles of work which do not guarantee support for their preferred conclusions. It is not hard to choose terms which present the preferences of Gouldner or Fisher in a less attractive light than theirs, in the same way as they do for those they attack: an attraction to large statements unsupported by systematic data, deliberate bias to preferred values – and that's only the methodological ones!

The argument is not that sociology should not be related to political concerns, but that for clarity of thought it is desirable to distinguish those from concerns about such matters as the basis for plausibility in reaching empirical conclusions. For our purposes here, the political agenda is relevant only because it seems to have led some writers in directions which are not helpful to explanation. To explain what actually happened, one needs to consider alternative possible lines of development chosen for their historical plausibility, not their ideological attractiveness. We conclude that, in the field of research methods, the counter-factual possibilities sketched above are more plausible. If they are, it follows that the role of external funding has been important in relation to methods, but not so determinative or so independent of factors internal to the discipline as some writers have suggested.

CHAPTER 6

Social structures of
academic life

No sociologist should doubt that the social structures of academic life are relevant to understanding its intellectual processes, though they figure surprisingly little in histories of sociology, where disembodied ideas tend to march in orderly Whig succession. The social units given much the most attention are departments, and there is a conventional version of the history of US sociology which can be summarised thus: Chicago, then Harvard and Columbia. This entails a number of assumptions which may be questioned, of which the most salient is the overwhelming importance of the most prominent departments. (In the next chapter we discuss some of the processes of creation of such reputations.) Importance for what? Fame, certainly; hegemony, maybe; quantitative dominance, not necessarily; Stephen Turner's work on Giddings' students and 'mainstream sociology' (S. P. Turner 1994) makes clear that there may be currents which, for whatever reason, have at least as much practical significance as those commonly identified.

An alternative type of account deals in 'schools', which may or may not coincide with departments, and the utility of such accounts is considered below. Only in the case of the 'Chicago School' is there a clear reference to methods, though they are also implied in the selection of Columbia, since BASR was so evidently part of what made it important. It is conceivable that the units relevant for methods are different from those relevant for theory or substantive specialisms; if that is so, accounts criticised in relation to the material here are only undermined by those criticisms insofar as they claim, explicitly or implicitly, to cover method too. In this chapter we shall not attempt to cover every aspect of the social structures of academic life as they bear on research methods, but to sketch a general outline, pick out significant features and highlight some which merit more attention than they have often received.

(The funding system, which is certainly part of the relevant structures, is omitted here because covered in chapter 5.)

I start by looking at departments, their internal unity and its bases and their consequentiality for their graduates; in doing so, we are concerned with what it is about the department that produces effects, since this raises questions of interpretation and of method in the history of sociology. The background to this account of the role of some departments is a national academic system which was (and is) highly differentiated and stratified. For our purposes we are mainly concerned with the 'research universities', initially a relatively small number, but becoming a much larger one in the postwar expansion, which was an expansion of style as well as of numbers. (The role of funding changes in this is discussed in chapter 5.) These included both private institutions such as Chicago and Harvard, and major state universities such as those of California, Minnesota and Wisconsin. These universities traditionally competed with each other for faculty, students, funding and reputation, though the major focus of that competition was likely to be other institutions at the same level or in the same region. Such competition requires some sense of institutional or departmental identity, though it also creates a counter-tendency to uniformity as each tries to establish a claim to strength in major areas, sometimes by buying in faculty from rivals.

DEPARTMENTS

The school of doctoral training is commonly regarded as conferring a shared identity, to be carried through a career whatever the form that takes; it does not follow that departmental images always give a correct impression of intellectual style. Some graduate departments seem to have been consequential for their students, if not always in relation to method, especially if they had a distinctive technique or theory to transmit. Columbia under Merton and Lazarsfeld has been much written about;[1] it was clearly BASR as much as or more than the formal department which counted as an

---

[1] See Glock 1979, Coleman 1980. Columbia under Giddings is before our period, but S. P. Turner (1994) has made the case for it as having a clear long-term methodological influence; Camic and Xie (1994), however, draw attention to the extent to which the statistical styles advocated there were not specific to the department but shared across several fields at Columbia.

intellectual and social unit. BASR was united by the interests and the charisma of Lazarsfeld, which created a setting in which there was a network of working relationships linking staff and students in both practical research and the development of methodological thought and writing, and supported theoretically by his cooperation with Merton. (Not every member of the department was happy with a situation which some saw as placing BASR and its concerns too much at the centre, in ways which excluded those with other interests.)[2] Alumni of BASR went out and founded survey research units elsewhere in their turn. It was probably particularly important that Columbia provided a theory and a method and, in contrast to many other settings, a strong link between them, which meant that its influence could be carried into many fields.

Harvard at the same period provides an instructive contrast. The former department of sociology had been succeeded by the Department of Social Relations, and its structure as a multi-disciplinary department meant that it contained several different intellectual traditions; moreover, there were also important links with other units at Harvard such as the Business School, and maverick individuals such as Zipf and Bridgman could offer courses within it. The Laboratory of Social Relations, its research facility under Stouffer, was an umbrella organisation rather than a unit, and Stouffer, though distinguished and congenial, did not create working relationships as Lazarsfeld did – J. A. Davis (1984), a student there, remarked: 'He was a fine man, a perfect gentleman, but just not particularly interested in students or disciples' – and so had less influence (J. Platt 1986c: 108–9). The links at Harvard seem to have followed theoretical lines, with the network centring on Parsons, though most of his students did not go on to do theoretical work of the same kind as his own;[3] his lack of methodological

---

[2] 'the push toward methodology, because of ambitiousness and love of promotion on the part of Paul and Merton, has had unfavorable effects. In the first place, it has created a group of "second class" students – those who do not rate as useful research workers or who do not care to make methodology their major. It has led to the neglect of teaching and de-emphasis of content' (Abel, *Journal of Thoughts and Events*, 11: 45, 1950). Abel went so far as to take the opportunity to criticise his colleagues (for their undue empiricism) to Wormser of the Congressional Special Committee to Investigate Tax-Exempt Foundations (on which see also pp. 165–6).

[3] We may note also that an intellectually very consequential set of relationships depended on someone at Harvard but outside the department: Henderson, a physiologist who had a longstanding interest in social theory, ran a discussion group on Pareto in which several key sociologists, including Parsons, took part (Heyl 1968).

commitments gave this no consequences for method. He is not generally thought of first for his political and fundraising skills but, as recent work has shown, he possessed these in abundance and used them in ways which established his influence, on the national scene as much as within the department.[4]

The interwar Chicago department was a very meaningful unit for its members, not so much because there was a shared viewpoint or method as because research was treated as a communal activity (Bulmer 1984a: chs. 8, 11; J. Platt 1994a); despite the statistics versus case study cleavage, data were shared and theses and monographs typically used multiple methods and data sources. However, it could be misleading to think of this as a setting adequately described in terms of what lay within the department's formal boundaries, since as a research base it was closely integrated with social workers and reformers in its local community, who were also conducting research and often employed graduate students on it (J. Platt 1994a.). Bulmer (1983c) has documented the interwar importance of the department's Society for Social Research both in cementing internal links and in maintaining contacts with Chicago students now located elsewhere. After the Second World War there was still a sense of unity, and of a shared identity as an empirically oriented department contrasted with the more theoretical style of Harvard though this no longer rested, in a much larger group, on primary-group links (J. Platt 1995a). The department nonetheless contained highly divergent research styles, associated with different research subgroupings, and the greater specialisation of method meant that the old tradition of students using the whole range of methods died away. The wider Chicago community was less relevant as research had become more professionalised and university-based.

The department at the University of Washington under Lundberg was a meaningful social unit, with Lundberg at the centre socially as well as organisationally, and it had many practices which promoted this. His former graduate students describe how there were regular parties at his house to which they were invited, at which sociology was discussed; his bachelor status at the time made him socially more available to students than the average professor. There was a compulsory weekly seminar for students and

[4] See Klausner and Lidz 1986.

faculty at which work in progress was presented, and the sense of communal effort and commitment to research was shown in the practice of circulating offprints of publications to every member of the department. In another sense departmental identity was sealed by the production of a departmental textbook (Lundberg, Schrag and Larsen 1954); the recruitment of Larsen to contribute to this while still a student (replacing a professor who left) again shows the extent to which students were involved. Graduate students who took on undergraduate teaching were not teaching assistants, but had their own classes, a symbolic recognition of equality. The research climate was such that most graduate students had publications before they completed the doctorate. The orientation was a cosmopolitan one, to sociology nationally rather than inwards to the university, and at Lundberg's parties students often met distinguished visitors such as Lazarsfeld who were passing through. There were three different organisational focuses for research, which provided jobs and dissertation topics for many students: Calvin Schmid's population laboratory, Delbert Miller's work for the Air Force, and the Washington Public Opinion Laboratory (WPOL) directed by Stuart Dodd. When students were ready to move on, Lundberg put effort into placing them well; Lyle Shannon (1993) reports that when he told Lundberg of the job he had found for himself he made him resign it, saying: 'I didn't put all that effort in for you to take a job like that – I'll get you one in the Big Ten' – which he did. In consequence, Shannon recounts, when there was a big reunion in Seattle some years later of the cohort who got their degrees around 1951 they had all made full professor, and some were already head of department or even Dean. This departmental cohesion did not, however, last; Lundberg died relatively young in 1966, Dodd became increasingly eccentric, WPOL lost funding as state and military sources declined, and the department's expansion destroyed its primary-group character. There is still, however, contact among some of the surviving students of the period, who keep the memory of Lundberg green.[5]

What was the continuing intellectual influence of this socially vibrant setting? One of its more striking features is the

[5] This is reflected by the fact that when I sent a draft paper on Lundberg and his circle to one member it was circulated to several others, so that I received useful unsolicited comments on it. The same happened with a paper on Lazarsfeld.

unimportance of Dodd's work, despite his centrality to the department. He was well liked, but had few if any disciples, and even those who did their dissertations with him could, like Larsen, avoid using his system of symbols. Lundberg is certainly seen as a continuing inspiration by some, but this does not lead them to do work identifiable as the product of his school, except in the sense of a generalised identification with 'science'. (Catton, for instance, has had a career in environmental sociology in which he has done work which he sees as Lundbergian in spirit in its commitment to crossing boundaries between social and biological science (Catton 1993), but this is not similar to Lundberg's own work.) But that is perhaps the normal fate of programmatic writers; what Lundberg had to transmit was a stance rather than a technique or a theory.

In departments with some real unity of character, that unity did not always rest on shared sociological ideas of the kind conventionally thought of when defining 'schools'. A leading example of this point is the University of North Carolina under Howard Odum, where it seems evident that commitment to Southern regional identity was the crucial focus, uniting those who used demographic data in quantitative delineation of the region with those who, like Odum himself, analysed folksongs and wrote up their material in semi-fictional modes (see e.g. Odum 1928). His Institute for Research in Social Science had an interdisciplinary regional remit.[6] The departmental journal, *Social Forces*, makes this very clear in editorial matter as well as the type and authors of articles. An article in the 25th anniversary celebration issue (Odum 1945) reviews the history of their approach. This identity does not obviously point in any particular methodological direction as conventionally defined, though in that article Odum states his position that regionalism is a methodological approach inasmuch as it implies that 'the folk-regional society or culture' is the appropriate unit for social study.(1945: 253). However, the regional concern created some specialisation in ecological approaches, and the department was for other reasons 'a bastion of correlational methods' (S. P. Turner and J. H. Turner 1990: 52). The regional concern also ensured considerable interest in issues related to

---

[6] For an excellent history of this, see B. Johnson and M. M. Johnson 1980. More useful historical material on all aspects of the department at UNC is given in the vol. 23, March 1945 issue of *Social Forces*.

206 SOCIOLOGICAL RESEARCH METHODS IN AMERICA

agriculture and rural life, a concern present in most of the large land-grant universities because of their setting and the nature of the relationship to their communities. The institutional segregation of rural sociology encouraged the maintenance of relatively distinct research traditions which, especially in the Agricultural Experiment Stations, were influenced by other disciplines represented there, including natural sciences.[7] Rural sociology had a strong quantitative tradition, which one may impute partly to this intellectual setting, combined with the resources to collect data when others did not have them; S. P. Turner and J. H. Turner (1990: 79) suggest also that the political constraints of their situation led to the pursuit of methodological rigour as a way of avoiding the political issues their data could raise.

Most of the departments mentioned above are well documented and, without fresh research, one cannot make a strong case about the character or significance of undocumented departments. However, significant numbers of students were taught and future professors and researchers trained in other departments. For instance, the figures show a steady contribution to the total numbers of doctorates in sociology being made by Ohio State[8] and by Catholic University. Other more prominent departments which have also contributed steadily to the totals, but hardly figure in historical accounts, include Cornell, Michigan, New York University, Wisconsin and Yale.[9] The students and staff at these other

[7] Rural sociologists had their own journal, *Rural Sociology*, from 1936, and the Rural Sociological Society, founded in 1937, developed from the earlier rural sociology section within the American Sociological Society.

[8] A ten-page xeroxed history of the department, written by its former chairman Raymond Sletto, is available from the University Archives. This shows a number of relatively well-known sociologists on the faculty (some, such as Kurt Wolff and Melvin Seeman, before they were established as such), but noone who figures largely in general histories of the discipline. A. Meier (1977: 265) remarks that it produced a disproportionate number of the total black PhDs in the 1950s which, given the difficulty for blacks even then in finding jobs in research universities, might do something to account for this particular case.

Some sources on other less-known departments are Martindale 1976 and Fine and Severance 1985 (Minnesota), Angell 1976? (Michigan), McGuire and Dawes 1983 (North Dakota), Sica 1983 (Kansas), Hill 1988 (Nebraska). Some of these are somewhat tendentious, as much concerned to give the authors' standpoint on events as to provide systematic data.

[9] Each of these probably provided approximately the same number of doctorates as Harvard over the period 1934–47, as did Catholic University. Different sources (e.g. listings in the *American Journal of Sociology* and the Association of Research Libraries' publications) give different numbers, so precise figures are not offered. The most easily accessible source, Sibley (1963: 65–6), covers only 1950–60; its figures are consistent with the general

departments may have been less productive and original in research than those at the best-known institutions, but even if they were that would not justify historical neglect; mundane research and routine methods are also part of the picture.

In relation to the role of departments in research outcomes, the methodological issue of the counterfactual needs to be raised: what would have happened otherwise? So many different aspects of departments are potentially relevant that this is very hard to answer. At least one small aspect can, however, be addressed: did individuals entering graduate work have already formed methodological predispositions which they simply continued to follow? Systematic data on this are not available, but my interview responses suggest that, although some cases look as though they fit that model, many others do not. Students could end up in a particular department more or less accidentally, or choose one because a member of faculty was there who turned out, once they arrived, to have left. Moreover, even in the departments with a pronounced character different students took different routes through them; R. Freed Bales' students would have different experiences of Harvard from Samuel Stouffer's, Everett Hughes' students would have different experiences of Chicago from Philip Hauser's. Some students, moreover, may choose influences from people not present in the department. Thus Winkin (1988) shows how Goffman, often seen as a distinctive Chicago product, was strongly influenced by people in the Toronto department before he went to Chicago and by Kenneth Burke who was not at Chicago (and not a sociologist).[10] Hubert Blalock (1984) said that among those who influenced him most were George Homans and Herbert Simon, despite the fact that he never met them.

But departmental character is not defined only by the members of faculty present, though that is the aspect easiest to collect data on. Numbers of people mention the importance of other students; these may be especially significant when, as in the well documented case of the Chicago department in the immediate postwar period, there is a large student cohort and an unfavourable staff–student

impression conveyed in the text, though at that time Harvard production had expanded relatively. Numerically it shows Ohio State ranking seventh.

[10] Goffman also got bad grades in his early years at Chicago, did not get on with Blumer, was not approved by Hughes, and did his doctoral fieldwork at Edinburgh and wrote the material up in Paris without returning to Chicago!

ratio; several members of that cohort have said that it was really other students who taught them (J. Platt 1995a). Also relevant to departmental character, if in a somewhat Pickwickian sense, are the resources to which students have access in other departments of the same institution, whether through compulsory minors, optional courses or less formal individual relations. Camic and Xie (1994) have shown how at Columbia in 1890–1915 the cross-departmental contacts and climate were crucial to the formation of a distinctive interest in statistical work. Bulmer (1984a: 190–202) has shown the importance of cross-disciplinary contacts at Chicago in the 1920s; G. H. Mead is commonly regarded as a formative figure in the Chicago department – but he was not a member of it (J. D. Lewis and R. L. Smith 1980). Probably similar stories could be told of other institutions. It is striking how many among the committed methodologists mention contacts with psychologists, philosophers, anthropologists or economists as important to their learning.

Those professors who seem to have had most lasting practical influence on students were those who involved them in ongoing empirical work, for which they had funding to provide employment opportunities, and these were not necessarily the same ones as the prominent advocates. At Chicago, for instance, several people mentioned how important Ernest Burgess was in that way after the end of the major Rockefeller funding; he probably had much more importance than Blumer, though not personally so inspiring and figuring much less in historical accounts oriented to theory and to programmatic statements. The research done in the departments was also important in another way: it was heavily drawn on for teaching material, and not only as a source of examples to illustrate general points. Several respondents who did graduate work at leading departments mention that they were hardly taught there about the work done at the other leading departments,[11] which tended to be mentioned only disparagingly (see below), though one may presume that only the largest departments could limit their teaching to local work. Naturally some students read more widely,

---

[11] Rainwater (1984) said of his time as a graduate student at Chicago that: 'It was almost institutionalised in Chicago, the feeling that we were in competition with and better than Merton and his crew, so unless you wanted to be a critic, if you were interested in tools, you tended not to read that stuff very much.'

but this surely limited their initial perspectives on the field, though it would only make an important difference to the outcome if the work done in the various places was of different enough character. It was assumed to be, at any rate: 'We were hired two people from Columbia and two people from Chicago, a sort of Noah's Ark way of establishing an outpost in North Dakota' (Rossi 1984). Such hirings, like the famous recruitment from Columbia to Chicago in the 1950s, could diversify the receiving department and so support greater homogeneity.

Many authors have discussed patterns of stratification within the discipline, which usually imply dominance of some departments by leading others (e.g. Gross 1970, Knudsen and Vaughan 1969, Shichor 1973, Shils 1980). Some forms of 'dominance' are purely quantitative: it is hardly surprising if departments producing more doctorates supply more of the discipline's faculty than do those producing fewer, and if those faculty members publish a higher proportion of all articles than do the smaller number of those with other origins.[12] The emphasis on Chicago in the literature has been historically justifiable on purely numerical grounds, though some versions give the impression that its prominence was simply due to merit; its postwar 'decline' also reflects a relative numerical decline as departments elsewhere expanded or started up (J. Platt 1995a). To the extent that large departments have more resources, they are always likely to be able to buy in talent from smaller ones and so to concentrate the 'best', whatever its origins.

Non-numerical modes of dominance are matters of status or hegemony – not always easy to separate empirically from numerical bases.[13] The model of centre and periphery has been used to describe the situation, and it has obvious attractions, though the connotations of shared values which Shils attaches to the model

---

[12] Sibley shows (1963: 72–3) that a higher proportion of the graduates of the most prestigious departments found employment in university teaching, and that their graduates predominated among the chairmen of departments offering doctoral degrees and earned more in both academic and non-academic jobs. This, of course, does not demonstrate that the department *produced* the effect, though it is consistent with that conclusion.

[13] Status has traditionally been measured by either reputational studies or citation studies, both appropriate if interpreted as saying what data of that type will bear; more relevant to influence on practical method, however, would be imitation, which needs to be measured by observing the methods actually used. Those, however, do not say where they came from, unless there is an innovation clearly contributed by one individual or group, which is often not the case.

may not be appropriate; at the periphery, jealousy and resentment may accompany or overwhelm respect and deference. The early relationship between Chicago and lesser midwestern universities, and perhaps between Columbia and other New York area institutions, can be seen as fitting the model, but the resentment of Chicago dominance, leading to the foundation of the *American Sociological Review* and the promotion of rival candidates for president of the American Sociological Association, is well known (Lengermann 1979). Lengermann suggests a cleavage of interests between those in more and less secure positions within the profession. At least before the Second World War sociology was, like the rest of national life in the era before easy routine flight,[14] highly regionalised, and this counteracted national centralisation; journal articles were less important and, as S. P. Turner and J. H. Turner (1990) have argued, the emphasis on textbooks as a key mode of publication meant that authors looked outwards to a wider constituency more than they do when more specialist types of publication are to the fore.

One notable aspect of stratification and hegemony is the need felt, at least by candidates for leadership among departments, to define what they possess as different from, and superior to, what other candidates for leadership offer. Listening to respondents who were in graduate school in the 1950s, when there was real competition, one can see how they learned and/or were taught to revere the local styles and exemplars and to criticise their rivals. For instance:

to the graduate student, there was no discipline of sociology outside Columbia . . . There was a sociological literature of some importance . . . but except for the work of Talcott Parsons, which Merton admitted to it, that literature was all written by Europeans no longer alive. The effective absence of a discipline west of the Hudson River was most strongly emphasised by the absence of interest in reading or publishing in the journals. (Coleman 1990: 79)

I still remember virtually sneaking into the campus bookstore for my copy of Merton's *Social Theory and Social Structure* because the rivalry between

---

[14] Minor technology can make important differences to communications in other respects; the archives show how before xeroxing papers were not easily reproducible, and so even their authors could have not enough copies to meet the requests of their colleagues.

the Columbia and Chicago sociology departments discouraged undue interest in Columbia authors. (Gans 1990: 449)

There was an elitist attitude at Harvard; they felt Chicago was a second-rate place because it was so empirical . . . [a friend] told me that Parsons asked him at his PhD exam 'What theoretical developments can you expect from Chicago?', and he said 'None' and Parsons said 'That's the right answer.' (K. Geiger 1984)

This boundary-work almost necessarily entailed the creation of questionable stereotypes – of both parties. One may speculate that this process is one of the mechanisms by which reputations are made. (Reputations may have real consequences, but one would be rash to assume that they are always well founded.) At the same time as this, departments might recruit stars, or promising younger people, from elsewhere as part of the competitive process, and this would create pressures towards homogeneity. Thus Chicago clearly felt that it too needed a survey research organisation, and so brought in NORC; moreover, a key role in initiating this was played by Louis Wirth, who was far from being personally sympathetic to or interested in survey method, but was a realistic and competent academic politician (LW 1). Ideally, of course, a hegemonic department needs either to offer something distinctive which is unequivocally the best, or to be the best in each specialist area even if others also offer the same specialisms; one can see Chicago trying to do both, despite the strain between them (cf. Camic and Xie 1994).

This discussion of departments has suggested that not all departments have the same effects, and that sometimes their character and consequences are not due to strictly departmental factors. However, we need to go beyond this to look at extra-departmental patterns of social relations if we are to understand the social processes involved. We start by presenting an intensive case study of a group significant but relatively unfamiliar in historical writing, and showing some of the factors relevant in this instance. This, in conjunction with less detailed material on other groupings, many more widely known, will provide the basis for suggesting some alternative interpretations. The group in question is that which centred on George Lundberg who, as documented above, ran a department that was a very real unit; nonetheless, we cannot describe his setting adequately by looking only at his department.

THE LUNDBERG GROUP

From the 1930s Lundberg had a close intellectual relationship of mutual admiration with Stuart C. Dodd, who initially was based at the American University of Beirut. They met when Dodd visited the US, after having sent Lundberg his *A Controlled Experiment on Rural Hygiene in Syria* (Dodd 1934), which reported a study inspired by his reading of Lundberg's *Social Research*. As a result they agreed to write a joint book; this eventually became Dodd (1942) and Lundberg (1939a), described as companion volumes. In 1946, Lundberg recruited Dodd to the Washington department, and they cooperated closely for the rest of their careers. Indeed, this went well beyond even close cooperation of a usual kind. Dodd describes how at an early stage in their time together at Washington they made a 'Twenty-year pact':

> We agreed that, rather than trying to write co-authored books, each of us would supplement the other's talents. He wrote well while I wrote poorly . . . He powerfully advocated improved measuring instruments, while I invented and tested them. He ably publicised the need for better scientific methodology, while I designed and administered projects developing those methods. Pursuant to this policy, George undertook no new field work projects . . . I would eschew indigestible monographs, overly packed with statistical formulations and seldom read . . . I would seek instead wider professional communicating via journal articles . . . each of us would publish around 1967 a summarising volume or two before retirement. (Dodd 1973: 10–13)

Not only was this division of labour put into practice, but they also regularly exchanged manuscripts and comments at every stage of work. Thus in many ways it makes sense to treat their later careers as one joint one. The departmental joke was that 'There is one Dodd, and Lundberg is his prophet.' Lundberg has quite often been criticised, or at least joked about, for advocating a programme which he did not act upon, but in the light of this pact it seems less reasonable to treat that as inconsistent; Dodd was doing it for him. Dodd published extensively on empirical topics, and organised empirical work within the department, while Lundberg engaged in general evangelism for their viewpoint and was more active in the wider profession and its affairs.

Lundberg and Dodd were members of a group of men who shared their commitment to the idea that natural-science methods should be applied in the social sciences. This chapter argues that this group was a meaningful intellectual circle which was more significant for its sociological members, in relation to the issues we are concerned with here, than relationships confined to sociology. Since it has received little or no historical attention, we describe its composition, interests and links.

At the centre of the group, in addition to Dodd and Lundberg, were John Q. Stewart and George K. Zipf. Jacob L. Moreno could also be seen as a more marginal member.[15] None of these others were formally sociologists, though all of them published in social-scientific journals and were known to sociologists at the time. Stewart was an astrophysicist at Princeton, initially a conventional one who published in the field and was a joint author of a standard textbook, and thus in a strong position to claim to speak for natural science. The Dodd–Stewart correspondence shows that they knew each other, and had shared ideas, when Dodd was a student at Princeton; the acquaintance lapsed when Dodd went abroad, but was taken up again on his return. Stewart was interested in the idea of applying natural science to sociological problems from the 1920s, when he organised some informal discussion meetings at Princeton, but without success in interesting others. However, he became increasingly drawn to what he called 'social physics', in 1939 hitting what he saw as 'pay-dirt' with the concept of 'potential of population' (Stewart 1948a). By the end of the 1940s all his research was in social physics, and he had found some support; he published a number of articles in both natural-science and mainstream social-

---

[15] Moreno, the most marginal member of the group as a group, was of Viennese origin, but emigrated to the USA in 1925. His background was in medicine and psychiatry, but he had developed highly idiosyncratic interests, including the use of 'psychodrama' as a therapeutic technique. The feature of his work most relevant here is his invention of 'sociometry'. This was a technique for plotting group structure, quantitatively and graphically, from data about members' declared preferences or relationships. For Lundberg, sociometry showed that inner realms were not, as some had previously argued, inaccessible to science; it 'helped open up and objectify a large area of important phenomena which had hitherto largely been subject only to imaginative and subjective approaches', as well as being useful in various practical problems (Larsen 1968: 14–15). Lundberg published an unsolicited review of Moreno's *Who Shall Survive?* (1934) in the *American Sociological Review* (Lundberg 1937), which he thought was one of the first things to call the attention of sociologists to it; it soon became widely known. When Moreno founded *Sociometry* in 1937 Lundberg had a paper using Moreno techniques in the first volume.

science journals (including *Sociometry* under Lundberg's editorship), had a team of research assistants collecting and collating social data, and held a grant from the Rockefeller Foundation to organise working conferences on it. His conferences were attended by numbers of natural scientists, and a minority of social scientists; that minority included on various occasions Dodd, Lundberg and Zipf, who all signed a 'declaration of interdependence in research' between natural and social science resulting from one of his earlier meetings (Stewart 1950).

Zipf was formally a Germanist, with his PhD in comparative philology, and taught at Harvard. At an early career stage he developed unconventional methodological interests. The preface to his first book, *The Psycho-Biology of Language*, says:

Nearly ten years ago, while studying linguistics at the University of Berlin [during his PhD work], it occurred to me that it might be fruitful to investigate speech as a natural phenomenon ... in the manner of the exact sciences, by the direct application of statistical principles to the objective speech-phenomena. (Zipf 1935: xi)

The result was a book which the introduction to the reprint of 1965 characterised thus: 'Zipf was the kind of man who would take roses apart to count their petals; if it violates your sense of values to tabulate the different words in a Shakespearean sonnet, this is not a book for you' (Miller 1965: v). These studies revealed some striking empirical regularities, which led Zipf in subsequent work into fields of data no longer confined to language; his 1949 book *Human Behavior and the Principle of Least Effort* (where Lundberg is one of the small number of people thanked in the preface for his long-term support) has chapters with titles such as 'The distribution of economic power and social status'. He taught courses at Harvard, outside philology, related to these interests. On Zipf's premature death, Dodd and Lundberg wrote a highly laudatory obituary in the *American Sociological Review*. Bain (on whom see below) wrote to Stewart:

I hope that the mantle that Zipf bore so gallantly will fall on you . . . I suspect engineers – people like Mayo and C. J. Barnard and J. Q. Stewart [n.b. none of these were literally engineers] may do more for sociology than the old type word jugglers like Weber and Sorokin. The tradition stemming from Comte thru Quetelet, Le Play, Mayo-Smith to Dodd-Zipf-Stewart is the line that will produce social *science*. (Bain 1951)

This group can meaningfully be described as a social unit, because its members had multiple links which went well beyond mere recognition of shared intellectual interests or positions: they frequently cooperated in organised activities to promote the shared 'scientific' viewpoint which they saw as not held by most other colleagues, they held a shared political position, and there were social links between their families. Material on these points is summarised below. It is argued that these links distinguish them from the general sociological community, and show that even the subset of those within it with scientistic commitments had significant divisions.

Stewart developed a group around him, with a small centre of disciples and active participants in his programme of work, and a periphery of others who attended at least some of the meetings he organised without necessarily being committed to his ideas. Dodd and Lundberg took part in his meetings and recommended others who might be interested; Lundberg's disciple Raymond Bassett was one of Stewart's active co-workers. There was a 'Committee on Social Physics', whose function may only have been to provide a list of names of supporters which could be invoked, though in Stewart's files it is sometimes called a committee of the AAAS. Both Stewart and Lundberg were very actively involved in the AAAS, seeing it as an appropriate forum for promoting their concerns to a wider audience; it was one of the few settings in which it was normal for natural and social scientists to be present at the same conference. Only Zipf's death prevented his participation in a session at its 1950 annual meeting, planned by them, under the joint auspices of the Social Sciences and Engineering sections; at the 1953 meeting Bridgman (on whom see below) and Bassett presided at sessions on social physics at which Dodd and Stewart were among those giving papers. The 'declaration of interdependence' mentioned above appeared in *Science*, the journal of the AAAS. The correspondence between Lundberg and Zipf is often almost conspiratorial in tone, especially on Zipf's part. He suggests PR campaigns with, for example, anonymous letters to the press to draw attention to his work, and Lundberg appears to have cooperated in this.

These activities show some of the ways in which the very active evangelism[16] for their ideas in which they engaged was conducted; this evangelistic style is a significant shared feature. Some of the evangelism took conventional academic forms, notable only because of its planning and intensity. Lundberg, thus, wrote general books which put forward his viewpoint, drew attention to work by others of which he approved, and published in semi-popular as well as in purely academic contexts. He showed in private a modest conception of his own role:

I think it should be recognised that my own contribution, if any, to the general subject [of social physics] has been and is perhaps destined to be that of a sort of John the Baptist, crying in various wildernesses, of those who are to come after me who are greater than I. My work has been largely a polemic attempt to bridge the gap between the physical and the social sciences and to do it in terms that would appeal at least to social scientists. (Lundberg 1954)

This self-consciousness extended to deliberate strategy. An introductory textbook (Lundberg, Schrag and Larsen 1954) was produced to spread the word at levels that might not be reached in other ways, and he writes to Bentley (on whom see below) explaining why his writing has not been addressed to very sophisticated versions of the issues: 'I have been struggling hard to move the crowd I am writing for only part of the way to begin with' (Lundberg 1944b). He took on the editorship of *Sociometry*, he explained to Zipf,

partly to get a hearing before a rather good representation of six or seven departmental fields who are fascinated by Moreno's work, and partly to get an outlet for papers on social measurement in which I am deeply interested and which will have to develop if we are to make good the main thesis. (Lundberg 1941)

The group used whatever networks they had access to in pursuit of

---

[16] Moreno too was very actively concerned to propagandise for his cause, if by such relatively traditional mechanisms as holding conferences, publishing manifestos and getting people with established reputations to join editorial and advisory boards. But the most striking feature of his and his collaborators' message is the untraditionally evangelistic tone, and the sweeping claims made for the capacity of sociometry to solve all problems; it had the style of a religious sect. Moreno had in fact published several religious works before he came to the USA, one of which, as he himself points out, had when published in the USA 'aroused, in scientific circles, some controversy as to my sanity' (Moreno 1955: 80). His relentless self-promotion appears, nonetheless, to have had considerable success, even if one discounts his own claims about it.

their goals. The AAAS was an important forum. The Vienna Circle had always been actively concerned to recruit across disciplines, and developed its own networks; in the US they shared enough interests with the Lundberg group to use each others' networks. Lundberg drew on subgroups within sociology such as the Sociometric Group (entirely unconnected with Moreno's 'sociometry'), which included probably all the small number of sociologists in the interwar period who were committed to quantitative empirical work, and the Sociological Research Association (SRA), an elitist body within the membership of the American Sociological Association which provided a forum for those active in research and judged worthy. Stewart drew on natural-science and Princeton networks and, less predictably, the community of people, including many senior academics, who also had summer cottages in New Hampshire.[17] Both Dodd and Lundberg were very actively involved in their later years with a body known as the Behavioral Science Council (which appears to have developed from an employer-funded organisation which funded the diffusion of right-wing views on economic matters). Its formal remit was, however, to provide 'access to an unbiased source dedicated solely to the business of reporting scientifically on the probable costs and consequences of alternate proposed policies and solutions'; its conception of science is declared to be that following the general positions of Peirce, James, Dewey, Bentley and the Vienna Circle's *International Encyclopedia for Unified Science* (SCD 5).

Their shared political position was a right-wing one,[18] and they referred to it as such themselves; they saw it as a natural consequence of their more general intellectual positions. It was characterised by an impatience with moralism and do-gooding, a conviction that more 'scientific' approaches to public policy were necessary and more likely to be realistically successful, and a belief that there were relevant general laws to be discovered which would have implications for policy. It is not evident that these views are intrinsically right-wing – indeed, similar ones have traditionally been held by left-wingers in support of their belief in social

[17] Cf. Heims (1991) for another case where the summer-cottage intellectual community was significant.
[18] Nash (1976: 342) makes it clear that their particular right-wing position was by no means the only possible one; he lists the fundamental prejudices on which right-wing intellectuals agreed after 1945, and the list includes hostility to positivism.

planning. They themselves, however, saw them as having right-wing implications, and it is likely, although I have no specific evidence in support of this, that the shared perspective helped to create a social solidarity among them which went beyond what their purely academic interests alone would have created.[19]

The particular issues on which they shared views were hostility to the New Deal and Keynesian economics, a 'revisionist' stance on American participation in the two World Wars (which they saw as brought about by deception of the public by politicians), and an anti-Zionism – perhaps shading over into anti-Semitism – which went with a general perception of the inevitability of 'organic-contiguous' nations (Zipf 1941) striving to eliminate cultural islands of difference in their midst. This, obviously, had much in common with traditional isolationism and hostility to 'hyphenated Americans' who maintained their identification with their countries of origin. Such positions set them apart from the broadly liberal or left-wing views of most sociologists which, Lipset and Ladd's (1972) data on a later period suggest, were probably more strongly held by the more prominent members of the discipline. These views also grated with the patriotic motives for participation in the wartime effort of many colleagues, especially those involved in its social research, who included many of those who were most committed to empirical research and quantification and/or who became dominant in the postwar period. Some saw Lundberg as sympathetic to fascism, or holding views which led in that direction even if he did not follow them there (Bannister 1992: 191–4). The hothouse political atmosphere of the McCarthyite period must have made such themes more salient. Even if the Lundberg group was not really anti-Semitic, it was certainly perceived as such by some contemporaries, and of course numbers of sociologists were Jewish, with the proportion probably increasing as the tradition of a tacit quota for Jewish students in many universities became discredited after the Holocaust which, together with the wartime role of negroes, also led to the production of much important post-war research on issues of ethnic discrimination. It seems likely, therefore, that this was indeed a significant line of cleavage.

---

[19] Lundberg's correspondence shows some sympathetic interchanges on political issues, national and disciplinary, with several colleagues whose intellectual work is in quite a different style from his.

Social meetings between members of the group other than Lundberg and Dodd were limited by geographical distance, and tend to have been associated with summer cottages and conferences. However, there were even second-generation links among members of the group and its close contacts. Stewart's son Jack was a graduate student in physics at Harvard with Bridgman; there he was an acquaintance of Duane H. D. Roller, also in physics, the son of Duane Roller senior. The latter was a physicist at Wabash College and, as editor of *Science*, responsible for publishing there some material on social physics; he was one of Stewart's supporters and, with his son, attended at least one of his conferences. Dodd's son Peter was an undergraduate at Princeton and did his senior dissertation with Stewart on social physics. (He went on to do graduate work in the Department of Social Relations at Harvard, and later followed in his father's footsteps at the American University of Beirut.) Robert Zipf, G. K. Zipf's son, wrote after his death to Dodd to ask for advice about a career in empirical social science, and was warmly invited to the University of Washington. (I have not found whether he took up the invitation.) No doubt Lundberg too would have contributed to this nexus if he had not been disadvantaged by late marriage, which meant that his son was rather younger than those of the other members!

Some other people who were significant in the intellectual circles of this group, though without being central members of it, were Read Bain, Arthur F. Bentley, Percy W. Bridgman, Joseph L. Walsh, Warren Weaver and several members of the Vienna Circle of philosophers of science. A few words on each of these are necessary to sketch in the background.

Read Bain, a sociologist, based at Miami University (Ohio), whom Lundberg met at an early stage and who became a career-long intellectual ally and correspondent; they shared a robust polemical style, and Lundberg was pleased to give him a regular column in *Sociometry* in which to exercise it. Bain's publications were mainly theoretical and methodological, and he took a strong line in support of his conception of scientific method. (For comments on him as a teacher, see Strodtbeck 1980.)

Arthur F. Bentley, a political scientist not always in a university job, who had a lifelong concern with philosophical issues.[20] He

---

[20] For more information about him, see Ratner 1957.

published a book which tried to draw implications for the social
sciences from relativity theory (Bentley 1926); he corresponded
with Bridgman and Lundberg on issues of scientific method;
he donated money to the AAAS to set up a prize for social-
scientific work 'along those methodological lines that have
been most prominent in the established sciences', for which
Lundberg was one of the early judges.[21] (The prize was
donated anonymously, but AAAS records reveal his identity.)

Percy W. Bridgman, a Nobel Prize-winning physicist at Harvard,
with a name familiar to social scientists because of his
invention of 'operationism', which was enthusiastically taken
up by psychologists in particular. What they and positivist
philosophers made of it was, as Walter has shown, far from his
original intentions, and it became 'a monster to which he had
only a historical connection' (Walter 1990: 175).[22] Nonetheless
Bridgman, while remaining a working physicist, became
strongly interested in philosophical aspects of social issues; he
wrote a book bearing on them (*The Intelligent Individual and
Society*, 1938), took part in discussions of philosophy of science
which included social scientists, and at one point offered a
course on the establishment of operational definitions of social
abstractions in the Dept. of Social Relations (Walter 1990:
294). He took part in several of Stewart's meetings, and
allowed his name to appear on the list of his Committee on
Social Physics.

Joseph L. Walsh, a mathematician at Harvard and former
president of the American Mathematical Society; he took part
in many of Stewart's meetings, and his extensive help is also
warmly acknowledged in Zipf's *National Unity and Disunity* and
Human Behavior and the Principle of Least Effort.

Warren Weaver, a mathematician with a PhD in mathematical
physics who headed the Rockefeller Foundation's natural

---

[21] Lundberg wanted to award it to Dodd, and was extremely annoyed to be outvoted; he
wrote to Stewart expressing his embarrassment at being apparently associated with the
decision to give it to Arnold Rose (Lundberg 1953).

[22] It addressed the intellectual problems caused for an experimental physicist of Bridgman's
style by relativity theory, and for him it saved empiricism; B. F. Skinner, his Harvard
colleague and a leading behaviourist psychologist, lamented that: 'My efforts to convince
you of the possibility of extending the operational method to human behavior have long
since suffered extinction' (Skinner 1956).

science division, and in that capacity was responsible for an unsolicited offer of funds to Stewart for his meetings. He saw these activities as potentially analogous to the very fruitful move to take physical approaches into biology in which he had played a significant role. Initially, at least, he took a strong personal interest in Stewart's work, though later he became disillusioned with it. He also took an interest in Zipf, 'because of our overlapping personal interest in communication and word frequencies' (Weaver 1950), which for Weaver had been expressed in work on the mathematical theory of communication (C. E. Shannon and Weaver 1962).

Several members of the Vienna Circle of philosophers of science, and their American associates, had multiple connections with both the natural and the social scientists in the network; Herbert Feigl, who first came to the USA on a grant to work with Bridgman, was prominent among them, as were Gustav Bergmann, Carl Hempel and Ernest Nagel. Their commitment to the idea of 'unified science' made them interested in anything which looked like a move in that direction. They also had connections with many other social scientists; indeed, their ideas had been more warmly received by social than natural scientists in the USA. Lundberg was a very keen and active proponent of their ideas, and corresponded with them.[23]

The essential tie among the wider circle was an active interest in the idea of applying the successful methods of natural science to the social sciences. Obviously this may not have had quite the same meaning for the natural scientists that it had for the social scientists. (A number of the natural scientists involved were emeritus which, together with the summer-cottage connection, suggests an element of hobbyism in the theme for them.) It would be rash to assume that even the natural scientists had a consensus on conceptions of scientific method – a topic generally much less explicitly discussed among natural scientists; we may note, however, that the natural scientists involved were all mathematicians or physicists, and in particular that there were no biologists, who might have brought different models to bear. The period was, of course, one of physical triumphalism in the aftermath of the wartime successes of physics, and physicists were moving into

---

[23] For more detail on them and the relationship with Lundberg, see Platt and Hoch 1995.

biology; it was also one in which cross-disciplinary work was advocated by many, and being promoted by some leading figures in funding agencies. (This group might be compared with that involved in the development of cybernetics (Heims 1991).) It is striking that there are several comments in Lundberg's papers about the more favourable reception for his and Dodd's ideas which he claims to find among natural scientists.[24]

It will be noted that only two of the others listed are social scientists, and only one a sociologist. It is also perhaps worth noting that some sociologists whom one might have thought equally eligible on purely intellectual grounds for membership in this circle do not appear to have belonged to it as a circle, even though they had contact with some of its members, in particular Lundberg; these include William F. Ogburn, and the less well-known Hornell Hart.[25] This suggests, though it is certainly not enough to demonstrate, that the Dodd-Lundberg circle faced inwards, bound by multiple ties beyond the purely academic, and also faced towards those natural scientists and philosophers who shared their methodological interests, as much as towards mainstream sociology. That statement may, however, put the matter too much as if it were a matter of their choice; there were also probably elements of intellectual and political exclusion from dominant sociological circles.

What does this case study show for our larger theme? It shows that the intellectual community relevant in this case was not confined to either the department or the discipline, that the circle making up this community had only partial overlap with what might have been seen as the Lundberg 'school', that non-intellectual ties were probably significant in defining its boundaries,

---

[24] 'Dodd and I have . . . concluded contracts with the Operations Research Office . . . I have been peddling the same proposal to all the important foundations for some years without any success, and . . . some top flight physicists . . . at once saw merit in the proposal and made arrangements for substantial support' (Lundberg 1949).

[25] Hart was for the latter part of his pre-retirement career at Duke in North Carolina. In addition to the paper on logistic trends already cited he was the author of such other works as 'Operationism analyzed operationally' (1940) and 'Measuring degrees of verification in sociological writings' (1947), and *A Laboratory Manual for Introductory Sociology* (1960b). These show an extreme version of mechanical positivism. On the other hand, he also declared in favour of religious and spiritual values, wrote popular works of psychological self-improvement, and criticised positivistic sociologists for their neglect of creative imagination and values. This demonstrates the point that methodological stances do not all come in predictable standard packages.

and that sociologists may belong to a variety of networks which help to define their identities. Some of these other networks are regional or national ones, and so constitute larger social structures. One cannot assume that the structures within which other sociologists are located will follow just the same pattern, but this sensitises us to the need to look for such features.

OTHER SOCIAL NETWORKS

In the sociological community there were important extra-academic bases of solidarity which could have academic consequences. Politics was mentioned in relation to the Lundberg group, and that is not the only one where it is known to have been relevant. For the earliest generation with which we are concerned, the Progressive movement, of which the growth of social science was in a sense just one part, was broadly relevant. Also well documented is the New York socialist background which was significant in at least the early career of a number of prominent postwar sociologists.(On this, see Cooney 1986, Wald 1987.) In the McCarthy era socialism was dangerous, but those who were touched by McCarthyite accusations included deeply improbable candidates for anti-Americanism like Parsons and Stouffer; many of the accusations made were so unrelated to reality that they probably did not tap political positions genuinely in common.[26] Perhaps one of the most important ways in which the hysteria of this time touched sociology was in the research into the phenomenon which it generated (Stouffer 1955, Lazarsfeld and Thielens 1958).

In both the Progressive and the New York socialist milieux religion was also involved, in rather different ways. In the Progressive period, the Social Gospel was part of the inspiration towards social work and social science, and many of the early surveys were on religious subjects or religiously motivated. (Vidich and Lyman (1985) have argued that key ideas of modern American sociology emerged from a distinctively Protestant style of worldly utopianism, and that modern sociological positivism, seen as pursuing social redemption through science, is in its direct line of

---

[26] This context did, however, provide opportunities for animosities arising from intellectual differences to be expressed in political terms.

descent. Whether or not their interpretation is convincing, it does not imply meaningful community among Protestants as such at our period.) The New York socialists were from a Jewish immigrant community where Judaism was important as ethnicity rather than as religion. In the interwar period, an unselfconsciously open anti-Semitism was institutionalised in academic life; anyone who scans the archives will find innumerable letters discussing appointments which use such phrases as 'He is a Jew, but . . . '. John Useem (1984) suggests that this was in part a response to the socio-intellectually marginal position of sociology within the universities, which made it particularly necessary to appear conventionally acceptable in other ways (male, tall, dressed right, WASP, . . .). Some Jews did, nonetheless, get academic jobs, but it was not easy.[27] Lazarsfeld was very conscious of the prejudices he faced as a Jew – and Rossi (1984) reports being present when Lundberg told Lazarsfeld that he was a good fellow although he was Jewish. (Lundberg's presidential address to the American Sociological Association (1944a) made a truly impressive effort to cause the maximum possible offence by criticising, in addition to amateurs and do-gooders as opposed to scientific experts, Jews, Catholics and anyone who holds that values are more than just data.)[28] There was a journal *Jewish Social Studies*, though it was not specifically sociological. For obvious reasons most of the refugees from Hitler were Jewish as well as German or

---

[27] There was also, of course, systematic discrimination against women, but some of them did get jobs nonetheless.

[28] It is not strictly true to say that he criticised Jews as such. Nor was it Catholics as such that he criticised, but a pronouncement made in New York by the Administrative Board of the National Catholic Welfare Conference. What he did was to criticise those who 'demand legislation prohibiting criticism and . . . international action outlawing anti-Semitism, instead of reckoning with the causes of the antagonism' (Lundberg 1944a: 3). He does not say there what he thinks the causes are, but what he says elsewhere suggests that he supported Zipf's (1941) argument that the Jews as a 'psychological nation' inevitably succeed at the expense of others who then persecute them, while 'organic-contiguous' nations inevitably strive to eliminate cultural islands in their midst – so that anti-Semitism and Hitler might be regarded as 'cure' rather than 'disease', while US anti-Nazi activities before entry into the Second World War interfere with the drive towards equilibrium. (Zipf immediately goes on to say that essentially the same applies to other national minorities within the USA, and his tone is in part one of admiration for Jewish success and cohesion.) Lundberg correctly predicted that his comments would lead to accusations of anti-Semitism, which he denied. The offensive language in which he went on to describe the activities of those he had in mind might suggest otherwise, though that was quite consistent with his usual knockabout polemical style on any subject – questionably appropriate in a presidential address as that may have been. He was greeted with what may be the only recorded heckling at an ASA presidential address.

Austrian, and quite often socialists; some of them maintained strong contacts with others they had known in their countries of origin, though others, like the philosopher Bergmann, chose to dissociate themselves from a rejected past background (Bergmann 1993). After the war, shared Jewish identity continued to be a basis of solidarity, for instance in the Chicago department *c.* 1945–55 (J. Platt 1995a: 101). Those who worked with the American Jewish Committee researching inter-group relations were Jewish, even if their Jewish identity was not salient in their work in other ways.[29]

There was certainly discrimination against Jews, but they were not the only ones affected by religious or ethnic identities. The position of blacks is too obvious to require much discussion. Although a few became prominent in the discipline, black sociologists were generally forced to make careers in the black college sector, where there were fewer research opportunities and they were likely to get drawn into administrative roles instead.[30] Both the discrimination and the shared institutional memberships made them a distinct and self-conscious group, even if one that perforce had few consequences for research. Less familiar is the effective prewar requirement by some universities of relatively orthodox Christianity.[31] Where it was not required there could nonetheless be considerable external social pressures; Odum, for instance, based in the Bible Belt, had in early years to defend *Social Forces* against accusations of atheism and blasphemy from local clergy. It is said that there has been a marked Mormon presence in

---

[29] For a little more about this, see Sklare 1963, Lipset 1955.

[30] The career of Charles S. Johnson exemplifies this pattern; see also A. M. Platt (1991) on E. Franklin Frazier. A. Meier (1977) suggests that the peculiar role of Charles S. Johnson, who effectively concentrated the available funding in his fief at Fisk so that it was not available to others, was relevant postwar, though the lack of interest at the major research universities in race issues at that time also contributed. This may have had something to do with methodological trends to quantification which did not lend themselves to community studies of race relations. Lieberson (1980) however shows that quantitative data could be highly relevant to such concerns.

[31] 'While we should not hire anyone here who is not an avowed Christian, in the sense of accepting the ideals of Jesus, yet noone here is under any denominational or sectarian constraint' (Ellwood 1931). This letter was part of the courtship of Hornell Hart, whom Ellwood was anxious to attract to Duke, and responded to Hart's expressed unwillingness to have his freedom in the search for religious truth hampered. Moral as well as religious criteria could be deemed relevant. Odum's papers reveal a case in the 1920s in North Carolina where a colleague was found guilty of drunken driving; it is clear that if the charge had been believed true, which it was not, he would have lost his job.

the sociology of the family, which one may presume has affected the directions it has taken.

Catholicism has clearly been important. There were separate Catholic colleges, many staffed by members of religious orders. The American Catholic Sociological Society (ACSS) was founded in 1938; its journal, the *American Catholic Sociological Review*, followed in 1940. John Useem (1984) reports that this was in response to a comment by Bain, in a meeting attended by many Catholics who immediately walked out, that Catholics were educated beyond their intelligence. More formal comments in public reminiscence by those involved show that more diffuse and long-term factors were relevant. Ralph Gallagher SJ, the founding president of the ACSS, declared in his presidential address that:

There is such a thing as a Catholic sociology . . . those whose approach is different from ours . . . have much to contribute in the fields of method and research . . . [but] We deny much of their theory and condemn the lack of principle so evident in much of their work. (Gallagher 1938: 319)[32]

Loretta Morris (1989: 323) reports that at that period 'the sociological establishment regarded *anyone* committed to a specific set of religious beliefs and a specific religious institution as incapable of genuinely scientific research', and so Catholics felt frozen out; many of them were also unhappy with the ASA because it paid so little attention to teaching, which was a salient concern in the small colleges in which they worked. Several participants describe how comfortable they felt in the relatively small and welcoming setting of the ACSS meetings, as compared with the ASA. However, changes in the general position of Catholics and Catholicism in American society have led to changes within sociology. The ACSS declined, and in 1970 it transformed itself into the Association for the Sociology of Religion; meanwhile its journal had in 1964 become *Sociological Analysis*, renouncing any mission of a distinctively Catholic sociology.[33] Although there has been a specifically Catholic line on a number of sociological issues, and an entirely distinct textbook literature for that reason, this hardly touched

---

[32] This address is reprinted, along with several other relevant historical documents and some specially written reminiscences, in *Sociological Analysis* 50: 4.

[33] Andrew Greeley, a Catholic priest who became a mainstream sociologist, has described some of the difficulties which he experienced in this transition (Greeley 1990).

the field of methods,[34] though the Jesuit Furfey's metasociological work (Furfey 1953) has been widely used in the mainstream.

All these extra-academic identities affected who was where, but few if any of them were directly associated with methodological cleavages, though they had some consequences for theoretical concerns and for choices of substantive topic which may also have had indirect effects. More likely to be associated with method-ological cleavages were the academic-related bodies people joined as an expression of intellectual taste or interest: the Sociometric Group, the Society for Applied Anthropology (SAA), the Society for the Study of Social Problems, the American Association for Public Opinion Research (AAPOR), the Society for the Study of Symbolic Interaction, American Sociological Association sections (on this see the discussion of sub-disciplines in chapter 4). Such groupings are a meaningful part of the social structure of the discipline, but confirm rather than creating intellectual identities; they pre-sumably have some relevance in providing social support and legitimation.[35] The felt need for a separate body indicates lines of cleavage; sometimes, as probably with AAPOR, this may only be one of specialist shared interests, but in other cases, such as SAA (on which see also chapter 2), there is a partially methodological agenda even if the title does not make this evident. AAPOR was the locus of methodologically significant links outside sociology: the public-opinion research community was one which not only cut across disciplinary boundaries, but also linked academic and commercial groups. Another set of links of a similar kind was among demographers and social statisticians, though here those outside academic life were in branches of the government service, particularly the Census; a number of people such as Margaret Hagood and Philip Hauser moved between jobs in the two sectors, and played important roles in diffusing practices. (See also chapter 5, pp. 153–4, on this.) For this group the linking learned society was the American Statistical Association. In this context the SRA, founded in 1936, is of some interest. It is an elitist body, with a fixed

---

[34] The 50-year index of *Sociological Analysis* shows that of the 1,034 articles listed only 18 under the head 'methodology' come from 1960 or earlier, and most of their titles suggest nothing distinctively Catholic.

[35] Other voluntaristic links, with potential for influence on students, are those expressed by the invitations to visiting professors for summer sessions; these would lend themselves to a sociometric or network approach, but await systematic study.

total size, whose members are chosen by nomination. It originated formally to bring together those who, as distinguished from other members of the ASA, were seen as serious researchers, so that they could hold meetings which expressed their interests; the felt need for such a body shows the extent to which research was not then taken for granted.[36] The choice of members came to have much of academic politics without reference to the research/non-research distinction about it, and as research grew more salient in the discipline it has gradually become a purely honorific body with no distinct activities. Lengermann (1979) sees the SRA's unofficial purpose as having been the defence of an elitist Chicago/ quantitativist coalition against the encroachments of the rebels against Chicago dominance, who were united by the under- standable career anxiety of those in more marginal positions during the Depression.

But it seems likely that none of these groupings or academic structures were as important as the wartime research effort in having a lasting impact on methodological developments. This research was carried out by several different teams within changing organisational structures, but here their differences are not important, not least because there was considerable contact among them as well as some interchange of personnel. Much about the social aspects of the research made it consequential for those involved and for the whole discipline. It used almost all those who were prominent in practical research method in one capacity or another, and it recruited to work with them the cream of their graduate students[37] – at the same time as graduate schools generally emptied as the young men went off to the war. It provided resources and opportunities for research on a scale never before available, with ample replication and chances to try new things and learn from experience. The work was done under great pressure, sometimes in dangerous conditions, which helped to forge group

---

[36] In 1930, only 30 per cent of the members of the ASA declared an interest in research on their membership forms (Lundberg 1931: 460).

[37] It may be significant that those involved included social psychologists as much as sociologists, thus helping to communicate the methodological traditions of psychology, some of which were more systematically elaborated than those of sociology. Not all of these were, as one might suspect, scientistic; for instance, Charles Cannell, who was a graduate student of Carl Rogers of non-directive therapy fame, was recruited to the Division of Program Surveys to help train interviewers in techniques of open-ended questioning (Cannell 1983).

solidarity. It was self-evidently important work, with effects on crucial matters of policy. Thus the atmosphere was one of high commitment and intellectual excitement. From the point of view of method, this performed the function of an extremely intensive workshop, which both made important technical advances and gave a strong practical training to younger people. At the same time it created powerful social bonds among them. In consequence, at the end of the war some teams arranged to stay together in academic life, while others kept in touch though now in separate institutions. The work done had high disciplinary prestige, cemented by the publication of the *American Soldier* volumes. Modern survey method had in effect been created, and was both institutionalised in the survey research units now in universities and theorised in the spate of publications on method which followed; it was also now associated, as it had not previously been, with substantively significant topics and with theoretical developments. (Contrary to widespread assumption, though, survey method was certainly not the only area of method used and developed during the war.) Alumni of the wartime work had reason to stay in areas which drew on their experience and, though some returned to graduate school after the war, were excellently placed a little ahead of later cohorts to take the jobs which opened up to cater for the enormous university expansion under the GI Bill. Their prospects were surely not hindered by the jobs several of their former colleagues also took up with key foundations.

The impact of this wartime experience depends on a particular set of historical events, and so it does not fit well into any general theoretical account which rests on factors of permanent relevance; it cannot for that reason be ignored. Probably no other historical event has been of nearly equal importance, but we should be alert to the possibility that some may have affected developments on a smaller scale. At the smallest possible scale are the events of the individual career. Graduate school may have considerable impact on the students' skills, interests, sense of what is possible or ordinary, and so on, but these are no more than predispositions which they carry with them into new settings or periods where other influences may also impinge. A personal intellectual career has its own dynamics, leading on from one problem to another and building intellectual capital or providing experience which suggests new directions. In addition, though, there are contextual factors.

Funding sources open up or close, new colleagues have different backgrounds, new courses to be taught open up fresh vistas, innovations made elsewhere can be taken up. An empirical analysis of methodological career patterns, differentiated by cohort, would be extremely interesting; unfortunately we are not in a position to provide one. We may, however, note the bearing of one relatively well-known pattern. Firsthand empirical research is less often carried out as academics advance in their careers. For some, this is because their jobs emphasise teaching; for those of more relevance here it is because fieldwork is better suited to a younger person with few ties and time commitments, and/or because they now supervise the work of others funded by their grants – who may not themselves in turn find academic jobs. Gans suggested in the later 1960s that an apparent revival of participant observation was simply because an earlier group had reached the career stage where they had graduate students whom they had trained in the methods they preferred, so that more such people were now currently active in the profession (H. S. Becker, B. Geer and E. Hughes 1968: 301). Some patterns of change in the methods in use may, thus, perhaps be imputed to changes in the age structure of the profession, reflecting the expansion and contraction of recruitment over time, combined with cohort effects.

We would argue that, though departments have undoubtedly sometimes been very important units, their importance has varied; they have contained major internal differences, there have been affiliations which crosscut them, and non-academic units have been equally or more significant. Insofar as they have been important in questions of method, that has depended not only on the extent to which there were distinctive methods and method was treated as important in the definition of identity, but also on practical rather than ideological features of the departmental situation (on which see chapter 4).

SCHOOLS

The implication of the material presented so far is that the social structures of academic life provide a framework which has consequences for commitments and practices, including methodological ones. This is not in itself a novel observation. However, some important general accounts pay little attention to such matters, or discuss them in ways which take for granted relationships between the intellectual and the social which would benefit from a closer look. In particular, historians of social science, especially writers oriented to theory or the history of ideas, often discuss their subject in terms of units such as 'school', 'paradigm' or 'tradition'. These terms are usually not closely defined and, though it might be possible to identify consensus on some central uses, are not clearly distinguished from each other; we can, thus, for our purposes here, treat them all together under the head of 'school' in order to raise questions about the utility, and the practical applicability, of such terms.

At a minimum, terms such as 'school' imply that those who belong to one have something significant in common which distinguishes them from those who do not. But what is it that they have in common? Are schools relatively unusual phenomena, or does everyone belong to one? Do members of a school have to know that they belong to it? Such questions are not new, and some of the issues below have been raised by Szacki (1975) and Harvey (1987a, b), but this is one of those areas where sophisticated new models of the wheel are regularly reinvented and so the same queries need to be raised over again. Let us look at some examples of usage and see what they imply.

There are many books, of which we may take Sorokin (1966) and Martindale (1961) as widely known examples, which give general reviews of periods of sociology classifying the tendencies into categories. Thus Sorokin has a section called 'The nominalistic-singularistic-atomistic trend in contemporary sociology', and Martindale one on 'The formal school of sociological theory'. Although their subject matters overlap, the categories they use are quite different. Moreover, Sorokin sees (unacknowledged) predecessors of recent ideas at distant times and places and recognises the coexistence of many competing tendencies, while Martindale treats his schools as broadly consecutive stages in historical development. Despite these important differences, they have a significant methodological similarity: their categories are their own, and were not usually used by those whose work they analyse. This means that writers may be identified as members of the same school who would not have recognised each other as such, and may not even have been aware of each others' existence. (In Szacki's terms, this is a 'typological' school.) Clearly the phenomena thus defined are not the same as when there is a self-conscious group with which people deliberately associate themselves.

Historians using such units in their accounts have identified them operationally in different ways. Mullins (1973) examines eight 'theory groups'; he has first to identify the groups, and then their individual members. He defines as a theory a position that meets minimum intellectual criteria *and* is held by a recognisable group in American sociology (1973: 5), although acknowledging that other positions meeting the minimum criteria have also existed. Both his own judgments and those observed in the community, as well as citation of similar sources and known collegial relations between the authors, are used to identify similar intellectual content; the relative weight given to different criteria is not clear. He then lists as important members of each group those who met criteria including past and present institutional location and co-authorships. It is hardly surprising that he found confirmation for a model of the process of theory development which attached importance to factors such as institutional location, or that theory *groups* loom large in his picture of the life of sociology, since his operational definitions guaranteed their salience. His procedure gives lists with some names that anyone who knows the field – surely including the owners of the names – would regard as misplaced, because it is known that they were not actually associated with the theoretical position under which they appear – as indeed he admits in the appendix ; this generally seems to be the result of co-authorship, and implies that that is a poor operational definition of theoretical affiliation.[38] As Mullins also points out, it may sometimes have occurred as a result of shared institutional location. This strange amalgam of social and intellectual criteria makes it impossible within his frame of reference to ask questions about the relationships between them.

Alexander and Colomy, in a range of joint and separate publications (e.g. Alexander 1979, Alexander and Colomy 1992, Colomy and Brown 1995), have expounded a 'post-positivist model of knowledge cumulation and decline' whose units are 'traditions'

---

[38] Another possible reason for this is that they have changed their intellectual positions over time. This draws attention to Mullins' tacit assumption that each individual has a permanent commitment such that co-authorship at one stage may be used as an indicator of that person's longer-term stance.

(equated with 'schools') defined by their theoretical cores, which limit the options seen as available at other levels of discourse even if the links made are not logically imperative. (Note the implication that the units are not identified by Colomy and Alexander's criteria of coherence.) It is assumed that everyone belongs to one tradition or another. Each tradition is seen as containing both abstract generalised discourse, whose empirical referents may not be immediately evident, and research programmes, which treat abstract issues as unproblematic and are organised around concrete problems. They add that most traditions contain some fundamental disagreements about the school's general pro-gramme, and divisions into distinct tradition segments. Alexander and Colomy work within the 'theory' rather than the 'history' mode, so they offer no explicit criteria by which they decide what consti-tutes a tradition and who belongs to it; it is plain, however, that their own intellectual judgments play a key role in their imputations. It is easier to see everyone as belonging to some tradition if these are allowed to contain disagreements; it is easier to see comprehensive theory/research packages if the theory and the research do not have either to imply each other logically or to make overt reference to each other, since this means that no specific evidence of the connection is required. There are evident dangers here.

Tiryakian (1979) gives a general account of 'major' schools, listing the social characteristics they share. (The limitation to the 'major' means that this scheme is not required to fit the whole range of sociological work.)[39] For him they consist of a charismatic leader and followers (including an organiser and a populariser) with shared convictions; a paradigm is formulated and the group proselytises and attracts students so that its influence spreads beyond the initial shared location. A manifesto, a journal under their control, and exemplary works, are required for the new paradigm to become institutionalised. A problem with this list is that it is not clear whether items on it are parts of a definition, or empirical generalisations about instances defined on other criteria;

---

[39] Tiryakian's list of the 'major' is one which would win widespread recognition, but it is still worth raising the question of how such a categorisation is achieved. One may suspect that having the sort of organisation described by Tiryakian is very helpful in the process, in which case there is a potential circularity here too. On this, see chapter 7.

nor is it clear how cases such as that of Bogardus at the University of Southern California (with leader, followers and journal but no institutionalisation at the level of the discipline)[40] are to be dealt with. A question not raised is under what circumstances people identify themselves as a school. (Amsterdamska (1985) and Collins (1989), as well as more recent general discussions of 'boundary work', suggest that the felt need to distinguish oneself from others is probably important.) As with both Mullins and Alexander/Colomy, there are risks of circularity, with propositions which follow from the operational definitions used being reported as though they were findings: it seems likely that a grouping which did not have most of the characteristics listed would not be counted as a school.[41]

These cases show 'school' used in at least three different ways: the school of current social membership, the school of retrospective identification, and the school of imputation. The main functions performed by these seem to be, respectively, empirical description, legitimation, and support for teaching or 'systematics' (study of the systematic substance of ideas). It does not follow that only the first use is appropriate for the historian, though she of course always

[40] Bogardus was a relatively well-known figure in the discipline, serving as President of the American Sociological Association in 1931; Odum (1951: 158) describes this as in part recognition of his 'distinctive regional pioneering', like his own presidency of the year before. Bogardus was a prolific publisher, especially of textbooks, including two on methods (Bogardus 1918, 1925), and Pauline V. Young, also the author of a prominent methods text, was a member of his department. My respondents, however, showed little awareness of or interest in his work; it was evidently not taken very seriously as an intellectual contribution. The description of his department by one of them as oriented to local community professionals such as social workers, rather than to the cosmopolitan national sociological world, is probably correct, despite Bogardus' continuing connection with Robert Park, whose student and then collaborator on the Pacific Race Relations Survey he was (Young 1939: 33–9). Robert Ellis (1991), who taught there in 1955–7, recounts that he was the first person to teach social psychology there who did not use Bogardus' book. Most of the faculty had been Bogardus' students, and the cult of him as leader was exemplified even after his retirement when he gave a talk on his trip to Iceland in the Mormon church with the candles lit and everybody went; one can see this style reflected in early issues of *Sociology and Social Research*, the department's journal.

[41] Collins (1989: 114–15) rejects the criterion of having ideas in common as adequate, and uses all three of his other potential criteria: intellectual influences among members, networks of personal contact, and shared organisational membership. He dismisses possible queries about the satisfactoriness of this as an operational definition in a rather cavalier manner; that is justified for his immediate problem by the sparsity of data on the cases he is considering. He is dealing with 'schools' of philosophy, not sociology, so his picture cannot be related to our substantive material. We note, however, that he too distinguishes 'major' figures in terms of their recognition and relationships, raising again the possibility of circularity in some of his apparently empirical propositions.

needs to ask how far the accounts implied fit the historical facts. The school of retrospective identification is an interesting historical phenomenon in its own right (on which see also chapter 7) and, though very likely to give a misleading version of the glorious past invoked, defines a group of current membership; the 'history' here serves the purposes of contemporary systematics. The school of imputation is also likely to mislead, though in more sophisticated ways. When used in textbooks, a key role is simply to wrap ideas up in tidy packages easily transmitted (preferably one per lecture) and memorised. The telescope is not concerned with what the microscope might reveal, so the question of validity in the detection of 'real' intellectual commonalities is not easy to address. This facilitates the proliferation of alternative schemes, which may provide a relatively low-effort means of achieving novelty and establishing a reputation; only published sources are required, not tedious archival work. It has often been pointed out that such textbook versions also socialise the young into approved belief systems, commonly providing suitably Whig versions of disciplinary history.

To the extent that the school of imputation appears as part of systematics rather than mere textbook work, it raises the issue of the status to be given to actors' models. To identify shared ideas that the people who held them may not have been aware of can be a very valuable contribution – but how far is it a historical one? The great danger of this kind of history is that using our categories instead of theirs may lead to neglect of the ideas that were steering developments in favour of ones which might have been but weren't. A fine example of this is provided by Bales (1984), who describes his own 'Interaction Process Analysis' on small groups in the laboratory as partly inspired by Durkheim's emphasis on the importance of rates of behaviour; this could hardly have been guessed by a reader of his work. (This provides a pleasing obverse to the commoner case of claimed influences from Durkheim which did not actually take place.) More typically, the risk is that it is too easy to apply anachronistic categories which look convincing from the perspective of the present (cf. Q. Skinner 1974, Kragh 1987, S. P. Turner 1983). This is, of course, a danger from the viewpoint of the historian, but not from that of the theorist, for whom it might even be a valued source of creativity. For systematics, indeed, to assign past thinkers to schools on the basis of actors' models can be unhelpful. Colomy and Alexander's acceptance as units of analysis of generally recognised packages which they do not regard as intellectually coherent prevents critical questions about the composition of the packages being discussed; it also means that the issue of *why* apparently incoherent packages should have arisen, interesting both historically and systematically, does not get asked.

In part we are here merely applying to 'schools' a point made long ago by Merton (1967), about the need to distinguish history and systematics. When we do so, we find it hard to avoid recognising that there have been many different bases of social and/or intellectual solidarity in meaningful groups of social scientists and, in particular, that 'fundamental' ideas are not necessarily involved or may not have been at all salient for the actors. Faithfulness to historical detail may mean accepting that shared membership of a survey organisation (such as Columbia's Bureau of Applied Social Research) or of a department with a commitment to a salient regional identity (such as that under Odum at North Carolina) has sometimes been more important than shared philosophy. It is common to assume that fundamental ideas can be inferred from practices, so that they can be treated as present even when not stated; this is historically rash, both because of the risk of anachronism and because it does not follow that if they *should* have held appropriate fundamental ideas, they were consistent (by your criteria) and actually did so. (See Chapter 4 for detailed general discussion of this issue.) It is unwise to allow oneself to be swallowed by one's own reified teaching materials.

History has often been approached from the angle of systematics, whether by intellectual preference or because of the pragmatic demands of teaching. Perhaps the time has come to try approaching it with the presupposition of incoherence, eclecticism and lack of pattern? Quentin Skinner (1969) has pointed out the fallacy of imputing coherence or system to the work of individual thinkers where it may not have been present. One of the reasons why moderately plausible alternative accounts of intellectual groupings can be given is surely that there are often individual positions that combine several influences, have multiple affiliations, or are ambiguous.[42] But being influenced by a tendency is not the

---

[42] There are also, if one shifts the focus to the classifier rather than the classified, different bases on which distinctions can be made, and alternative positions from which one may wish to distinguish the one in question. Thus, for instance, my own work on the US

same as belonging to a school. Moreover, it is not only individual social scientists who may lack coherence. Periods and places may contain divergent trends and specialisms with little mutual contact, and the presumption that all periods can be treated as like those where there is a clear dominant paradigm is again rash. The effort to do so forces resort to high levels of abstraction with little relevance to the work of many mundane practitioners. It is historically risky to assume that social reality fits consistent principles, or intellectually exhaustive schemata without large boxes, of the kind familiar in survey questionnaires, for 'other' or 'miscellaneous'. It is safer to start from the assumption that different social and intellectual groupings may come together on different bases and that, although the social and the intellectual have a strong tendency to influence each other, they do not automatically correspond.

Some of the concepts of 'school' which are current work much better as ideal types or sensitising concepts than they do as historical descriptions, and if they were only used as such the problems would be reduced; it does not advance understanding to discuss whether an instance meeting only some criteria from a list is 'really' a school. However, this is not an argument against theorising or causal accounts in intellectual history. Quite the reverse: it is only if we distinguish between descriptions and causal propositions (as Bulmer (1985) does in discussing why a school was successfully established at Chicago) that interpretations of particular cases, and generalisations, can be tested against the data. In order to do that, it is also necessary to have operational definitions which do not create tautologies like those in some instances mentioned above. Some of the problems noted seem to arise because authors start with preconceptions about the existence of particular groupings, rather than defining what they are interested in and then looking for instances; this can put them at the mercy of the processes of the social construction of perceived 'schools', which arguably might better be treated as part of the subject matter for study.

reception of Durkheim (J. Platt 1995b) shows some authors classifying him with Tarde in 'the French school', while others contrast the two thinkers. Cosmopolitan writers such as Sorokin, with wide and multilingual frames of reference, draw boundaries differently from those who are only aware of a narrower range of work.

Some of the terms current – paradigm, specialism, tradition – have primary reference to the sphere of ideas. At least one other – invisible college ('network of productive scientists linking separate groups of collaborators in a research area' (Crane 1972: 54)) – has primary reference to social relations. A key problem with 'school' is that it has both, and so begs the question of connections. It could seem desirable to limit its application to literal 'schools', where shared institutional membership might or might not lead to shared and distinctive intellectual positions. This would leave us without a term for groups with both social and intellectual ties who see themselves and are seen as distinctive. Perhaps having no term is better than using such an ambiguous one? But in the end it is not terminology as such that matters. Whatever the particular terms we use, they need to allow us to distinguish among shared institutional location, shared ideas, joint work on specific projects, and membership of the same communication network, and to discuss the connection with these of actors' identifications, others' perceptions of intellectual similarities and differences, and patterns of disciplinary hegemony and centre/periphery relations.

We have shown that departments, even where they had some socially and intellectually unifying features, did not necessarily constitute uniform environments with intellectual relations confined to, and explicable by, their boundaries. Moreover, different departments had different bases of unity, as well as different relations to their communities, other parts of their own institution, and the national structure of the discipline. (In some fields such as sampling, additionally, there were important intellectual developments outside the universities which eventually fed back into them.) The idea of 'school' as the key grouping is not a helpful one, since it carries a variety of unclarified meanings and, when applied in empirically plausible ways, covers only a small proportion of the discipline. Other social structures and groupings, both professional and personal, have also affected solidarities. All this means that any account which omits extra-departmental factors is as deficient as one which includes only those. Of crucial significance in relation to research methods was a historical episode quite outside the academic system, and, as is shown in chapter 5 on research funding, other less fundamental historical changes have also made important differences. The history of sociology cannot be understood without looking outside sociology, whether that is defined as a system of ideas or as a set of university departments with that title.

CHAPTER 7

Reputation, exemplars
and origin myths

It has been shown in earlier chapters how unconvincing retrospective claims may be made to newly prestigious ancestry,[1]and
how practices may have a less than perfect fit with the declared
principles on which reputations appear to be based. It has also
been shown how the social structures of academic life can channel
knowledge of the field. We attempt now to characterise and account
for such phenomena in the creation of images of sociological work
and groupings. Much has been written in recent years on the social
construction of memories and reputations, and the processes
observed in other fields are equally relevant to sociological research
methods and the memories of sociologists. It is always to be
expected that memory should be selective and purposeful, and that
the past should be used for present ends. We shall not attempt here
to review this whole literature, or to do justice to the accounts given
of the particular cases studied by other authors, but only to refer
briefly to some highlights of direct bearing on our material before
demonstrating how these processes are exemplified in it. The
construction of reputations and the choice of exemplars are the
product of selection made by the collective disciplinary memory
from the total number of sociologists, institutions and research, and
we are concerned to explore some of the consequences of this
selection for the historical picture.

There is a range of general work on the memory of broad
historical events. Middleton and Edwards (1990) provide examples
showing how people construct and retrieve memories for current

---

[1] The direct analogy with the traditional parvenu's practice of buying 'ancestral' portraits
for the walls of his new house is painfully obvious here. In academic life, however, to fail
to provide any portraits can be seen as disrespectful to the ancestors one must surely have
had.

purposes, tell stories to create a community of shared knowledge, remodel images of the past to fit newer concerns, sustain memories collectively or lose them through turnover. Barry Schwartz (1982) shows, in relation to statues of political figures on the Capitol, how within the constraints of recorded history different aspects are selected at different times to use commemoratively, but with meanings which relate to contemporary needs. Hobsbawm and Ranger (1983) offer a number of examples from British history of 'invented traditions', characterised by a set of rule-governed ritual or symbolic practices which make unfounded claims to continuity with a historic past to legitimate values or norms of behaviour. Doug McAdam (1992) argues that the greater salience for women in the construction of personal identity of their participation in Freedom Summer is due to its incorporation into the story of the origins of the women's movement, which has continued when other movements equally relevant to men have not. Schuman and Scott (1989) show that memories of large political and social events are generationally structured, with events that took place when subjects were in their teens and early twenties being remembered as the most important. Fred Davis (1984) considers the processes by which decades come to be labelled as having had a certain character ('me decade', 'jazz age'). He suggests that one element in the selection of such labels is the way in which their succession can be made to fit into narrative plots such as innocence/transgression/retribution/redemption, so that collective 'memory' becomes the creation of familiar fundamental stories about the past.

Thus this work shows a general pattern in which 'memories' are chosen for their significance to the group remembering, and sometimes remodelled, or created, to serve purposes such as legitimation or identity when the available material does not do so well; they are also likely to be selected for their fit to models of an appropriate story. There is also a literature on the reception of intellectual work which relates to these concerns, reviewed below.

Lamont (1987) takes as her problem the success of Derrida's interpretive theory in winning legitimacy in the two very different cultural markets of France and the USA. A preliminary requirement for legitimation in the French philosophical community was a sophisticated rhetoric, a theoretical trademark to distinguish his system from others, but sufficient connection to current major

debates to be recognised as contributing to them. He drew
attention to it by describing it himself as answering fundamental
questions and transcending classic work. Packaging his theory as
a sophisticated cultural good gave it access to the distinctively
French upper middle class for which intellectual symbols of status
boundaries are important, and his links to prestigious institutions
helped to diffuse it to this group; his publications were increasingly
in general cultural and literary journals rather than those of
academic philosophy, and publications about his work came
increasingly from those fields. The American intellectual scene was
very different, but it happened that his work there too found
existing agendas and traditions, and a prestigious base among
literary critics at Yale – while much less interest was shown by
philosophers. A latent function of the interest was to legitimate a
theoretical orientation. Here the base was academic, but in a field
with general cultural connections which assisted wider diffusion;
the concurrent interest in other French scholars helped his
visibility and diffusion. The general argument is that the treatment
of a theory as important depends not only on its content in isolation,
but also on the fit between the work and a structured cultural and
institutional system.

   Clegg, following humorously but not unseriously in Lamont's
footsteps, has analysed the career and reputation of Anthony
Giddens as a sequence of strategies for establishing 'legitimacy as
a high-status good in the intellectual market place' (1992: 577) and
so achieving fame. Giddens is seen as having started by establishing
himself in Britain (at a time of sharp expansion in student
numbers) as an expositor of classic authors, extending his market
by linking them to the standard British topic of class, at the same
time as he offered the US market risk-free access to Marx. His
introduction of the concept of 'structuration' provided product
differentiation, and it was vague enough to be widely applicable and
not to constrain its users. As the market shrank with student
numbers, he maintained his position by strategic forays into other
disciplines which extended his market range. Finally, his production of a comprehensive introductory text promises to impose
his viewpoint as 'normal science' on those who set the framework
within which the novice approaches more advanced levels, and so to
lead them on to the more sophisticated material he can offer for
later stages.

Fuller (1992) studies the reception of Kuhn's *The Structure of Scientific Revolutions* (1962) and, in particular, its uses beyond its original obvious audience in the history of science. He argues that, quite contrary to Kuhn's intentions, his model of science provided 'a free-floating legitimation narrative . . . that could be used by any discipline in need of boosting its status' (1992: 269); this accounts for Kuhn's disavowal of most of the consequences others saw as following from his arguments. The book appeared to provide for members of any one discipline access to interesting material from others which they could connect with their concerns, and so had a wide appeal. Moreover, its weaknesses of argument are clear and so invite the reader to continue the discussion by correcting them, and so remaining within its frame of reference.

Megill (1987) has studied the reception of Foucault's work by historians. He shows that this was different in France and abroad, and that early and late reception varied, with some works attracting wide attention only some time after they were originally published. For French historians that kind of intellectual was less of a novel phenomenon, so they did not attempt to come to grips with his project in general, but took account of particular points in it when their own interests developed in directions to which they had relevance. Foreigners showed more interest initially, and translations were important in the growth of his fame. The special success of a later book led people back to an earlier work, which only then received much recognition. His vogue led foreign historians to feel a need to confront his work, if only to reveal his historical errors; those who did so were particularly likely to be from the professionally marginal groups of historians of ideas and of science. Foucault's work is such that it cannot be fitted into the matrix of any one discipline, but some of its concerns cut across disciplinary boundaries and so have points of connection with many.

Baehr and O'Brien (1994, chapter 5) have a valuable review and discussion of the literature on how it is that some works receive recognition as classics. Their conclusions are documented with data on the changing reception of Simmel and Weber in particular. They suggest that a first condition for classic status is that the author be dead, or at least silent, so that the work is available for use as collective property and can be freely subjected to multiple readings. Suitable work will have some cultural resonance, and also a certain 'textual suppleness' (perhaps due to its bulk or ambiguity) so that the range of interpretive options is increased. Readers need to be able to appropriate the material for their own concerns, though in doing so they may misunderstand it, and there must be agencies of social transmission and diffusion such as a 'school', translators, or dedicated admirers. Success in achieving classic status depends on the presence of such factors, and not just on the 'influence' of the work's intellectual content.

Nock (1993) has studied the social construction of reputation in Canadian sociology. He shows that in key general texts the authors cited reflect not just the fields of interest of the writers, but also regional networks and personal networks past and present. Equally relevant work, equally or more frequently cited in the literature, was mentioned less often if its authors were not connected with these networks (or not congenial theoretically or method-ologically).

Camic (1992) has studied the processes at work in Talcott Parsons' selection, in *The Structure of Social Action* (1937), of four European social thinkers as predecessors. Camic outlines as an orthodoxy in accounting for such selection the 'content-fit' model, which assumes that predecessors are chosen because their ideas fit the concerns of the thinker making the choice. He points out that to understand what is going on one needs also to know if other previous writers, who might have fitted equally well, have been rejected as choices; if they have been, fit alone cannot explain the outcome. In Parsons' case, he argues that there were indeed other equally or even more suitable choices among American insti-tutional economists, with whose work Parsons was closely familiar. Why, then, did he exclude them? Camic maintains that this was because they were in low repute in his local Harvard context, where neo-classical economics was dominant, while the thinkers he did choose were of good or growing standing. To choose locally credible predecessors makes it more likely that one's own work will be given credibility; to do so can therefore be seen as a rational strategy, though the decision may have been unconsciously made if one's perception of the alternatives is formed by the social environment. A 'reputational' model rather than the 'content-fit' one corresponds to these mechanisms. Camic goes on to argue that the 'content-fit' model is more likely to be appropriate in fields with high mutual dependence, where acceptable knowledge claims rest on close coordination with the work of specialist colleagues; the 'reputational' model applies better in fields where validity claims do not rest on such systematic coordination, and so mutual dependence is low. Mutual dependence is greater when fields are more autonomous and institutionalised as distinct specialisms; these conditions were not met in sociology at the time when Parsons came on the scene.[2]

Those considerations shift the discussion to the social conditions affecting differential outcomes.[3] Some other writers have addressed the issue of the mechanisms by which the continuance of reputations is ensured. Gladys and Kurt Lang (1988) demonstrate, in their study of the reputation of women etchers, the significance of a range of factors in ensuring the continuance of a reputation. Fame during one's lifetime was a good start, since merit is more likely to be recognised if associated with a respected 'brand label'. Any link to important artistic circles or to a political or cultural elite helped; one would be remembered for one's connection to them, if only as a leader or follower. It was particularly useful if the link was to a literary figure who wrote about one's work or used one as an illustrator. Symbolic association with otherwise famous things depicted, or with a region or group whose identity the work could be taken to symbolise, helped an artist to be singled out. Those whose work was congruous with ideological themes which enabled

---

[2] Camic takes it for granted, as most sociologists would, that the selection made by Parsons in *The Structure of Social Action* has been consequential for subsequent sociology; his predecessors have become ours, and moreover their status as such has survived the fluctuations of his reputation. However, as he barely notes in passing, it is only two of Parsons' four who have become ours; why, if Parsons was so influential, do we not teach Marshall and Pareto along with Weber and Durkheim? That is a rhetorical question here, to which no answer will be attempted, but it could merit study. We may also note that it is worth asking why any of Parsons' choices have become ours; he was not a prominent figure in the profession when his book was published. Perhaps the perception of him as having been so influential is also a retrospective reconstruction of history in the light of his later repute?

[3] There is a considerable body of work related to these themes in the older sociology of science, though most of this is concerned with short-term status rather than long-term reputation. Thus Diana Crane (1965) showed that location at a major university played a significant role in creating visibility and gaining recognition for scientists. Robert K. Merton suggested that there is a 'Matthew effect' by which those who are better known already receive more of the credit for new work. Cole and Cole (1973: 191–215) found that in the sample of natural scientists whom they studied significant work tended to be recognised whoever had produced it, but that the whole work of those seen as leading figures was more widely diffused, so that even their minor work which, done by others, would have received little attention, was known. The pattern is one in which social stratification makes the work of those who rank higher more salient.

it to serve a broader cause were more likely to be remembered, or resurrected later when the theme came to prominence. After death, the availability of others with a stake in preserving the reputation is often crucial; these are close allies who take some responsibility for the memory of an artist after her or his death. They show that the women they studied were less likely to be married than the men or, if married, were likely to outlive their husbands; they were, thus, less likely to leave behind anyone who would organise retrospective exhibitions, make donations to galleries, save papers, and so on. The consequence is that, of women and men of equal repute during their lives, the men are more often remembered now.

In those cases family was important, but the same role can be played by other groups, and in academic life more commonly is. Laub and Sampson (1991) have studied the posthumous reputation of Sheldon and Eleanor Glueck, and argue that little justice has been done to them historically in their debate with Edwin Sutherland. They suggest that this is not due to the relative merits of their research findings. A key factor was their institutional location. Sheldon Glueck was a professor of criminology in the Harvard Law School, where research on the causes of crime was not a valued or usual activity; Eleanor Glueck was unable to obtain any teaching position at Harvard, and for more than thirty years had only a research post in the Law School. Thus they had no opportunity to train graduate students and 'Quite simply, no-one had a stake in defending the Gluecks' (Laub and Sampson 1991: 1427).

Laub and Sampson also draw attention to other factors, of both intellectual and social significance. The Gluecks were handicapped as far as influencing *sociology* was concerned. Harvard sociology for much of their time showed little or no interest in the study of crime, and was heavily theoretically oriented, while their work was atheoretical and, indeed, hostile to theory. They stressed faithfulness to the data, which drove them in the direction of explanation in terms of multiple causes not all of which fitted into any one disciplinary framework. Sutherland, on the other hand, was not only an established sociologist but attacked the Gluecks' work to put forward his own purely sociological version of crime causation. Hence he had greater plausibility within sociology and, although many of his criticisms of their work were unfounded or tendentious, he won the argument for sociological posterity. (The relevance of disciplinary boundaries will be considered further below.)

Another case, documented by Bulmer (1991), is that of W. E. B. Du Bois. He was the author of *The Philadelphia Negro* (1899), a remarkable study for its time which received almost no attention from sociologists then and has figured little in historical accounts. He published a number of further monographs, carried out with inadequate resources, and was a serious scholar despite heavy teaching pressures which gave him little time for research. He had started his career promisingly, with a Harvard degree and graduate work including two years in Berlin. But he was black, and his race meant that he could not hope for a job in a research university; thus he could not have the opportunity to train research students who would carry his legacy to the mainstream of white sociology. In mid-career, he became so disillusioned that he left academic life and turned to political activism; an additional consequence of this was that his earlier work became seen from that perspective, and defined as not really an academic contribution.

Many writers have written about the functions of the invocation of classics. Jones (1980) brilliantly demonstrates that this can be presented as a system of Durkheimian religious ritual and myths, reaffirming the collective identity through sacred rites; the fact that his presentation is in the form of a spoof does not make it less telling. Stinchcombe (1982) lists uses of classics, from badges to indicate what tradition one is working in to shared disciplinary ritual. (There are also more purely normative discussions, such as those of Alexander (1987). Here the normative aspects are not to the point.) The debate between 'presentist' and 'historicist' approaches, in which the former favour continuing use for current purposes of 'classic' authors while the latter want them to be understood in terms of the meanings they had in their original contexts, is usefully summarised in Seidman (1985) and Jones (1985). This discussion is normally conducted about theoretical classics, but is equally applicable to methodological ones. Thus the 'memories' represented by the selection and invocation of classics can often be seen as disciplinary social rituals, or as in other ways serving purposes quite distinct from those of history.

The general picture painted by the authors cited is one where relevant factors include the nature of the original work, the original writer's entourage and the intellectual setting of later potential users. The original work can make claims and provide labels which will be used to characterise it, can offer handles for commentary or unanticipated uses, and can associate itself with prestigious themes and groups. The writer who leaves a surviving entourage with a stake in the continuity of the original reputation is more likely to have steps taken which enhance memory. From among available sources, later potential users are likely to choose those which confer credit or serve other current purposes in their immediate setting. Against this background, we turn now to consider the choices memory has made on questions of method.

EXEMPLARS

Far more works are published than ever receive detailed attention from many readers. Of those that are published, a minority are singled out for special status: books the well-informed sociologist should have read this year, cult works for a particular group, aunt sallies that the sociologist *au courant* will attack, founding fathers, symbols of a particular intellectual position. The rest vanish from sight, or are referred to only by specialists in their fields. Those that remain are, with hindsight, defined as the important ones. Whether or not they are always worthy of that status, at least some become objectively important in the sense that their ideas are influential and they provide a basis for future work. This is true even though the inspiration taken from them may rest on misinterpretation,[4] or selective attention to aspects not the most salient for the original author. (A few of those forgotten will later be resurrected, and may then come to the fore.)[5]

Kuhn has written about exemplars/paradigms and their role in natural science. By 'exemplar' he means:

[4] Parkin (1974), in his spoof Althusserian-Marxist analysis of a children's story, provides a truly inspiring example of what can be done in the way of creative reading to find exemplification of the points one wants.

[5] Such predecessor-selection has been made, in our field, by Deutscher (1973), who argues that a historic study by LaPiere provides a better model than most subsequent work; a very interesting problem is raised, but Deutscher does not really solve it, which may be why his resurrection attempt has not had widespread success. Another possible example is Webb, Campbell, Schwartz and Sechrest (1966). Here the examples used are not necessarily old, but the purpose of the book is to introduce a new concept ('unobtrusive method'), and it redefines existing work – not previously seen as similar – as exemplifying unobtrusiveness. This redefinition has had considerable success; it is not hard to apply, and the moral drawn is not hard to act on.

the concrete problem-solutions that students encounter from the start of their scientific education, whether in laboratories, on examinations, or at the ends of chapters in science texts. To these shared examples ... should be added at least some of the technical problem-solutions found in the periodical literature ... that also show them by example how their job is to be done. (Kuhn 1970)

It may be questioned whether there are 'exemplars' in sociology in the full Kuhnian sense. However, Kuhn's account of textbooks reconstructing history to create a 'tradition' of exemplary works leading to the latest developments is obviously consistent with some of the phenomena in sociology to which we have drawn attention.

The use of the term 'exemplar' here is not intended to carry all Kuhn's connotations, but to be broader and vaguer because, while examples and exemplars may be distinguished in principle, they are often not distinguished in practice. In the normative literature on method examples are naturally likely to be chosen from instances regarded as exemplary; when a work is innovative, or exceptionally skilled, it may be both exemplary and the only available example of a general point. Even where that is not so examples tend to be drawn from works commonly regarded as exemplary, simply because those are likely to be already known to readers or easily accessible. A work not initially seen as exemplary may become such through the salience given to it by use as an example. In this section we are concerned with the examples treated in the methodological literature as significant, perhaps only by subgroups.

Which empirical works are drawn on in methodological writing, and how are they chosen? Certain examples recur: *Life and Labour of the People in London* (Booth 1892–97), *The Polish Peasant* (W. I. Thomas and Znaniecki 1918–20), *Middletown* (Lynd and Lynd 1929), *The Jack-Roller* (Shaw 1930), *The Family Encounters the Depression* (Angell 1936), *Mental Disorders in Urban Areas* (Faris and Dunham 1939), *The Unemployed Man and his Family* (Komarovsky 1940), *Street Corner Society* (Whyte 1943), *The People's Choice* (Lazarsfeld, Berelson and Gaudet 1944), *The American Soldier* (Stouffer, Guttman, Suchman et al. 1949–50),[6] *Suicide* (Durkheim 1951). These tend to be used not

---

[6] There has been a tendency among later writers to regard this as an unchallenged leader and formative influence; several respondents, however, gave accounts of a packed and dramatic meeting at Chicago at which it was strongly criticised, as well as similar criticisms made elsewhere. See Lerner in Merton and Lazarsfeld 1950 for a systematic analysis of tendencies in its reception.

merely as examples, but as exemplars. They are all books which made their mark for non-methodological reasons too, but that is not a sufficient cause for a work to become used in this way. Not all the books listed were equally emphasised as exemplars by everyone, and articles and other shorter works are also sometimes used as in this way as exemplars. Lundberg and his sympathisers, for instance, had as their own special exemplars Dodd's *A Controlled Experiment on Rural Hygiene in Syria* (1934) and Stouffer's 'Intervening opportunities: a theory relating mobility and distance' (1940); in sharp contrast, Everett Hughes' postwar Chicago students looked to his *French Canada in Transition* (1943).

Textbook writers are likely, both for pedagogical reasons and for reasons of personal familiarity, to choose as their exemplars or examples works on striking subjects of general interest; the aficionado will favour cases of more specialist interest. The ideal methodological exemplar is in principle one which is a clear case of a category, without confusing features; books with mixed methods are less likely to be suitable. However, that will not stop the user treating books with mixed methods as though they only had one if that is convenient to the purpose in hand; stereotypes may develop which have little connection with the whole book as it was actually written. (Hughes is, rightly, looked back to as a leader in qualitative work, but *French Canada in Transition* contains, in addition to much fieldwork material, 49 tables and 19 figures.)

Examples may substitute for analysis; an empirical study can be used as ostensive definition of what is meant, as happened in much of the 'case-study' literature. A concrete instance may be worth many words of abstract definition, but it may also mean that the reader is left not at all clear which features of the instance are the crucial ones.[7] Does that matter? Maybe not. If the point is to hold out an ideal, there may be no existing work which fully exemplifies it. Any work which makes the required point will do if one already knows what the point to be made is; the example may

[7] A fluctuation of use in methodological discussion is shown in relation to *Middletown*, which appears as an example sometimes of a 'survey' and sometimes of a 'case study'. It was available for use in this way because it had some of the defining features of each category. This brings out characteristics of the categories, not just of the book; they had different bases of definition.

then be chosen at random intellectually – which probably means that it will be far from random socially. If, however, the writing represents new methodological thought, its content will be affected by the nature of the examples used, which may, indeed, have sparked off reflection on a new issue. The symbiotic relationship between examples and general ideas is one of the factors which shapes the overall pattern of writing done, but it would be rash to assume that there is always an optimal intellectual match between them.

For some of the exemplars, one can be reasonably sure that the reason they were chosen is that the author has explicitly treated methodological issues, in the text and/or in closely associated other publications. *An American Dilemma* (Myrdal 1944), for instance, achieved equal or greater prominence, but is seldom mentioned in methodological contexts. This is presumably because its focus is not on presenting the details of the data in a technically social-scientific way. If the book is mentioned, that is likely to be in the context of the role played by the social scientist's values and biases, because that is an issue which Myrdal does discuss. Other factors are also relevant, as some examples show. *Street Corner Society* did not become an exemplar of participant observation until Whyte contributed a chapter on 'Observational fieldwork methods' to the second volume of Jahoda, Deutsch and Cook in 1951 and, more importantly, the second edition of 1955 added the famous methodological appendix. It is particularly interesting that this, with its emphasis on the relational problems of fieldwork and its place in Whyte's personal life, led to the book's methodological meaning being interpreted in significantly different ways from some of those which had seemed most relevant before. There has been little or no commentary within sociology on its connections with obviously behaviouristic and positivistic orientations to observation and to study of small groups, despite some clues given in the text and in the Jahoda et al. chapter. Argyris, in a little-known contemporary booklet whose contents had been approved by Whyte, linked him with other 'interactionists' (n.b. certainly *not* symbolic interactionists):

The interactionists, following Bridgman and other positivists, insist . . . that the most fruitful area of discourse is that which is given to immediate experience (i.e. that which is objective) and that which can be measured by certain specific concrete operations . . . Whyte agrees that all feelings of individuals can be inferred from changes in their basic interaction pattern. (Argyris 1955: 41, 45)[8]

However, as Whyte has explained (Whyte 1981: 359), he wrote the appendix as he did to meet what he and his then colleagues felt as the teaching need for realistic descriptions of the experience of field research. The consequence was not merely a new salience for the book, but also a new perception of its methodological meaning.

Another example is Durkheim's *Suicide*, which was hardly available for exemplary status until it was translated in 1951, though originally published long before. Selvin's classic article (1958) helped to establish it as a methodogical exemplar. It established it, however, as an ancestor of multivariate analysis of the kind associated with his close colleague Lazarsfeld, and thus shifted the interpretation of its methodological meaning away from the more philosophical aspects on which it stated general positions shared with the author's *Rules* (1895, 1938). (This way of relating it to current concerns was the methodological equivalent of the shift in interpretation of the *Rules* and *Suicide* from earlier versions to one which connected them theoretically with functionalism and substantively with deviance; for more on this see J. Platt 1995b.)

Such striking shifts of interpretation have not occurred for all the exemplars. For some the process of selection looks very simple: both *The Family Encounters the Depression* and *The People's Choice* report research which was in part motivated by methodological interest in a somewhat novel strategy, and so they exemplified a point not equally available elsewhere as well as writing about it fully; as it happens they were also substantively about topical issues of wide interest, even though from the point of view of the authors that was not important and the substantive subject could have been different. Some books, particularly *The Jack-Roller* and *Mental Disorders in Urban Areas*, are especially suitable as examples because they are unusually pure and correct specimens of a current theoretical category. *Life and Labour of the People of London*, *The Polish Peasant* and *Middletown* did not all stand alone as books presenting data collected in that way on their subjects, but they certainly had the advantage of relatively few rivals, as did the Chicago monographs

---

[8] For more and more easily accessible information on the intellectual context which this reflects, see Homans 1985: 162–5.

of the 1920s. Just how few the rivals were, however, may be questioned; it is, of course, precisely because these works have been used as exemplars that we are well aware of them and much less familiar with their contemporaries.

Examination of the way in which one category has been used and exemplified in the literature will throw further light on these issues. 'Case-study method' was a concept of key importance in interwar methodological discourse, but it is often not clear just what it includes and excludes. The term was sometimes used, for instance, as if it were synonymous with the use of 'personal documents' as data, while at other times it was used as if it included any intensive study of a small number of cases whatever the type of data. On the assumption that it would be wrong to conclude from this either that it had no specific meaning, or that one of the apparent meanings was the correct or fundamental one, I set out to explore its meaning by the analysis of exemplars. The practical meaning of a methodological category, especially one without an explicitly operationalised procedure, depends heavily on the instances seen as exemplifying it. Strategically chosen instances may, therefore, put flesh on the bones of abstract definitions. The strategy was to choose the most diverse possible instances used as examples of it in the methodological literature, and to compare them with both the abstract definitions offered and the most super-ficially similar examples not used as examples. If rational principles of classification are being used, with categories which are internally homogeneous and clearly distinct from each other, this should enable one to infer the *fundamentum divisionis*.

This logically attractive strategy did not turn out to be very useful for its intended purpose, because it became clear that 'rational principles of classification' were not being used. Some of those cases used as instances of 'case study' had rather little in common with the abstract definitions of it. That is not in itself very problematic, since there is nothing unusual in practice failing to live up to an ideal, or not corresponding perfectly to a constructed type. More worrying is the fact that no purely methodological criterion could be identified which enabled one to distinguish between the cases which were and were not used as instances. Indeed, some of the examples not used fitted the abstract type *better* than did some which were used. Thus the pattern cannot be accounted for by the making of arbitrary choices from among equally eligible candidates, which suggests that social rather than intellectual factors must be involved.

To explore this further, a list was made of criteria which, on whatever ground, looked plausible as a basis for discriminating among at least some of the cases; these criteria ranged from features commonly found in agreed 'case studies' but not treated as part of its definition (e.g. use of social-work records) to social background features (e.g. association with Ernest Burgess). No feature distinguished all members of one group from all of the other, but two factors covered much of the ground. The first of these was the availability of some other methodological category, also current at the time, which could be applied to the instance in question; almost any study of a community could be called 'survey' or 'ecological' instead, and it makes sense for this ambiguity to make such studies less eligible to exemplify one of the categories. The other feature cannot be justified logically: it is that the study was done at Columbia, stereotyped as the home of the 'statistical method' counterposed to the case-study method associated with its rival Chicago. Moreover, two had an additional feature to dissociate them from Chicago. One, Lundberg, Komarovsky and McInery's *Leisure* (1934), was by an author already well known as a critic of the case study and proponent of quantification. Another, Caroline Ware's *Greenwich Village*, has an appendix on method which appears to dissociate itself deliberately from the Chicago style. Great emphasis is given to the importance of evaluating the evidence critically as a historian does, and this is surely a dig at Chicago:

> The practice used in some studies of presenting excerpts of material, apparently on the assumption that the reader is in a position to interpret the material, fails to recognise the basis necessary for interpretation and relieves the author of a responsibility which is rightly his.

She also implies that what she sees as the full-length case study is psychological rather than sociological, and most appropriate to behaviour problems such as delinquency (Ware 1935: 433, 429). The two other instances are Willard Waller, *The Old Love and the New* (1930), and Theodore Abel, *Why Hitler Came Into Power* (1938); both are very suitable as examples in that they draw heavily on rich qualitative life-history data. I asked Herbert Blumer why he thought Abel's use of life-history material should have received so little attention at Chicago, and he replied that Abel was known mainly as a theorist, particularly of German sociology (Blumer 1982). Perhaps another suggestion might be that his subject had more reverberations in the New York intellectual community, which had many Jews and refugees from Hitler and was nearer to Europe psychologically as well as geographically. No such reason can be offered for the neglect of Waller, who had even done graduate work under Burgess at Chicago, and described his own book as a case study.[9]

The Columbia connection could have operated in at least two ways. First, it could have made the Chicago-based writers responsible for much of the methodological literature less likely to be familiar with the works, even though they were published, because they would not have been present in the vicinity when the work was being done or had it drawn to their attention by daily contact with the authors. Second, anyone familiar with the stereotypically contrasted departmental reputations would be less likely to perceive work coming from Columbia as central to the case-study tradition, or even part of it.

If the relevant issue is not whether a work is an example of a category, but just whether it is good, interesting or distinctive for its method, it is harder to look systematically for instances of use or non-use to compare. It is, nonetheless, still worth considering whether the choices made in some unsystematically identified cases are intellectually consistent. Parallel with the case-study instances studied is the strange absence of the well-known study by Blau (1955) from discussions of participant observation, despite the fact that he used it successfully at the same period as the studies which are frequently cited. A rather different example, which could have been made the basis of a standard methodological argument, is the study by Gillin (1937) of prisoners, in which he ingeniously addressed the question of causation by adopting a design in which each prisoner in his sample was compared with his non-prisoner brother. Margaret J. Hagood's *Mothers of the South* (1939) has a sophisticated strategy for using qualitative data, locating each illustrative case in relation to the mode and extreme values on the

---

9 It is striking how much less Pauline Young's *Pilgrims of Russian-Town* is referred to than the other methodologically comparable monographs in the Chicago series. Is this because, despite her Chicago connections, it was not written in Chicago? Or because it does not fit the stereotype of the series because its data were collected in Los Angeles?

variable of concern, which happily combines statistical and case-study logics. Du Bois' *The Philadelphia Negro* is, Bulmer (1991) suggests, a study unique in its intensity of detail on an urban community, addressed with theoretical and methodological sophistication. One does not need to evaluate these studies as wholly outstanding to think that they were at least as worthy of citation as methodological examples as some which have commonly been used for that purpose.

Barry Barnes (1982), in a general discussion, proposes a 'finitist' conception of knowledge which sees the application of concepts as decided *ad hoc* in particular cases, and current definitions as depending upon community consensus on a body of shared examples, from which application to new cases cannot be conclusively predicted. He argues that linguistic usage in any culture 'tends towards conditions of maximum cognitive laziness' (1982: 105), and social interaction enables rules to be left implicit. This conception has a very good fit to what appears to have happened. It predicts that it will be difficult to infer exactly what the shared understandings were from the written generalisations made by members of intellectual subcultures based upon close social contacts, and it is highly consistent with, if it does not directly predict, a situation where potential exemplars arising outside the relevant social network are ignored. It also implies that more precise and explicit statements of principle are likely to be made as the relevant community becomes larger and more diverse and social relations thinner, which one could reasonably maintain is what has happened in methodological writing in sociology.

REPUTATIONS

The reputed 'great schools' of research method in sociology in our period have been Chicago/qualitative and Columbia/survey. Obviously both the groupings referred to have had important features other than method, so the whole phenomenon is not done justice by our focus on method – but nor is it done justice by the commoner focus on theory. For this chapter, we consider not their merits or the magnitude of their objective contributions but how it comes about that they are generally accepted as great schools of method, while other places and focuses of intellectual interest have received much less attention. It is taken for granted here that merely being truly meritorious and large contributors is not a sufficient explanation, even if it is a necessary condition for such recognition. It is especially important that this position should be taken, since our perceptions of their 'objective' merit are likely to have been formed by the same historical processes.

It seems highly likely that substantive characteristics of the work done help to draw attention to its methodological strengths. If methodological strength alone were sufficient one might, for instance, expect Minnesota under Chapin and his students to have had a comparable reputation, but his substantive work was not seen as of particular interest, and much of it related to social work as much as to sociological topics. Burt (1982: 125–8) shows, in relation to a more recent group of methodologists, that groups within a network were more prominent if they worked closely together in the same substantive area; elite experts not involved in such substantive relationships were invisible as a group, though prominent as individuals.

Sheer size of the groups in question must be a necessary condition to be seen as a prominent school, though that is not sufficient, since there have been other large departments whose reputations have not been at all comparable. Size not only helps visibility in the eyes of others, but provides more graduates to spread the word. Chicago and Columbia each had a charismatic leader, Park and Lazarsfeld respectively, who is agreed to have been the cause of work by others which they would not have produced without that facilitation. Robert Park was generally known as a supervisor who could squeeze theses out of students (Bulmer 1984a: 97–9, 103); Nels Anderson (quoted in Matthews 1977: 109), one of his students, remarked that: 'Some he drains so dry they never piss another drop.' Lazarsfeld's reputation has laid less stress on the extent to which he provided a framework which carried students through substantive studies, as well as directing them to problems, but it is fair to suggest that some of his colleagues were dependent on him for the work for which they are best known. Where there is such a relationship, those whose standing has depended on their leader are most likely to feel loyalty and to have a stake in the continuance of his reputation. That capacity, and that style of work, are thus the ones which are most likely to leave a faithful group.

Whatever the limitations of the literature on schools, it brings out the potential significance of conscious groupings which provide for the creation, diffusion and transmission of traditions. Equally good ideas and practices will have different fates if they are or are not associated with such a grouping; for recognition, the ideas or practices also require to be labelled, not merely tacitly transmitted, though tacit transmission may have an equal or greater effect on practice. The comparison of Stouffer and Lazarsfeld is useful to bring out some of these points. Both are recognised as very important figures, who played a leading role in methodological developments. Stouffer was widely respected and liked, and had his base at first one and then another of the leading graduate departments as well as participating actively in key roles extra-departmentally, but he has not had the same kind of posterity; his reputation is an individual one, which has not been seen as having consequences beyond his lifetime. Why is that?

There are a number of converging reasons, probably more than are necessary to account for the outcome. He died relatively young, which might be relevant; he cooperated so closely with Lazarsfeld over many years, and both were so much associated with the survey, that it is possible that his reputation became subsumed under Lazarsfeld's, despite the real differences in their work (J. Platt 1986c: 100–3). It was only in the wartime research that Stouffer first took an active part in surveys, and he continued to advocate experimentation as preferable, even though he did not himself act on this recommendation. He did not write much about survey method as such, while Lazarsfeld, who was associated with it for longer, wrote a lot on various aspects of it. When the survey came to have such vogue, therefore, it was Lazarsfeld who was more obviously relevant.

Stouffer worked cooperatively in three centrally important enter-prises: the series of monographs on social aspects of the Depression, *An American Dilemma* (Myrdal 1944), and the wartime research which eventually produced *The American Soldier*. Each produced highly respected publications, but none led to continuing institutionalised groupings, though there were individual contacts and alliances. Before the war Stouffer participated in the research life of the Chicago department, where he fitted into the demographic/statistical subgrouping; the data used in that area are normally available statistics such as Census data, and so data collection did not create a social base. (There was work particularly concerned with the Chicago area, on which data were compiled, but this was not his field.) It was others who established units which carried forward the relationships of the war. After the war, he went to head the Laboratory of Social Relations in the newly founded Department of Social Relations at Harvard. This was an umbrella organisation whose function was to facilitate the research of all members of the department, and they worked in a great variety of styles. He did not dominate or guide the body of work done there, and kept his own research to himself. He wanted to be close to his own data, as is shown by the many anecdotes about him set in the machine room as the results came through. He had his students, and they have marked his memory, but there was no memorial volume with contributions from others. Instead, Lazarsfeld wrote an introduction to a collection of Stouffer's papers, which he had put together himself before his death; in this introduction Lazarsfeld not only praised Stouffer's contribution to the growth of sociology as a science, but undertook to signpost its key features. This was a useful function to perform because Stouffer did not do it himself: 'When he had an important idea he developed it so that it would enter into the collective stream of scholarly work' (Stouffer 1962: xxxi).

Lazarsfeld, in contrast, was not only a builder of institutions but also famous for his keenness to recruit others to work on problems he was interested in. Thus in the postwar period he had many more who were dependent on him and/or worked with him, and who had stakes in his BASR. A study of citations to the work of the two men showed, suggestively, that over the time 1940–60 when both were active Lazarsfeld received more citations from authors with whom he had some kind of personal contact – most of them, moreover, not accountable for by the citing and the cited work coming from the same field (J. Platt 1986c: 108). Lazarsfeld's colleagues have left innumerable memorials to him, as well as imitating the institutions he created (Merton, Coleman and Rossi 1979, Sills 1987). He had his festschrift, though his continuing activity made it so late that it became a memorial volume, and there have been further publications since his death. (He had the advantage of leaving a widow who was a colleague, and so could participate actively in the production of these volumes.)[10] As an émigré who became famous

---

[10] However, his own institution, BASR, did not have the conditions which enabled it to survive, so that vehicle for maintaining his reputation has gone, and even his junior

in his new country he was a source of pride to Austrians, who have also helped to maintain his posthumous repute. Perhaps more important in Europe generally was that he played a prominent role in exporting the survey there, under the Ford Foundation and UNESCO auspices which were significant in the American hegemony of the post-Second World War settlement. Any flagging in his American base could be compensated by European support. His personal commitment to analysing and labelling methodological issues, as contrasted with Stouffer, means that his contributions can be easily identified, and may even be overestimated because he has made explicit what others left implicit. It has also been suggested that the historical writing in which he became interested late in his career (see Oberschall 1972) constructed a picture which overestimated the significance of the work of himself and his associates. If so, nothing could be more normal. Thus everything about Lazarsfeld's style of operation was likely to promote the recognition and continued reputation of his contribution.

Other issues than the prominence of individuals and graduate schools are raised by our study. Among the factors affecting the transmission of reputations and the collective memory are the disciplinary boundaries drawn in constructing the history of sociology. The history of *sociology* is assumed to be about 'sociologists', which implies the exclusion from it of other people. Mrs Ethel Sturges Dummer's name hardly figures in the history of sociology; when it does appear, that has almost invariably been with reference to her role in funding various activities related to sociology. However, in Chicago in the 1920s and in the American Sociological Association she played a much wider role than that suggests. She was a wealthy woman who did indeed fund many activities to do with social betterment, among them sociological ones. But she did not only fund them; she frequently initiated them. In particular, she was responsible not just for commissioning W. I.

---

colleagues there have now reached retirement age. He will not be forgotten, but his special association with method, and in particular a method so successful that it has become universal and has been worked on by many successors who have developed it in their own directions, leaves his memory at some disadvantage as compared with those especially associated with a substantive specialism. He is especially associated with communication research, but the extent to which this has now developed as a distinct discipline, rather than a specialism within sociology, means that that does little for his general sociological reputation.

Thomas to undertake the work for *The Unadjusted Girl* (1923), but also for contributing data and ideas to it. She published an article on the Soviet Five-Year Plan in the *American Journal of Sociology* (Dummer 1933), and organised several symposia which led to publications quite well known at the time. She kept up an extensive intellectual correspondence, and frequently circulated copies of articles she thought important to academics she thought should know about them. Her activity in the American Sociological Association included involvement in the foundation of the Section on the Family; she organised, chaired and gave reports at its sessions, and was its secretary in 1925–26. She was a member of the executive committee of the ASA from 1927–30. All this (and much more)[11] was done without her ever holding a paid job, although she was practically and intellectually as important to the discipline as many who held a job title. History has rewarded her by remembering only her money. This surely is largely because she was not formally a 'sociologist'.

That is a handicap which Mrs Dummer shares with a considerable number of other people in the earlier stages of the development of empirical sociology. Most of these, though not all, were women, and Deegan (1988) has documented the processes by which some, such as Jane Addams and others associated with her circle around the Hull-House settlement she founded in Chicago, were at first regarded as sociologists and then redefined as social workers or, if in academic posts, relegated to departments with titles such as 'household administration' or 'home economics'. The University of Chicago Department of Sociology in the 1920s was part of a wider context in the city of Chicago which was of considerable importance to it. However, in accounts of the department by its own members and by historians the significance of this context has been downgraded. It is quite frequently mentioned, but normally in a way which takes it for granted that the university sociologists were the important and leading figures, at least as far as research was concerned. That is quite a misleading picture, as J. Platt (1994a) documents. Here we concentrate on one aspect of the way in which the sociologists were given priority; in this case it is literal priority, in time.

The Chicago sociologists of the 1920s are generally described as

---

11 For more details about Mrs Dummer, see J. Platt 1992a.

pioneers in research methods: the first to use systematic empirical data, and the inventors of new methods, especially participant observation and the collection and mapping of quantitative ecological data. The university certainly engaged in large-scale data-collection. But how pioneering were they, and did they invent these methods? The earlier 'social survey movement' had of course collected much quantitative data. Several authors have pointed out that the women of the Hull-House settlement were collecting systematic data about Chicago before the sociology department did (Deegan 1988: 33–69, Fish 1985, Sklar 1985). Social workers of the period, including those in Chicago, frequently carried out research, which was seen as a normal part of their training. The Juvenile Protective Association (JPA) in Chicago employed investigators who collected large amounts of data. The JPA was part of the nexus of institutions which led to the setting up of the first child guidance clinic, under Dr William Healy (recruited and funded by Mrs Dummer). His many published case studies of children, such as *The Individual Delinquent* (1915), were frequently drawn on by sociologists, as were those of the pioneering California social worker Miriam van Waters (e.g. van Waters 1926). The university was, thus, by no means alone, or first, in the field. What about specific methods?

Let us cite some extracts from publications to exemplify the methods in use:

'another investigator (a man) was employed to visit . . . restaurants and music halls, and by treating the women to drinks to get them to tell their own stories . . . investigators spent some time watching prostitutes, either at their professional haunts or at common lodging houses and other places where they talked among themselves when off duty.'

Investigators 'mingled with the men and girls, sat in the saloons, danced in the halls, and talked with manager, employees and patrons. Their observations were carefully noted on cards prepared for the purpose and filed daily'.

The investigation included the personal histories of '200 department store girls, of 200 factory girls, of 200 immigrant girls, of 200 office girls, and of girls employed in over one hundred hotels and restaurants'.

I think that anyone broadly familiar with the 'Chicago School' work of the 1920s would find that these accounts sounded familiar, and assume that they came from the university department. None of them does. The first is from Royden (1916: 13–14), the second from Bowen (1917: 3), and the third from Jane Addams' book on prostitution (1912: x). Maude Royden was a British feminist and preacher;[12] she reports the work of several contributors to an inquiry originally begun 'for social workers specially interested in discovering how far economic causes contribute to the making of prostitutes' (Royden 1916: 12). Louise de Koven Bowen was a Chicago society lady, the daughter of a banker, who in the 1890s started to be involved in many of the activities of Hull-House and the JPA, and was also active on many civic issues (Bowen 1926, Sicherman and Green 1980). In the quotation she is reporting work done by the JPA. Both Royden's and Bowen's enquiries also collected quantitative data on a large scale, in addition to the systematic participant observation reported above. Thus we see that just those methods, and indeed topics,[13] which were characteristic of the 'Chicago School' were equally characteristic of social workers and voluntary activists who were in the field somewhat sooner.

A closer investigation reveals that in the town of Chicago it is, indeed, often not easy to distinguish between the 'sociologists' and the rest. Several of the graduate-student authors of the classic university monographs supported themselves for some of the time by working for bodies such as the JPA, several of their professors were actively involved in the world of social work and reform, and university publications often rested to a striking extent on data provided by full-time participants in that world. Nor is it, as we perhaps tend parochially to assume, evident that it was necessarily the university people who were dominant in their contacts. The two groups were so intertwined that it might be more appropriate to regard them as one.

The official volumes about social-science research at the university (T. V. Smith and White 1929, Wirth 1940) give due credit to city predecessors, but define their work as an earlier stage on which more systematic and scientific university work has built; current connections with civic reformers and social agencies are treated as

---

[12] British and American workers in these fields were closely in touch at this period (J. Platt 1991).

[13] For more on this, see J. Platt 1994a.

a source of funding, sometimes for work done as public service rather than academic priority. Park's chapter (T. V. Smith and White 1929: 13–14) which sketches some of the relevant history, refers to the work of the Juvenile Court and Healy without mentioning at whose initiative they took place, thus implicitly co-opting them for the university in a way which does little justice to their origins. One can understand why it should be that celebratory volumes emphasise the contribution of the groups celebrated, but it would be a little naive to treat those versions at face value as simply the history of what happened. Accounts written from within sociology, as history of sociology, generally treat both other disciplines, and groups outside the academy, as parts of the background.[14] They are seen as instrumental to the main ends of sociologists, or as introducing distortions into the natural or appropriate course of pure sociological development. That is the perspective one expects when groups write their own history. In the case of 1920s Chicago, at least, this is singularly inappropriate, and it does not make sense either to draw a sharp boundary between 'sociology' and other activities, or to treat the latter as subsidiary. It is only by doing so that the university department has been made to appear pioneering in its research methods. Where it did make a distinctive contribution was not in the practicalities of research, but in its theorisation; they named methods, analysed them and rationalised them, especially in discussions of 'case-study' method. To say that is not to belittle the department's pioneering role within sociology, where what it did in practice as well as theory was indeed novel.

It is probable that a greater novel contribution was actually made by the Chicago social scientists in the area of quantitative method, which is not what they have been collectively famous for in the later discipline.[15] Martin Bulmer (1981) has done something to correct

[14] Bulmer (1981: 313) has pointed out that developments which cut across disciplines, such as that of random sampling and other quantitative methods, tend to be neglected in disciplinary histories. Another example of groups outside the academic structure which have been historically neglected is provided by Taylor (1994).
[15] This latter assertion is made with confidence for historical writing; it is quite possible, however, that there is at least one different reputation orally transmitted among groups who have not contributed to the historical writing and are more interested in quantitative work. It is demonstrably the case that 'Chicago' symbolises different themes in relation to different substantive fields. Harvey (1987b: 9–13) reviews a number of different conceptions of 'Chicago School'. Marlene Shore's (1987) book on the influence of Chicago

the balance here. He documents how there was in fact an important and influential stream of quantitative work at interwar Chicago, supported by provision of appropriate resources such as calculators in a statistical laboratory. Why should it be that the reputation of the department has been so overwhelmingly one for qualitative method, when there was always a significant commitment to quantitative work too? Bulmer suggests that one reason is that those committed to quantitative work are much less interested in their history. They see the development of their field as cumulative advance, and so do not legitimate their activities by reference to ancestors. Others do, however, and it is clear that a significant role has been played by the use of the 'Chicago School' as what we have called a school of retrospective identification. How has this happened?

There is current in American sociology, especially among those favouring qualitative approaches, an image of the early 'Second Chicago School' after the Second World War as a brilliant continuation of an established Chicago tradition of commitment to symbolic interactionism and participant observation.[16] This tradition is, however, seen as sadly shattered by the introduction of faculty from the survey camp in the 1950s, after which the department is perceived as having declined. There are considerable problems with this image. There is no doubt that there were, among the postwar cohorts at Chicago, some graduate students

---

in Canada shows an angle on familiar material where social ecology looms particularly large, and Hughes and McKenzie, with Canadian connections, become the most prominent figures. She also suggests (1987: 270) that Hughes was a particularly acceptable influence in some of the French-language universities because the French intellectual tradition of human geography, demography and Le Play had also been relevant to Chicago thinking. In the preface to his anthology of symbolic-interactionist work, Arnold Rose felt the need to remark that, while some used the term 'Chicago tradition' to refer to the Park/Burgess ecological and urban sociology, 'only those who had little or no direct contact with the University of Chicago's sociology department think of it as being primarily associated with ecological theory and research. Actually the Chicago sociologists always regarded ecology as a minor sub-field of sociology' (Rose 1962: viii). It would be rash to treat this as a simple statement of historical fact.

[16] It is interesting to consider that a plausible claim could be made for a Harvard school of fieldworkers, who took their message to Chicago; Warner and Whyte had both established themselves as fieldworkers at Harvard before moving to Chicago. *Applied Anthropology*, the journal of the Society for Applied Anthropology (which involved many of those committed to qualitative fieldwork), was based at Harvard, though associated with the Business School rather than social-science departments, and Arensberg and Chapple were its first editor and book review editor. Its early authors were heavily drawn from Harvard, and it had many articles from the Western Electric studies.

who did important participant-observation work and who wrote about its methods and rationale. The questions are whether they were typical or dominant, whether the pattern of methods used at Chicago was distinctive, and how far this represented continuity with the prewar period.

The faculty at Chicago were notoriously divided on questions of method, with numbers doing work which was predominantly quantitative in character, and controversy between the two groups. There were several faculty members who were prominent in demography and ecology, and they had a corresponding group of students. A study of a sample of theses submitted in 1946–62 shows that at each stage within that period approximately half of the theses used almost entirely quantitative methods; around a third were almost entirely qualitative, and of those only about half used fieldwork or participant observation.[17] That certainly does not show a qualitative majority among the theses, but it could still be that Chicago was stronger in the qualitative field than other universities. It is not practicable to compare theses, so a comparison has been made between both the sample of Chicago theses and a sample of 1945–59 journal articles, the latter divided into those which are by members of the Chicago cohort in question and the rest. This shows a very slight lead for Chicago in qualitative methods, and slightly more survey method elsewhere – but despite that two-thirds of even the Chicago articles are quantitative, 40 per cent of them using surveys. It is, thus, hard to sustain the argument that Chicago had a very distinctive output. It could be suggested that books would give a different impression, and they might; we note, however, that those best known for their qualitative books, such as Howard S. Becker, are also well represented among the articles.

Those who were present in the department at the time do not describe it as overwhelmingly qualitative in style (or committed to symbolic interactionism), though they did feel that it had a certain unity related to methodological issues. What they mention as unifying is the idea that it was possible to be scientific about society, with 'scientific' having the connotation of staying close to the data and only making well-founded assertions, and a strong commitment to empirical work rather than theory. Otis Dudley

---

[17] The detailed data, for this and subsequent such statements, are presented in J. Platt 1995a.

Duncan, a leader in quantitative work, described meeting Erving Goffman, famous for his qualitative work, after the celebrations for the 50th anniversary of the Social Science Research Building, and agreeing that despite their totally different styles of work they both felt like part of Chicago tradition: 'it was not a methodological style, but a kind of curiosity they had about human life' (Duncan 1984).

That part of the story of the golden age of qualitative method which sees the golden age as followed by decline also needs to be questioned, on numerical grounds. (Not everyone, of course, would accept that for less important qualitative work to be done was in itself a decline, if it was replaced by good quantitative work, though some see it in that way.) Chicago had historically been the largest single department. After the war, the GI Bill caused huge expansion everywhere. For 1947–50, the period when the maximum number of those well known for qualitative work were simultaneously present at the university, Chicago produced over 20 per cent of the total doctorates recorded in sociology. Its proportion then declined markedly, but this was not so much because Chicago numbers fell as because those elsewhere rose. That is just what one would expect in a time of expansion, when established schools would experience it first and then others grow to meet the demand, so that the original leaders have a lower proportion of the total number of students and become members of what is now a larger leading group. When an exceptionally large cohort of students graduates, it is normal, not a sign of decline, for them to disperse and take their messages elsewhere – perhaps to induct their students in turn into the traditions they carry. After the exceptionally large cohort, there will be smaller cohorts – and probably fewer academic jobs to keep them in the discipline, as demand declines and the large cohort get the available jobs first. It does not make sense, therefore, for the presence of fewer leading workers in the qualitative tradition at Chicago through the 1950s to be interpreted as showing decline; there were then both fewer doctorates being produced, and Chicago was providing a smaller proportion of the national total.

If those were the practical realities, why does the myth of the golden age have such currency? One answer is that it serves other current purposes than those of history. It is an origin myth, used to legitimate contemporary preferences by providing them with an

honourable past. This use is epitomised in the choice of the title
'Chicago Irregulars' by a California-based group of sociologists
committed to ethnographic styles of research. The journal *Urban
Life and Culture*, declaredly committed to an 'urban ethnography'
which seeks understanding through participant observation and
intensive interviewing, emerged from that group (Manning 1978),
and has repeatedly referred back to Chicago for inspiration.[18] It
may be noted that there is an interesting conflation of two Chicago
periods here. The urban theme has much more connection with the
famous interwar monographs, most obviously continued in the postwar period in the quantitative work done by the demographic group
at the Chicago Community Inventory, while the methods theme
connects more with postwar writings not on particularly urban
topics.

Another answer is that, though fieldworkers were never dominant at Chicago, there was a noticeable small cluster there when
there was no equivalent at other leading departments, so this could
reasonably be seen as a distinguishing feature. There are several
different ways in which methodological contributions and reputations can be made: carrying out empirical work treated as
exemplary by others, creating innovative methods in substantive
work, writing directly about method, researching method. Postwar
Chicago contributed in all these ways, with two senior faculty
members (Blumer and Hughes) and three graduates (Strauss,
Goffman and Becker) playing leading roles. Consciousness of
difference from what was becoming the mainstream led to the
elaboration of explicit justifications for what they were doing. Once
these justifications were written, they helped to create the rather
unbalanced conception of 'Chicago' on which we have commented.
Writers always tend to draw examples from work with which they
are already closely familiar, whether their own or that of colleagues,
and so to publicise it and draw exemplars from it; this is especially
likely to happen when, like most of these men, they are writing from
personal research involvement, not just as abstract methodological
discussion. Substantive works which stress issues of method are also
more likely to have it noticed and written about by others,
especially if, as with some of those from Chicago, they write well
about striking topics and so have many non-specialist readers.

[18] See Lofland 1980, and the whole issue of vol. XI, no. 4, 1983.

A small number of methodologically self-conscious writers in one place can, thus, have a multiplier effect on public images, as this group appears to have done. That would naturally be assisted, in this case, by the general prominence and total reputation of the department. It helped in this process historically that the New Left and counter-cultural movement from the late 1960s, in which many younger sociologists were involved, had as part of its ethos a hostility to 'science' and quantification which encouraged them to take up alternatives. The fact that many of the postwar Chicago studies focused on deviant groups, and pictured them sympathetically, also gave them a special appeal. This made 'Chicago' an ideal symbolic banner to rally round. For purposes of legitimation, association with the unquestioned leading role of the interwar department helped in what would otherwise have been an excessively youthful movement; even revolutionaries like to claim appropriate ancestors. Such claims have probably helped to sustain the reputation of the earlier Chicago School, and its perceived contemporary relevance, beyond what would otherwise have occurred.[19]

Baxandall (1985: 58–62) has argued that discussion of the relationship between two artists in terms of 'influence' is misleading, because the word reverses the roles of agent and patient. In reality, the second comer's behaviour is better described in such terms as 'draw on', 'adapt', 'face up to', or even 'parody' or 'distort'. We see that the same could be said of collective versions of the methodological history of sociology. They start, of course, from the basic 'facts', but from those selections are made to create origin myths for current use. Sub-groups within the discipline choose their own

---

[19] I have been struck, as I have worked over the years on what I define as the history of research methods, and therefore written some papers that relate to Chicago, by the frequency with which other people have defined it as working on the Chicago School; colleagues have appeared to find it hard to see the more general theme, because Chicago is so salient to them. It is interesting to note that not only has a disproportionate amount of historical work been (intentionally) about the Chicago School, but also that a disproportionate amount of it has been British (Bulmer 1984a, Harvey 1987b, Rock 1979, D. Smith 1988); there is a topic there too for the historian or sociologist of knowledge. Quite recently, historical attention has turned to Columbia; see, for instance, Sztompka 1986, Crothers 1987, 1990, forthcoming, S. P. Turner and J. H. Turner 1990, Camic and Xie 1994, S. P. Turner 1994. This could be interpreted as the natural progression from thesis to antithesis, attacking established emphases, or as simply indicating a turn to topics not yet exhausted.

preferences, and the discipline as a whole focuses on the history of sociology and omits those outside it who have played a part. Exemplars are chosen for reasons other than their perfect match to the ideas exemplified, and individual reputations have greater chances of survival if their holders have the right personal style and structural location. Some widely current interpretations rest on such processes. Some of these interpretations fit into larger patterns recognisable as stories with narrative plots of the kinds cited by Fred Davis (1984). Martin Bulmer (1981: 328) has identified the Whig and Inverse Whig patterns, in which the past is seen as leading directly to a glorious present, or as error which has now been triumphantly overcome. Non-Whig – if hardly Tory! – stories, in which the present is not glorious but a decline, are commonly told by those for whom a political agenda rather than a method-ological one is salient. For us, all these stories are themselves part of the data to be studied and analysed.

CHAPTER 8

Conclusion

Earlier chapters have tried to deal with a range of questions about the history of US sociological research methods. Here we do not so much summarise the material presented there as draw on it to construct an overall picture of the implied trajectory of development up to 1960. The development with which we are concerned is in both the practice of method and in its conceptualisation and theorisation; these cannot be dissociated from the wider sociological setting.

A changing background of historical events had direct consequences for sociological research; the key ones were the Depression, the Second World War and the postwar GI Bill expansion of the universities. The political response to the Depression enlarged research opportunities, both because much Depression-related research was funded and because work-relief meant that it could be staffed on a scale seldom practicable before. The war both led to further research mobilisation and concentration, and created a radical break in graduate-school continuity which made room for fresh influences from outside the academy and a change of direction; in addition, the success of the wartime research programme gave social science a prestige which encouraged funding support. The postwar expansion provided a cohort of graduate students of unprecedented size to carry forward what they were taught, and created academic job opportunities for them. As the role of government grew, the salience for sociologists of the important earlier constituency of social reformers and social workers diminished. Large economic and political events affected the role of government initiatives; more localised ones such as tax regimes and the invention of radio affected the availability of private sources of research funding such as foundations and commercial bodies. Funding was extremely important in enabling

272   SOCIOLOGICAL RESEARCH METHODS IN AMERICA

research to be done, but it does not follow that it constrained methods, or distorted the methodological patterns which would have been suggested by sociologists' free intellectual preferences.

At the level of practice, the significance of research methods increased considerably, simply because research became part of the normal role-expectations of far more academic sociologists. Concomitantly, the level of theorisation of research method, and self-consciousness about it, increased. Courses on it became universally required, even at the undergraduate level; textbooks and monographs were written; the convention that method should be carefully described when results were reported evolved. The availability of funding for research also increased, both from universities and from outside bodies, some interested in supporting 'basic' research and others not. This made more ambitious topics and methods, which did not need to rely on data already collected by others, accessible. Statistical theory as applied to social-scientific subjects made important advances. The emergence of the modern survey made it possible for the first time for quantification to explore correlations at the individual as well as the area level with large numbers of cases. The social technology of the survey research unit, with its breakdown of the research process into distinct stages and its corresponding division of labour among specialists, was created. In addition, the physical technology for dealing with some research tasks, especially those involving the processing of large numbers of items of information or the carrying out of complex calculations, developed enormously.

The research which sociologists published in journals, and probably also their research more generally, became increasingly quantitative in character, and its quantification took more sophisticated forms, though experts repeatedly had reason to complain of the failure of their colleagues to use appropriate available methods. Some of this transition, in the earlier part of the period, indicated not so much the choices made between empirical methods as the choice of systematic empirical methods where previously undocumented assertions had been common. The repertoire of known standard methods of data-collection expanded to include the modern survey and content analysis, and techniques of unstructured interviewing and structured observation were elaborated; the use of 'personal documents' and available records such as those of social workers went out of normal practice.

Questionnaire and interview data became increasingly common as the modern survey model was diffused, and concomitantly random sampling became normal. Ideas about the logic of experimental design were elaborated and applied to sociology, and design and analysis became more salient concerns. More radical, and less apparently cumulative, change took place in the way in which methods were conceptualised. A basic quantitative/qualitative antithesis was maintained (whether or not that had a good logical fit to the nature of what was actually being distinguished) while much else changed. It appears that technical change in the repertoire of methods led to reconceptualisation of the nature of the differences between them in order to allow the antithesis to be maintained when old boundaries became blurred. As a result, the modern category of 'participant observation' emerged to prominence in the set of perceived alternatives.

The ways in which these categories were applied and exemplified sometimes reflected socially shared stereotypes of different departmental research styles; such stereotypes could be quite misleading about the range of what was happening in the departments in question. Nonetheless, images such as those of Chicago as the home of qualitative method were very persistent. Leading departments cultivated unfavourable stereotypes of their rivals, and defined the world of sociological discourse differently for their students. The social functions served by that are obvious, but such labels were also used for the other function of defining the identity, and choosing the preferred ancestors, of current groupings on the basis of elective affinity. Accounts based uncritically on these images are not helpful as history, but the perceived divisions which they reflect can be seen as intellectually fruitful and even necessary: much methodological writing has moved forward by the critical analysis of previous positions, so that the long-term pattern is one of ebb and flow, or challenge and response.

Methodological writing has also been closely related to research practice, in that a high proportion of its new contributions appear to arise from the critical analysis of practice. But not all practical innovation is equally likely to be written about. External circumstances such as the need to defend oneself against the criticism of intellectual rivals or to explain and justify a new development which looks vulnerable, or the demand for training materials, have been significant. So also have the less socially structured personal agendas of strategically placed individuals, who have chosen to promote methodological writing by others as well as engaging in it themselves. Of the total methodological innovations made in practice, not all were documented; some which were documented only achieved that status some time after their invention and establishment in practice at their places of origin; some which were documented, at least in the sense that work using them was published, were not flagged by the authors as innovatory or given a clear capsule formulation, and so were not widely noticed as innovatory. On the other hand, some practices presented as innovations in the sociological literature were not new, in that others had already used them, though they were new to sociology.

The last point draws attention to a general issue, that of the boundaries between sociology and other parts of the world. Within the university, many methodological developments have drawn on ideas from other disciplines – often practices truly current in them, but sometimes ideas like 'science' whose authentically representative status is more questionable. Some universities may have ivory towers intellectually cut off from the surrounding society, but some departments of sociology, like the interwar University of Chicago one, have had sufficiently close relations with outside groups for it not to be clear where, or whether, the boundaries should be drawn. Similarly, parts of the world of the large foundations, and of governmental data-collection, have had close enough interchanges of personnel and ideas, and interdependence of interests, with university social scientists for it to make more sense to regard them as one community rather than as two for some purposes. Under these circumstances the history of sociology cannot sensibly be written separately from that of these links. The 'internal'/'external' distinction loses some of its force, and it is hardly appropriate to see the influence of the outside world as introducing distortion into the otherwise pure world of sociology. That comment is, however, an empirical one; the idea of distortion usually carries a normative weight independent of historical description. It would be desirable, in the interests of clarity, to separate the evaluative from the descriptive components.

Other factors draw boundaries within academic sociology. Differences between departments have been mentioned above, but there were also differences within them, often ones which corresponded to differences within the larger sociological community.

These included differences in methodological preferences, sometimes stated as such and sometimes associated with the intellectual traditions of particular specialisms; there have been national organisations corresponding to some of these subgroupings. One dividing line of particular importance is that of the academic division of labour among theorists, methodologists and empirical researchers. The notional intellectual interdependence of their activities does not mean that any one person is normally adept or interested in each of their spheres; hence it does not follow automatically, though it may be the case, that the practical relation among them is that which might seem logical. In particular, research methods may on the level of theory, when theory is consciously involved at all, reflect intellectual *bricolage* or *post hoc* justifications rather than the consistent working through of carefully chosen fundamental assumptions. Frequently methodological choices are steered by quite other considerations, some of a highly practical nature, and there are independent methodological traditions with their own channels of transmission. It cannot be taken for granted that what is done in particular research projects has a clear relationship even to the stated abstract positions of those carrying them out, let alone to the positions of others whose views might be seen as characterising their institution or era. In many cases general theoretical/methodological stances are just stances: slogans, hopes, aspirations, not guidelines with clear implications that are followed in practice. Programmatic statements cannot, therefore, be taken as descriptions; they are of interest in their own right, but practice has to be studied directly in *its* own right.

Sociological research methods are, thus, closely implicated with many other aspects of the discipline and the wider society. Their development and theorisation nonetheless has its own dynamics, which cannot be fully subsumed under other heads.

Interviews

The table below lists those whom I interviewed for this research; not all of them are cited in the text, but what all of them told me has contributed to my descriptions and interpretations. Only the names of those explicitly cited appear in the list of references. With some I had lengthy formal interviews, with others there was a fairly swift conversation snatched as the opportunity arose; the boundary between these is not clearcut, but where it seemed more appropriate the interchange has been described as 'conversation' rather than 'interview' to indicate its relative brevity and less systematic character.

The final column gives miscellaneous information to indicate the broad character of the sample in relation to the themes of this book, and the connections in which the material has been used. 'Methods with which associated' in some cases refers to a career-long commitment and expertise, while in others it indicates only an early publication or research practice which appears in the methodological literature; it should be interpreted, therefore, as showing something about why I chose to see that particular person rather than as an accurate general characterisation of them. Length of career was also, of course, a relevant factor, especially for the older generation. Where people are listed with prime disciplinary affiliations other than sociology, that is usually because they have been involved in work commonly referred to in the sociological literature, even often treated as sociological. Sol Tax was seen because he could throw light on the relation between sociology and anthropology at Chicago in the interwar period; those associated with funding bodies were seen to throw light on the funding relationship from their side.

Name	PhD date	PhD institution	Main later institutions	Background if not sociological, methods with which associated, other connections
Theodore Abel	1929	Columbia	Columbia	Life histories
C. Arnold Anderson	1932	Minnesota	Harvard, Iowa State, Kentucky, Chicago	Rural sociology
Odin Anderson	1948	Michigan	Michigan, Western Ontario, Health Information Foundation	—
Robert C. Angell	1924	Michigan	Michigan	Analytical induction, personal documents
R. Freed Bales	1945	Harvard	Harvard	Interaction process analysis
Allen Barton	1957	Columbia	Columbia	Survey, BASR
Howard S. Becker	1951	Chicago	Northwestern	Participant observation
Mrs L. Bergmann (re Gustav Bergmann)	—	—	Iowa	Vienna Circle (philosopher)
Hubert Blalock	1954	North Carolina	Michigan, Yale, UNC, Washington	Quantitative methods, textbook author
Herbert Blumer	1928	Chicago	Chicago, Berkeley	Qualitative methods
Jerome Bruner	1941	Harvard	Harvard	Psychologist; DPS, OPOR
Charles Cannell	1952	Ohio State	Michigan	Psychologist; survey; DPS, ISR
Ruth Shonle Cavan	1926	Chicago	Chicago, Northern Illinois	Case study
John Clausen	1949	Chicago	NIMH, Berkeley	*American Soldier*
Joseph Cohen	1936	Michigan	Washington	—
James Coleman	1955	Columbia	Johns Hopkins, Chicago	Mathematical sociology, BASR

Name	PhD date	PhD institution	Main later institutions	Background if not sociological, methods with which associated, other connections
Leonard Cottrell	1933	Chicago	Cornell, Russell Sage Foundation	*American Soldier*
James Davis	1955	Harvard	Chicago, Dartmouth, Harvard	Survey; NORC
John T. Doby	1956	Wisconsin	Wofford, Emory	Textbook author
Otis Dudley Duncan	1949	Chicago	Michigan, Chicago	Demography, mathematical sociology
Robert Ellis	1956	Yale	Oregon, Georgia	—
Ronald Freedman	1947	Chicago	Michigan	Demography
Eliot Freidson	1952	Chicago	New York	—
Herbert Gans	1957	Pennsylvania	Columbia	Participant observation
Burleigh Gardner	1936	Harvard	Chicago, Social Research Inc.	Qualitative methods
Laurence Garfinkel	—	—	—	American Cancer Society
Kent Geiger	1955	Harvard	Tufts, Wisconsin	—
Jacob Getzels	1951	Harvard	Chicago	Psychologist
Charles Glock	1952	Columbia	Columbia, Berkeley	Survey, BASR
Raymond Gold	1954	Chicago	Montana	Participant observation
Leo Goodman	1950	Princeton	Chicago	Quantitative methods
Edward Gross	1949	Chicago	Washington State, Minnesota, Washington	—
Robert Habenstein	1954	Chicago	Missouri	—
Oswald Hall	1948	Chicago	Toronto	—
Archibald Haller	1954	Wisconsin	Wisconsin	Survey

Name	PhD date	PhD institution	Main later institutions	Background if not sociological, methods with which associated, other connections
Philip Hauser	1929	Chicago	Chicago	Demography, quantitative methods, case study; Census
Paul Horst	1931	Chicago	Procter and Gamble, Washington	Psychologist; quantitative methods
Robert Kahn	1952	Michigan	Michigan	Psychologist; Census, survey, ISR
Daniel Katz	1928	Syracuse	Michigan	Psychologist; survey, DPS, ISR
Patricia Kendall	1954	Columbia	Queens, NY	survey, BASR
Leslie Kish	1952	Michigan	Census, Michigan	Survey sampling, DPS, ISR
Florence Kluckhohn	1941	Radcliffe	Harvard	Anthropologist; participant observation
Frank Kohout	1970	Case Western Reserve	Iowa	Iowa symbolic interactionism
Mirra Komarovsky	1940	Columbia	Columbia (Barnard)	—
Otto Larsen	1955	Washington	Washington	—
Arthur Lumsdaine	1949	Stanford	US Air Force, UCLA, Washington	Psychologist; *American Soldier*
Russell Middleton	1956	Texas	Florida State, Wisconsin	—
Frank Miyamoto	1950	Chicago	Washington	—
Charles Page	1940	Columbia	City College of NY, Smith, Princeton, Massachusetts	—
Bernard Phillips	1956	Cornell	Boston	Textbook author
Lee Rainwater	1954	Chicago	Social Research Inc., Harvard	—

Name	PhD date	PhD institution	Main later institutions	Background if not sociological, methods with which associated, other connections
Albert Reiss	1949	Chicago	Chicago, Vanderbilt, Michigan, Yale	—
Peter Rossi	1951	Columbia	Harvard, Chicago, Massachusetts	Survey, BASR, NORC
Irwin Sanders	1938	Cornell	Alabama, Kentucky, Ford Foundation, Boston.	Rural sociology
David Schneider	1949	Harvard	Chicago	Anthropologist; DPS
Morris Schwartz	1951	Chicago	Brandeis	Census, DPS; participant observation
William H. Sewell	1939	Minnesota	Oklahoma State, Wisconsin	Rural sociology, quantitative methods
Frederick Seymour	1958	Chicago	Northern Illinois	Demography
Lyle Shannon	1951	Washington	Wisconsin, Iowa	Quantitative methods
Paul Sheatsley	—	—	NORC	Survey, NORC
James Short	1951	Chicago	Washington State	—
Anselm Strauss	1945	Chicago	Chicago, California San Francisco	Qualitative methods
Francis X. Sutton	1950	Harvard	Ford Foundation	Ford Foundation
Frank Sweetser	1941	Columbia	Boston	Ecology/ demography
Sol Tax	1935	Chicago	Carnegie Institution, Chicago	Anthropologist
John Useem	1939	Wisconsin	S. Dakota, Wisconsin, Michigan State	—
Murray Wax	1959	Chicago	Kansas, Washington U. (St. Louis)	Participant observation

Name	PhD date	PhD institution	Main later institutions	Background if not sociological, methods with which associated, other connections
William F. Whyte	1943	Chicago	Chicago, Cornell	Participant observation
Robin Williams	1943	Harvard	Cornell	Rural sociology, *American Soldier*
Hans Zeisel	1928	Vienna	Columbia, Chicago	Vienna Circle

References

ARCHIVAL SOURCES

The main archives used, with their short titles, have been: the Department of Special Collections, Joseph Regenstein Library, University of Chicago (Chicago); the Oral History Archive, Columbia University (Oral History); the Ford Foundation Archives in New York (Ford); the Harvard University Archives (Harvard); the University of Iowa archives (Iowa); the University of Michigan's Michigan Historical Collection, Bentley Historical Library (Michigan); the University of Minnesota Library's archive section (Minnesota); the University of North Carolina archives (UNC); the Manuscripts Division, Department of Rare Books and Special Collections, Princeton University Libraries; the Rockefeller Archive Center (Rockefeller); the Schlesinger Library, Radcliffe College (Schlesinger); the University of Washington Libraries Manuscripts and University Archives Division (Washington). Where these are not salient in the text, that is because they were used in earlier publications which are summarised in this book (with cross-references) without the full supporting detail given in the original. Particularly valuable sources for various purposes have been: the papers held at Chicago of both members of faculty (Burgess, Hauser, Hughes, Wirth) and the administration; the Columbia Oral History materials on foundations; the Dodd and Lundberg papers at Washington; the Ford archives; the Angell, Bain and ISR papers at Michigan; the Chapin papers and teaching materials at Minnesota; the Odum papers in North Carolina; the Stewart papers at Princeton; the Dummer papers at Radcliffe; the Rockefeller Archive.

ABBREVIATIONS USED IN ARCHIVAL REFERENCES

AJC   American Jewish Committee
CAE   Charles A. Ellwood papers, 1873–1946 (Duke University Archives)
CCOH Carnegie Corporation Oral History Project (Oral History)
ESD   Ethel Sturges Dummer papers (Schlesinger)
FFOH Ford Foundation Oral History Project (Oral History)
GAL   George A. Lundberg papers (Washington)

HHS   Harold H. Swift papers (Chicago)
HWO   Howard W. Odum papers (UNC)
JQS   John Q. Stewart papers (Princeton)
LW   Louis Wirth papers (Chicago)
PMH   Philip M. Hauser papers (Chicago)
PWB   Percy W. Bridgman papers (Harvard)
RAC   LSRM or Rockefeller Foundation papers (Rockefeller)
RFOH Rockefeller Foundation Oral History Project (Oral History)
SCD   Stuart Carter Dodd papers (Washington)
SFOH Spencer Foundation Oral History Project (Oral History)
SSRC Social Science Research Council files

Archival references which do not clearly have an individual author in the conventional sense are referred to in the text, and listed here, by number under the relevant archive. Where there is a conventional author, the item is listed in the general reference list, with the source archive indicated by the appropriate abbreviation.

AJC

American Jewish Committee, Department of Scientific Research and Program Evaluation, Budget 1950.

CAE

Letter from Ellwood to Hornell Hart, 12 Nov. 1931.

CCOH

1 Charles Dollard
2 Frederick Osborn
3 Bernard Berelson
4 Donald Young
5 Guy Johnson

FFOH

Bernard Berelson

Ford

1 'A Report on "leading contributions" to the scientific study of human behavior, 1930–1956', November 1956, reel 23, Appendix to Bernard Berelson Oral History, Transcript.
2 Statement by Senator Eastland, quoted by Fulton Lewis on radio in talk

given 5 Oct. 1955, Law and the behavioral sciences reel 5336, Grant
550-0122.

GAL

1 Letter to Lundberg, 24 July 1938, box 4, folder 14.
2 Letter from Lundberg to Chapin, 30 July 1938, box 4, folder 14.
3 Letter from Lundberg to Robert Bierstedt, 9 Aug. 1951, box 13, folder
  14.
4 Letter from Lundberg to Bentley, 4 Dec 1944, box 3 folder 8.
5 Letter from Bergmann to Lundberg, 19 April 1944, box 3, folder
  10.
6 Letter to Rashevsky, 21 Jan. 1939, box 11, folder 5.
7 Letter from Lundberg to Zipf, 15 July 1941, box 14, folder 8.
8 Letter from Longman's, 30 Mar. 1953, box 8, folder 21.
9 'Classroom circulations as related to illustrations in introductory
  sociologies', General Correspondence, Hornell Hart, box 6, folder
  19.
10 Box 36, folder 4.
11 Letter from Lundberg to Stewart, 8 March 1954, box 12, folder 12.
12 Letter from Lundberg to Barnes, 21 Feb. 1949, box 2, folder 23.
13 'Citations to Lundberg's work in sociological journals', no date, box 25,
   folder 6.

HHS

1 'An inventory of fund-raising resources and suggested procedure', p.17;
  box 83, folder 13.
2 Letter from Swift to Trevor Arnett, 19 May 1924, box 177, folder 11.

HWO

Letter from Odum to Beardsley Ruml, 29 Sept. 1926, folder 110.

Iowa

University of Iowa Archives, Liberal Arts 50–51, correspondence folder A
(1).

JQS

1 Letter from Stewart to Dodd, 1 Dec. 1957, box 13.
2 Letter from Stewart to Lundberg, 11 July 1949, box 21.
3 Letter from Lundberg to Stewart, 30 Jan. 1953, box 21.
4 Letter from Read Bain to Stewart, 25 April 1951, box 8.

These extracts are published with permission of the Princeton University Libraries, courtesy of their Manuscripts Division, Department of Rare Books and Special Collections.

LW

1 Memorandum to Acting Dean and others, 2 November 1946, box XXVII, folder 5.
2 Report on the History of the Social Science Research Council, box XXXII, folder 2.
3 Minutes of SSRC Committee on Problems and Policy, 8–9 Dec. 1950, box XXXIII, folder 7.
4 Box LX, folder 17: 1, 5; memo from LW to SSRC Committee.

PMH

1941 program, Department of Agriculture Department of Mathematics and Statistics, box 8, folder 11.

PWB

1 Letter from Stewart to Bridgman, 25 April 1951, 4234.10, box V.
2 Letter from Skinner to Bridgman, 10 May 1956, 4234.10, box VI.

RAC

1 Diary entry, Weaver, 15 Dec. 1949, 1.2, 200D, box 212, folder 213.
2 Memo, Weaver to JHW, 15 June 1950, 1.2, 200D, box 212, folder 213.
3 TBA, memo, 14 Feb. 1936, RG 3.1, 900, box 21, folder 160.
4 Chester Barnard, memo to principal officers, 9 Mar. 1950, p. 3, RG 3.2, 900, sub-series Pro-42, box 28, folder 155.
5 Interview by JHW, University of Chicago, 29 May 1940, p. 4, RF 1.1, 216, sub-series S, box 25, folder 341.
6 'Program and policies in social sciences', 1/3/29, p. 29039, RF 3.1, box 1, folder 1.
7 'Study of delinquency', dockets for meeting of 26 Jan 1928, p. 2, LSRM 25, series 1, box 4, folder 31.
8 LSRM 25, series 1, box 4, folder 30, dockets for meeting of 15 Dec. 1927, p. 2.
9 'Harvard University – Research in the Social Sciences', Mar. 1938, p. 1, RG 1.1, 200, sub-series S, box 347, folder 4131.

RFOH

Warren Weaver

SCD

1 Dodd, letter to Lundberg, 4 Nov. (1936), box 1, folder 1.
2 Dodd, 'Dimensions of Lundberg's society as foundations for Dodd's sociology', paper given at the Pacific Sociological Society conference, 1967, xeroxed.
3 Letter from Margenau to Dodd, 4 Dec. 1969, box 5, correspondence folder Marganau [sic].
4 *'Stuart Dodd: a seminar at Brown University, Sep 16–17, 1973'*; xeroxed.
5 Behavioral Science Council (n.d.), Values papers, POL vol. 3, box 32.

SFOH

1 Lloyd N. Morrissett
2 Kathleen Carlson,
3 Daniel Griffiths

UNC

IRSS minutes, 10 Dec. 1951, p. 3.

SECONDARY SOURCES

Abel, Theodore (1931–57) *Journal of Thoughts and Events* (Theodore Abel papers, Rare Book and Manuscript Library, Columbia University)
(1938) *Why Hitler Came Into Power*, New Jersey: Prentice Hall
(1947) 'The nature and use of biograms', *American Journal of Sociology* 53: 111–18
(1983) Interview
Achinstein, Paul and S. F. Barker (1969) *The Legacy of Logical Positivism*, Baltimore: Johns Hopkins University Press
Ackoff, Russell (1953) *The Design of Social Research*, Chicago: University of Chicago Press.
Ackroyd, Stephen and John A. Hughes (1981) *Data Collection in Context*, London: Longman.
Adams, Richard N. and Jack J. Preiss, eds. (1960) *Human Organization Research*, Homewood, IL.: Dorsey Press
Addams, Jane (1912) *A New Conscience and an Ancient Evil*, New York: Macmillan
Adorno, Theodor, Else Frenkel Brunswik, D. J. Levinson and R. Nevitt Sanford (1950) *The Authoritarian Personality*, New York: Harper
Ahmad, Salma (1991) 'American foundations and the development of the social sciences between the wars: comment on the debate between Martin Bulmer and Donald Fisher', *Sociology* 25: 511–20

Alchon, Guy (1985) *The Invisible Hand of Planning*, Princeton, NJ: Princeton University Press

Alexander, Jeffrey C. (1979)'Paradigm revision and "Parsonianism"', *Canadian Journal of Sociology* 4: 343–58

    (1982) *Theoretical Logic in Sociology*, Berkeley: University of California Press

    (1987) *Sociological Theory Since 1945*, London: Hutchinson

Alexander, Jeffrey C. and Paul Colomy (1992) 'Traditions and competition: preface to a postpositivist approach to knowledge cumulation', pp. 27–52 in George Ritzer (ed.), *Metatheorizing*, Beverly Hills, CA: Sage

Alihan, Milla A. (1938) *Social Ecology: A Critical Analysis*, New York: Columbia University Press

Allport, Gordon W. (1942) *The Use of Personal Documents in Psychological Science*, New York: SSRC Bulletin 49

Alpert, Harry (1939) *Emile Durkheim and his Sociology*, New York: Columbia University Press

    (1954) 'The National Science Foundation and social science research', *American Sociological Review* 19: 208–11

    (1955) 'The social sciences and the National Science Foundation: 1945–1955', *American Sociological Review* 20: 653–61

    (1968) 'George Lundberg's social philosophy: a continuing dialogue', pp. 48–62 in A. de Grazia et al. (eds.), *The Behavioral Sciences: Essays in Honor of George A. Lundberg* (Behavioral Research Council, Great Barrington, MA)

Amsterdamska, Olga (1985) 'Institutions and schools of thought: the neogrammarians', *American Journal of Sociology* 91: 332–58

Anderson, C. Arnold (1984) Interview

Anderson, Nels (1923) *The Hobo*, Chicago: University of Chicago Press

Angell, Robert C. (1936) *The Family Encounters the Depression*, reprinted 1965, Gloucester, MA: Peter Smith

    (1954) 'Comment on discussion of the analytic induction method', *American Sociological Review* 19: 476–7

    (1976?) 'The Sociology Department, 1940–1975' (Michigan)

Argyris, Chris (1952) *An Introduction to Field Theory and Interaction Theory*, New Haven: Yale University Labor and Management Center

Arnove, R. F. (ed.) (1980) *Philanthropy and Cultural Imperialism: The Foundations at Home and Abroad*, Bloomington, IN: Indiana University Press

    (ed.) (1982) *Philanthropy and Cultural Imperialism*, Bloomington, IN: Indiana University Press

Aronovici, Carol (1916) *The Social Survey*, Philadelphia: Harper

Baehr, Peter and Mike O'Brien (1994) 'Founders, classics and the concept of a canon', *Current Sociology* 42, 1

Bain, Read (1928) 'An attitude on attitude research', *American Journal of Sociology* 33: 940–57

(1950) Review of Zipf, *Human Behavior and the Principle of Least Effort*, *Social Forces* 28: 340–1

(1951) JQS 4

Baldamus, W. (1976) *The Structure of Sociological Inference*, London: Martin Robertson

Bales, R. Freed (1950) *Interaction Process Analysis*, Cambridge, MA: Addison Wesley

(1984) Interview

Bannister, Robert C. (1987) *Sociology and Scientism*, Chapel Hill: University of North Carolina Press

(1992) 'Principle, politics, profession: American sociologists and fascism 1930–1950', in Stephen Turner and Dirk Käsler (eds.), *Sociology Responds to Fascism*, London: Routledge

Barnard, Chester I. (1938) *Functions of the Executive*, Cambridge, MA: Harvard University Press

Barnes, Barry (1982) *T. S. Kuhn and Social Science*, London: Macmillan

Barnes, Harry E. (ed.) (1948) *An Introduction to the History of Sociology*, Chicago: University of Chicago Press

Barnes, Harry E. and Howard P. Becker (1938) *Social Thought From Lore to Science*, Washington, DC: Harren Press

Baxandall, Michael (1985) *Patterns of Intention*, New Haven: Yale University Press

Beach, Walter G. (1939) *The Growth of Social Thought*, reprinted 1967, Port Washington, NY: Kennikat Press

Becker, Howard P. (1948) review of Lundberg, *Can Science Save Us?*, *American Journal of Sociology* 54: 170–1

Becker, Howard S. (1958) 'Problems of inference and proof in participant observation', *American Sociological Review* 23: 652–60

(1982) Conversation

(1990) Letter to J. Platt

Becker, Howard S. and Blanche Geer (1957) 'Participant observation and interviewing: a comparison', *Human Organization* 16: 28–32

Becker, Howard S., Blanche Geer and Everett Hughes (1968) *Making the Grade*, New York: Wiley

Becker, Howard S., Blanche Geer, David Riesman and Robert S. Weiss (1968) *Institutions and the Person: Papers Presented to Everett C. Hughes*, Chicago: Aldine

Bell, E.T. (1942) Review of Dodd, *Dimensions of Society*, *American Sociological Review*, 7: 707–9

Ben David, J. (1973) 'The state of sociological theory and the sociological community', *Comparative Studies in Society and History* 15: 448–72

Bennett, James (1981) *Oral History and Delinquency: The Rhetoric of Criminology*, Chicago: University of Chicago Press

Bentley, Arthur F. (1926) *Relativity in Man and Society*, New York: Putnam

Berelson, Bernard R. (1952) *Content Analysis in Communication Research*, Glencoe, IL: Free Press
  (1956) Ford 1
  (1968) 'Behavioral sciences', ed. D. L. Sills, *International Encyclopedia of the Social Sciences* 2: 41–5
Berelson, Bernard R., Paul F. Lazarsfeld and William N. McPhee (1954) *Voting*, Chicago: University of Chicago Press
Berger, Bennett M. (ed.) (1990) *Authors of Their Own Lives*, Berkeley: University of California Press
Berger, Joseph, David G. Wagner and Morris Zelditch (1989) 'Theory growth, social processes and metatheory', pp. 19–42 in Jonathan H. Turner (ed.), *Theory Building in Sociology*, Newbury Park, CA: Sage
Bergmann, Gustav (1944) GAL 5
Bergmann, Leola (Mrs Gustav Bergmann) (1993) Conversation
Bernard, Luther L. (1945) 'The teaching of sociology in the US in the last 50 years', *American Journal of Sociology*, 50: 534–48
Bernard, Luther L. and Jessie Bernard (1943) *The Origins of American Sociology*, reissued 1965, New York: Russell and Russell
Bernert, Christopher (1983) 'The career of causal analysis in American sociology', *British Journal of Sociology* 34: 230–54
Bierstedt, Robert (1981) *American Sociological Theory*, New York: Academic Press
Bingham, W. Van Dyke and B. V. Moore (1931) *How to Interview*, New York: Harper
Bird Dogs, The (1961) 'The evolution of the Office of Naval Research', *Physics Today* 14 (8): 30–5
Black, Max (ed.) (1961) *The Social Theories of Talcott Parsons*, Englewood Cliffs, NJ: Prentice Hall
Blalock, Hubert M. (1984) Interview
  (1988) 'Socialization to sociology by culture shock', pp. 107–18 in Matilda White Riley (ed.), *Sociological Lives*, Beverly Hills: Sage
  (1989) 'The real and unrealized contributions of quantitative sociology', *American Sociological Review* 54: 447–60
Blankenship, Albert B. (1943) *Consumer and Opinion Research*, New York: Harper
Blankenship, Albert B. (ed.) (1946) *How to Conduct Consumer and Opinion Research*, New York: Harper
Blau, Peter M. (1955) *The Dynamics of Bureaucracy*, Chicago: University of Chicago Press
Blau, Peter M. and Duncan, Otis D. (1967) *The American Occupational Structure*, New York: Wiley
Bloor, David (1976) *Knowledge and Social Imagery*, London: Routledge and Kegan Paul
Blumer, Herbert (1937) 'Social psychology', pp. 144–98 in Emerson P. Schmidt (ed.), *Man and Society*, Englewood Cliffs, NJ: Prentice-Hall

References

(1939) *An Appraisal of Thomas and Znaniecki's 'The Polish Peasant in Europe and America'*, New York: Social Science Research Council

(1969) *Symbolic Interactionism*, Englewood Cliffs, NJ: Prentice Hall

(1979) 'Introduction to the Transaction edition', reissue of *An Appraisal of Thomas and Znaniecki's 'The Polish Peasant in Europe and America'*, New Brunswick NJ: Transaction

(1982) Interview

Bogardus, Emory S. (1918, 1925) *Making Social Science Studies*, Los Angeles: Jesse Ray Miller

(1926) *The New Social Research*, Los Angeles: Jesse Ray Miller

(1936) *Introduction to Social Research*, Los Angeles: Suttonhouse

(1953) 'Erle Fiske Young, sociologist', *Sociology and Social Research* 38: 71–9

Bogue, Donald J. (1992) Letter to J. Platt

Booth, Charles (1892–7) *Life and Labour of the People in London*, London: Macmillan

Bowen, Louise de K. (1917) *The Public Dance Halls of Chicago*, Chicago: Juvenile Protective Association

Bridgman, Percy W. (1927) *The Logic of Modern Physics*, New York: Macmillan.

(1931) *Dimensional Analysis*, New Haven: Yale University Press

(1938) *The Intelligent Individual and Society*, New York: Macmillan

Brooks, Harvey (1983) 'The effect of sponsorship upon social science research', *Items* 37: 43–6

Brown, E. R. (1979) *Rockefeller Medicine Men: Medicine and Capitalism in America*, Berkeley: University of California Press

Brown, J. S. and Gilmartin, B. (1969) 'Sociology today: lacunae, emphases and surfeits', *The American Sociologist* 4: 283–91

Bruyn, Severyn T. (1966) *The Human Perspective in Sociology*, Englewood Cliffs, NJ: Prentice-Hall

Bryant, Christopher G. A. (1985) *Positivism in Social Theory and Research*, London: Macmillan

Bryman, Alan (1984) 'The debate about quantitative and qualitative research: a question of method or epistemology', *British Journal of Sociology* 35: 75–92

(1988) *Quantity and Quality in Social Research*, London: Unwin Hyman

Bulmer, Martin (1980) 'The early institutional establishment of social science research: the Local Community Research Committee at the University of Chicago, 1923–30', *Minerva* 18: 51–110

(1983a) 'The methodology of early social indicator research: William Fielding Ogburn and *Recent Social Trends*', *Social Indicators Research* 13: 109–30

(1983b) 'The methodology of *The Taxi-Dance Hall*: an early account of Chicago ethnography from the 1920s', *Urban Life* 12: 95–120

(1983c) 'The Society for Social Research: an institutional underpinning to the Chicago School of Sociology in the 1920s', *Urban Life* 11: 421–39

(1984a) *The Chicago School of Sociology*, Chicago: University of Chicago Press

(1984b) 'Philanthropic foundations and the development of the social sciences in the early twentieth century: a reply to Donald Fisher', *Sociology* 18: 572–9

(1985) 'The Chicago School of Sociology: what made it a "school"?', *History of Sociology* 5: 61–77

(1991) 'W. E. B. Du Bois as a social investigator: *The Philadelphia Negro* 1899', pp. 170–88 in Bulmer, Bales and Sklar (eds.), q.v

Bulmer, Martin and Bulmer, Joan (1981) 'Philanthropy and social science in the 1920s: Beardsley Ruml and The Laura Spelman Rockefeller Memorial, 1922–29', *Minerva* 19: 347–407

Bulmer, Martin, Kevin Bales and Kathryn Kish Sklar (eds.) (1991) *The Social Survey in Historical Perspective*, Cambridge: Cambridge University Press

Burgess, Ernest W. and Leonard S. Cottrell (1939) *Predicting Success or Failure in Marriage*, New York: Prentice Hall

Burt, Ronald S. (1982) *Toward a Structural Theory of Action*, New York: Academic Press

Buxton, William (1985) *Talcott Parsons and the Capitalist Nation-State*, Toronto: University of Toronto Press

Calhoun, Donald W. (1942) 'With the operationalists' (review of Lundberg, *Foundations of Sociology* and Dodd, *Dimensions of Society*), *Social Forces* 20: 498–504

Camic, Charles (1992) 'Reputation and predecessor selection: Parsons and the institutionalists', *American Sociological Review* 57: 421–445

Camic, Charles and Yu Xie (1994) 'The statistical turn in American social science: Columbia University, 1890 to 1915', *American Sociological Review* 59: 773–805

Campbell, Donald T. (1957) 'Factors relevant to the validity of experiments in social settings', *Psychological Bulletin* 54: 297–312

Cannell, Charles (1983) Interview

Cantril, Hadley (1947) *Gauging Public Opinion*, Princeton: Princeton University Press

Capecchi, Vittorio (1978) 'Paul F. Lazarsfeld: a link between American and European methodology', *Quality and Quantity* 12: 239–54

Cappell, Charles L. and Thomas M. Guterbock (1992) 'Visible colleges: the social and conceptual structure of sociology specialties', *American Sociological Review* 57: 266–73

Cartwright, Nancy (1987) 'Philosophical problems of quantum theory: the response of American physicists', pp. 417–35 in Lorenz Krüger, Gerd Gigerenzer and Mary S. Morgan (eds.), *The Probabilistic Revolution*, vol. II, Cambridge, MA: MIT Press

Catton, William R. Jr. (1966) *From Animistic to Naturalistic Sociology*, New York: McGraw-Hill

(1968) 'An assessment of Lundberg's substantive inquiries', pp. 23–33 in de Grazia, Handy, Harwood et al. (eds.), q.v

(1993) Letter to J. Platt

Cavan, Ruth Shonle (1982) Interview

Chapin, F. Stuart (1920) *Field Work and Social Research* (Appleton-Century, New York)

(1938) GAL 1

(1947) *Experimental Designs in Sociological Research*, New York: Harper

Chapin, F. Stuart and Stuart A. Queen (1937) *Research Memorandum on Social Work in the Depression*, Social Science Research Council, Bulletin 39

Chapoulie, Jean-Michel (1991) 'La seconde fondation de la sociologie française, les Etats Unis et la classe ouvrière', *Revue française de sociologie* 32: 321–64

Chapple, Eliot D. and Conrad Arensberg (1940) 'Measuring human relations: an introduction to the study of interaction of individuals', *Genetic Psychology Monographs* 22: 3–147

Christie, Richard and Marie Jahoda (eds.) (1954) *Continuities in Social Research: Studies in the Scope and Method of 'The Authoritarian Personality'*, Glencoe, IL: Free Press

Chubin, Daryl and James L. McCartney (1982) 'Financing sociological research: a future only dimly perceived', *The American Sociologist* 17: 226–35

Cicourel, Aaron V. (1964) *Method and Measurement in Sociology*, New York: Free Press of Glencoe

Clausen, John A. (1982) Interview

'Research on *The American Soldier* as a career contingency', *Social Psychology Quarterly* 47: 207–213

Clegg, Stewart (1992) 'How to become an internationally famous British social theorist', *Sociological Review* 40: 576–93

Cole, Jonathan R. and Stephen Cole (1973) *Social Stratification in Science*, Chicago: University of Chicago Press

Coleman, James S. (1980) 'Paul F. Lazarsfeld: the substance and style of his work', pp. 153–74 in Merton and Riley (eds.), q.v

(1984) Interview

(1990) 'Columbia in the 1950s', pp. 75–103 in B. M. Berger (ed.), q.v

Collier, Gary, Henry L. Minton and Graham Reynolds (1991) *Currents of Thought in American Social Psychology*, New York: Oxford University Press

Collins, Randall (1977) Contribution to review symposium on Lewis A. Coser (ed.), *The Idea of Social Structure, Contemporary Sociology* 6: 150–54

(1989) 'Toward a theory of intellectual change: the social causes of philosophies', *Science, Technology and Human Values* 14: 107–40

Colomy, Paul and J. David Brown (1995) 'Elaboration, revision, polemic and progress in the Second Chicago School', pp. 17–81 in G. A. Fine (ed.), q.v.

Colvard, Richard (1976) 'Risk capital philanthropy: the ideological defense of innovation', in G. K. Zollschan and W. Hirsch (eds.), *Social Change: Explorations, Diagnoses and Conjectures*, New York: Wiley

Converse, Jean M. (1987) *Survey Research in the US: Roots and Emergence 1890–1960*, Berkeley: University of California Press

Cooney, Terry A. (1986) *The Rise of the New York Intellectuals: Partisan Review and its Circle*, Madison: University of Wisconsin Press

Coser, Lewis A. (1965) *Men of Ideas*, New York: Free Press
  (1971) *Masters of Sociological Thought*, New York: Harcourt, Brace Jovanovich

Cottrell, Leonard S. (1982) Interview

Crane, Diana (1965) 'Scientists at major and minor universities: a study of productivity and recognition', *American Sociological Review* 30: 699–713
  (1972) *Invisible Colleges*, Chicago: University of Chicago Press

Crawford, Elizabeth T. and Albert D. Biderman (1970) 'Paper money: trends of research sponsorship in American sociology journals', *Social Science Information* 9: 51–77

Cressey, Donald R. (1953) *Other People's Money*, Glencoe, IL: Free Press

Crothers, Charles (1987) *Robert K. Merton*, Chichester: Ellis Horwood
  (1990) 'The Columbia School of sociology: what made it a school?', paper given at ASA conference, Washington, DC
  (forthcoming) *The Columbia Tradition*

Danziger, Kurt (1990) *Constructing the Subject*, Cambridge: Cambridge University Press

Darley, John D. (1957) 'Psychology and the Office of Naval Research: a decade of development', *American Psychologist* 12: 305–23
  (1963) 'Five years of social science research: retrospect and prospect', pp. 3–15 in Harold Guetzkow (ed.), *Groups, Leadership and Men*, New York: Russell and Russell

Davis, Fred (1984) 'Decade labeling: the play of collective memory and narrative plot', *Symbolic Interaction* 7: 15–24

Davis, James A. (1984) Interview

Davis, Kingsley (1943) Review of Lundberg, *Social Research*, *American Sociological Review* 8: 100–1

de Grazia, A., Rollo Handy, E. C. Harwood et al. (eds.) (1968) *The Behavioral Sciences: Essays in Honor of George A. Lundberg*, Great Barrington, MA: Behavioral Research Council

Deegan, Mary Jo (1988) *Jane Addams and the Men of the Chicago School*, New Brunswick, NJ: Transaction

Denzin, Norman D. (1970) *The Research Act*, Chicago: Aldine

Deutscher, Irwin (1973) *What We Say/What We Do*, Glenview, IL: Scott, Foresman
  (1984) 'Choosing ancestors: some consequences of the selection from intellectual traditions', in R. M. Farr and S. Moscovici (eds.), *Social Representations*, Cambridge: Cambridge University Press

Dewey, F. A. (1915) 'An application of statistical method', *American Journal of Sociology* 21: 334–8

Doby, John T. (1954) *Introduction to Social Research*, Harrisburg, PA: Stackpole Press
(1991) Interview

Dodd, Stuart C. (1934) *A Controlled Experiment on Rural Hygiene in Syria*, Beirut: American University of Beirut
(1936) SCD 1
(1942) *Dimensions of Society*, New York: Macmillan
(1948) 'Developing demoscopes for social research', *American Sociological Review* 13: 310–19
(1950) 'The interactance hypothesis', *American Sociological Review* 15: 245–56
(1951) 'A measured wave of interracial tension', *Social Forces* 29: 281–9
(1955) 'Diffusion is predictable: testing probability models for laws of interaction', *American Sociological Review* 20: 392–401
(1967) SCD 2
(1973) SCD 4

Dollard, John (1935) *Criteria for the Life History*, New Haven: Yale University Press

Du Bois, W. E. B. (1899) *The Philadelphia Negro*

Dubin, Robert (1961) Obituary, Chester Barnard, *American Sociological Review* 26: 783–4

Dummer, Ethel Sturges (as Mrs W.F.) (1933) 'The philosophy back of the Five Year Plan', *American Journal of Sociology* 38: 595–602

Duncan, Otis Dudley (1959) 'Human ecology and population studies', pp. 678–716 in P. M. Hauser and O. D. Duncan (eds.), *The Study of Population*, Chicago: University of Chicago Press
(1966) 'Path analysis: sociological examples', *American Journal of Sociology* 72: 1–16
(1984) Interview
(1992) Letter to J. Platt

Duncan, Otis Dudley, W. R. Scott, Stanley Lieberson, Beverly Duncan et al. (1960) *Metropolis and Region*, Baltimore: Johns Hopkins Press

Durkheim, Emile (1938) *The Rules of Sociological Method*, reprinted 1950, Glencoe, IL: Free Press
(1951) *Suicide*, Glencoe, IL: Free Press

Easthope, Gary (1974) *History of Social Research Methods*, London: Longman

Eisenstadt, Shmuel N. and Curelaru, M. (1976) *The Forms of Sociology: Paradigms and Crises*, New York: Wiley

Ellis, Robert (1991) Interview

Ellwood, Charles A. (1931) CAE
(1933) *Method in Sociology: A Critical Study*, Durham, NC: University of North Carolina Press

Elmer, Manuel C. (1917) *The Technique of Social Surveys*, Los Angeles: Jesse Ray Miller

(1939) *Social Research*, New York: Prentice-Hall

England, J. Merton (1982) *A Patron for Pure Science*, Washington, DC: National Science Foundation

Ennis, James G. (1992) 'The social organization of sociological knowledge: modeling the intersection of specialties', *American Sociological Review* 57: 259–65

Faris, Robert E. L. (1967) *Chicago Sociology 1920–1932*, Chicago: University of Chicago Press

Faris, Robert E. L and H. Warren Dunham (1939) *Mental Disorders in Urban Areas*, Chicago: University of Chicago Press

Fay, Brian (1975) *Social Theory and Political Practice*, London: Allen and Unwin

Feagin, Joe R., Anthony M. Orum and Gideon Sjoberg (eds.) (1991) *A Case for the Case Study*, Chapel Hill: University of North Carolina Press

Feigl, Herbert (1969) 'The Wienerkreis in America', pp. 643–61 in D. Fleming and B. Bailyn (eds.), *The Intellectual Migration*, Cambridge, MA: Harvard University Press

Festinger, Leon and Daniel Katz (eds.) (1953) *Research Methods in the Behavioral Sciences*, New York: Holt, Rinehart and Winston

Filmer, Paul, Michael Phillipson, David Silverman and David Walsh (1972) *New Directions in Sociological Theory*, London: Collier Macmillan

Filstead, William J. (ed.) (1970) *Qualitative Methodology*, Chicago: Rand McNally

Fine, Gary A. (ed.) (1995) *A Second Chicago School?*, Chicago: University of Chicago Press

Fine, Gary A. and Janet S. Severance (1985) 'Great men and hard times: Sociology at the University of Minnesota', *Sociological Quarterly* 26: 117–34

Fish, Virginia Kemp (1985) 'Hull House: pioneer in urban research during its creative years', *History of Sociology* 6: 33–54

Fisher, Donald (1980) 'American philanthropy and the social sciences in Britain, 1919–1939: the reproduction of a conservative ideology', *Sociological Review* 28: 277–315

(1983) 'The role of philanthropic foundations in the reproduction and production of hegemony: Rockefeller foundations and the social sciences', *Sociology* 17: 206–33

(1984) 'Philanthropic foundations and the social sciences: a response to Martin Bulmer', *Sociology* 18: 580–7

(1993) *Fundamental Development of the Social Sciences*, Ann Arbor: University of Michigan Press

Form, William H. and William V. D'Antonio (1959) 'Integration and cleavage among community influentials in two border cities', *American Sociological Review* 24: 804–14

Freedman, Ronald (1948) Review of Lundberg, *Can Science Save Us?*, *American Journal of Sociology* 54: 226–8

Freidheim, E. A. (1979) 'An empirical comparison of Ritzer's paradigms and similar metatheories', *Social Forces* 58: 59–66

Freidson, Eliot (1984) Interview

Friedrichs, Robert W. (1970) *A Sociology of Sociology*, New York: Free Press

Fry, C. Luther (1934) *The Technique of Social Investigation*, New York: Harper

Fuller, Steve (1992) 'Being there with Thomas Kuhn: a parable for post-modern times', *History and Theory* 31: 241–75

Furfey, Paul Hanly (1953) *The Scope and Method of Sociology*, New York: Harper

Furner, Mary (1975) *Advocacy and Objectivity: A Crisis in the Professionalisation of American Social Science, 1865–1905*, Lexington: University Press of Kentucky

Gallagher, Ralph (1938) 'Presidential address, 1938', reprinted in *Sociological Analysis* 50: 319–20

Galliher, John F. and McCartney, James L. (1973) 'The influence of funding agencies on juvenile delinquency research', *Social Problems* 21: 77–91

Gans, Herbert J. (1990) 'Relativism, equality and popular culture', pp. 432–51 in B. M. Berger (ed.), q.v

Gardiner, Burleigh (1982) Interview

Gee, Wilson (1950) *Social Science Research Methods*, New York: Appleton-Century-Crofts

Gehlke, Charles E. (1935) Typescript of review of Simpson's translation of Durkheim, *The Division of Labor in Society*, for Columbia Law Review; Gehlke papers, Rare Book and Manuscript Library, Columbia University

Geiger, Kent (1984) Interview

Geiger, Roger L. (1986) *To Advance Knowledge: The Growth of American Research Universities, 1900–1940*, New York: Oxford University Press
    (1988) 'American foundations and academic social science, 1945–1960', *Minerva* 26: 315–41

Gerth, Hans H. and C. Wright Mills (eds.) (1946) *From Max Weber*, New York: Oxford University Press

Giddings, Franklin H. (1924) *The Scientific Study of Human Society*, reprinted 1974, New York: Arno Press

Gilbert, G. Nigel and Michael Mulkay (1984) *Opening Pandora's Box*, Cambridge: Cambridge University Press

Gillespie, Richard (1991) *Manufacturing Knowledge*, Cambridge: Cambridge University Press

Gillin, John L. (1937) 'Backgrounds of prisoners in the Wisconsin state prison and of their brothers', *American Sociological Review* 2: 204–12

Glaser, Barney G. and Anselm L. Strauss (1967) *The Discovery of Grounded Theory*, Chicago: Aldine

Glenn, John M., Lilian Brandt and F. Emerson Andrews (1946) *The Russell Sage Foundation 1907–1946*, New York: Russell Sage

Glock, Charles Y. (1979) 'Organizational innovation for social science research and training', pp. 23–36 in Merton, Coleman and Rossi (eds.), q.v

(1984) Interview

Goffman, Erving (1961) *Asylums*, New York: Doubleday

Gold, David (1957) 'A note on statistical analysis in the *American Sociological Review*', *American Sociological Review* 22: 332–3

Gold, Raymond L. (1958) 'Roles in sociological field observation', *Social Forces* 36: 217–23

(1984) Interview

Goode, William J. and Paul K. Hatt (1952) *Methods of Social Research*, New York: McGraw-Hill

Gottschalk, Louis, Clyde Kluckhohn and Robert Angell (1945) *The Use of Personal Documents in History, Anthropology and Sociology*, New York: SSRC Bulletin 53

Gouldner, Alvin W. (1971) *The Coming Crisis of Western Sociology*, London: Heinemann

Gouldner, Alvin W. and Timothy Sprehe (1965) 'Sociologists look at themselves', *Trans-Action* 2: 4: 42-4

Graham, Loren, Wolf Lepenies and Peter Weingart, (eds.) (1983) *Functions and Uses of Disciplinary Histories*, Dordrecht: Reidel

Greeley, Andrew (1990) 'The crooked lines of God', pp. 133–51 in B. M. Berger (ed.), q.v

Greenberg, Daniel S. (1969) *The Politics of American Science*, Harmondsworth, Middx.: Penguin

Greenwood, Ernest (1945) *Experimental Sociology*, New York: King's Crown Press

Gross, Edward (1956) 'Symbiosis and consensus as integrative factors in small groups', *American Sociological Review* 21: 174–9

(1984) Interview

Gross, George (1970) 'The organization set: a study of sociology departments', *The American Sociologist* 5: 25–9

Hader, J. J. and Eduard C. Lindeman (1933) *Dynamic Social Research*, New York: Harcourt Brace

Haerle, Rudolf K. (1991) 'William Isaac Thomas and the Helen Culver Fund for Race Psychology', *Journal for the History of the Behavioral Sciences*, 27: 21–41

Hagood, Margaret J. (1939) *Mothers of the South*, reprinted 1969, New York: Greenwood Press

(1941) *Statistics for Sociologists*, New York: Holt

(1947) 'Recent contributions of statistics to research methodology in sociology', *Social Forces* 26: 36–40

Halfpenny, Peter (1982) *Positivism and Sociology*, London: Allen and Unwin

Hall, Robert L. (1972) 'Agencies of research support: some sociological perspectives', pp. 193–227 in Saad Z. Nagi and Ronald G. Corwin (eds.), *The Social Contexts of Research*, New York: Wiley

Hallen, G. C. (ed.) (no date) *Essays on the Sociology of Parsons*, Meerut, India: *Indian Journal of Social Research*

Haller, Archibald (1984) Interview

Hammersley, Martyn (1992) 'On feminist methodology', *Sociology* 26: 187–206

Hansen, Morris H. (1987) 'Some history and reminiscences of survey sampling', *Statistical Science* 2: 180–90

Hansen, Morris H., W. N. Hurwitz and W. G. Madow (1953) *Sample Survey Methods and Theory*, New York: Wiley

Harrison, Shelby M. (1931) *The Social Survey*, New York: Russell Sage

Hart, Hornell (1940) 'Operationism analyzed operationally', *Philosophy of Science* 7: 288–313

(1946) 'Depression, war and logistic trends', *American Journal of Sociology* 52: 112–21

(1947) 'Measuring degrees of verification in sociological writings', *American Sociological Review* 12: 103–13

(1960a) GAL 9

(1960b) *A Laboratory Manual for Introductory Sociology*, Ann Arbor, MI: Edwards Brothers

Harvey, Lee (1987a) 'The nature of "schools" in the sociology of knowledge: the case of the "Chicago School"', *Sociological Review* 35: 245–78

(1987b) *Myths of the Chicago School of Sociology*, Aldershot: Avebury

Hauser, Philip M. (1941) PMH

(1961) Obituary of Stouffer, *American Journal of Sociology* 66: 364–5

(1968) 'Social accounting', pp. 839–75 in ed. Paul F. Lazarsfeld, William H. Sewell and Harold L. Wilensky (eds.), *The Uses of Sociology*, New York: Basic Books

(1982) Interview

Hawley, Amos H. (1992) 'The logic of macrosociology', *Annual Review of Sociology* 18: 1–14

Hawthorn, Geoffrey (1976) *Enlightenment and Despair*, Cambridge: Cambridge University Press

(1991) *Plausible Worlds*, Cambridge: Cambridge University Press

Healy, William (1915) *The Individual Delinquent*, Boston: Little, Brown

Heaven, John W. (1975) 'Functional and critical sociology: a study of two groups of contemporary sociologists', unpublished doctoral thesis, Duke University

Heims, Steve J. (1991) *The Cybernetics Group*, Cambridge, MA: MIT Press

Hempel, Carl G. (1959) 'The logic of functional analysis', pp. 271–307 in Llewellyn Gross (ed.), *Symposium on Sociological Theory*, New York: Harper and Row

(1966) *Philosophy of Natural Science*, Englewood Cliffs, NJ: Prentice Hall

Hempel, Carl G. and Paul Oppenheim (1936) *Der Typusbegriff im Lichte der neuen Logik*, Leiden: Sijthoff

Hertzler, Joyce O. (1947) Review of Lundberg, *Can Science Save Us?*, *Social Forces* 26: 100–1

Heyl, Barbara (1968) 'The Harvard Pareto Circle', *Journal for the History of the Behavioral Sciences* 4: 316–34

Hill, Michael R. (ed.) (1988) 'The Foundations of Nebraska Sociology', special issue, *Mid-American Review of Sociology* 13: 2

Himelhoch, J. and Sylvia F. Fava (1955) *Sexual Behavior in American Society*, New York: Norton

Hindess, Barry (1973) *The Use of Official Statistics in Sociology*, London: Macmillan

Hinkle, Roscoe C. (1994) *Developments in American Sociological Theory 1915–1950*, Albany, NY: State University of New York Press

Hinkle, Roscoe C. Jr. and Gisela J. Hinkle (1954) *The Development of Modern Sociology*, New York: Random House

Hobbs, A. H. (1951) *The Claims of Sociology: A Critique of Textbooks*, Harrisburg, PA: Stackpole

Hobsbawm, Eric and Terence Ranger (1983) *The Invention of Tradition*, Cambridge: Cambridge University Press

Hollingshead, August B. (1949) Review of Zipf, *Human Behavior and the Principle of Least Effort*, *American Sociological Review* 14: 822–3

Holt, A. E. (1926) 'Case records as data for studying the conditioning of religious experience by social factors', *American Journal of Sociology* 32: 227–36

Holton, Gerald (1988) *Thematic Origins of Scientific Thought*, Cambridge, MA: Harvard University Press

Homans, George C. (1947) 'The small warship', *American Sociological Review* 11: 294–300

(1951) 'The strategy of industrial sociology', *American Journal of Sociology* 54: 330–7

(1985) *Coming To My Senses*, New Brunswick: Transaction

Horst, Paul K. (ed.) (1941) *The Prediction of Personal Adjustment*, New York: Social Science Research Council

(1982) Interview

House, Floyd N. (1936) *The Development of Sociology*, New York: McGraw-Hill

Hovland, Carl I., Arthur A. Lumsdaine and Fred D. Sheffield (eds.) (1949) *Experiments on Mass Communication*, Princeton, NJ: Princeton University Press

Hughes, Everett C. (1943) *French Canada in Transition*, Chicago: University of Chicago Press

Hughes, John A. (1976) *Sociological Analysis: Methods of Discovery*, London: Nelson

Hunt, Morton M. (1961) 'How does it come to be so?' [profile of R. K. Merton], *New Yorker* 36, 28 Jan.: 60

Hyfler, Robert (1984) *Prophets of the Left*, Westport, CT: Greenwood Press

Hyman, Herbert H. (1954) *Interviewing in Social Research*, New York: Free Press

(1955) *Survey Design and Analysis*, New York: Free Press

(1991) *Taking Society's Measure*, New York: Russell Sage Foundation

Inkeles, Alex (1986) 'The intellectual consequences of federal support for the social sciences', pp. 237–46 in Klausner and Lidz (eds.), q.v

Irvine, J., Ian Miles and J. Evans (1979) *Demystifying Social Statistics*, London: Pluto Press

Jacobs, G. (ed.) (1970) *The Participant Observer*, New York: George Braziller

Jahoda, Marie, Morton Deutsch and Stuart Cook (1951) *Research Methods in Social Relations*, New York: Dryden Press

Johnson, Benton and Johnson, M. M. (1986) 'The integrating of the social sciences', pp. 131–9 in Klausner and Lidz (eds.), q.v

Johnson, D. Gale (1979) 'Theodore W. Schultz', p. 708 in vol. xviii, ed. David L. Sills, *International Encyclopedia of the Social Sciences*, New York: Free Press

Jones, Robert A. (1980) 'Myth and symbol among the Nacirema Tsigoloicos: a fragment', *American Sociologist* 15: 207–12

(1983) 'On Merton's "History" and "Systematics" of sociological theory', pp. 121–142 in Graham, Lepenies and Weingart (eds.), q.v

(1985) 'Presentism, anachronism and continuity in the history of sociology: a reply to Seidman', *History of Sociology* 6: 153–60

Junker, Buford H. (1960) *Field Work: An Introduction to the Social Sciences*, Chicago: University of Chicago Press

Kahn, Robert L. (1983) Interview

Kahn, Robert L. and Charles F. Cannell (1957) *The Dynamics of Interviewing*, New York: Wiley

Karl, Barry D. (1969) 'Presidential planning and social science research: Mr Hoover's experts', *Perspectives in American History* 3: 347–412

Karl, Barry D. and Stanley N. Katz (1981) 'The American private philanthropic foundation and the public sphere, 1890–1930', *Minerva* 19: 236–70

Katz, Elihu and Paul F. Lazarsfeld (1955) *Personal Influence*, Glencoe, IL: Free Press

Keat, Russell and Urry, John (1975) *Social Theory as Science*, London: Routledge and Kegan Paul

Kendall, Patricia and Paul F. Lazarsfeld (1950) 'Problems of survey analysis', pp. 133–196 in Merton and Lazarsfeld (eds.), q.v

Kennedy, Raymond and Ruby Kennedy (1942) 'Sociology in American colleges', *American Sociological Review* 7: 661–75

Kinsey, Alfred C., Wardell B. Pomeroy and Clyde E. Martin (1948) *Sexual Behavior in the Human Male*, Philadelphia: Saunders

Kirkendall, R. S. (1966) *Social Scientists and Farm Politics in the Age of Roosevelt*, Columbia, MS: University of Missouri Press

Kirkpatrick, Clifford (1940) Review of Lundberg, *Foundations of Sociology*, *American Sociological Review* 5: 438–40

Kish, Leslie (1983) Interview

Klausner, Samuel Z. and Victor M. Lidz (1986) *The Nationalization of the Social Sciences*, Philadelphia: University of Pennsylvania Press

Knudsen, Dean D. and Ted R. Vaughan (1969) 'Quality in graduate education: a re-evaluation of the rankings of sociology departments in the Cartter report', *The American Sociologist* 4: 12–19

Kohler, Robert E. (1991) *Partners in Science*, Chicago: University of Chicago Press

Kohout, Frank (1993) Interview

Kohn, Melvin L. (1969) *Class and Conformity*, Homewood, IL: Dorsey

Komarovsky, Mirra (1940) *The Unemployed Man and His Family*, reprinted 1971, New York: Octagon Books

(ed.) (1957) *Common Frontiers in the Social Sciences*, New York: Free Press

(1964) *Blue-Collar Marriage*, New York: Random House

Kragh, Helge (1987) *An Introduction to the Historiography of Science*, Cambridge, Cambridge University Press

Kuhn, Thomas S. (1962) *The Structure of Scientific Revolutions*, Chicago: University of Chicago Press

(1970) *The Structure of Scientific Revolutions* (2nd edn), Chicago: University of Chicago Press

Kurtz, Lester R. (1984) *Evaluating Chicago Sociology*, Chicago: University of Chicago Press

Ladinsky, Jack (1963) 'Careers of lawyers, law practice, and legal institutions', *American Sociological Review* 28: 47–54

Lagemann, Ellen Condliffe (1989) *The Politics of Knowledge: The Carnegie Corporation, Philanthropy and Public Policy*, Middletown, CT: Wesleyan University Press

Lamont, Michèle (1987) 'How to become a dominant French philosopher: the case of Jacques Derrida', *American Journal of Sociology* 93: 584–622

Lang, Gladys Engel and Kurt Lang (1988) 'Recognition and renown: the survival of artistic reputation', *American Journal of Sociology* 94: 79–109

Larsen, Otto N. (1968) 'Lundberg's encounters with sociology and vice versa', pp. 1–22 in A. de Grazia, Handy, Harwood et al., q.v

(1984) Interview

(1992) *Milestones and Millstones: Social Science at the National Science Foundation, 1945–1991*, New Brunswick, NJ: Transaction

Larson, Olaf F. and Edward O. Moe (1990) 'Pioneering in the development and practice of sociology in the USDA's Division of Farm Population and Rural Life – a Dialogue', paper given at the annual meeting of the American Sociological Association, Washington, DC

Laszlo, Ervin (1979) 'Bertalanffy, Ludwig von', pp. 56–9 in vol. xviii, ed. David L. Sills, *International Encyclopedia of the Social Sciences*, New York: Free Press

Latour, Bruno and Steve Woolgar (1979) *Laboratory Life: The Social Construction of Scientific Facts*, Beverly Hills: Sage

Laub, John H. and Robert J. Sampson (1991) 'The Sutherland-Glueck debate: on the sociology of criminological knowledge', *American Journal of Sociology* 96: 1402–40

Lazarsfeld, Paul F. (1948) 'The use of panels in social research', *Proceedings of the American Philosophical Society*, 92: 405–10

    (1961) 'Reminiscences of P. F. Lazarsfeld' (Oral History)

    (1962) 'Philosophy of science and empirical social research', in E. Nagel, P. Suppes and A. Tarski (eds.), *Logic, Methodology and Philosophy of Science*, Stanford: Stanford University Press

    (ed.) (1954) *Mathematical Thinking in the Social Sciences*, New York: Free Press

Lazarsfeld, Paul F. and Allen H. Barton (1951) 'Qualitative measurement in the social sciences' pp. 155–93 in Daniel Lerner and Harold Lasswell (eds.), *The Policy Sciences*, Stanford, CA: Stanford University Press

    (1955) 'Some functions of qualitative analysis in social research', *Frankfurter Beiträge zur Soziologie* 1: 321–61

Lazarsfeld, Paul F., Bernard Berelson and Hazel Gaudet (1944) *The People's Choice*, New York: Columbia University Press

Lazarsfeld, Paul F. and Morris Rosenberg (eds.) (1955) *The Language of Social Research*, Glencoe, IL.: Free Press

Lazarsfeld, Paul F. and Wagner Thielens Jr. (1958) *The Academic Mind: Social Scientists in a Time of Crisis*, New York: Free Press

Lengermann, Patricia M. (1979) 'The founding of the *American Sociological Review*: the anatomy of a rebellion', *American Sociological Review* 44: 185–98

Lewin, Kurt (1951) *Field Theory in Social Science*, New York: Harper

Lewis, Jane (1991) 'The place of social investigation, social theory and social work in the approach to late Victorian and Edwardian social problems: the case of Beatrice Webb and Helen Bosanquet', pp. 148–69 in Bulmer, Bales and Sklar (eds.), q.v.

Lewis, J. David and Richard L. Smith (1980) *American Sociology and Pragmatism: Mead, Chicago and Symbolic Interaction*, Chicago: University of Chicago Press

Lieberson, Stanley (1980) *A Piece of the Pie: Blacks and White Immigrants Since 1880*, Berkeley: University of California Press

Lindeman, Eduard C. (1924) *Social Discovery*, New York: Republic

Lindesmith, Alfred (1947) *Opiate Addiction*, Bloomington, IN: Principia Press

    (1952) 'Comment on W. S. Robinson's "The logical structure of analytical induction"', *American Sociological Review* 17: 492–3

Lipset, Seymour M. (1955) 'Jewish sociologists', *Jewish Social Studies* 17: 177–8

(1993) 'Jeremiah Kaplan, The Free Press and post-war sociology', *Footnotes* 21: 8, p. 7

Lipset, Seymour M. and Everett C. Ladd (1972) 'The politics of American sociologists', *American Journal of Sociology* 78: 67–104

Lipset, Seymour M. and Smelser, Neal (1961) 'The setting of sociology in the 1950s', pp. 1–13 in Lipset and Smelser (eds.), *Sociology: The Progress of a Decade*, Englewood Cliffs, NJ: Prentice Hall

Lipset, Seymour M., Martin Trow and James S. Coleman (1956) *Union Democracy*, Glencoe, IL: Free Press

Lofland, John (1970) 'Interactionist imagery and analytic interruptus', pp. 35–46 in Tamotsu Shibutani (ed.), *Human Nature and Collective Behavior*, Englewood Cliffs, NJ: Prentice-Hall

(1971) *Analysing Social Settings*, Belmont, CA: Wadsworth

(1980) 'Reminiscences of classic Chicago: the Blumer–Hughes talk', *Urban Life* 9: 251–81

Lundberg, George A. (1929, 1942) *Social Research*, New York: Longmans, Green

(1931) 'The interests of members of the American Sociological Society, 1930', *American Journal of Sociology* 37: 458–60

(1937) review of Moreno, *Who Shall Survive*, *American Sociological Review* 2: 542–4

(1938) GAL 2

(1939a) *Foundations of Sociology*, New York: Macmillan (reprinted in abridged edition New York: David McKay, 1964)

(1939b) GAL 6

(1941) GAL 7

(1944a) 'Sociologists and the peace', *American Sociological Review* 9: 1–13

(1944b) GAL 4

(1945) 'The growth of scientific method', *American Journal of Sociology* 50: 502–13

(1947) *Can Science Save Us?*, New York: Longmans, Green

(1949) GAL 12

(1951) GAL 3

(1953) JQS 3

(1954) GAL 11

(1955) 'The natural science trend in sociology', *American Journal of Sociology* 61: 191–202

(1956) 'Some convergences in sociological theory', *American Journal of Sociology* 62: 21–7

(no date) GAL 13

Lundberg, George A. and Virginia Beazley (1948) '"Consciousness of kind" in a college population', *Sociometry* 11: 59–74

Lundberg, George A. and Lenore Dickson (1952a) 'Selective association among ethnic groups', *American Sociological Review* 17: 23–35

(1952b) 'Inter-ethnic relations in a high-school population', *American Journal of Sociology* 58: 1–10

Lundberg, George A., Virginia Beazley Hertzler and Lenore Dickson (1949) 'Attraction patterns in a university', *Sociometry* 12: 158–69

Lundberg, George A., Mirra Komarovsky and Mary A. McInery (1934) *Leisure: a Suburban Study*, New York: Columbia University Press

Lundberg, George A., Clarence Schrag and Otto Larsen (1954, 1958) *Sociology*, New York: Harper

Lundberg, George A and Mary Steele (1938) 'Social attraction-patterns in a village', *Sociometry* 1: 375–419

Lynd, Robert S. (1939) *Knowledge For What?*, New Jersey: Princeton University Press

Lynd, Robert S. and Helen M. Lynd (1929) *Middletown*, New York: Harcourt Brace

Lyons, Gene M. (1969) *The Uneasy Partnership*, New York: Russell Sage Foundation

McAdam, Doug (1992) 'Gender as a mediator of the activist experience: the case of Freedom Summer', *American Journal of Sociology* 97: 1211–40

McCall, George J. and J. L. Simmons (1969) *Issues in Participant Observation*, Reading, MA: Addison-Wesley

McCartney, James L. (1970) 'On being scientific: changing styles of presentation of sociological research', *The American Sociologist* 5: 30–5
    (1971) 'The financing of sociological research: trends and consequences', pp. 384–97 in Edward A. Tiryakian (ed.), *The Phenomenon of Sociology*, New York: Appleton-Century-Crofts

McCormick, Thomas C. (1941a) *Elementary Social Statistics*, New York: McGraw-Hill

(1941b) Review of Zipf, *National Unity and Disunity*, American Sociological Review 6: 745–6

McCormick, Thomas C. and Roy G. Francis (1958) *Methods of Research in the Behavioral Sciences*, New York: Harper

McGee, Reece (1985) 'The sociology of sociology textbooks', pp. 175–201 in F. L. Campbell, Hubert M. Blalock and Reece McGee (eds.), *Teaching Sociology*, Chicago: Nelson-Hall

McGuire, Patrick and Kenneth Dawes (1983) 'Sociology as social contribution: University of North Dakota as a case study of the contradictions of academic sociology', *Sociological Quarterly* 24: 589–603

MacIver, Robert M. (1942) *Social Causation*, New York: Ginn

Mackenzie, Donald A. (1981) *Statistics in Britain 1865–1930*, Edinburgh: Edinburgh University Press

McKinney, John C. (1954) 'Constructive typology and social research', pp. 139–94 in Doby, q.v

McNemar, Quinn (1946) 'Opinion-attitude methodology', *Psychological Bulletin* 43: 289–374

Madge, John (1963) *The Origins of Scientific Sociology*, London: Tavistock
Mann, Michael (1981) 'Socio-logic', *Sociology* 15: 544–50
Manning, P. (1978) 'Editor's remarks', *Urban Life* 7: 282–4
Margenau, Henry (1969) SCD 3
Martindale, Don (1961) *The Nature and Types of Sociological Theory*, London: Routledge and Kegan Paul
    (1976) *The Romance of a Profession*, St Paul, MN: Windflower Publishing
    (1982) *Personality and Milieu*, Houston: Cap and Gown Press
Matthews, Fred H. (1977) *Quest For an American Sociology: Robert Ezra Park and the Chicago School*, Montreal: McGill-Queen's University Press
Mayo-Smith, Richmond (1895) *Statistics and Sociology*, New York: Macmillan
Mazon, Brigitte (1987) *Aux origines de l'Ecole des Hautes Etudes en Sciences Sociales: le role du mécénat américain*, Paris: Editions du Cerf
Meier, August (1977) 'Black sociologists in white America', *Social Forces* 56: 259–70
Meier, Richard L. (1961) Preface, *General Systems* (Yearbook of the Society for General Systems Research), 6: iii
Megill, Allan (1987) 'The reception of Foucault by historians', *Journal of the History of Ideas* 48: 117–41
Meltzer, Bernard N., John W. Petras and Larry T. Reynolds (1975) *Symbolic Interactionism*, London: Routledge and Kegan Paul
Menzies, Ken (1982) *Sociological Theory in Use*, London: Routledge and Kegan Paul
Meroney, W. P. (1933) 'The use of textbooks in the introductory course in sociology', *Journal of Educational Sociology* 7: 54–67
Merton, Robert K. (1949) *Social Theory and Social Structure*, Glencoe, IL: Free Press
    (1967) 'On the history and systematics of sociological theory', in Merton, *On Theoretical Sociology*, New York: Free Press
    (1984) Letter to J. Platt
    (1990) 'Introduction to the second edition', pp. xiii–xxxi in Merton, Fiske and Kendall, q.v
Merton, Robert K., James S. Coleman and Peter Rossi (eds.) (1979) *Qualitative and Quantitative Social Research*, New York: Free Press
Merton, Robert K., Marjorie Fiske and Patricia L. Kendall (1956, 1990) *The Focused Interview*, New York: Free Press
Merton, Robert K. and Paul F. Lazarsfeld, (eds.) (1950) *Continuities in Social Research: Studies in the Scope and Method of 'The American Soldier'*, Glencoe, IL: Free Press
Merton, Robert K., George Reader and Patricia Kendall (1957) *The Student Physician: Introductory Studies in the Sociology of Medical Education*, Cambridge, MA: Harvard University Press
Merton, Robert K. and Matilda White Riley (eds.) (1980) *Sociological Traditions From Generation to Generation*, Norwood, NJ: Ablex

306 *References*

Middleton, D. and Derek Edwards (eds.) (1990) *Collective Remembering*, Beverly Hills, CA: Sage

Middleton, Russell (1984) Interview

Miller, G. A. (1965) 'Introduction', pp. v–x in G. K. Zipf, *The Psychobiology of Language* (Cambridge, MA: MIT Press)

Miller, Roberta Balstad (1982) 'The social sciences and the politics of science: the 1940s', *The American Sociologist* 17: 205–9

Miller, L. Keith and Robert L. Hamblin (1963) 'Interdependence, differential rewarding, and productivity', *American Sociological Review* 28: 768–78

Mills, C. Wright (1942) Review of W. L. Warner and Lunt, *The Social Life of a Modern Community*, *American Sociological Review* 7: 263–71

(1959) *The Sociological Imagination*, New York: Oxford University Press

Mitchell, G. Duncan (1968) *A Hundred Years of Sociology*, London: Duckworth

Morawski, Jill G. (1992) 'There is more to our history of giving: the place of introductory textbooks in American psychology', *American Psychologist* 47: 161–9

Moreno, Jacob L. (1934, 1953) *Who Shall Survive?*, Beacon, NY: Beacon House

(1955) *Preludes to my Autobiography*, Beacon, NY: Beacon House

Morris, Loretta M. (1989) 'Secular transcendence: from ACSS to ASR', *Sociological Analysis* 50: 323–347

Mosteller, Frederick, Herbert H. Hyman, P. J. McCarthy et al. (1949) *The Pre-Election Polls of 1948*, New York: Social Science Research Council, Bulletin 60

Mulkay, Michael J. and Bryan S. Turner (1971) 'Over-production of personnel and innovation in three social settings', *Sociology* 5: 47–61

Mullins, Nicholas C. (1973) *Theories and Theory Groups in Contemporary American Sociology*, New York: Harper and Row

Münch, Richard (1991) 'American and European social theory: cultural identities and social forms of theory production', *Sociological Perspectives* 34: 313–35

Myers, Howard B. (1936) 'Research with relief funds – past, present and future', *American Sociological Review* 1: 771–80

Myrdal, Gunnar (1944) *An American Dilemma*, New York: Harper

Nagel, Ernest (1961) *The Structure of Science*, New York: Harcourt, Brace and World

Nash, George H. (1976) *The Conservative Intellectual Movement in America Since 1945*, New York: Basic Books

Nelson, Lowry (1969) *Rural Sociology: Its Origin and Growth in the US*, Minneapolis: University of Minnesota Press

Nisbet, Robert (1966) *The Sociological Tradition*, New York: Basic Books

(1976) *Sociology as an Art Form*, London: Heinemann

Nock, David A. (1993) *Star Wars in Canadian Sociology*, Halifax, Nova Scotia: Fernwood

Oberschall, Anthony (ed.) (1972) *The Establishment of Empirical Sociology*, New York: Harper and Row

Odum, Howard W. (1926) HWO

(1928) *Rainbow Round My Shoulder*, Indianapolis: Bobbs-Merrill

(1945) 'From community studies to regionalism', *Social Forces* 23: 245–58

(1951) *American Sociology*, reprinted 1969, New York: Greenwood

Odum, Howard W. and Katharine Jocher (1929) *An Introduction to Social Research*, New York: Holt

Ogburn, William F. (1929) 'The folkways of a scientific sociology', *Papers of the American Sociological Society* 24: 1–11

Opler, Morris E. (1942) Review of W. L. Warner and Lunt, *The Status System of a Modern Community*, *American Sociological Review* 7: 719–22

Ozanne, Henry (1943) 'Critique of a critique: further comment on S. C. Dodd's *Dimensions of Society*', *American Journal of Sociology* 49: 604–8

Palmer, Vivien (1928) *Field Studies in Sociology*, Chicago: University of Chicago Press

Parkin, Rosa and Charley (1974) [Frank Parkin] 'Peter Rabbit and the Grundriße', *Archives européennes de sociologie* 15: 181–3

Parsons, Talcott (1937) *The Structure of Social Action*, New York: McGraw-Hill, reprinted 1949, Glencoe, IL: Free Press,

(1942) Review of Dodd, *Dimensions of Society*, *American Sociological Review*, 7: 709–714

(1949) *Essays in Sociological Theory*, Glencoe, IL: Free Press

(1951) *The Social System*, Glencoe, IL: Free Press

Parsons, Talcott and Robert F. Bales (1955) *Family, Socialization and Interaction Process*, New York: Free Press

Parsons, Talcott, Robert F. Bales and Edward Shils (1953) *Working Papers in the Theory of Action*, Glencoe, IL: Free Press

Parsons, Talcott and Edward Shils (1951) *Toward a General Theory of Action*, Cambridge, MA: Harvard University Press

Parten, Mildred (1950) *Surveys, Polls and Samples*, New York: Harper

Payne, Stanley L. (1951) *The Art of Asking Questions*, Princeton, NJ: Princeton University Press

Pearl, Raymond (1924) *Studies in Human Biology*, Baltimore: Williams and Wilkins

Pearson, Karl (1892) *The Grammar of Science*, London: Walter Scott (revised and reprinted several times with various publishers)

Phillips, Bernard S. (1966, 1976) *Social Research: Strategy and Tactics*, New York: Macmillan

Phillips, Bernard S. (1984) Interview

Platt, Anthony M. (1991) *E. Franklin Frazier Reconsidered*, New Brunswick: Rutgers University Press

Platt, Jennifer (1981) 'The social construction of "positivism" and its significance in British sociology 1950–1980', pp. 73–87 in Philip Abrams et al. (eds.), *Practice and Progress: British Sociology 1950–1980*, London: Allen and Unwin

  (1983) 'The development of the "participant observation" method in sociology: origin myth and history', *Journal of the History of the Behavioral Sciences* 19: 379–93

  (1985) 'Weber's verstehen and the history of qualitative research', *British Journal of Sociology* 36: 448–66

  (1986a) 'Qualitative research for the state', *Quarterly Journal of Social Affairs* 2: 87–108

  (1986b) 'Functionalism and the survey: the relation of theory and method.', *Sociological Review* 34: 501–36

  (1986c) 'Stouffer and Lazarsfeld: patterns of influence', pp. 99–117 in Henrika Kuklick and Elizabeth Long (eds.), *Knowledge and Society*, vol. VI

  (1991) 'Anglo-American contacts in the development of research methods before 1945', in Bulmer, Bales and Sklar (eds.) q.v.

  (1992a) '"Acting as a switchboard": Mrs Ethel Sturges Dummer's role in sociology', *The American Sociologist* 23 (3): 23–36

  (1992b) 'The SSRC's 1940s restudy of Robert Angell's cases from *The Family Encounters the Depression*', *Journal for the History of the Behavioral Sciences* 28: 143–57

  (1992c) '"Case study" in American methodological thought', *The Case Method in Sociology, Current Sociology* 40 (1): 17–48

  (1994a) 'The Chicago School and firsthand data', *History of the Human Sciences* 7: 57–80

  (1994b) 'Has funding made a difference to research metods?', University of Sussex, mimeo

  (1995a) 'Research methods and the second Chicago School', pp. 82–107 in Gary A. Fine (ed.), q.v

  (1995b) 'The US reception of Durkheim's The Rules of Sociological Method', *Sociological Perspectives* 38: 77–105

Platt, Jennifer and Paul Hoch (1995) 'The Vienna Circle in the USA and empirical research methods in sociology', pp. 224–45 in Mitchell G. Ash and Alfons Söllner (eds.), *Forced Migration and Scientific Change*, New York: Cambridge University Press

Ploch, Donald R. (1978) 'Research funding for sociology in the NSF', pp. 54–62 in Jerry Gaston (ed.), *Sociology of Science*, San Francisco: Jossey-Bass

Pollak, Michael (1979) 'Paul F. Lazarsfeld: Fondateur d'une multinationale scientifique', *Actes de la recherche en sciences sociales* 25: 45–59

Provus, Severn (1942) Review of Lundberg, *Social Research*, *Social Forces* 21: 119–20

Rainwater, Lee (1965) *Family Design*, Aldine: Chicago

(1959) *Workingman's Wife*, New York: Oceana Publications

(1984) Interview

Rapoport, Anatol (1979) 'Rank-size relationship', pp. 319–323 in David L. Sills (ed.), *International Encyclopedia of the Social Sciences*, New York: Free Press

Rashevsky, Nicholas (1951) Review of Zipf, *Human Behavior and the Principle of Least Effort*, *American Journal of Sociology*, 57: 92

Ratner, S. (1957) 'A. F. Bentley's inquiries into the behavioural sciences and the theory of scientific inquiry', *British Journal of Sociology* 8: 40–58

Reinharz, Shulamit (1992) *Feminist Methods in Social Research*, New York: Oxford University Press

(1995) 'The Chicago School of Sociology and the founding of the Brandeis University graduate program in sociology: a case study in cultural diffusion', pp. 273–321 in Gary A. Fine (ed.), q.v

Reiss, Albert L. (1984) Interview

Rhoades, Lawrence J. (1981) *A History of the American Sociological Association 1905–1980*, Washington: American Sociological Association

Rhoads, G. (1972) 'On Gouldner's *Crisis of Western Sociology*', *American Journal of Sociology* 78: 136–54

Rice, Stuart A. (ed.) (1931) *Methods in Social Science: A Case Book*, Chicago: University of Chicago Press

Riecken, Henry W. (1983) 'The National Science Foundation and the social sciences', *Items* 37 (2, 3): 39–42

Riemer, Svend (1942) Review of Zipf, *National Unity and Disunity*, *American Journal of Sociology* 48: 285–7

Riley, Matilda W. (1963) *Sociological Research*, New York: Harcourt, Brace and World

Riley, Matilda W., John W. Riley and Jackson Toby (1954) *Sociological Studies in Scale Analysis*, New Brunswick, NJ: Rutgers University Press

Ritzer, George (1975) 'Sociology: a multiple paradigm science', *The American Sociologist* 10: 156–7

Robinson, Marshall (1983) 'The role of the private foundations', *Items* 37: 35–9

Robinson, W. S. (1950) 'Ecological correlations and the behavior of individuals', *American Sociological Review* 15: 351–7

(1951) 'The logical structure of analytical induction', *American Sociological Review* 16: 812–18

Rock, Paul (1979) *The Making of Symbolic Interactionism*, London: Macmillan

Rose, Arnold M. (ed.) (1962) *Human Behavior and Social Processes*, New York: Houghton Mifflin

Rosenberg, Charles E. (1976) *No Other Gods*, Baltimore: Johns Hopkins University Press

Ross, Dorothy (1991) *The Origins of American Social Science*, Cambridge: Cambridge University Press

Ross, F. A. (1931) 'On generalisation from limited social data', *Social Forces* 10: 32–7

Rossi, Peter (1959) 'Four landmarks in voting research', pp. 5–54 in Eugene Burdick and Arthur J. Brodbeck (ed.), *American Voting Behavior*, Glencoe, IL: Free Press

(1984) Interview

Rothman, Robert A. (1971) 'Textbooks and the certification of knowledge', *The American Sociologist* 6: 125–7

Royden, A. Maude (1916) *Downward Paths*, London: Bell

Russett, Cynthia E. (1966) *Equilibrium in American Social Thought*, New Haven: Yale University Press

Sanders, Irwin (1984) Interview

Sapolsky, Harvey M. (1990) *Science and the Navy: The History of the Office of Naval Research*, Princeton, NJ: Princeton University Press

Sarbin, Theodore R. (1943) 'A contribution to the study of actuarial and individual methods of prediction', *American Journal of Sociology* 48: 593–602

Schatzman, Leonard and Anselm L. Strauss (1973) *Field Research*, Englewood Cliffs, NJ: Prentice Hall

Schmid, Calvin (1984) Conversation

Schuman, Howard and Jacqueline Scott (1989) 'Generations and collective memories', *American Sociological Review* 54: 359–81

Schwartz, Barry (1982) 'The social context of commemoration: a study in collective memory', *Social Forces* 61: 374–402

Seidman, Steven (1985) 'Classics and contemporaries: the history and systematics of sociology revisited', *History of Sociology* 6: 121–36

Selvin, Hanan C. (1958) 'Durkheim's *Suicide* and problems of empirical research', *American Journal of Sociology* 63: 607–19

'Durkheim's *Suicide*: further thoughts on a methodological classic', pp. 113–36 in Robert A. Nisbet (ed.), *Emile Durkheim*, Englewood Cliffs, NJ: Prentice Hall

'Durkheim, Booth and Yule: the non-diffusion of an intellectual innovation', *Archives européennes de sociologie* 17: 39–51

Sewell, William H. (1983) Interview

Seybold, Peter (1987) 'The Ford Foundation and the transformation of political science', pp. 185–98 in M. Schwartz (ed.), *The Structure of Power in America*, New York: Holmes and Meier

Seymour, Frederick (1982) Interview

Shanas, Ethel (1942) 'A critique of Dodd's *Dimensions of Society*', *American Journal of Sociology* 48: 214–30

(1943) 'Rejoinder', *American Journal of Sociology* 49: 608–11

Shannon, C. E. and Warren Weaver (1962) *The Mathematical Theory of Communication*, Urbana: University of Illinois Press

Shannon, Lyle (1993) Interview

Shaw, Clifford R. (1930) *The Jack-Roller*, Chicago: University of Chicago Press

Shichor, David (1973) 'Prestige and regional mobility of new PhDs in sociology', *The American Sociologist* 8: 180–6

Shils, Edward A. (1980) *The Calling of Sociology*, Chicago: University of Chicago Press

Shore, Marlene (1987) *The Science of Social Redemption: McGill, the Chicago School and the Origins of Social Research in Canada*, Toronto: University of Toronto Press

Short, James F. and Fred L. Strodtbeck (1963) 'The response of gang leaders to status threats', *American Journal of Sociology* 68: 571–9

Sibley, Elbridge (1963) *The Education of Sociologists in the United States*, Russell Sage Foundation, New York

　(1974) *Social Science Research Council: The First Fifty Years*, New York: Social Science Research Council

Sica, Alan (1983) 'Sociology at the University of Kansas, 1889–1983: a historical sketch.', *Sociological Quarterly* 24: 605–23

Sicherman, Barbara and Carol H. Green (eds.) (1980) *Notable American Women*, Cambridge, MA: Harvard University Press

Sills, David L. (1987) *Paul F. Lazarsfeld: A Biographical Memoir*, Washington, DC: National Academy Press

Silva, Edward T. and Sheila T. Slaughter (1984) *Serving Power: The Making of the Academic Social Science Expert*, Westport, CT: Greenwood Press

Simpson, George (1949) 'The assault on social science', *American Sociological Review* 14: 303–11

Sjoberg, Gideon, Norma Williams, Ted R. Vaughan and Andrée F. Sjoberg (1991) 'The case study approach in social research', pp. 27–79 in Feagin, Orum and Sjoberg (eds.), q.v.

Skinner, B. F. (1956) PWB 2

Skinner, Quentin (1969) 'Meaning and understanding in the history of ideas', *History and Theory* 8: 3–53

　(1974) 'Some problems in the analysis of political thought and action', *Political Theory* 2: 277–302

Sklar, Kathryn Kish (1985) 'Hull-House as a community of women reformers in the 1890s', *Signs* 10: 657–77

Sklare, Marshall (1963) 'The development and utilization of sociological research: the case of the American Jewish community', *Jewish Journal of Sociology* 5: 167–86

Smith, Dennis (1988) *The Chicago School: A Liberal Critique of Capitalism*, Basingstoke: Macmillan

Smith, Laurence D. (1987) *Behaviorism and Logical Positivism*, Stanford: Stanford University Press

Smith, T. V. and Leonard D. White (eds.) (1929) *Chicago: An Experiment in Social Science Research*, Chicago: University of Chicago Press

Snizek, William E. (1975) 'The relationship between theory and research: a study in the sociology of sociology', *Sociological Quarterly* 16: 415–28

(1976) 'An empirical assessment of "Sociology: a multiple paradigm science"', *The American Sociologist* 11: 217–19

Sorokin, Pitirim A. (1940) review of Lundberg, *Foundations of Sociology*, *American Journal of Sociology* 45: 795–8

(1956) 'Changes in sociology during the past 50 years', *Sociology and Social Research* 40: 404–10

(1958) *Fads and Foibles in Modern Sociology*, London: Mayflower

(1966) *Sociological Theories of Today*, New York: Harper and Row

Spengler, J. J. and O. D. Duncan (eds.) (1956) *Demographic Analysis*, Glencoe, IL: Free Press

Stephan, Frederick F. (1948) 'History of the uses of modern sampling procedures', *Journal of the American Statistical Association* 43: 12–39

Stephan, Frederick F. and Philip J. McCarthy (1958) *Sampling Opinions*, New York: Wiley

Stewart, John Q. (1947) 'Suggested principles of "social physics"', *Science* 106 (NS):179–80

(1948a) 'Demographic gravitation: evidence and applications', *Sociometry* 11: 31–58

(1948b) 'Concerning "social physics"', *Scientific American* 178 (2): 20–3

(1949) JQS 2

(1950) 'The natural sciences applied to social theory', *Science* 111: 500

(1951) PWB 1

(1957) JQS 1

Stinchcombe, Arthur L. (1982) 'Should sociologists forget their mothers and fathers?', *American Sociologist* 17: 2–10

Stouffer, Samuel A. (1930) 'Experimental comparison of a statistical and a case-history technique of attitude research', *Publications of the American Sociological Society* 25: 154–6

(1940) 'Intervening opportunities: a theory relating mobility and distance', *American Sociological Review* 5: 845–67

(1950) 'Afterthoughts of a contributor', pp. 197–211 in Merton and Lazarsfeld (eds.) q.v

(1955) *Communism, Conformity and Civil Liberties*, New York: Doubleday

(1962) *Social Research To Test Ideas*, New York: Free Press

Stouffer, Samuel A., Louis Guttman, Edward A. Suchman et al. (1949–50) *Measurement and Prediction*, Princeton, NJ: Princeton University Press

Strodtbeck, Fred L. (1980) *A Study of Husband-Wife Interaction in Three Cultures*, reprinted New York: Arno Press

Sulek, Antoni (1994) 'Paul Lazarsfeld and Polish Sociology: 60 years of influence', Paper given at RC 08, XIIIth World Congress of Sociology, Bielefeld

Sutherland, Edwin (1939) *Principles of Criminology*, Philadelphia: Lippincott

Sutton, Francis X. (1986) 'Report of the Acting President', pp. 13–30 in *Social Science Research Council Annual Report*, New York: SSRC
(1993) Interview

Swift, Harold H. (1924) HHS 2

Szacki, J. (1975) '"Schools" in sociology', *Social Science Information* 12 (4): 173–82
(1979) *The History of Sociological Thought*, Westport, Conn.: Greenwood Press

Sztompka, Piotr (1986) *Robert K. Merton: An Intellectual Profile*, London: Macmillan

Szymanski, Albert (1971) 'Towards a radical sociology', pp. 93–107 in J. D. Colfax and J. L. Roach (eds.), *Radical Sociology*, New York: Basic Books

Taylor, Brian (1994) 'The Anglican clergy and the early development of British sociology', *Sociological Review* 42: 438–51

Thomas, Dorothy S. (1931) 'An attempt to develop precise measurements in the social behavior field', *Sociologus* 8: 435–56

Thomas, Dorothy S. and associates (1929) *Some New Techniques for Studying Social Behavior*, New York: Teachers' College, Columbia

Thomas, Dorothy S., Alice M. Loomis and Ruth E. Arrington (1933) *Observational Studies of Social Behavior*, New Haven: Yale University Press

Thomas, William I. (1923) *The Unadjusted Girl*, Boston: Little, Brown

Thomas, William I. and Florian Znaniecki (1918–20) *The Polish Peasant in Europe and America*, Boston: Badger

Thurstone, Louis L. and E. J. Chave (1929) *The Measurement of Attitudes*, Chicago: University of Chicago Press

Timasheff, Nicholas S. (1950) 'Sociological theory today', *American Catholic Sociological Review* 11: 25–33

Tiryakian, Edward A. (1979) 'The significance of schools in the development of sociology', pp. 211–233 in ed. W. E. Snizek, *Contemporary Issues in Theory and Research*, Westport: Greenwood Press

Torgerson, Warren S. (1958) *Theory and Methods of Scaling*, New York: Wiley

Truesdell, Leon E. (1965) *The Development of Punch Card Tabulation in the Bureau of the Census*, Washington, DC: Bureau of the Census

Turk, Herman (1963) 'Social cohesion through variant values: evidence from medical role relations', *American Sociological Review* 28: 28–37

Turner, Ralph H. (1947) 'The navy disbursing officer as a bureaucrat', *American Sociological Review* 12: 342–8
(1954) 'The quest for universals in sociological research', *American Sociological Review* 18: 604–11

Turner, Stephen P. (1983) '"Contextualism" and the interpretation of the classic sociological texts', pp. 273–91 in *Knowledge and Society*, vol. IV, Greenwich, CT: Greenwood Press
(1994) 'The origins of "mainstream sociology" and other issues in the history of American sociology', *Social Epistemology* 8: 41–67

Turner, Stephen P. and Jonathan H. Turner (1990) *The Impossible Science: an Institutional Analysis of American Sociology*, Newbury Park, CA: Sage

Useem, John (1984) Conversation

Useem, Michael (1976) 'Government influence on the social science paradigm', *Sociological Quarterly* 17: 146–61

van Elteren, Mel (1990) 'Psychology and sociology of work in the Netherlands within the Anglo-American orbit, 1945–1980', mimeo

van Waters, Miriam (1926) *Youth in Conflict*, London: Methuen

Vaughan, Ted R. and Larry T. Reynolds (1968) 'The sociology of symbolic interactionism', *The American Sociologist* 3: 208–14

Veblen, Thorstein (1931) *The Theory of the Leisure Class*, New York: Viking

Verhoeven, Jef C. (1994) 'An interview with Erving Goffman, 1980', *Research on Language and Social Interaction* 26: 317–48

(1995) 'Some reflections on cross-cultural interviewing', paper given at ESRC seminar, University of Warwick; Papers in Theoretical Sociology and Sociology of Education, Department of Sociology, University of Leuven

Vidich, Arthur J and Stanford M. Lyman (1985) *American Sociology: Worldly Rejections of Religion and their Directions*, New Haven: Yale University Press

Wald, Alan M. (1987) *The New York Intellectuals*, Chapel Hill, NC: University of North Carolina Press

Waller, Willard (1930) *The Old Love and the New*, Carbondale: Southern Illinois University Press, reprinted 1967

Walter, Maila (1990) *Science and Cultural Crisis: An Intellectual Biography of Percy Williams Bridgman*, Stanford: Stanford University Press

Ware, Caroline (1935) *Greenwich Village*, New York: Harper and Row, reprinted 1965

Warner, W. Lloyd and Paul S. Lunt (1941) *The Social Life of a Modern Community*, New Haven: Yale University Press

Warntz, William (1984) 'Trajectories and coordinates', pp. 134–50 in M. Billinge et al. (eds.), *Recollections of a Revolution*, London: Macmillan

Watson, John B. (1919) *Psychology from the Standpoint of a Behaviorist*, Philadelphia: Lippincott

Weaver, Warren (1949) RAC 1

(1950) RAC 2

Webb, Eugene J., Donald T. Campbell, Richard D. Schwartz and Lee Sechrest (1966) *Unobtrusive Measures*, Chicago: Rand McNally

Weber, Max (1949) *The Methodology of the Social Sciences*, Glencoe, IL: Free Press

Weinberg, S. Kirson (1952) 'Comment on W. S. Robinson's "The logical structure of analytical induction"', *American Sociological Review* 17: 493–4

Wells, Richard H. and J. Steven Picou (1981) *American Sociology: Theoretical and Methodological Structures*, Washington, DC: University Press of America

Westie, Frank R. (1993) 'Race stratification and the culture of legitimization', pp. 255–82 in J. H. Stanfield II (ed.), *A History of Race Relations Research*, Newbury Park, CA: Sage

Whyte, William F. (1943, 1955, 1981) *Street Corner Society*, Chicago: University of Chicago Press

   (1982) Conversation

Williams, Robin (1984) Interview

Wilner, Patricia (1985) 'The main drift of sociology between 1936 and 1984', *History of Sociology* 5: 1–20

Winkin, Yves (1988) *Erving Goffman: les moments et leurs hommes*, Paris: Editions du Seuil

Wirth, Louis M. (1937) LW 2

   (ed.) (1940) *Eleven Twenty-Six: A Decade of Social Science Research*, Chicago: University of Chicago Press

   (1946) LW 1

Woofter, T. J. (1933) 'Common errors in sampling', *Social Forces* 11: 521–5

Woolston, Howard (1942) Review of Dodd, *Dimensions of Society*, *Annals of the American Academy of Political and Social Science* 221: 231

Wormser, R. A. (1958) *Foundations: Their Power and Influence*, New York: Devin-Adair

Wright, Erik Olin (1989) *The Debate on Classes*, London: Verso

Young, Pauline V. (1932) *The Pilgrims of Russian-town*, Chicago: University of Chicago Press

   (1935) *Interviewing in Social Work*, New York: McGraw-Hill

   (1939, 1949, 1956) *Scientific Social Surveys and Research*, New York: Prentice-Hall

Zeisel, Hans (1947) *Say It With Figures*, New York: Harper

   (1968) 'L'école viennoise des recherches de motivation', *Revue française de sociologie* 9: 3–12

   (1990) Interview

Zetterberg, Hans L. (1954, 1965) *On Theory and Verification in Sociology*, Stockholm: Almquist and Wiksell

Zipf, George K. (1935) *The Psycho-Biology of Language*, New York: Houghton Mifflin

   (1941) *National Unity and Disunity: The Nation as a Bio-Social Organism*, Bloomington, Indiana: Principia Press

   (1949) *Human Behavior and the Principle of Least Effort*, reprinted 1965, New York: Hafner

Znaniecki, Florian (1934) *The Method of Sociology*, New York: Farrar and Rinehart

Index

Abbreviations are not listed in this index; please see the list of abbreviations for the corresponding entry. Fleeting references, of a kind not likely to be of interest to a reader concerned with that person or institution as such, are not listed. Publications cited are listed here under the name of each author named in the bibliography, but only very exceptionally under the title of a book. The sole-authored publications come first, followed by joint-authored ones where the person is the first author, and then those where s/he is not or the publication is a contribution to an edited volume. The 'publications' include the interviews which are part of the data.

Abel, Theodore, 277
  hostility to Merton and Lazarsfeld, 202
  and Znaniecki, 51
  Abel 1938, 51, 254–5
  Abel 1941, 89
  Abel 1947, 51
Achinstein (Paul) and Barker 1969, 79
Ackoff (Russell) 1953, 35
Ackroyd (Stephen) and Hughes 1981, 4, 118
Adams (Richard N.) and Preiss 1960, 16, 29–30, 62
Addams, Jane 261
  Addams 1912, 263
Adorno, Theodor, 49
  Adorno et al. 1950, 26, 149
age as a factor in choices of method, 230
Agricultural Experiment Stations
  encouraging study of diffusion of innovations, 130
  quantitative tradition of, 153, 206
  research opportunities in, 151–2
Agriculture, Department of, see US Department of Agriculture
Ahmad (Salma) 1991, 184
Air Force, see US Air Force
Alchon (Guy) 1985, 142, 165

Alexander (Jeffrey) 1979, 110, 232; 1982, 107; 1987, 247
Alexander and Colomy 1992, 107, 111, 232–3
Alihan (Milla) 1938, 17
Allport (Gordon) 1942, 14, 21, 146
Alpert (Harry) 1939, 69; 1954, 157; 1955 157; 1968, 93
American Association for the Advancement of Science, 101, 215, 217, 220
American Association for Public Opinion Research, 59, 227
American Catholic Sociological Society, 226
American Council for Judaism, 95, 149
American Jewish Committee, 149
American Sociological Association
  interests within, 131, 228
  membership of, 52–3
  Mrs Dummer and, 260–1
  Presidents of, 19, 78, 210, 224, 234
  sections, 131, 227, 261
American Sociological Review, 210
American Sociological Society, see American Sociological Association
American sociology, influence of, 2–3
American Soldier research, see also Stouffer et al., Hovland et al.
  Carnegie funding of, 147, 189

and methodological publications, 24, 59–60
reception of, 60, 249
and survey, prominence of, 60, 229
American Statistical Association, 19, 227
Amsterdamska (Olga) 1985, 234
analytical induction, 18, 48
ancestors, intellectual, choice of, 3, 7, 32, 244–5, 267–70
Anderson, C. Arnold, 277
Anderson 1984, 152, 181
Anderson, Nels, 257
Anderson 1927, 119
Anderson, Odin, 277
Andrews, F. Emerson: Glenn, Brandt and Andrews 1946, 144
Angell, Robert C., 49, 277
re-study of cases from Angell 1936, 58, 136
Angell 1936, 14, 18, 48, 252
Angell 1954, 18
Angell 1976?, 206
Gottschalk, Kluckhohn and Angell 1945, 14, 58, 146
anti-Semitism, 218, 224–5
Arensberg, Conrad, 265
Chapple and Arensberg 1940, 12
Argyris (Chris) 1952 (revised ?1955), 251–2
Arnove (R. F.)1982, 142
Aronovici (Carol) 1916, 14, 17
Arrington, Ruth E.: Thomas, Loomis and Arrington 1933, 14, 18–19, 42
Authoritarian Personality, The, 26, 149

Baehr (Peter) and O'Brien 1994, 243–4
Bain, Read, 219, 226
influence on Strodtbeck, 96
Bain 1928, 99
Bain 1950, 97
Bain 1951, 214–15
Baldamus (W.) 1976, 114
Bales, Kevin: Bulmer, Bales and Sklar 1991, 39
Bales, R. Freed, 277
funding not needed, 194
influenced by Durkheim, 235
and scientism, 102
Bales 1950, 15, 23, 54
Bales 1984, 102
Parsons and Bales 1955, 101
Parsons, Bales and Shils 1953, 102
Bannister (Robert C.) 1987, 67, 76, 77; 1992, 218
Barker, S. F.: Achinstein and Barker 1969, 79
Barnard, Chester I., 177
Barnard 1938, 177

Barnes (Barry) 1982, 256
Barnes (H. E.) 1948, 3
Barnes and Becker 1938, 4
Barton, Allen, 277
Lazarsfeld and Barton 1951, 1955, 13
Bassett, Raymond, 215
Baxandall (Michael) 1985, 269
Beach (Walter G.) 1939, 3
Beazley, Virginia: Lundberg and Beazley 1948, 83–4
Becker, Howard P.
confused with H. S. Becker, 118
Becker 1948, 92
Barnes and Becker 1938, 4
Becker, Howard S., 277
on Blumer's method, 120
and Chicago stereotype, 268
confused with H. P. Becker, 118
and funding, 190
as influence, 130
reasons for methodological writing, 62
and symbolic interactionism, 121
Becker 1958, 50
Becker 1982, 62
Becker 1990, 121
Becker and Geer 1957, 50
Becker and Geer 1960, 62–3
Becker, Geer and Hughes 1968, 190, 230
Becker, Geer, Riesman and Weiss 1968, 121, 133
Behavioral Research Council, 95
Behavioral Science Council, 217
Behavioral Sciences, *see* Ford Foundation
behaviourism, 17, 47, 71
Bell (E. T.) 1942, 94
Ben David (Joseph) 1973, 114
Bennett (James) 1981, 133–4
Bentley, Arthur F., 90, 219–20
Bentley 1926, 220
Berelson, Bernard, 283
and foundations, 167, 171, 179
Berelson 1952, 15, 24, 61
Berelson 1956, 168–9
Berelson 1968, 148
Berelson, Lazarsfeld and McPhee 1954, 174
Lazarsfeld, Berelson and Gaudet 1944, 249, 252
Berger, Joseph: Berger, Wagner and Zelditch 1989, 111
Bergmann, Gustav, 75, 221, 225, 277
Bergmann 1944, 90
Bergmann 1993, 225
Bernard, Jessie: Bernard and Bernard 1943, 4

Bernard (L. L.) 1945, 53
  Bernard and Bernard 1943, 4
Bertalanffy, Ludwig von, 101
Biderman, Albert D.: Crawford and
  Biderman 1970, 157, 158, 180, 191
Bierstedt, Robert, 89
  Bierstedt 1981, 69
Bingham (W. Van Dyke) and Moore 1931,
  24
biograms, 51
Bird Dogs (The) 1961, 155
Black (Max) 1961, 112
black sociologists, 206, 225, 247
Blalock, Hubert M., 277
  influences on, 207
  mathematical background, 195
  Blalock 1984, 93, 132, 133, 207
  Blalock 1988, 57, 195
  Blalock 1989, 31, 130, 139–40
Blankenship (Albert B.) 1943, 22; 1946, 22
Blau (Peter M.) 1955, 255
Bloor (David) 1976, 5
Blumer, Herbert, 277
  and Chicago stereotype, 268
  critic of American Soldier, 60
  as football player, 46
  influence of, 208
  and symbolic interactionism, 120–1
  versus Lundberg, 65, 104
  Blumer 1939, 14, 20–1, 58, 146
  Blumer 1969, 120
  Blumer 1982, 120, 254–5
Bogardus, Emory S.
  and department at University of
    Southern California, 36, 234
  Bogardus, 1918, 34, 35, 234
  Bogardus, 1925, 34, 35, 234
  Bogardus, 1926, 35
  Bogardus, 1936, 35
Bogue, Donald J.
  and Stewart, 96
  Bogue 1992, 96
books, their methods unlike those of
  articles, 125–6
Booth, Charles, 31, 39
  Booth 1892–7, 249, 252
Bowen, Louise de K., 263
  Bowen 1917, 263
  Bowen 1926, 263
Brandeis University, Hughes and Chicago
  influence at, 62
Brandt, Lilian: Glenn, Brandt and Andrews
  1946, 144
Bridgman, Percy W.
  and Department of Social Relations, 202

and Lundberg group, 90, 215, 220
and Vienna Circle, 71
  Bridgman 1931, 80
  Bridgman 1938, 220
Brooks (Harvey) 1983, 157
Brown (E. R.) 1979, 142
Brown, J. D.: Colomy and Brown 1995, 232
Brown, J. S.: and Gilmartin 1969, 124, 126
Bruner, Jerome, 277
Brunswik, Else Frenkel: Adorno et al. 1950,
  149
Bruyn (Severyn) 1966, 30
Bryant (Christopher G. A.) 1985, 68, 70
Bryman (Alan) 1984, 110; 1988, 106
Bulmer (Martin) 1980, 135, 145; 1981, 264–5,
  270; 1983a, 76, 145; 1983b, 119; 1983c,
  203; 1984a, 4, 51, 145, 160, 184, 203, 208,
  257, 269; 1984b, 142, 160; 1985, 237; 1991,
  247, 256
  Bulmer and Bulmer 1981, 144, 160, 169,
    184, 187, 191
  Bulmer, Bales and Sklar 1991, 39
Bureau of Agricultural Economics, 150
Bureau of Applied Social Research
  and American Jewish Committee, 149
  books associated with, 61, 136
  funding of, 156, 157, 171–2, 175
  group identity, 259
  intellectual style, 133
  and Lazarsfeld influence, 236
Burgess, Ernest W.
  and case study, personal documents, 13,
    48, 49, 63–4, 254–5
  and early survey, 144
  encouraging writing by others, 56, 58, 64,
    146
  as influence, 130, 208
  and SSRC, 13
  Burgess and Cottrell 1939, 79
Burt (Ronald S.) 1982, 138, 257

Calhoun (Donald W.) 1942, 91, 94
Camic (Charles) 1992, 244, 245
  Camic and Xie 1994, 201, 208, 211, 269
Campbell (Donald T.) 1957, 44
  Webb et al. 1966, 19, 30, 248
Canadian sociology, 244, 265
Cannell, Charles F., 277
  Cannell 1983 228
  Kahn and Cannell 1957, 16, 24, 61
Cantril (Hadley) 1947, 14, 22, 60
Capecchi (Vittorio) 1978, 2
capitalism and sociology, 67, 113, 159–66
Cappell (Charles L.) and Guterbock 1992,
  131

Carlson, Kathleen, 167
Carnegie Corporation
  and libraries, 163
  method, lack of interest in, 189
  and Myrdal 1944, 147, 170
  and Parsons and Shils 1951, 190
  and social science, 147, 172, 177
Cartwright (Nancy) 1987, 88
case study
  decline of category, 37, 39, 41, 50
  choice of exemplars for, 253–5
  social-work origins, 46
  unpublished monograph on, 58
  versus statistical method, 22, 36, 45–6, 128
Catholics in sociology, 224, 226
Catholic University, doctoral productivity, 206
Catton, William R.
  and Dodd, 99, 205
  Catton 1966, 99
  Catton 1968, 83, 93
  Catton 1993, 205
Cavan, Ruth Shonle, 277
  Cavan 1982, 120
Census
  and data processing, 136
  and methodological writing, 15
  and social science, 49, 153
Center for Advanced Study in the
    Behavioral Sciences, 101, 148, 168, 196
centre and periphery in sociology, 209–10
Chapin, F. Stuart
  author of both textbook and monograph
    on method, 57
  in Giddings line of descent, 76, 137–8, 195
  reputation limited by substantive work, 257
  Chapin 1938, 89
  Chapin 1947, 15, 22–3
  Chapin and Queen 1937, 23
Chapoulie (Jean-Michel) 1991, 2
Chapple, Eliot D., 265
  Chapple and Arensberg 1940, 12
Chave, E. J.: Thurstone and Chave 1929, 12
Chicago Irregulars, 268
Chicago, University of
  and case-study method, 49, 254–5
  Chicago School, 200, 262, 265–9
  and city, 261–5
  departmental style, 132–3, 200, 203, 254
  division on methods, 45–6, 63
  dominance, 210
  fall in relative size, 49, 209, 267
  and Free Press, 55–6

  and funding, 144, 174, 184
  and Goffman, 207, 267
  Jewish students at, 225
  reception of Lundberg, 104
  methods teaching, courses, 30, 53
  methods textbooks, 34, 36
  monograph series, 38, 39
  qualitative researchers at, 62, 117–21, 266–8
  reputation of, 257, 260–9
  versus Columbia, rivalry, 17–18, 63, 211, 254
  versus Columbia, stereotype, 51, 65, 208–9
  versus Harvard, 133, 203, 211
Christie (Richard) and Jahoda 1954, 12, 15
Chubin (Daryl) and McCartney 1982, 182
Cicourel (Aaron V.) 1964, 30
Clausen, John A., 277
  Clausen 1984, 154, 179
Clegg (Stewart) 1992, 242
Cohen, Joseph, 277
Cole (Jonathan) and Cole (Stephen) 1973, 245
Coleman, James S., 277
  engineering background, 132, 195
  Coleman 1980, 201
  Coleman 1984, 132, 133,195
  Coleman 1990, 210
  Lipset, Trow and Coleman 1956, 132
  Merton, Coleman and Rossi 1979, 13, 259
Collins (Randall) 1977, 140; 1989, 65, 234
Colomy, Paul
  Colomy and Brown 1995, 232
  Alexander and Colomy 1992, 107, 111, 232–3
Columbia Project for Advanced Training in
    Social Research, 29
Columbia University
  departmental style, 133, 201–2, 210
  Giddings period, 76, 208
  and funding, 144
  methods courses, 53
  methods textbooks, 34, 36
  reputation of, 257–60
  research on, 269
  versus Chicago, *see* Chicago, versus Columbia
  versus Michigan, 133
  versus North Carolina, 133
Colvard (Richard) 1976, 178
Commercial research agencies, 13, 22, 58, 128, 134, 227
Committee on the Appraisal of Research, 146

Committee on Human Relations in Industry, 62
Committee on the Measurement of Opinion, Attitudes and Consumer Wants, 58, 146
Committee on Scaling Theory and Methods, 59, 146
Committee on Social Adjustment, 58
concepts, methodological, *see* methods, concepts used for
Congressional Special Committee to Investigate Tax-Exempt Foundations, 165–6
Converse (Jean M.) 1987, 4, 25, 27, 58, 73, 99, 135, 151, 153, 154, 157, 179
Cook, Stuart
  Jahoda, Deutsch and Cook 1951, 35, 36, 40–2, 149, 251
  Selltiz, Jahoda, Deutsch and Cook 1959, 35
Cooley, Charles H., 3
  influence on qualitative method, 118–19
Cooney (Terry A.) 1986, 223
Coser (Lewis A.) 1971, 3
Cottrell, Leonard S., 28, 278
  Cottrell 1982, 52
  Burgess and Cottrell 1939, 79
Crane (Diana) 1965, 245; 1972, 238
Crawford, Elizabeth T.: Crawford and Biderman 1970, 157, 158, 180, 191
Cressey (Donald R.) 1953, 18
Cressey, Paul G., 119
criminology, 130
critical analysis of method, 25–7, 31
Crothers (Charles) 1987, 269; 1990, 269; forthcoming, 269
Culver, Helen, funding of *The Polish Peasant*, 143
Curelaru, M.: Eisenstadt and Curelaru 1976, 113
curve fitting, logistic curves, 85

D'Antonio, William V.: Form and D'Antonio 1959, 172
Danziger (Kurt) 1990, 108
Darley (John D.) 1957, 155; 1963, 155
Davis (Fred) 1984, 241, 270
Davis, James A., 278
  Davis 1984, 54, 93, 115, 202
Davis (Kingsley) 1943, 92
Dawes, Kenneth: McGuire and Dawes 1983, 206
de Grazia, A.: de Grazia et al. 1968, 82
deduction and induction, 36, 72, 79, 86–7
Deegan (Mary Jo) 1988, 261, 262

Deming, W. S., 151
Denzin (Norman K.) 1970, 57
departments
  importance of, 200–11
  neglected in history, 206
  rivalry or conflict between, 17–18, 63, 201, 203, 210–11
  self-selection of students, 207
  stereotypes of, 51, 65, 208–9, 273
  stratification of, 201, 209–11
Depression, the, 49, 52, 271
Derrida, Jacques, reception of, 241–2
design of research, 13, 28, 37
Deutsch, Morton
  Jahoda, Deutsch and Cook 1951, 35, 36, 40–2, 149, 251
  Selltiz, Jahoda, Deutsch and Cook 1959, 35
Deutscher (Irwin) 1973, 248; 1984, 120
deviant cases, 18, 48
Dewey (F. A.) 1915, 32
Dickson, Lenore: Lundberg, Hertzler and Dickson 1949, 83–4
diffusion or non-diffusion of ideas, 31, 33, 136–7
Division of Program Surveys, 134, 151, 182, 228
Doby, John T., 278
  Doby 1954, 35, 36, 74
  Doby 1991, 54, 73–4
Dodd, Stuart C., 219
  biography of, 212
  citations, 94
  empirical work, 85–6
  and funding, 149, 204
  lack of disciples, 205
  and the Lundberg circle, *see* Lundberg
  Project Revere, 85, 156
  S-theory, 80–1, 94, 97, 100
  Dodd 1934, 212, 250
  Dodd 1936, 89
  Dodd 1942, 80–2, 86, 93–4, 212
  Dodd 1948, 86
  Dodd 1950, 81, 85
  Dodd 1951, 85
  Dodd 1955, 85
  Dodd 1967, 89
Dollard, Charles, 283
Dollard (John) 1935, 14, 20, 57, 128
Dubin (Robert) 1961, 177
Du Bois, W. E. B., 247
  Du Bois 1899, 247, 256
Dummer, Ethel Sturges
  funding of *The Unadjusted Girl*, 143
  role in sociology, 260–2
  Dummer 1933, 261

Duncan, Beverly: Duncan, Scott, Lieberson and Duncan 1960, 96
Duncan, Otis Dudley, 278
and Dodd, 96
as influence, 130
and Sewell, 137
and Stewart, 96
and Zipf, 96
Duncan 1959, 96
Duncan 1984, 93, 196, 267
Duncan 1992, 96
Duncan, Scott, Lieberson and Duncan 1960, 96
Spengler and Duncan 1956, 96
Duncan, Otis Durant, 137
Dunham, H. Warren: Faris and Dunham 1939, 249, 252
Durkheim, Emile, 3, 31, 32, 102, 235, 237, 245
and scientism in US sociology, 69–70
Suicide as exemplar, 249, 252
Durkheim 1895, 252
Durkheim 1938, 65, 69–70, 252
Durkheim 1951, 249

Easthope (Gary) 1974, 4, 118
ecological fallacy, 32
ecology, ecological approach, 17–18, 39
Edwards, Derek: Middleton and Edwards 1990, 240–1
Eisenstadt, S. N.: Eisenstadt and Curelaru 1976, 113
election polls, 59
Ellis, Robert, 278
and Vienna Circle, 74
Ellis 1991, 74, 130, 234
Ellwood, Charles A., 225
Ellwood 1933, 14, 17, 18, 72
Elmer, Manuel C.
author of both textbook and monograph on method, 57
Elmer 1917, 14, 17, 42, 144
Elmer 1939, 35
England (J. Merton) 1982, 157
Ennis (James G.) 1992, 131
epistemology, 106
Evans, J.: Irvine, Miles and Evans 1979, 142
ex post facto design, 23
exemplars, choice of, 42, 79, 129–30, 210, 248–56
experimentation, experimental design, 22–3, 128

Faris (Robert E. L.) 1967, 4
Faris and Dunham 1939, 249, 252

Fava, Sylvia: Himelhoch and Fava 1955, 12, 16, 26
Fay (Brian) 1975, 107
Feagin, Joe R.: Feagin, Orum and Sjoberg 1991, 105
Feigl, Herbert, 71, 221
feminism, and method, 122–3, 126
Festinger, Leon
Festinger and Katz 1953, 35, 36
Jahoda et al. 1951, 41
Filmer, Paul: Filmer, Phillipson, Silverman and Walsh 1972, 107, 113
Filstead (William J.) 1970, 30
Fine, Gary A.: Fine and Severance 1985, 206
Fish (Virginia Kemp) 1985, 262
Fisher, Donald, 164, 170
Fisher 1980, 142, 183
Fisher 1983, 142, 144, 159, 183–4
Fisher 1984, 142, 144, 160
Fisher 1993, 67, 68, 142, 144, 146, 169, 179, 180, 184, 198
Fisher, R. A., 151
Fisk University, 225
Fiske, Marjorie: Merton, Fiske and Kendall 1956, 16, 23–4, 136
Ford Foundation
attacked, 178
Behavioral Sciences programme, 147–8, 179, 195
block grants, 169
civil rights support, 163
grant for *Field Work*, 62, 190
policy of complementarity, 178
projects funded, 62, 175, 190
Form, William H.: Form and D'Antonio 1959, 172
Foucault, Michel, reception of, 243
foundations, 5, 95, 144–50, 159–79, *see also* Carnegie, Ford, Rockefeller, Spencer
and establishment, 179
and methods, 189–90
officers, 167–8, 176–9
trustees, role of, 164–5, 176–7
Francis, Roy G., 138
Mc Cormick and Francis 1958, 35, 138
Frankfurt School, 49
Frazier, E. Franklin ,225
Free Press, The, 55
Freedman, Ronald, 278
Freedman 1948, 92
Freidheim (E. A.) 1979, 111
Freidson, Eliot, 109, 278
and symbolic interactionism, 121
Freidson 1984, 121, 132–3

Friedrichs(Robert W.) 1970, 4, 70
Fry (Luther) 1934, 35, 47
Fuller (Steve) 1992, 243
functionalism, 75
    and survey method, 113–17
funding, 135, 271–2, *see also* foundations
    and commercial sources, 158–9
    and government, 150–8, 180–2
    individual benefactors, 143
    and quantification, 142, 182–98
    unfunded research, 190–4
Furfey (Paul H.) 1953, 35, 227
Furner(Mary) 1975, 4

GI Bill, 52, 229, 267, 271
Gallagher, Ralph, 226
    Gallagher 1938, 226
Galliher, John F.: Galliher and McCartney
    1973, 173, 198
Galpin, Charles J., 150
Gans, Herbert, 133, 211, 278
    Becker, Geer and Hughes 1968, 230
Gardner, Burleigh, 134, 158, 278
    Gardner 1982, 159
Garfinkel, Laurence, 278
Gaudet, Hazel: Lazarsfeld, Berelson and
    Gaudet 1944, 249, 252
Gee (Wilson) 1950, 35, 37
Geer, Blanche
    Becker and Geer 1957, 50
    Becker, Geer and Hughes 1968, 190,
    230
    Becker, Geer, Riesman and Weiss, 1968
    121, 133
Gehlke (Charles E.) 1935, 65
Geiger, Kent, 278
    Geiger 1984, 133, 211
Geiger (Roger L.) 1986, 178
    Geiger 1988, 173, 175
general systems, 101
Gerth, Hans H.: Gerth and Mills 1946, 37
Getzels, Jacob, 278
Giddens, Anthony, reception of, 242
Giddings, Franklin H., 3, 76, 137, 195, 201
    Giddings 1924, 34
Gilbert, G. Nigel: Gilbert and Mulkay 1984,
    110
Gillespie (Richard) 1991, 139
Gillin (John L.) 1937, 255
Gilmartin, B.: Brown and Gilmartin 1969,
    124, 126
Glaser, Barney G.: Glaser and Strauss 1967,
    18, 30
Glenn, John M.: Glenn, Brandt and
    Andrews 1946, 144

Glock, Charles, 278
    Glock 1979, 175, 201
    Glock 1984, 93, 158
Glueck, Sheldon and Eleanor, versus
    Sutherland, 246–7
Goffman, Erving
    and Chicago, 207, 267
    and Chicago stereotype, 268
    commercial work, 158
    method and funding, 135
    method without rules, 32–3
    and symbolic interactionism, 120–1
Gold (David) 1957, 125
Gold, Raymond L., 62, 172, 278
    Gold 1958, 44
    Gold 1984, 62
Goode, William J.: Goode and Hatt 1952, 35,
    36, 72
Goodman, Leo, 93, 155, 195, 278
Gottschalk, Louis: Gottschalk, Kluckhohn
    and Angell 1945, 14, 58, 146
Gouldner, Alvin, 149
    Gouldner 1971, 4, 106, 159
    Gouldner and Sprehe 1965, 104
government funding, *see* funding
government, sociologists in, 49, 150–4, 227
graphics, 39, 65
Greeley (Andrew) 1990, 226
Green, Carol H.: Sicherman and Green
    1980, 263
Greenberg (Daniel S.) 1969, 158
Greenwood (Ernest) 1945, 14, 23, 61
Gross, Edward, 278
    Gross 1956, 156
    Gross 1984, 133, 156
Gross (George) 1970, 209
Gumplowicz, Ludwig, 3
Guterbock, Thomas M.: Cappell and
    Guterbock 1992, 131
Guttman, Louis, 28, 39, 137
    Stouffer, Guttman, Suchman et al. 1950,
    15, 24–5, 59, 147, 189, 249
Guttman scales, 25, 28

Habenstein, Robert, 278
Hader, J. J.: Hader and Lindeman 1933, 14,
    17
Haerle (Rudolf K.) 1991, 143
Hagood, Margaret J., 150, 227
    Hagood 1939, 255–6
    Hagood 1941, 150
    Hagood 1947, 32
Halfpenny (Peter) 1982, 70
Hall, Oswald, 278
Hall (Robert L.) 1972, 157, 180, 181

Haller, Archibald, 278
  Haller 1984, 115, 136, 138, 152
Hammersley (Martyn) 1991, 122–3
Handy, Rollo: de Grazia et al. 1968, 82
Hansen, Alvin, 151
  Hansen 1987, 154
  Hansen, Hurwitz and Madow 1953, 15, 47
Harrison (Shelby M.) 1931, 144
Hart, Hornell, 222, 225
  Hart 1940, 222
  Hart 1946, 85
  Hart 1947, 222
  Hart 1960a, 91
  Hart 1960b, 222
Harvard University
  department of Social Relations, 114–15,
    147, 202–3, 220
  and fieldwork, 265
  and funding, 144
  intellectual settings at, 244, 246
  Laboratory of Social Relations, 147, 259
  methods courses, 53, 54
  recruiting in rural sociology, 137
  versus Chicago, *see* Chicago
Harvey (Lee) 1987a, 231; 1987b, 4, 264, 269
Harwood, E. C.: de Grazia et al. 1968, 82
Hatt, Paul K.: Goode and Hatt 1952, 35, 36,
  72
Hauser, Philip M., 46, 49, 151, 153, 227, 279
  Hauser 1961, 195
  Hauser 1968, 154
  Hauser 1982, 153, 154
Hawley, Amos, and Stewart, 96
  Hawley 1992, 96
Hawthorn (Geoffrey) 1976, 3; 1991, 197
Healy (William) 1915, 262
Heaven (John W.) 1975, 137
Heims (Steve J.) 1991, 101, 217, 222
Hempel, Carl G., 74, 75, 221
  Hempel 1959, 75
  Hempel 1966, 32
  Hempel and Oppenheim 1936, 75
Henderson, Laurence, 202
Hertzler (Joyce O.) 1947, 92
Hertzler, Virginia Beazley: Lundberg,
  Hertzler and Dickson 1949, 83–4
Heyl (Barbara) 1968, 202
Hill (Michael R.) 1988, 206
Himelhoch, J.: Himelhoch and Fava 1955,
  12, 16, 26
Hindess (Barry) 1973, 107
Hinkle, Gisela: Hinkle and Hinkle 1954, 4
Hinkle, Roscoe C.
  Hinkle 1994, 4, 50, 67, 68, 107
  Hinkle and Hinkle 1954, 4

histories of sociology 3–5
Hobsbawm, Eric: Hobsbawm and Ranger
  1983, 241
Hoch, Paul K.: Platt and Hoch 1995, 75, 78,
  221
Hollingshead (August B.) 1949, 97
Holton (Gerald) 1988, 66
Homans, George C.
  influence on Blalock, 207
  Homans 1947, 154
  Homans 1951, 48
  Homans 1985, 252
Horkheimer, Max, 149
Horst, Paul, 48, 279
  Horst 1941, 14, 21–2, 58
  Horst 1982, 55
House, Floyd N., 55
Hovland, Carl I.: Hovland, Lumsdaine and
  Sheffield 1949, 24, 59, 60, 115
Hughes, Everett C., 16
  and Canada, 265
  and Chicago stereotype, 268
  methods course, 30
  and participant observation, 62, 121
  Hughes 1943, 250
  Becker, Geer and Hughes, 190, 230
Hughes (J. A.) 1976, 107, 109
  Ackroyd and Hughes 1981, 4, 118
Hull-House, 261–2
human documents, *see* personal documents
Hunt (Morton M.) 1961, 116
Hurwitz, W. N., 151
  Hansen, Hurwitz and Madow 1953, 15, 47
Hyfler (Robert) 1984, 161
Hyman, Herbert H., 27
  Hyman 1954, 15, 24, 58
  Hyman 1955, 16, 28, 168
  Hyman 1991, 25, 33, 136
  Mosteller, Hyman and McCarthy 1949,
    15, 22, 59

induction, *see* deduction
industrial sociology, 130
Institute for Social Research, 24, 61, 135,
  151
Institute of Social and Religious Research,
  47
interviewing, 24, 228
interwar period, 4, 67
Iowa Margarine Incident, 181
Iowa State University
  and Office of Naval Research, 156
  methods courses, 53
  and symbolic interactionism, 121–2
Irvine, J.: Irvine, Miles and Evans 1979, 142

Jack-Roller, The, 46, 249, 252
Jacobs (G.) 1970, 30
Jahoda, Marie, 12, 15, 40, 149
  Jahoda, Deutsch and Cook 1951, 35, 36,
    40–42, 149, 251
  Selltiz, Jahoda, Deutsch and Cook 1959,
    35
Janowitz, Morris, 149
Jews, Jewish organisations, 40, 42, 218,
  224–5, *see* also anti-Semitism
  funding research, 95, 149
Jocher, Katharine: Odum and Jocher 1929,
  34, 35
Johnson, Benton: Johnson and Johnson
  1986, 116, 205
Johnson, Charles S., 225
Johnson (D. Gale) 1979, 181
Johnson, Guy, 283
Johnson, Miriam M.: Johnson and Johnson
  1986, 116, 205
Jones(Robert A.) 1980, 247; 1985, 247
Junker, Buford, 16, 29–30, 62
  Junker 1960, 190
Juvenile Protective Association, 262–3

Kahn, Robert L., 279
  Kahn 1983, 154
  Kahn and Cannell 1957, 16, 24, 61
Karl (Barry D.) 1969, 145
  Karl and Katz 1981, 164–5
Katz, Daniel 279
  Festinger and Katz 1953, 35, 36
Katz, Elihu: Katz and Lazarsfeld 1959, 158
Katz, Stanley N.: Karl and Katz 1981, 164–5
Keat, Russell: Keat and Urry 1975, 107, 113
Kendall, Patricia, 279
  Merton, Fiske and Kendall 1956, 16, 23–4,
    136
  Kendall and Lazarsfeld 1950, 44
  Merton, Reader and Kendall 1957 182
Kennedy, Raymond and Kennedy, Ruby:
    Kennedy and Kennedy 1942, 53
Kinsey Report, 26, 170
Kirkendall (R. S.) 1966, 181
Kirkpatrick (Clifford) 1940, 91, 92
Kish, Leslie, 279
  Kish 1983, 153
Klausner, Samuel Z.: Klausner and Lidz
  1986, 157, 203
Kluckhohn, Clyde: Gottschalk, Kluckhohn
  and Angell 1945, 14, 58, 146
Kluckhohn, Florence, 279
Knudsen, Dean D.: Knudsen and Vaughan
  1969, 209
Kohler (Robert E.) 1991, 181

Kohout, Frank, 279
  and Iowa symbolic interactionism, 121
  Kohout 1993, 121
Komarovsky, Mirra, 279
  Komarovsky 1940, 249
  Komarovsky 1957, 168
  Komarovsky 1964, 158
  Lundberg, Komarovsky and McInery
    1934, 254
Kornhauser, Arthur: Jahoda et al. 1951, 41
Kragh (Helge) 1987, 235
Kuhn, Manford, and Iowa symbolic
  interactionism, 121
Kuhn, T. S.
  reception of, 243
  Kuhn 1970, 248–9
Kurtz (Lester) 1984, 4

labelling ideas, 32–3, 43–4, 60, 260
Ladd, Everett C.: Lipset and Ladd 1972, 185,
  218
Ladinsky (Jack) 1963, 172
Lagemann (Ellen Condliffe) 1989, 167, 177,
  179
Lamont (Michèle) 1987, 241–2
Lang, Gladys Engel and Lang, Kurt: Lang
    and Lang 1988, 245–6
La Piere, Richard T., 248
Larsen, Otto N., 279
  Larsen 1968, 78, 213
  Larsen 1984, 92, 93
  Larsen 1992, 157
  Lundberg, Schrag and Larsen 1954, 1958,
    91, 204, 216
Larson, Olaf F.: Larson and Moe 1990, 150
Laszlo (Ervin) 1979, 101
Latour, Bruno: Latour and Woolgar 1979,
  110
Laub, John H.: Laub and Sampson 1991,
  246
Lazarsfeld, Paul F., 16, 22, 136
  and American Jewish Committee, 149
  attack by Wright Mills, 37
  encouraging writing by others, 56, 61, 64,
    148
  foundations, influence on, 148, 168
  and functionalism, 114–15
  influence, leadership, stimulation of, 13,
    15, 16, 29, 130, 202, 257, 259–60
  as Jew, 224
  mathematical background, 195
  as refugee from Hitler, 49
  reputation of, 259–60
  and Stouffer, 32, 258–60
  and Vienna Circle, 75

Lazarsfeld 1948, 58
Lazarsfeld 1954, 16, 28
Lazarsfeld 1961, 32
Lazarsfeld, Berelson and Gaudet 1944, 249, 252
Lazarsfeld and Rosenberg 1955, 16, 29, 32, 48, 168
Lazarsfeld and Thielens 1958, 223
Barton and Lazarsfeld 1951, 13
Barton and Lazarsfeld 1955, 13
Berelson, Lazarsfeld and McPhee 1954, 174
Jahoda et al. 1951, 41
Katz and Lazarsfeld 1959, 158
Kendall and Lazarsfeld 1950, 44
Merton and Lazarsfeld 1950, 12, 15, 24, 25–6, 59, 60, 249
Lengermann (Patricia M.) 1979, 210, 228
Lerner, Daniel: Merton and Lazarsfeld 1950, 60, 249
Levinson, D. J.: Adorno et al. 1950, 26, 149
Levy, Marion, member of Society for General Systems Research, 101
Lewin, Kurt, 49, 102
Lewin 1951, 102
Lewis, J. D.: Lewis and Smith 1980, 208
Lidz, Victor M.: Klausner and Lidz 1986, 157, 203
Lieberson (Stanley) 1980, 225
Duncan, Scott, Lieberson and Duncan 1960, 96
life histories, 14, 20, 51, 58, 119, *see also* personal documents
Likert, Rensis, 151
Lindeman (Eduard C.) 1924, 119
Hader and Lindeman 1933, 14, 17
Lindesmith (Alfred) 1952, 18
Lipset (Seymour M.) 1955, 225; 1993, 55
Lipset and Ladd 1972, 185, 218
Lipset and Smelser 1961, 114
Lipset, Trow and Coleman 1956, 132
Local Community Research Committee, 135
Lofland (John) 1970, 122; 1971, 30; 1980, 268
London School of Economics, 144
Loomis, Alice: Thomas, Loomis and Arrington 1933, 14, 18–19, 42
Loomis, Charles P., 150
Jahoda et al. 1951, 41
Lumsdaine, Arthur, 279
Hovland, Lumsdaine and Sheffield 1949, 15, 24, 59, 60
Lundberg, George A., 63, 216
anti-Semitic?, 218, 224

author of textbook and monograph on method, 57
biography, 77–8
citations, 91
correspondence with publishers, 55
departmental role, 203–5
and Dodd, their circle: activities, 215–17, 219; exemplars, 250; membership, 213–15, 219–22; politics, 217–18; reception of, 91–8; and scientism, 77–91
empirical work, 82–4
as evangelist, 216
and funding, 149
in Giddings line of descent, 137
influence of, 205
and Lazarsfeld, 99
position in US sociology, 99–100, 104
as representative of polar position, 65
and Vienna Circle, 74, 78–9
Lundberg 1929, 35, 36, 57, 71, 78
Lundberg 1931, 228
Lundberg 1934, 213
Lundberg 1937, 213
Lundberg 1938, 89
Lundberg 1939a, 14, 17, 78, 91
Lundberg 1939b, 90
Lundberg 1941, 89, 216
Lundberg 1942, 35, 78, 92
Lundberg 1944a, 224
Lundberg 1944b, 90
Lundberg 1945, 78
Lundberg 1947, 78, 92
Lundberg 1949, 222
Lundberg 1951, 89
Lundberg 1953, 220
Lundberg 1954, 216
Lundberg 1955, 78, 79
Lundberg 1956, 102, 182
Lundberg no date, 91
Lundberg and Beazley 1948, 83–4
Lundberg and Dickson 1952a, 84
Lundberg and Dickson 1952b, 84
Lundberg and Steele 1938, 82–3
Lundberg, Hertzler and Dickson 1949, 83–4
Lundberg, Komarovsky and Mc Inery 1934, 254
Lundberg, Schrag and Larsen 1954, 1958, 91, 204, 216
Lunt, Paul S.: Warner and Lunt 1941, 102
Lyman, Stanford M.: Vidich and Lyman 1985, 223
Lynd, Helen M.: Lynd and Lynd 1929, 249, 250, 252

Lynd, Robert, 60, 63
  Lynd and Lynd 1929, 249, 250, 252
  Lynd 1939, 17
Lyons(Gene M.) 1969, 156, 158

machines, role of, 135–6, 139
McAdam (Doug) 1992, 241
McCall, George J.: McCall and Simmons
  1969, 18, 30
McCarthy, Philip J.
  Mosteller, Hyman and McCarthy 1949,
    15, 22, 59
  Stephan and McCarthy 1958, 16, 27, 58
  Jahoda et al., 1951 41
McCartney, James L.
  McCartney 1970, 124, 126, 183
  Chubin and McCartney 1982, 182
  Galliher and McCartney 1973, 173, 198
McClung-Lee, Alfred, 60
McCormick, Thomas C., 138, 153
  mentor to Doby, 74
  and Zipf, 98
  Mc Cormick 1941a, 138
  Mc Cormick 1941b, 98
  Mc Cormick and Francis 1958, 35, 138
McGee (Reece) 1985, 34
McGranahan, Donald: Jahoda et al. 1951, 41
McGuire, Patrick: McGuire and Dawes
  1983, 206
McInery, Mary A.: Lundberg, Komarovsky
  and McInery 1934, 254
MacIver, Robert, 63, 65
  MacIver 1942, 14, 21, 73
Mackenzie (Donald A.) 1981, 136
McKinney (John C.) 1954, 65
McNemar (Quinn) 1946, 58
McPhee, William N.: Berelson, Lazarsfeld
  and McPhee 1954, 174, 252
Madge (John) 1963, 4, 67, 128
Madow, Lester, 151
  Hansen, Hurwitz and Madow 1953, 15, 47
Malinowski, Bronislaw, 119
Mann (Michael) 1981, 110
Manning (P.) 1978, 268
margarine, *see* Iowa Margarine Incident
Margenau, Henry
  and Dodd, 97
  Margenau 1969, 97
market research, *see* commercial research
  agencies
Martindale, Don Martindale 1961, 231
  Martindale 1976, 206
  Martindale 1982, 000
Marx, Karl and Marxism, 3, 69, 122
mathematics, 31

Matthews (Fred H.) 1977, 257
Mayo-Smith (Richmond) 1895, 34
Mazon (Brigitte) 1987, 2
Mead, G. H., 3, 208
Mead, Margaret, 39
Megill (Allan) 1987, 243
Meier (August) 1977, 206, 225
Meier (Richard L.) 1961, 101
Meltzer, Bernard: Meltzer, Petras and
  Reynolds 1975, 121–2
memory, social, 240–1
Menzies (Ken) 1982, 111
Merton, Robert K
  influence, leadership, stimulation, 140, 202
  and survey, 115
  Merton 1949, 69, 210
  Merton 1967, 236
  Merton 1984, 115–16
  Merton 1990, 128, 136
  Merton and Lazarsfeld 1950, 12, 15, 24–6,
    59, 60, 249
  Merton, Coleman and Rossi 1979, 13, 259
  Merton, Fiske and Kendall 1956, 16, 23–4,
    136
  Merton, Reader and Kendall 1957, 182
methods, *see also* exemplars, individual
  methods
  concepts used for, 33, 37, 44–52
  importance attached to, 34, 129–30
  improvement over time, 125, 127, 135,
    272–3
  monographs on, 11–33
  reasons for choice of, 131–6
  reasons for writing on, 52–63, 273–4
  reputations for, 29, 32–3, 60, 256–60,
    268–9
  and substantive specialisms, 129–31
  textbooks on, 33–44, 72
methods used in this book
  archives, 7
  counterfactual conditional, 10, 186, 197–8,
    207
  explanation, 10, 160–2, 186–8, 256–7
  interviews, 7–8
  samples, 8–9, 53,190–1, 266
  texts reviewed, 12–13
Michigan Survey Research Center, *see*
  Institute for Social Research
Michigan University, *see* Institute for Social
  Research
Middleton, D.: Middleton and Edwards
  1990, 240–1
Middleton, Russell, 279
  Middleton 1984, 194
migration and its impact, 2, 49, 70, 224–5

Miles, Ian: Irvine, Miles and Evans 1979, 142
Miller, Delbert, 156, 204
Miller (G. A.) 1965, 214
Miller (Roberta B.) 1982, 181
Mills, C. Wright
    attack on Lazarsfeld, 37
    Mills 1942, 102
    Mills 1959, 112
    Gerth and Mills 1946, 37
Minnesota, University of
    department, 76, 137, 257
    methods courses, 53
Mitchell (Duncan) 1968, 4
Miyamoto, Frank, 279
Moe, Edward O.: Larson and Moe 1990, 150
Moore, B. V.: Bingham and Moore 1931, 24
Moore, H. L., 195
Moreno, Jacob, 28, 56, 213, 216
    Moreno 1934, 1953, 14, 15, 19–20, 88, 89
    Moreno 1955, 216
Mormons in sociology, 225–6
Morris (Loretta) 1989, 226
Morrissett, Lloyd N., 167
Mosteller, Frederick: Mosteller, Hyman
    and McCarthy 1949, 15, 22, 59
Mulkay, Michael
    Gilbert and Mulkay 1984, 110
    Mulkay and Turner 1971, 63
Mullins (Nicholas J.) 1973, 23, 120, 232
Münch (Richard) 1991, 2
Myrdal (Gunnar) 1944, 147, 170, 181, 251, 258

Nagel, Ernest, 75, 221
    Nagel 1961, 75
Nash (George H.) 1976, 217
National Institute of Mental Health, 158,
    172
National Opinion Research Center, 36
National Science Foundation, 155, 156, 177,
    180–1
Nelson (Lowry) 1969, 152
networks, social and intellectual, 137–8, *see
    also* Lundberg and Dodd, their circle
New Deal, and research funding, 150, 153
Nisbet, Robert
    Nisbet 1966, 3
    Nisbet 1976, 66
Nock (David A.) 1993, 244
North Carolina, University of, 34, 225, 286
    departmental character, 205–6, 236
    and funding, 144

Oberschall (Anthony) 1972, 260
O'Brien, Mike: Baehr and O'Brien 1994,
    243–4

Odum, Howard
    and Bible Belt pressures, 225
    correspondence with publishers, 55
    Odum 1926, 56
    Odum 1928, 205
    Odum 1945, 205
    Odum 1951, 4, 53, 91, 234
    Odum and Jocher 1929, 34, 35
Office of Naval Research, 155–6
Office of Public Opinion Research, 22, 60–1
Ogburn, William F., 76–7
    and Census, 153
    in Giddings line of descent, 137–8, 195
    and Lundberg group, 222
    Ogburn 1929, 77
Ohio State University, doctoral production,
    206–7
operationism, 17, 74, 220
Opler (Morris E.) 1942, 102
Oppenheim, Paul: Hempel and Oppenheim
    1936, 75
Orum, Anthony M.: Feagin, Orum and
    Sjoberg 1991, 70, 105
Osborn, Frederick, 177, 283
Ozanne (Henry) 1943, 94

Pacific Coast Race Relations Survey, 38, 234
Page, Charles H., 279
Palmer (Vivien) 1928, 34, 35, 56
pan-sample, 86
panel studies, 41
Pareto Circle, 202
Park, Robert, 55, 56
    and biological ecology, 101
    mentor to Bogardus, 38, 234
    Pauline Young his student?, 38
    as supervisor, 257
    Smith and White 1929, 264
Parkin (Frank) 1974, 248
Parsons, Talcott, 112, 244–5
    changing perception of, 3
    and Chicago, 211
    choice of ancestors, 244–5
    and funding, 190, 203
    reception of, 74, 115, 210, 245
    and science, 101
    and survey, 114–16
    Parsons 1937, 69, 244, 245
    Parsons 1942, 94
    Parsons 1949, 115
    Parsons 1951, 115
    Parsons and Bales, 1955 101
    Parsons, Bales and Shils, 1953 102
    Parsons and Shils 1951, 190
Parten (Mildred) 1950, 15, 27

participant observation
at Chicago, 262–3, 265–8
and cohort effect, 230
emergence of category, 37, 44
in industrial sociology, 130
and meanings, 40, 47, 251–2
and positivism, 73
Street Corner Society as exemplar of, 251
and symbolic interactionism 120–2, 265
and Weber 117–19
writing on 30, 62–3
Payne (Stanley L.) 1951, 15, 27, 60
Pearl (Raymond) 1924, 85
Pearson, Karl, 76
personal documents, 20–1, 22, 44
Petras, John W.: Meltzer, Petras and
Reynolds 1975, 121–2
Phillips, Bernard S., 279
Phillips 1966, 56, 74
Phillips 1976, 106, 111, 113
Phillips 1984, 56, 73–4
Phillipson, Michael: Filmer, Phillipson,
Silverman and Walsh 1972, 107, 113
Picou, J. Steven: Wells and Picou 1981, 116,
125–6
Pitts, Jesse R.: Hallen no date, 101–2
Planned Parenthood, 134
Platt (Anthony M.) 1991, 225
Platt, Jennifer
Platt 1981, 70, 110
Platt 1983, 47, 73
Platt 1985, 117
Platt 1986a, 134, 142, 151, 161, 166
Platt 1986b, 116
Platt 1986c, 32, 202, 258, 259
Platt 1991, 263
Platt 1992a, 143, 261
Platt 1992b, 58, 136, 146
Platt 1992c, 43, 46, 119
Platt 1994a, 34, 47, 119, 143, 203, 261, 263
Platt 1994b, 169
Platt 1995a, 30, 49, 121, 203, 208, 209, 225,
266
Platt 1995b, 69, 237, 252
Platt and Hoch 1995, 75, 78, 221
Ploch (Donald R.) 1978, 180
polarities, 65
Polish Peasant in Europe and America, The, 14,
20–1, 46, 51, 143, 146, 249, 252
political sociology, 130
politicians and social science, 181–2
politics and sociology, 60, 67, 165–6, 198–9,
217–18, 223
Pollak (Michael) 1979, 2
positivism, 67–8, 70–71, 73, 109–10, 117

Preiss, Jack J.: Adams and Preiss 1960, 16,
29–30, 62
Procter, Charles H.: Jahoda et al., 1951 41
Procter and Gamble, 55
Progressive movement, 143, 223
Provus (Severn) 1942, 92
psychology, 12, 19, 28, 31, 40, 42, 71, 220, 228
Public Opinion Quarterly, 59
punchbags, intellectual, 65–6

qualitative research, interest in, 13, 30
qualitative/quantitative division, *see*
quantitative/qualitative division
quantitative/qualitative division, 13, 17, 45,
60, 65, 126, 273
quantification
and capitalism, 161, 165–6
and funding, 142, 182–97
increasing, 72, 123–5, 140, 272
Queen, Stuart: Chapin and Queen 1937, 23

Rainwater, Lee, 279
Rainwater 1959, 159
Rainwater 1965, 134
Rainwater 1984, 134, 149, 159, 208
RAND Corporation, 156
Ranger, Terence: Hobsbawm and Ranger
1983, 241
Rapoport, Anatol
and general systems, 101
and Zipf, 97
Rapoport 1979, 97
Rashevsky, Nicholas, 90
and general systems, 101
and Zipf, 97
Rashevsky 1951, 97
Ratner (S.) 1957, 219
Ratzenhofer, Gustav, 3
Reader, George: Merton, Reader and
Kendall 1957, 182
reception of intellectual work, 241–5
Reece, *see* Congressional Special
Committee to Investigate
Tax–Exempt Foundations
Reichenbach, Hans, 74
Reinharz, Shulamit
Reinharz 1992, 122
Reinharz 1995, 62
Reiss, Albert L., 280
Reiss 1984, 136
religion and sociology, 223–6
reputations, 256–69
Research Committee on Social Trends, 76,
145
Revere, Project, *see* Dodd

Reynolds, Larry T.
  Meltzer, Petras and Reynolds 1975, 121–2
  Vaughan and Reynolds 1968, 138
Rhoades (Lawrence J.) 1981, 53
Rhoads (G.) 1971, 109
Rice (Stuart) 1931, 14, 20, 57, 145
Riecken (Henry) 1983, 157
Riemer (Svend) 1942, 98
Riesman, David: Becker, Geer, Riesman
  and Weiss 1968, 121, 133
Riley, John W., 168
  Riley, Riley and Toby 1954, 16, 28, 156
Riley, Matilda W.: Riley, Riley and Toby
  1954, 16, 28, 156
Ritzer (George) 1975, 106–7, 111, 113
Robinson (Marshall) 1983, 181, 192
Robinson (W. S.) 1950, 32; 1951, 18
Rock (Paul) 1979, 120, 269
Rockefeller foundations, 183–4
  block grants, 169
  and Chicago, 174
  method, not interested in, 189
  policy of non-intervention, 170
  poor basis for generalisations, 164
  and Stewart, 214, 220–1
  topics funded, 163
Rogers, Carl, 228
Roller, Duane and Duane H. D., 219
Rose, Arnold M., 149
  and Chicago tradition, 265
  and definition of symbolic interactionism,
  120
  Rose 1962, 265
Rosenberg (Charles E.) 1976, 152
Rosenberg, Morris
  Lazarsfeld and Rosenberg 1955, 16, 29, 32,
  48, 168
  Jahoda et al. 1951, 41
Ross (Dorothy) 1991, 4, 68, 142
Ross, E. A., 3
Rossi, Peter, 63, 280
  Rossi 1959, 135
  Rossi 1984, 91, 114, 133, 171, 209, 224
  Merton, Coleman and Rossi 1979, 13, 259
Rothman (Robert A.) 1971, 34
Royden (Maude) 1916, 263
Ruml, Beardsley, 144, 174
rural sociology, 130, 150–2, 206
Russell Sage Foundation, 144, 168
Russett (Cynthia E.) 1966, 79, 101

Sage, Russell, *see* Russell Sage Foundation
sampling
  advances in, 151, 153–4
  textbooks on, 27

Sampson, Robert J.: Laub and Sampson
  1991, 246
Sanders, Irwin, 158, 280
  Sanders 1984, 152
Sanford, R. Nevitt: Adorno et al. 1950, 149
Sapolsky (Harvey) 1990, 155
Sarbin (Theodore R.) 1943, 47
scaling, 25, 28
Schatzman, Leonard: Schatzman and
  Strauss 1973, 114
Schmid, Calvin, 39, 54, 65, 204
Schneider, David, 280
schools (of thought), 112, 121, 230–7
Schrag, Clarence: Lundberg, Schrag and
  Larsen 1954, 1958, 91, 204, 216
Schultz, Theodore W., 181
Schuman, Howard: Schuman and Scott
  1989, 241
Schwartz (Barry) 1982, 241
Schwartz, Morris, 280
Schwartz, Richard D.: Webb et al. 1966, 19,
  30, 248
science, scientific method, 17, 36–7, 274
Schuman, Jacqueline: Schuman and Scott
  1989, 241
Scott, W. R.: Duncan, Scott, Lieberson and
  Duncan 1960, 96
Sechrest, Lee: Webb et al. 1966, 19, 30, 248
Second World War, 2, 24, 52, *see also*
  wartime research
  break between prewar and postwar, 25,
  36, 43, 45–50
Seidman (Steven) 1985, 247
Selltiz, Claire: Jahoda et al. 1951, 41
Selvin (Hanan C.) 1958, 69, 252; 1965, 32;
  1976, 31
Semmelweis, Ignaz, 32
Severance, Janet S.: Fine and Severance
  1985, 206
Sewell, William H., 152, 195, 280
  as influence, 130, 137–8
  Sewell 1983, 92–3, 195
Seybold, Peter: Seybold 1987, 148
Seymour, Frederick, 120, 280
  Seymour 1982, 42
Shanas (Ethel) 1941, 94; 1943, 94
Shannon, C. E.: Shannon and Weaver 1962,
  221
Shannon, Lyle, 73–4, 204, 280
  Shannon 1993, 74, 92, 93, 204
Shaw (Clifford) 1930, 46, 249, 252
Sheatsley, Paul B., 280
  Jahoda et al. 1951, 41
Sheffield, Fred D.: Hovland, Lumsdaine
  and Sheffield 1949, 15, 24, 59, 60

Shichor (David) 1972, 209
Shils, Edward A., 149, 179
  Shils 1980, 209
  Parsons, Bales and Shils 1953, 102
  Parsons and Shils 1951, 190
Shore (Marlene) 1987, 264–5
Short, James, 280
  Short and Strodtbeck, 1963 158
Sibley, Elbridge, 168
  Sibley 1963, 206, 209
  Sibley 1974, 146, 197
Sica (Alan) 1983, 206
Sicherman, Barbara: Sicherman and Green
  1980, 263
significance tests, use of, 133
Sills (David L.) 1987, 259
Silva, Edward T.: Silva and Slaughter 1984,
  68
Silverman, David: Filmer, Phillipson,
  Silverman and Walsh 1972, 107, 113
Simmons, J. L.: McCall and Simmons 1969,
  18, 30
Simon, Herbert, influence on Blalock, 132,
  207
Simpson (George) 1949, 91
Sjoberg, Andrée F.: Feagin, Orum and
  Sjoberg 1991, 70, 105
Sjoberg, Gideon: Feagin, Orum and Sjoberg
  1991, 70, 105
Skinner (B. F.) 1956, 220
Skinner (Quentin) 1969, 112, 236; 1974, 235
Sklar (Kathryn K.) 1985, 262
  Bulmer, Bales and Sklar 1991, 39
Sklare (Marshall) 1963, 225
Slaughter, Sheila T.: Silva and Slaughter,
  1984 68
Sletto, Raymond, 206
small-group research, 23
Smelser, Neal: Lipset and Smelser 1961, 114
Smith (Dennis) 1988, 4, 269
Smith (L. D.) 1987, 71
Smith, R. L.: Lewis and Smith 1980, 208
Smith, T. V.: Smith and White 1929, 263,
  264
Snizek (William E.) 1975, 124, 126; 1976, 111
Social Forces, 205, 225
social physics, 213
Social Research Association, 227–8
Social Research Inc., 134
Social Science Research Council, 144–9, *see
  also* names of its individual committees
  attacked by Reece Committee, 166
  and methodological writing, 13–16, 57–9
  and quantitative methods, 195–6
  and Rockefeller foundations, 169

Social Trends, Research Committee on, 76,
  145
social work, 13, 17, 24, 38, 143, 261–3
socialism, 223–4
Society for Applied Anthropology, 15, 62,
  227, 265
Society for General Systems Research,
  101
Society for the Psychological Study of Social
  Issues, 40
Society for the Study of Social Problems, 16,
  227
Society for the Study of Symbolic
  Interaction, 227
Sociological Research Association, 217
Sociometric Group, 217, 227
sociometry, 20, 39, 41, 84, 213
Sociometry (journal), 78, 95, 213, 216, 219
sophomores, sociology of, 194
Sorokin, Pitirim, 17, 137, 170, 237
  Sorokin 1940, 92
  Sorokin 1956, 99
  Sorokin 1966, 231
Spencer Foundation, 167
Spengler, Joseph J.: Spengler and Duncan
  1956, 96
Sprehe, Timothy: Gouldner and Sprehe
  1965, 104
statistics, 12, 37
  versus case study, *see* case study
Steele, Mary: Lundberg and Steele 1938,
  82–3
Stephan, Frederick F., 153
  Stephan 1948, 48
  Stephan and McCarthy 1958, 16, 27, 58
Stewart, John Q., 87–90, 213–14, 217, 219
  reception of, 95–7
  Stewart 1947, 88
  Stewart 1948a, 88, 213
  Stewart 1948b, 88
  Stewart 1949, 90
  Stewart 1950, 214
  Stewart 1951, 90
  Stewart 1957, 89
Stinchcombe (Arthur) 1982, 247
Stone, Gregory, 109
stories about sociology, 67
Stouffer, Samuel A., 202
  contributions labelled by Lazarsfeld, 32
  experimental method, advocacy of, 60,
    96
  and functionalism, 114–16
  Ogburn as inspiration, 195
  personal style, 258–9
  and survey, 258

Thurstone as mentor of, 132
Stouffer 1940, 79, 96, 250
Stouffer, Guttman, Suchman et al. 1950,
    15, 24–5, 59, 147, 189, 249
Jahoda et al. 1951, 41
Strauss, Anselm L., 158, 268, 280
Glaser and Strauss 1967, 18, 30
Schatzman and Strauss 1973, 114
Street Corner Society, 29, 251
Strodtbeck, Fred
and Stewart, 96
Strodtbeck 1980, 219
Short and Strodtbeck 1963, 158
strong programme in the sociology of
    science, 5
Suchman, Edward: Stouffer, Guttman,
    Suchman et al., 1950 15, 24–5, 59, 147,
    189, 249
Sulek (Antoni) 1994, 2
summer cottages, their intellectual role,
    217, 219, 221
Sumner, William G., 3
survey method
American Soldier and, 60
change of meaning, 44–5
community of researchers, 58–9
diffusion of, 2, 272–3
early 'survey', 17, 38, 41, 45, 262
and functionalism, 113–17
hegemony postwar, 49–50
and political sociology, 130
and scientism, 67
survey units and division of labour, 134
use of in articles, 123–6
writing about, 64
Survey Research Center, *see* Institute for
    Social Research
Sutherland, Edwin
vs. Gluecks, 246–7
Sutherland 1939, 18
Sutton, Francis X., 280
Sutton 1993, 177
Sweetser, Frank, 280
Swift, Harold H., 284
symbolic interactionism, 109
and participant observation, 120–2, 265
and social networks, 138
Szacki (J.) 1975, 3, 231
Sztompka (Piotr) 1986, 269
Szymanski (Albert) 1971, 113

Tarde, Gabriel, 3, 237
Tax, Sol, 277
Taylor (Brian) 1994, 264
Taylor, Carl C., 150

textbooks
audiences, 55
genre formulae, 33–4, 37, 42–4
graduate, 34
on scientific method, 72–3
reasons for writing, 52–7
sales, 37–8, 91
themata, 66
theory and practice, 11, 31–3, 65, 67–8, 105,
    275
Thielens, Wagner
Jahoda et al. 1951, 41
Lazarsfeld and Thielens 1958, 223
Thomas, Dorothy S., 39
Thomas and associates 1929, 14, 18–19,
    39–40
Thomas, Loomis and Arrington 1933, 14,
    18–19, 42
Thomas, William I., 3, 19, 39, 168
Thomas 1923, 143, 261
Thomas and Znaniecki 1918–20, 14, 20–1,
    46, 51, 143, 146, 249, 252
Thurstone, Louis L.
mentor to Stouffer, 132
Thurstone and Chave 1929, 12
Thurstone scale, 47
Timasheff (Nicholas S.) 1950, 91
Tiryakian (Edward) 1979, 233
Toby, Jackson: Riley, Riley and Toby 1954,
    16, 28, 156
Torgerson, Warren S., 16, 28
Trow, Martin: Lipset, Trow and Coleman
    1956, 132
True Story, funds research, 158, 159
Truesdell (Leon E.) 1965, 136
Turk, Herman, 172
Turner, Bryan: Mulkay and Turner, 1971 63
Turner, Jonathan H.: Turner and Turner
    1990, 4, 52, 67, 157, 169, 171–2, 205, 206,
    210, 269
Turner (Ralph H.) 1947, 154; 1954, 18
Turner, Stephen P.
Turner 1983, 235
Turner 1994, 4, 11, 137, 195, 269
Turner and Turner 1990, 4, 52, 67, 157,
    169, 171–2, 205, 206, 210, 269
typology, use of types, 18, 65

Unadjusted Girl, The, 143, 260–1
UNESCO 49, 260
University of, *see* substantive name
University expansion, 50, 52, 55, *see also* GI
    Bill
University of Southern California, 38
Urry, John: Keat and Urry 1975, 107, 113

US Air Force, and social science, 156
US Department of Agriculture, 150–1, 182
Useem, John, 280
  Useem 1984, 224, 226
Useem (Michael) 1976, 160, 184–5

van Elteren (Mel) 1990, 2
van Waters (Miriam) 1926, 262
Vaughan, Ted R.
  Feagin, Orum and Sjoberg 1991, 70
  Knudsen and Vaughan 1969, 209
  Vaughan and Reynolds 1968, 138
Veblen (Thorstein) 1931, 163
Verhoeven (Jef) 1993, 33, 135; 1995, 109, 120
verstehen, 117–18
Vidich, Arthur J.: Vidich and Lyman 1985, 223
Vienna, and its intellectual milieu, 40, 61, 75
Vienna Circle
  and Lundberg group, 217, 221
  and scientism in US sociology, 70–6
voting research, and surveys, 130, 135

Wagner, David G.: Berger, Wagner and Zelditch 1989, 111
Wald (Alan M.) 1987, 223
Wallace, Henry, 151
Waller (Willard) 1930, 254–5
Walsh, David: Filmer, Phillipson, Silverman and Walsh 1972, 107, 113
Walsh, Joseph L., 220
Walter (Maila) 1990, 71, 220
war, *see* Second World War, wartime research
Ward, Lester, 3
Ware (Caroline) 1935, 254
Warner, W. Lloyd
  as Harvard fieldworker, 265
  as industrial sociologist, 62, 121
  and Social Research Inc., 158
  Warner and Lunt 1941, 102
Wartime research, 13, 24–6, 59, 151, 154, 228–9, *see also American Soldier*
  alumni in foundations, 179
Washington, University of
  departmental character, 203–5
  methods courses, 53, 54
  reactions to Lundberg, 93
Washington Public Opinion Laboratory, 99, 204
Watson, J. B., 71
Wax, Murray, 280
Weaver, Warren, 220–1, 285
  Weaver 1949, 89
  Weaver 1950, 221
  Shannon and Weaver 1962, 221

Webb, Beatrice, 32, 38, 39
Webb, Eugene J.: Webb et al., 19, 30, 248
Weber, Max
  association with positivism, 37
  and participant observation, 117–19
  reception of, 243–4
Weinberg (S. Kirson) 1952, 18
Weiss, Robert S.: Becker, Geer, Riesman and Weiss 1968, 121, 133
Wellman, David, 120
Wells, Richard H.: Wells and Picou 1981, 116, 125–6
West coast, distance, 42, 93, 95, 101
Whig history, 140, 200, 235, 270
White, Leonard D.: Smith and White 1929, 263, 264
Whyte, William F., 281
  as Harvard fieldworker, 265
  and symbolic interactionism, 121
  Whyte 1943, 1955, 1981, 29, 249, 251–2
  Jahoda et al. 1951, 41
Wilensky, Harold, 172
Williams, Norma: Feagin, Orum and Sjoberg 1991, 70
Williams, Robin, 281
  Williams 1984, 152
Wilner (Patricia) 1985, 124–6
Winkin (Yves) 1988, 121, 207
Wirth, Louis
  and foundations, 174
  and NORC, 211
  and SSRC, 147
  Wirth 1940, 263
Wisconsin, University of
  departmental style, 74, 136, 138
  methods courses, 53, 54
  and Parsons, 115
Wolff, Kurt, 206
women, position of within sociology, 224
Woofter (T. J.) 1933, 32
Woolgar, Steve: Latour and Woolgar 1979, 110
Woolston (Howard B.) 1942, 94
Work Projects Administration, 153
World War, *see* Second World War
Wormser, Margot Haas: Jahoda et al. 1951, 41
Wormser, René, 202
  Wormser 1958, 165–6, 168
Wright (Erik Olin) 1989, 122

Xie, Yu: Camic and Xie 1994, 201, 208, 211, 269

Yale Institute of Human Relations, 19
Yankee City, 102
Young, Donald, 167, 283

Young, Erle Fiske, 38
Young, Kimball, 150
Young, Pauline V., 38–40, 234
  Young 1932, 38, 42, 255
  Young 1935, 24
  Young 1939, 35, 38–9, 234
  Young 1949, 35, 38–9, 72
  Young 1956, 35, 40
Yule, G. Udny, 31

Zander, Alvin Jahoda et al. 1951, 41, 42
Zeisel, Hans, 281
  Zeisel 1947, 12, 15, 22, 61
  Zeisel 1990, 75
Zelditch, Morris: Berger, Wagner and
  Zelditch 1989, 111

Zetterberg (Hans) 1954, 16, 28, 61; 1965,
  72
Zipf, George K., 87–90, 214–15, 219
  and Department of Social Relations,
    202
  reception of, 97–8
  and Weaver, 221
  Zipf 1935, 214
  Zipf 1941, 98, 218, 224
  Zipf 1949, 87, 97, 214
Znaniecki, Florian
  and Abel, 51
  analytical induction, 48
  Znaniecki 1934, 14, 17, 18, 73
  Thomas and Znaniecki 1918–20, 14, 20,
    46, 51, 249, 252

Ideas in Context

Edited by QUENTIN SKINNER (*General Editor*)
LORRAINE DASTON, WOLF LEPENIES, RICHARD RORTY
and J. B. SCHNEEWIND

1 RICHARD RORTY, J. B. SCHNEEWIND and QUENTIN SKINNER (eds.)
Philosophy in history
*Essays in the historiography of philosophy**

2 J. G. A. POCOCK
Virtue, Commerce and History
*Essays on political thought and history, chiefly in the eighteenth century**

3 M. M. GOLDSMITH
Private Vices, Public Benefits
Bernard Mandeville's social and political thought

4 ANTHONY PAGDEN (ed.)
The Languages of Political Theory in Early Modern Europe*

5 DAVID SUMMERS
The Judgment of Sense
*Renaissance nationalism and the rise of aesthetics**

6 LAURENCE DICKEY
Hegel: Religion, Economics and the Politics of Spirit, 1770–1807*

7 MARGO TODD
Christian Humanism and the Puritan Social Order

8 LYNN SUMIDA JOY
Gassendi the Atomist
Advocate of history in an age of science

9 EDMUND LEITES (ed.)
Conscience and Casuistry in Early Modern Europe

10 WOLF LEPENIES
Between Literature and Science: The Rise of Sociology*

11 TERENCE BALL, JAMES FARR and RUSSELL L. HANSON (eds.)
Political Innovation and Conceptual Change

12 GERD GIGERENZER *et al.*
The Empire of Chance
*How probability changed science and everyday life**

13 PETER NOVICK
The Noble Dream
*The 'objectivity question' and the American historical profession**

14 DAVID LIEBERMAN
The Province of Legislation Determined
Legal theory in eighteenth-century Britain

15 DANIEL PICK
Faces of Degeneration
A European disorder, c. 1848–c. 1918

16 KEITH BAKER
Approaching the French Revolution
*Essays on French political culture in the eighteenth century**

17 IAN HACKING
The Taming of Chance*

18 GISELA BOCK, QUENTIN SKINNER and MAURIZIO VIROLI (eds.)
Machiavelli and Republicanism*

19 DOROTHY ROSS
The Origins of American Social Science*

20 KLAUS CHRISTIAN KOHNKE
The Rise of Neo-Kantianism
German Academic Philosophy between Idealism and Positivism

21 IAN MACLEAN
Interpretation and Meaning in the Renaissance
The Case of Law

22 MAURIZIO VIROLI
From Politics to Reason of State
The Acquisition and Transformation of the Language of Politics 1250–1600

23 MARTIN VAN GELDEREN
The Political Thought of the Dutch Revolt 1555–1590

24 NICHOLAS PHILLIPSON and QUENTIN SKINNER (eds.)
Political Discourse in Early Modern Britain

25 JAMES TULLY
An Approach to Political Philosophy: Locke in Context*

26 RICHARD TUCK
Philosophy and Government 1572–1651*

27 RICHARD R. YEO
Defining Science
William Whewell, Natural Knowledge and Public Debate in Early Victorian Britain

28 MARTIN WARNKE
The Court Artist
The Ancestry of the Modern Artist

29 PETER N. MILLER
Defining the Common Good
Empire, Religion and Philosophy in Eighteenth-Century Britain

30 CHRISTOPHER J. BERRY
The Idea of Luxury
*A Conceptual and Historical Investigation**

31 E. J. HUNDERT
The Enlightenment's 'Fable'
Bernard Mandeville and the Discovery of Society

32 JULIA STAPLETON
Englishness and the Study of Politics
The Social and Political Thought of Ernest Barker

33 KEITH TRIBE
German Economic Thought from the Enlightenment to the Social Market

34 SACHIKO KUSUKAWA
The Transformation of Natural Philosophy
The Case of Philip Melancthon

35 Edited BY DAVID ARMITAGE, JACQUES HIMY and QUENTIN SKINNER
Milton and Republicanism

36 MARKKU PELTONEN
Classical Humanism and Republicanism in English Political Thought
1570–1640

37 PHILIP IRONSIDE
The Social and Political Thought of Bertrand Russell
The Development of an Aristocratic Liberalism

38 NANCY CARTWRIGHT, JORDI CAT, KAROLLA FLECK and THOMAS UEBEL
Otto Neurath: Philosophy between Science and Politics

39 DONALD WINCH
  Riches and Poverty
  An Intellectual History of Political Economy in Britain, 1750–1834*

40 JENNIFER PLATT
  A History of Sociological Research Methods in America 1920–1960

Titles marked with an asterisk are also available in paperback.